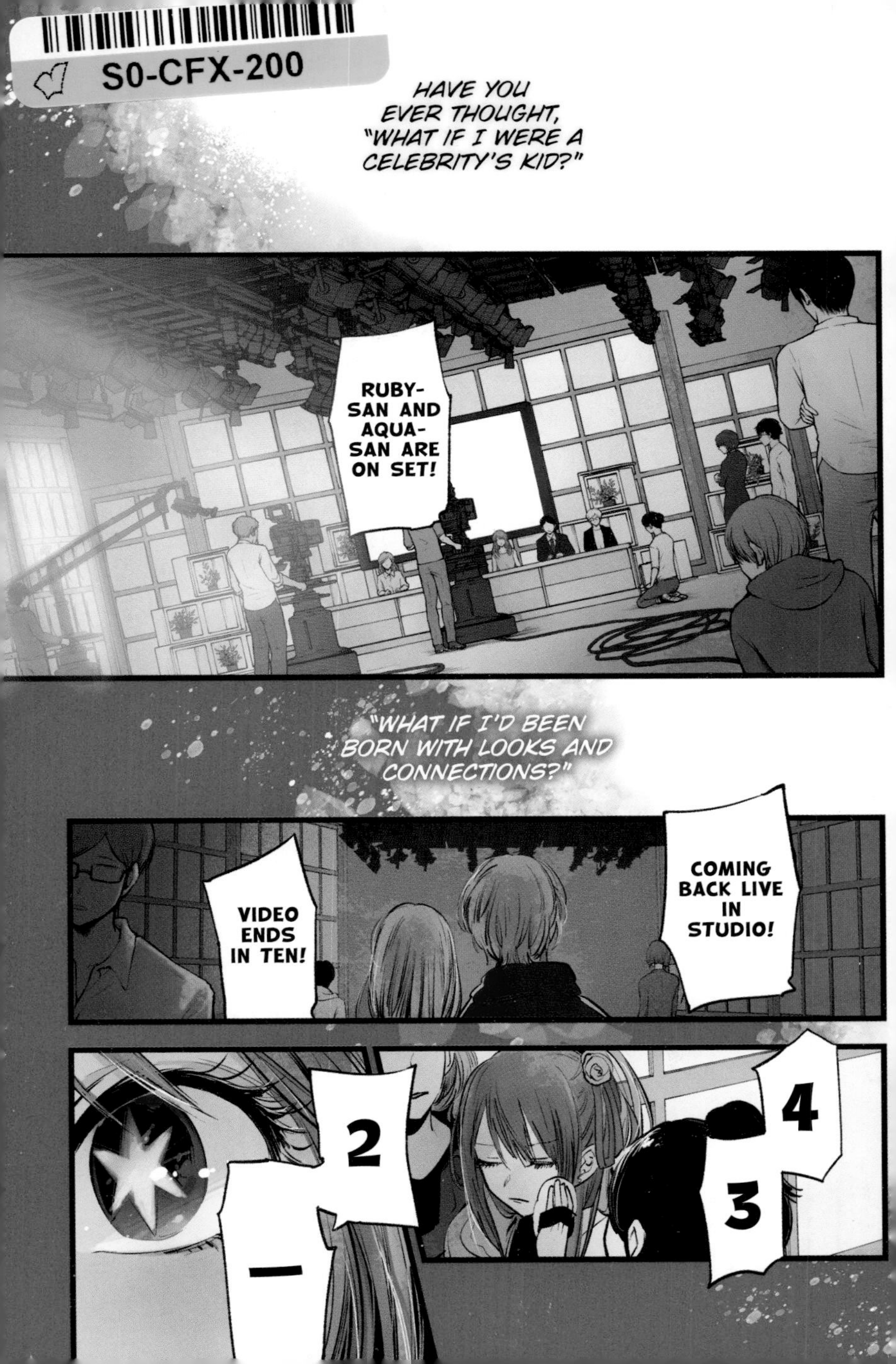
HAVE YOU EVER THOUGHT, "WHAT IF I WERE A CELEBRITY'S KID?"
RUBY-SAN AND AQUA-SAN ARE ON SET!
"WHAT IF I'D BEEN BORN WITH LOOKS AND CONNECTIONS?"
COMING BACK LIVE IN STUDIO!
VIDEO ENDS IN TEN!
4
3
2
—

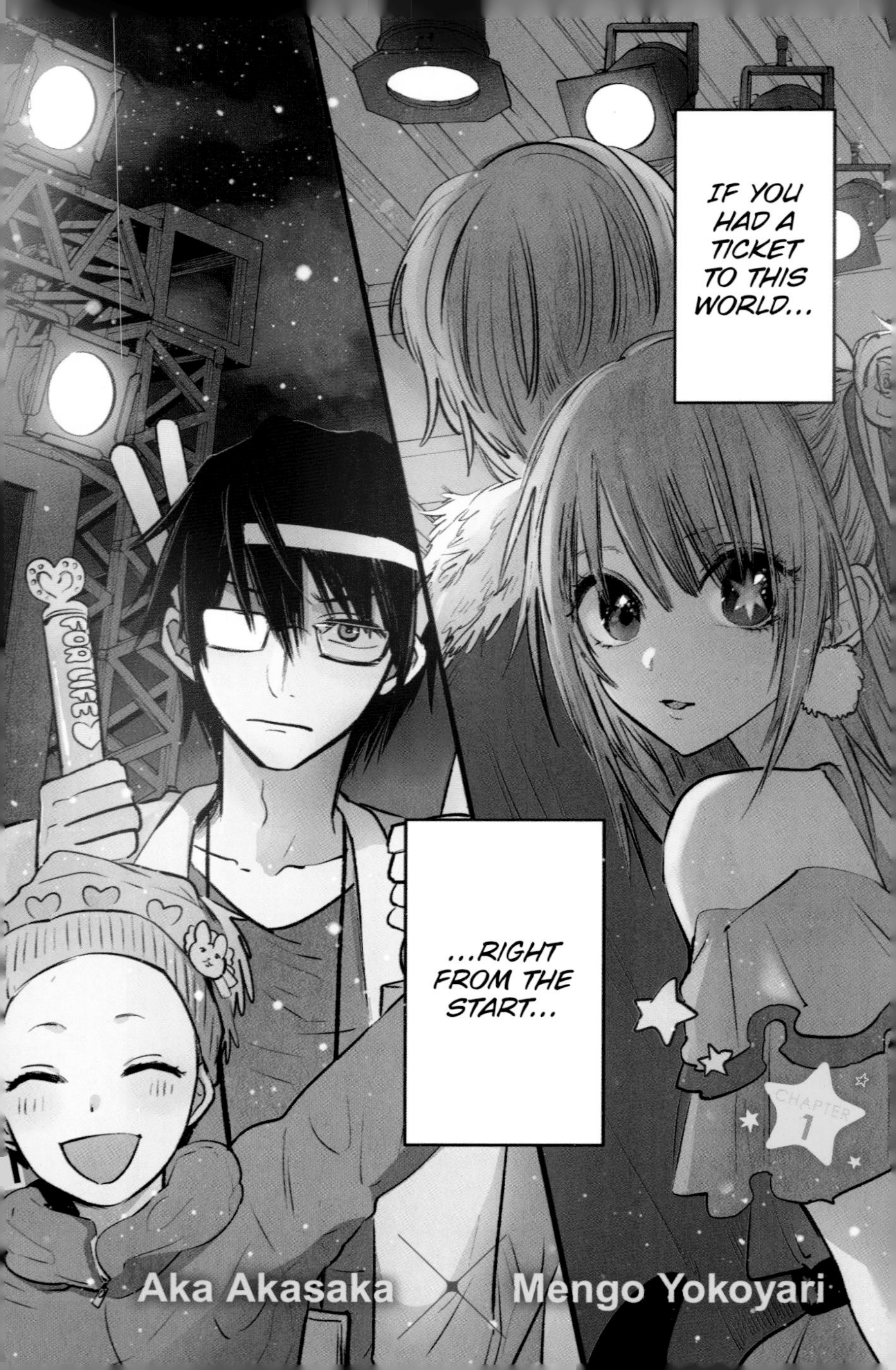
IF YOU HAD A TICKET TO THIS WORLD...
...RIGHT FROM THE START...
FOR LIFE
CHAPTER 1
Aka Akasaka
Mengo Yokoyari

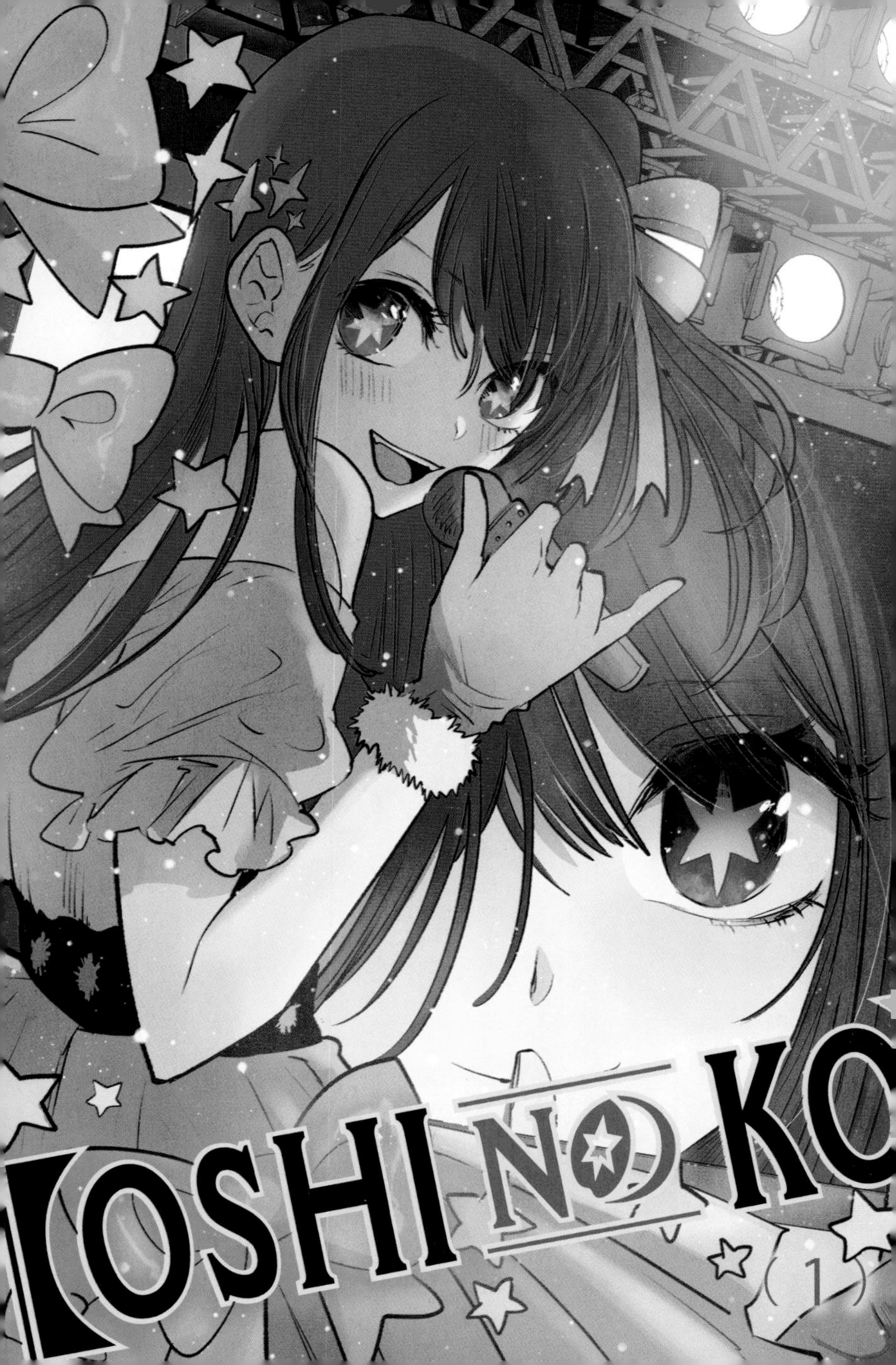
OSHI NO KO
(1)

OSHI NO KO ❶ CONTENTS

THIS STORY IS FICTION.

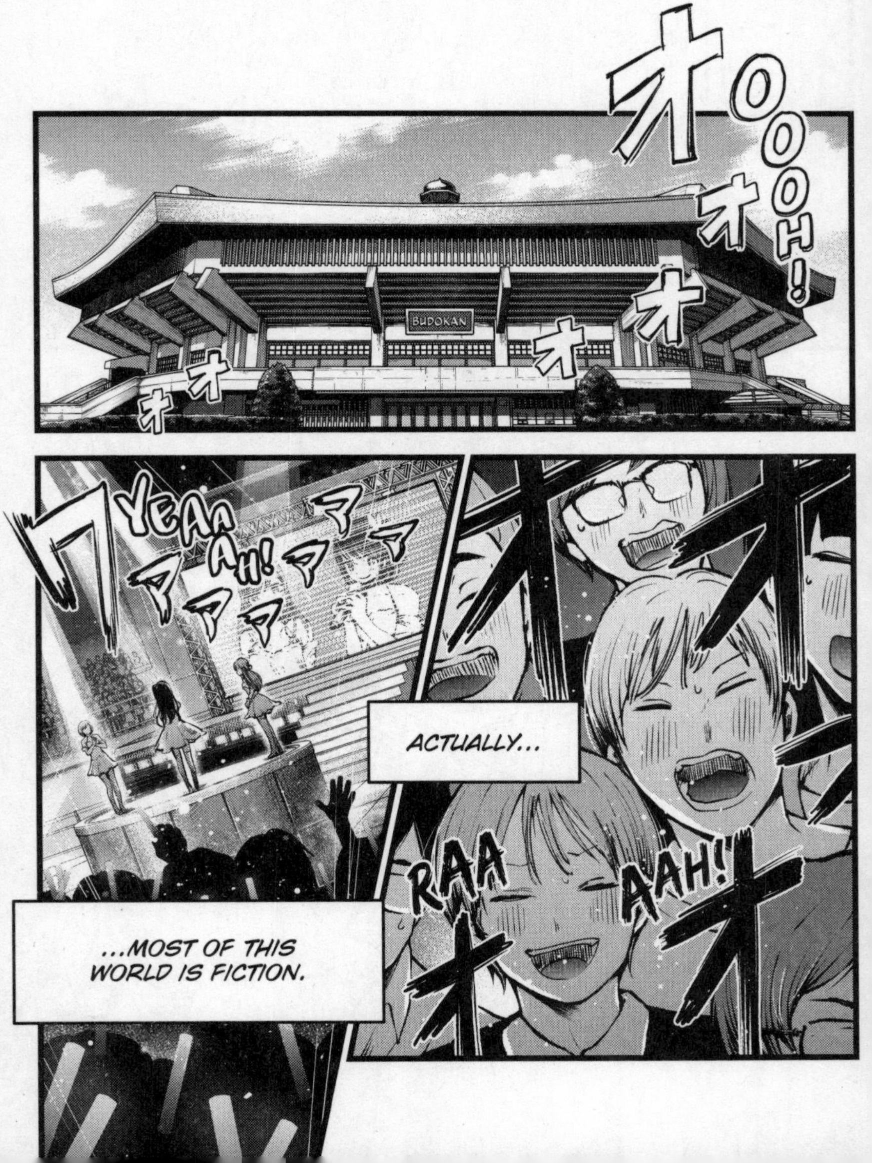
OOOOH!
BUDOKAN
RAA
AAH!
ACTUALLY...
YEAA
AAH!
...MOST OF THIS
WORLD IS FICTION.

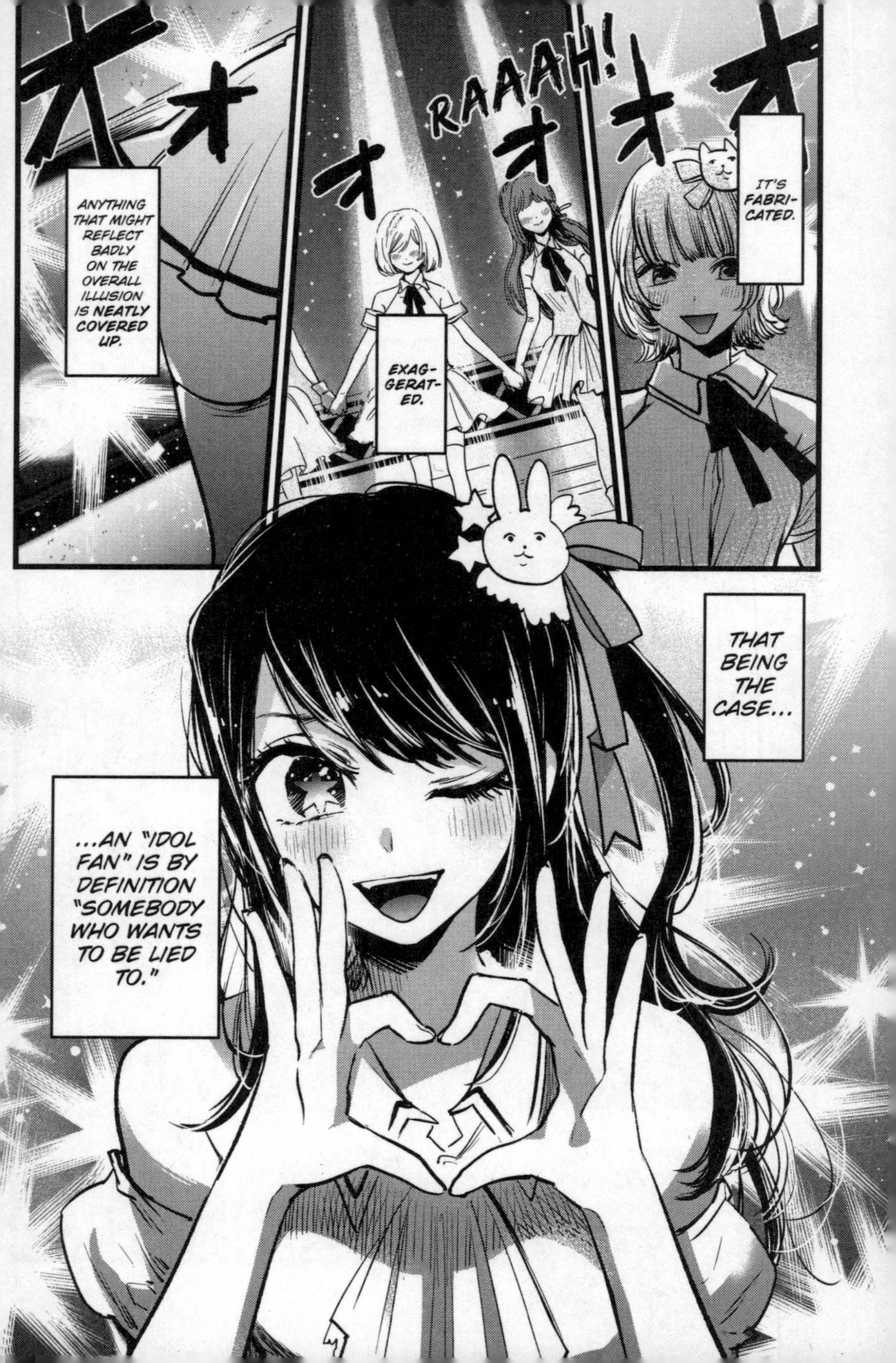
IT'S FABRICATED.
RAAAH!
EXAGGERATED.
ANYTHING THAT MIGHT REFLECT BADLY ON THE OVERALL ILLUSION IS NEATLY COVERED UP.
THAT BEING THE CASE...
...AN "IDOL FAN" IS BY DEFINITION "SOMEBODY WHO WANTS TO BE LIED TO."

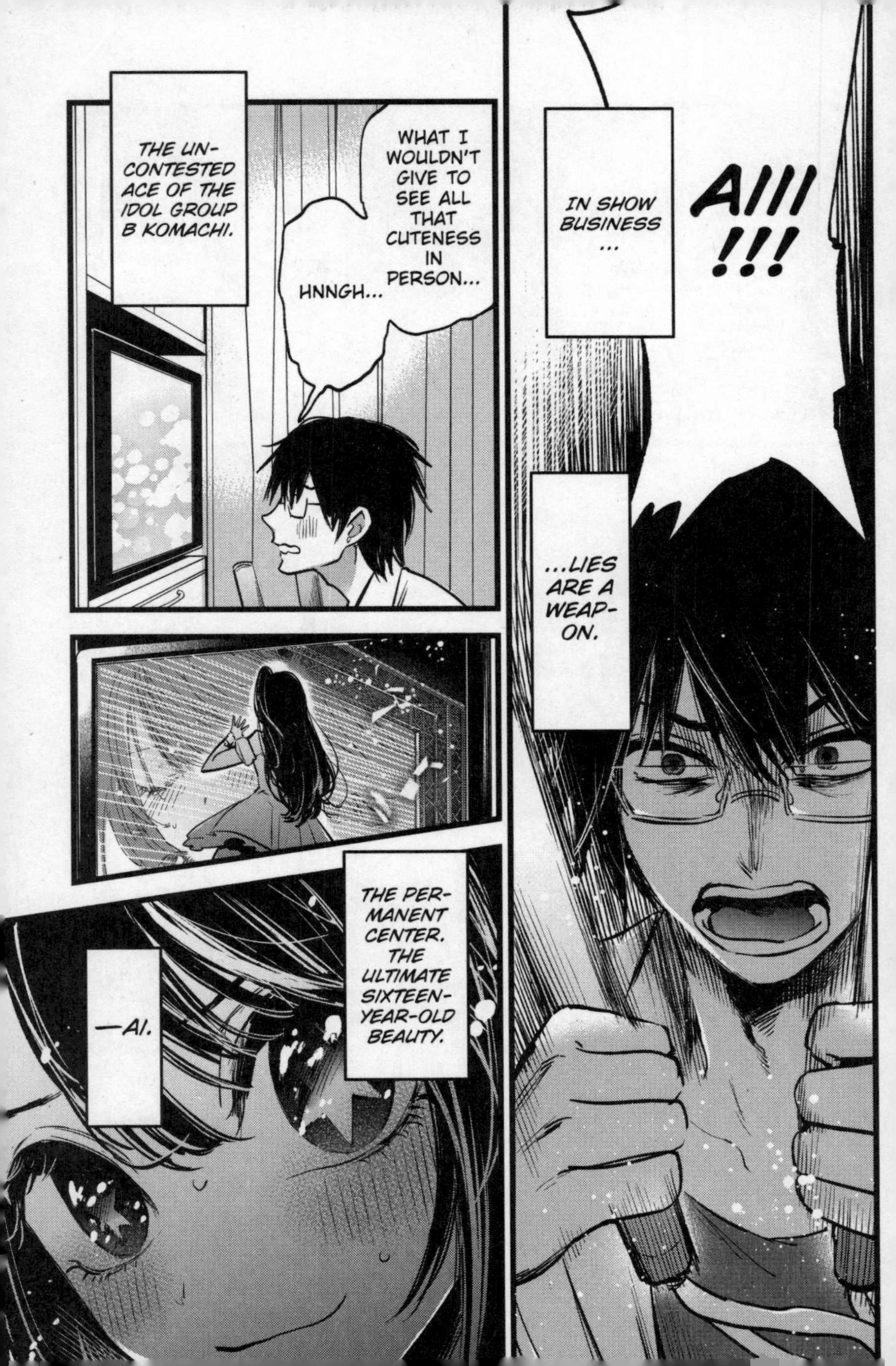
AIII !!!
IN SHOW BUSINESS ...
...LIES ARE A WEAP-ON.
WHAT I WOULDN'T GIVE TO SEE ALL THAT CUTENESS IN PERSON...
HNNGH...
THE UN-CONTESTED ACE OF THE IDOL GROUP B KOMACHI.
THE PER-MANENT CENTER. THE ULTIMATE SIXTEEN-YEAR-OLD BEAUTY.
—AI.

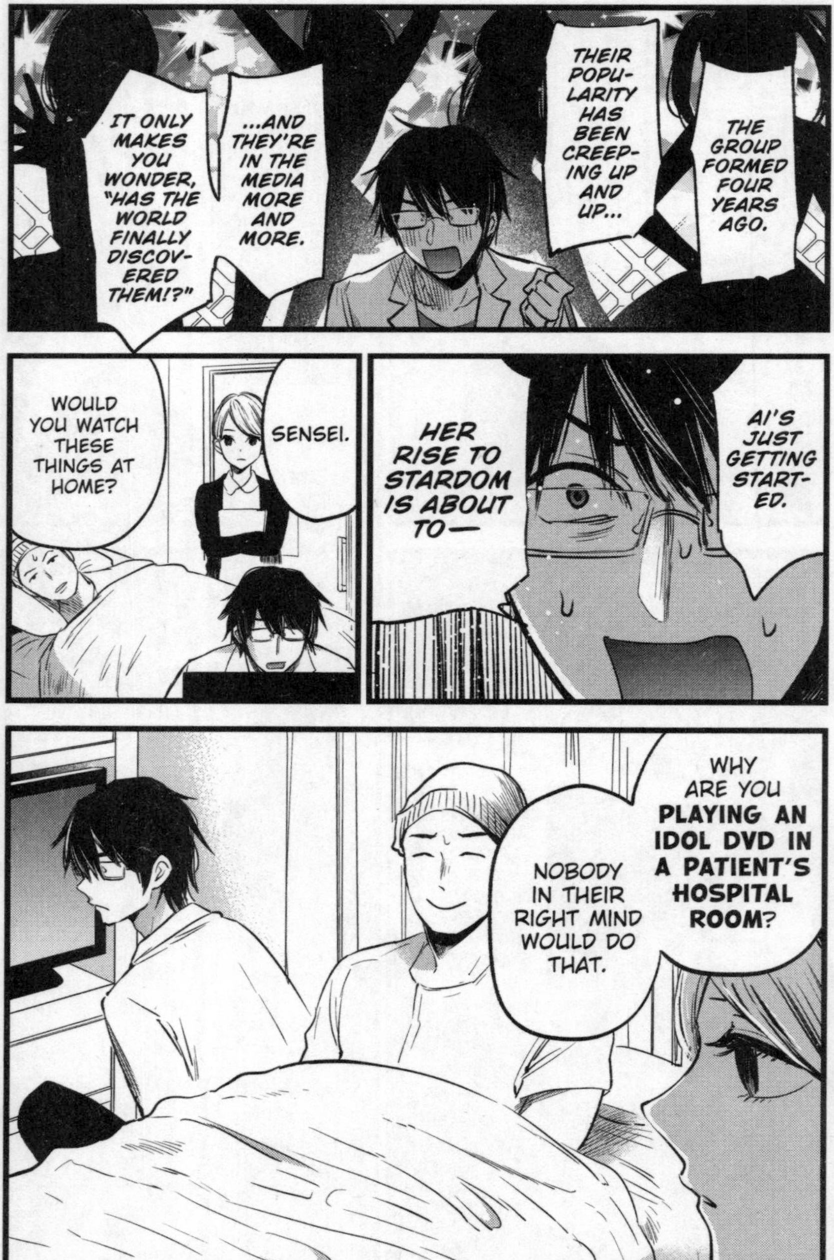
THE GROUP FORMED FOUR YEARS AGO.
THEIR POPULARITY HAS BEEN CREEPING UP AND UP...
...AND THEY'RE IN THE MEDIA MORE AND MORE.
IT ONLY MAKES YOU WONDER, "HAS THE WORLD FINALLY DISCOVERED THEM!?"
AI'S JUST GETTING STARTED.
HER RISE TO STARDOM IS ABOUT TO—
SENSEI.
WOULD YOU WATCH THESE THINGS AT HOME?
WHY ARE YOU **PLAYING AN IDOL DVD IN A PATIENT'S HOSPITAL ROOM?**
NOBODY IN THEIR RIGHT MIND WOULD DO THAT.

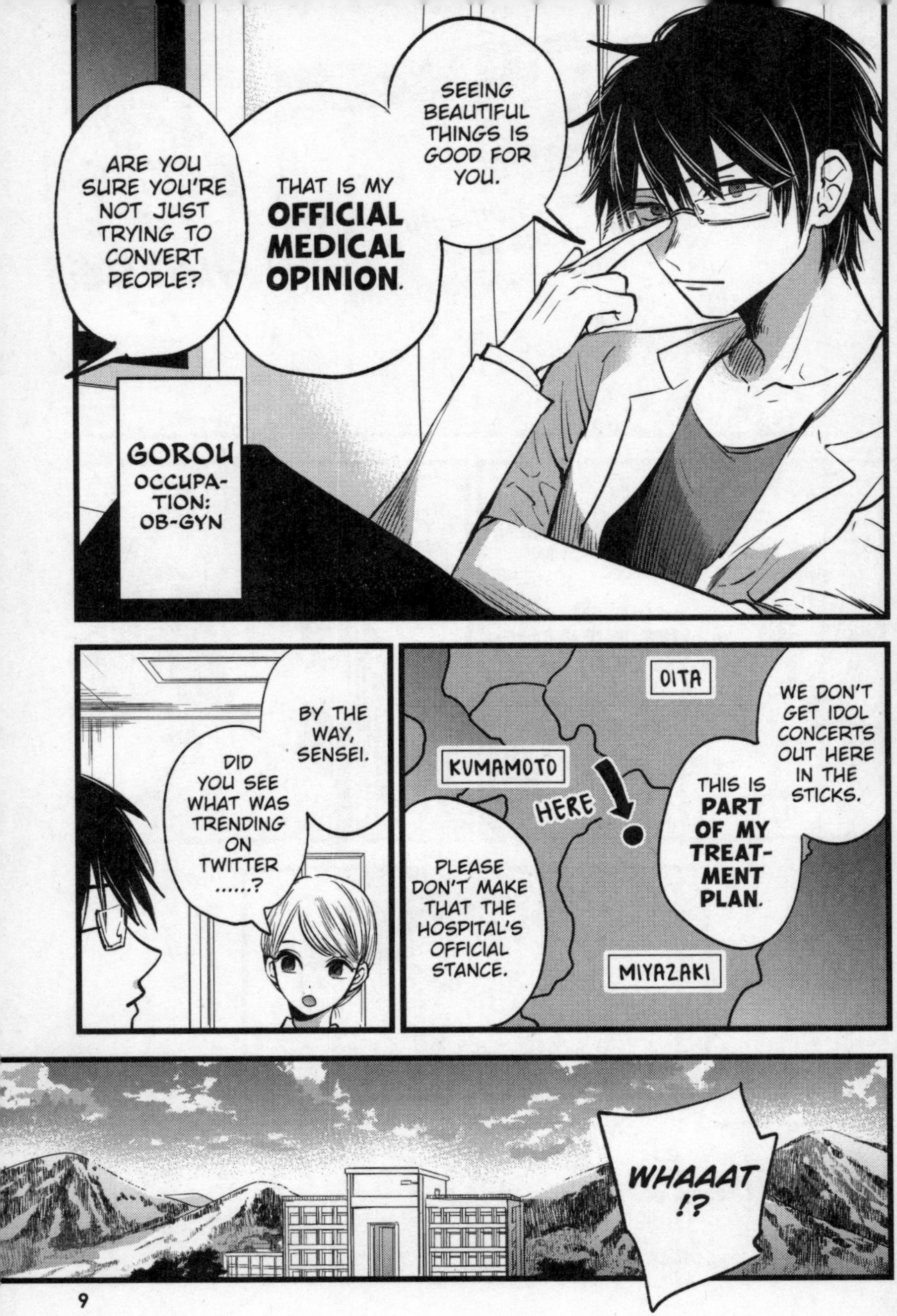
SEEING BEAUTIFUL THINGS IS GOOD FOR YOU.
THAT IS MY **OFFICIAL MEDICAL OPINION**.
ARE YOU SURE YOU'RE NOT JUST TRYING TO CONVERT PEOPLE?
GOROU OCCUPATION: OB-GYN
WE DON'T GET IDOL CONCERTS OUT HERE IN THE STICKS.
THIS IS **PART OF MY TREATMENT PLAN**.
OITA
KUMAMOTO
HERE
MIYAZAKI
PLEASE DON'T MAKE THAT THE HOSPITAL'S OFFICIAL STANCE.
BY THE WAY, SENSEI.
DID YOU SEE WHAT WAS TRENDING ON TWITTER ......?
WHAAAT !?

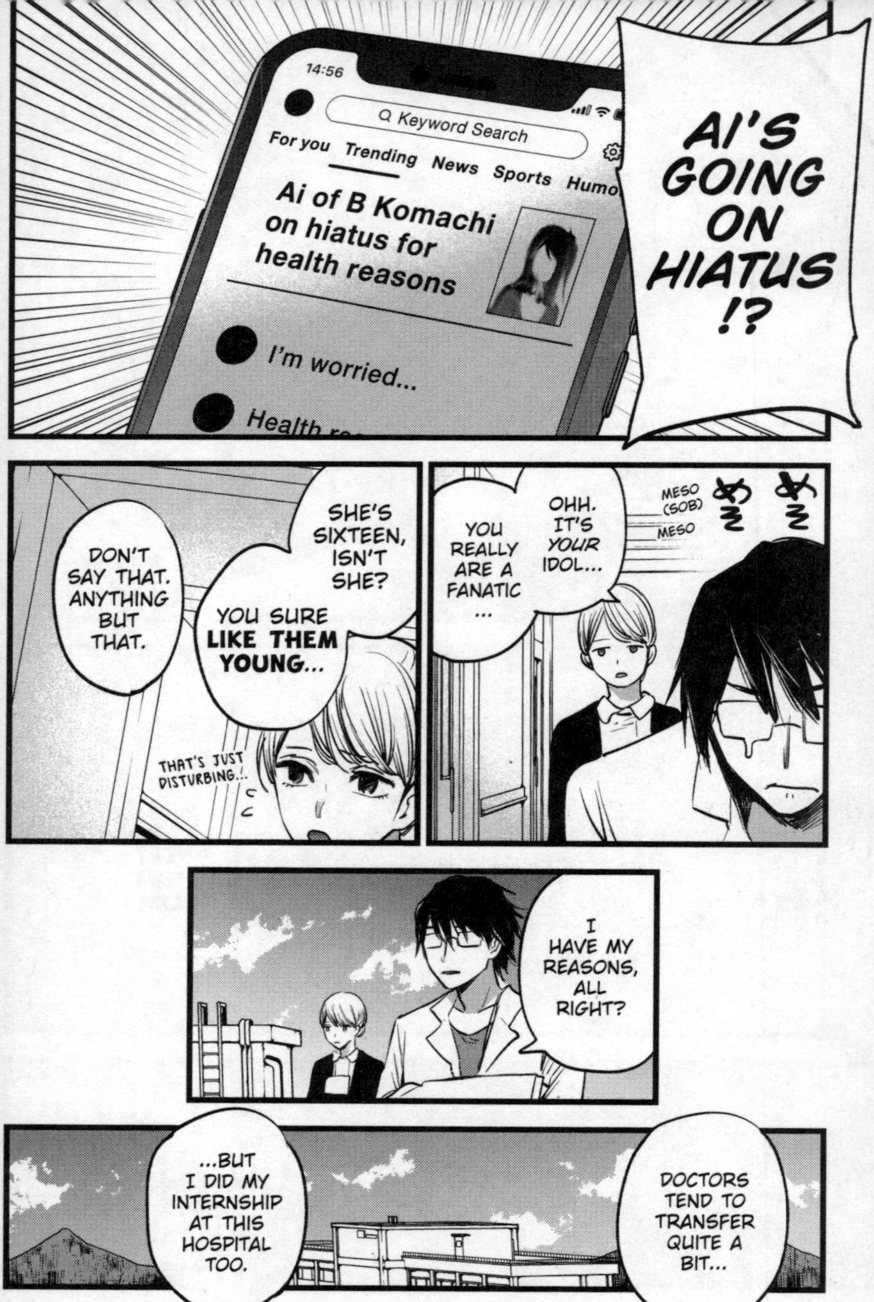
AI'S GOING ON HIATUS!?
14:56
Keyword Search
For you
Trending
News
Sports
Humo
Ai of B Komachi on hiatus for health reasons
I'm worried...
Health
めそ
めそ
MESO (SOB)
MESO
OHH. IT'S YOUR IDOL...
YOU REALLY ARE A FANATIC...
SHE'S SIXTEEN, ISN'T SHE?
YOU SURE LIKE THEM YOUNG...
DON'T SAY THAT. ANYTHING BUT THAT.
THAT'S JUST DISTURBING..!
I HAVE MY REASONS, ALL RIGHT?
DOCTORS TEND TO TRANSFER QUITE A BIT...
...BUT I DID MY INTERNSHIP AT THIS HOSPITAL TOO.

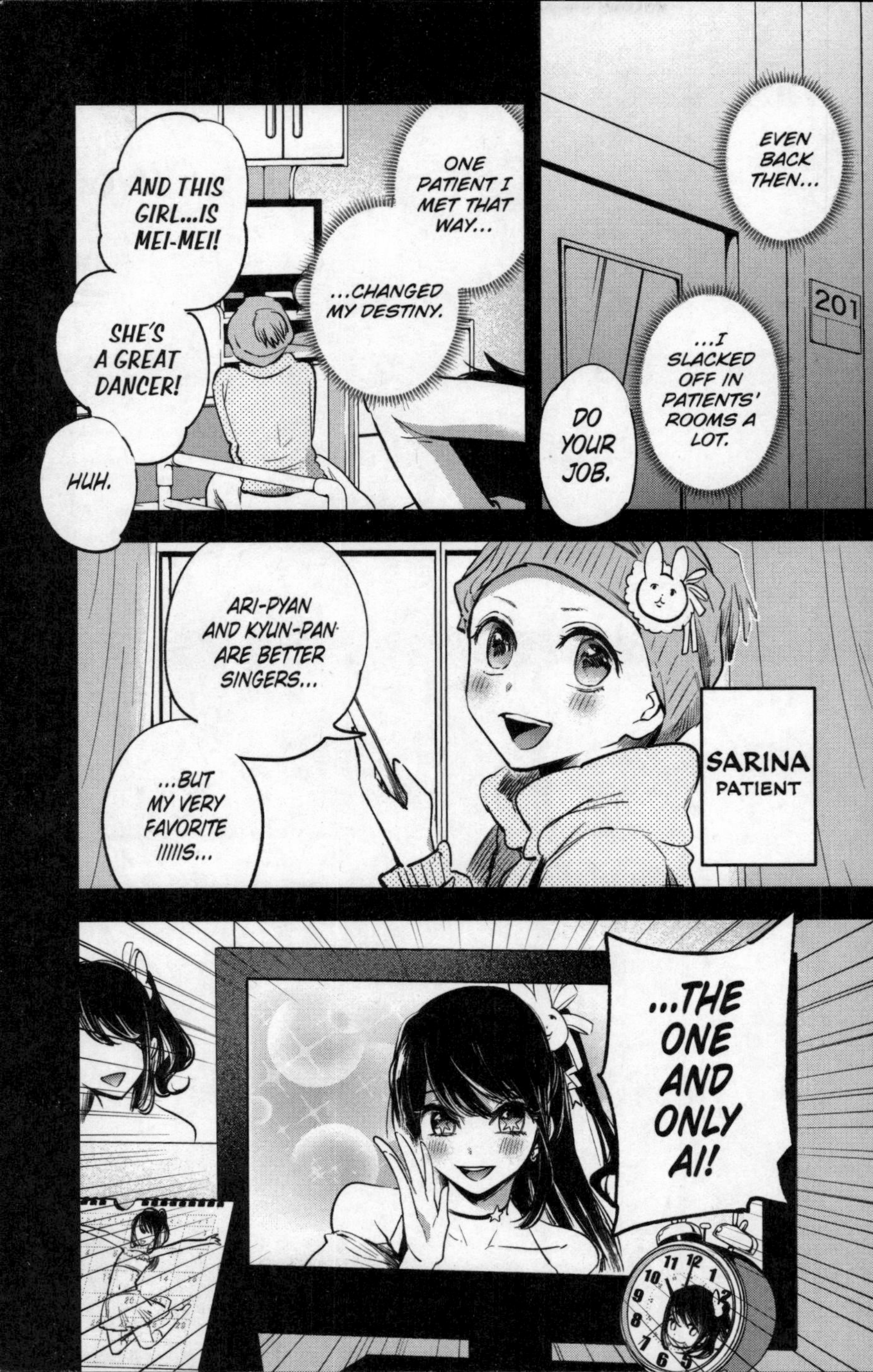
EVEN BACK THEN...
201
...I SLACKED OFF IN PATIENTS' ROOMS A LOT.
DO YOUR JOB.
ONE PATIENT I MET THAT WAY...
...CHANGED MY DESTINY.
AND THIS GIRL...IS MEI-MEI!
SHE'S A GREAT DANCER!
HUH.
SARINA
PATIENT
ARI-PYAN AND KYUN-PAN ARE BETTER SINGERS...
...BUT MY VERY FAVORITE IIIIIS...
...THE ONE AND ONLY AI!

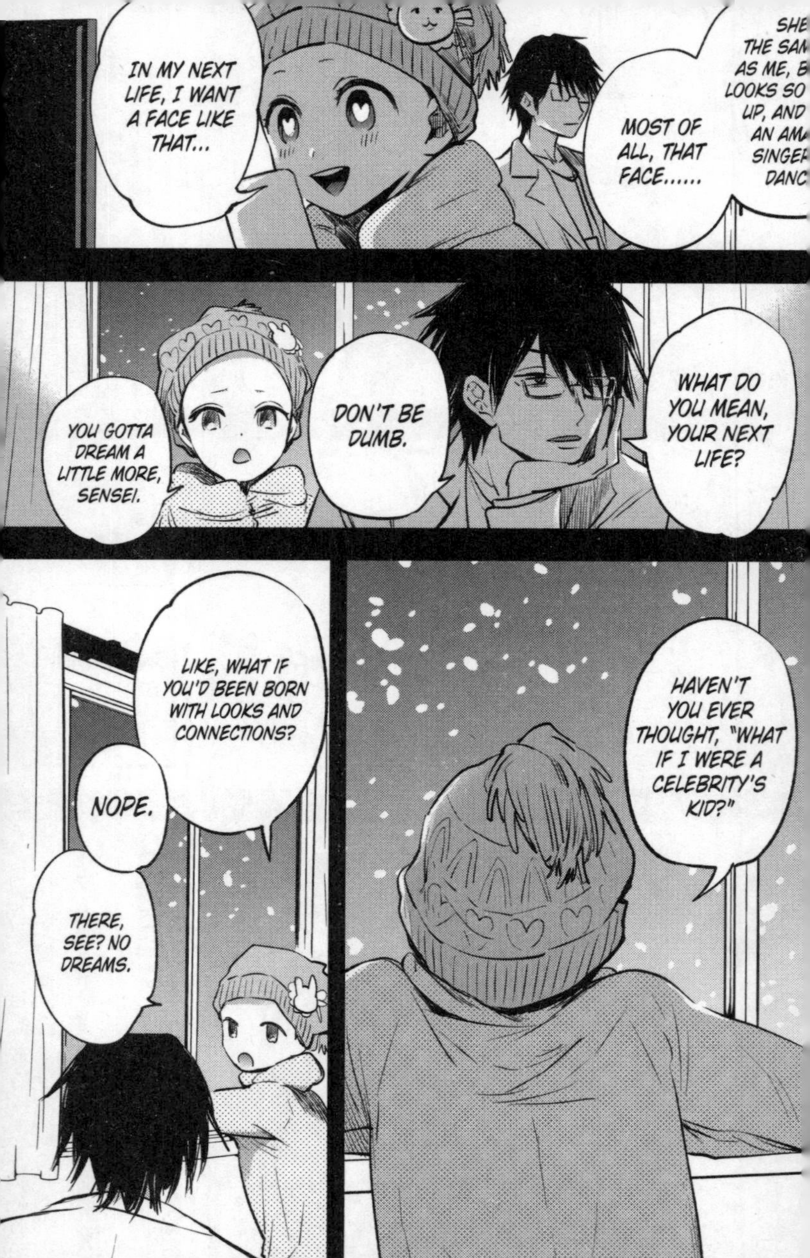
SHE THE SAM AS ME, B LOOKS SO UP, AND AN AMA SINGER DANC
MOST OF ALL, THAT FACE......
IN MY NEXT LIFE, I WANT A FACE LIKE THAT...
WHAT DO YOU MEAN, YOUR NEXT LIFE?
DON'T BE DUMB.
YOU GOTTA DREAM A LITTLE MORE, SENSEI.
HAVEN'T YOU EVER THOUGHT, "WHAT IF I WERE A CELEBRITY'S KID?"
LIKE, WHAT IF YOU'D BEEN BORN WITH LOOKS AND CONNECTIONS?
NOPE.
THERE, SEE? NO DREAMS.

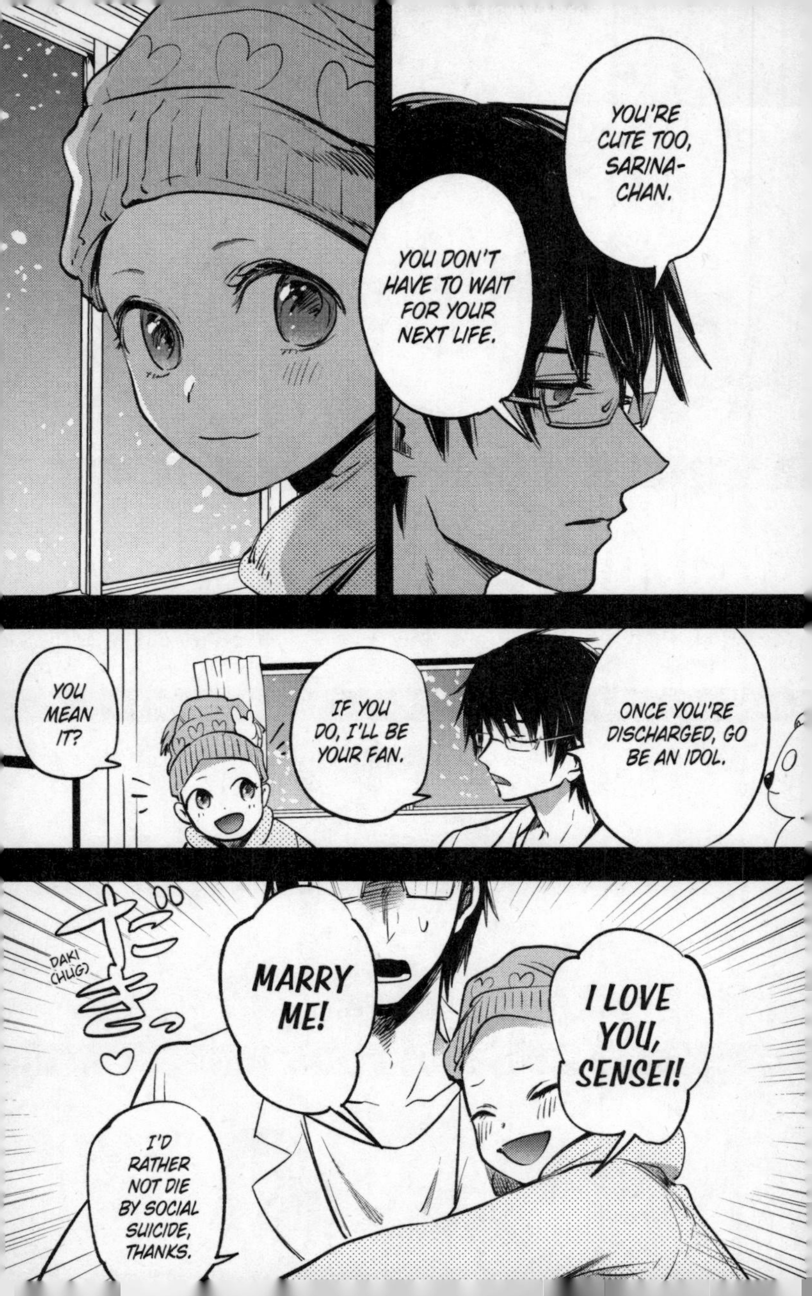
YOU'RE CUTE TOO, SARINA-CHAN.
YOU DON'T HAVE TO WAIT FOR YOUR NEXT LIFE.
ONCE YOU'RE DISCHARGED, GO BE AN IDOL.
IF YOU DO, I'LL BE YOUR FAN.
YOU MEAN IT?
I LOVE YOU, SENSEI!
MARRY ME!
DAKI (HUG)
I'D RATHER NOT DIE BY SOCIAL SUICIDE, THANKS.

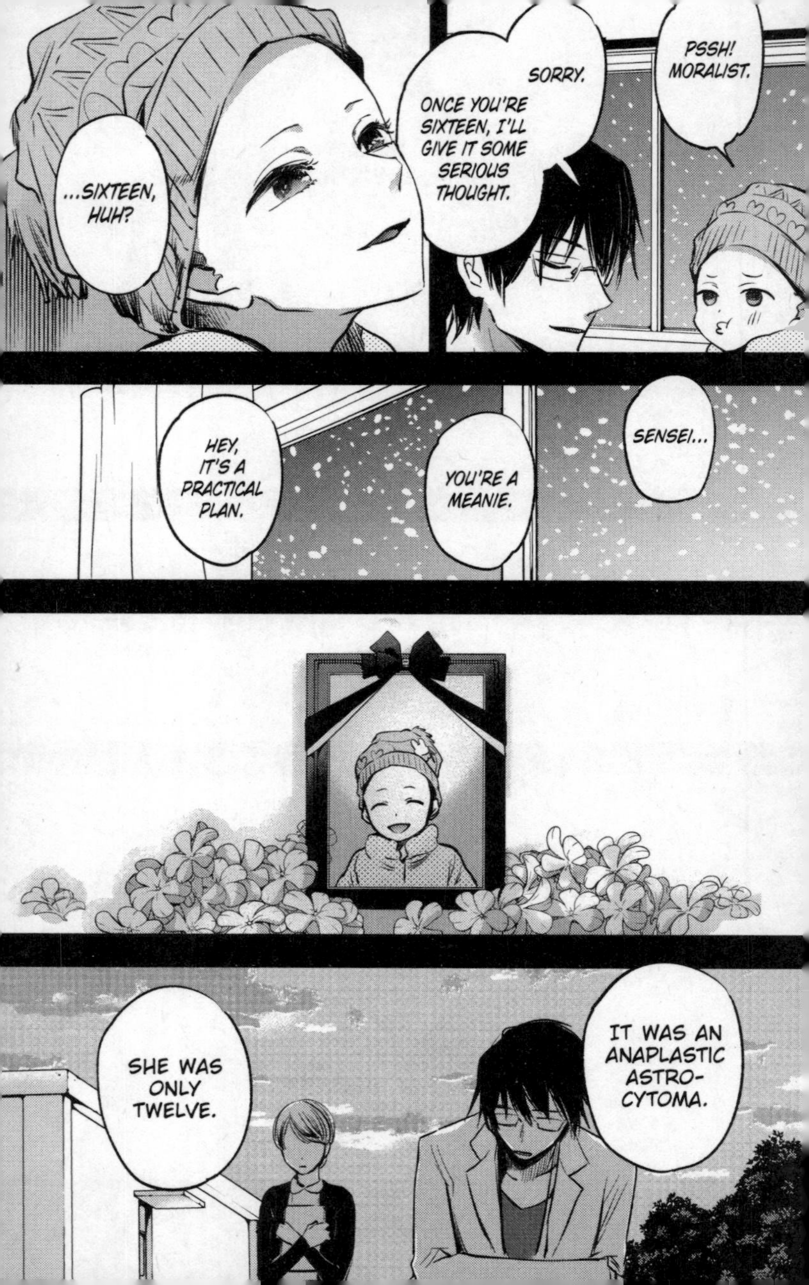
PSSH! MORALIST.
SORRY. ONCE YOU'RE SIXTEEN, I'LL GIVE IT SOME SERIOUS THOUGHT.
...SIXTEEN, HUH?
SENSEI...
YOU'RE A MEANIE.
HEY, IT'S A PRACTICAL PLAN.
IT WAS AN ANAPLASTIC ASTRO-CYTOMA.
SHE WAS ONLY TWELVE.

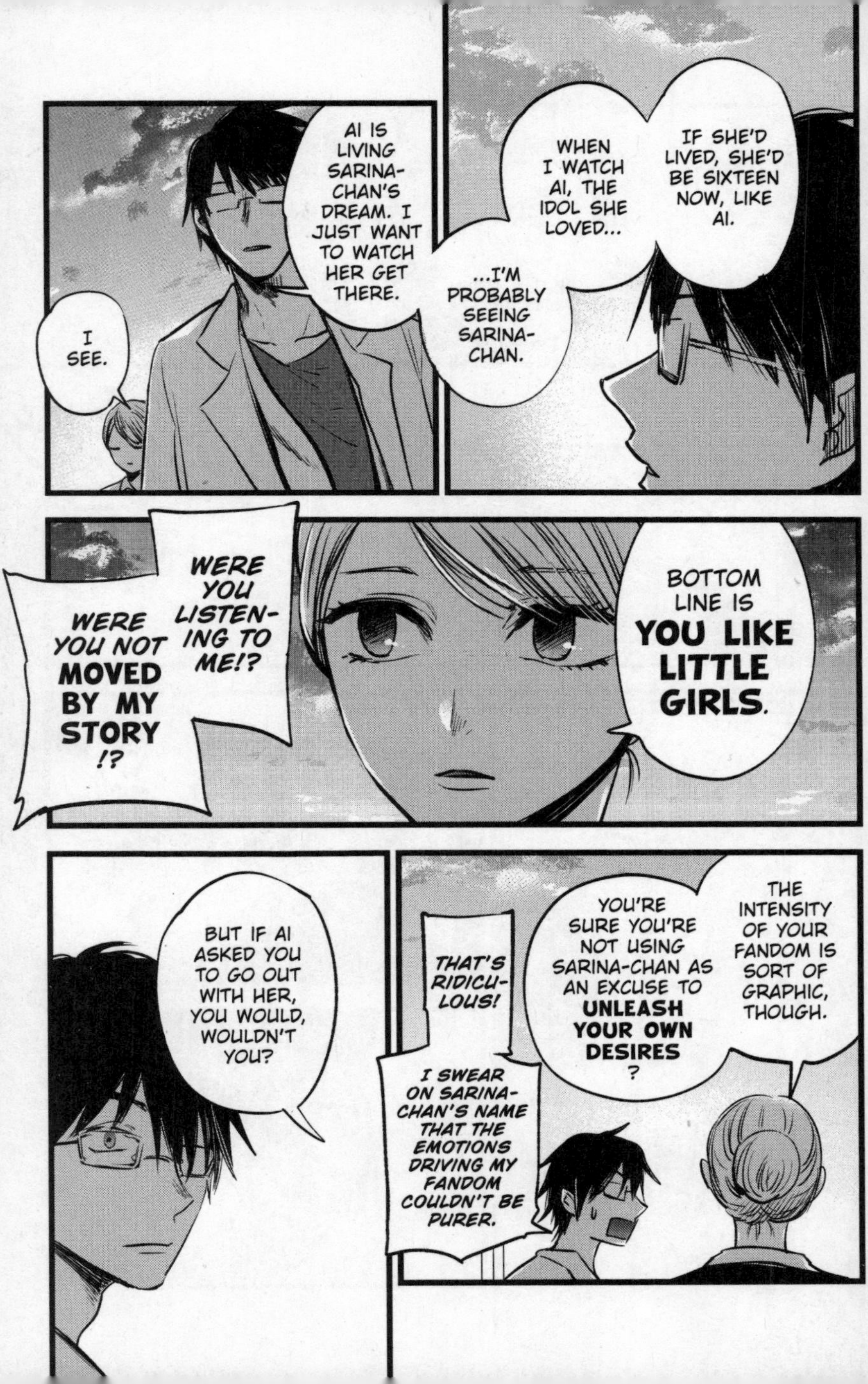
IF SHE'D LIVED, SHE'D BE SIXTEEN NOW, LIKE AI.
WHEN I WATCH AI, THE IDOL SHE LOVED...
...I'M PROBABLY SEEING SARINA-CHAN.
AI IS LIVING SARINA-CHAN'S DREAM. I JUST WANT TO WATCH HER GET THERE.
I SEE.
BOTTOM LINE IS **YOU LIKE LITTLE GIRLS**.
WERE YOU LISTENING TO ME!?
WERE YOU NOT **MOVED BY MY STORY** *!?*
THE INTENSITY OF YOUR FANDOM IS SORT OF GRAPHIC, THOUGH.
YOU'RE SURE YOU'RE NOT USING SARINA-CHAN AS AN EXCUSE TO **UNLEASH YOUR OWN DESIRES** ?
THAT'S RIDICULOUS!
I SWEAR ON SARINA-CHAN'S NAME THAT THE EMOTIONS DRIVING MY FANDOM COULDN'T BE PURER.
BUT IF AI ASKED YOU TO GO OUT WITH HER, YOU WOULD, WOULDN'T YOU?

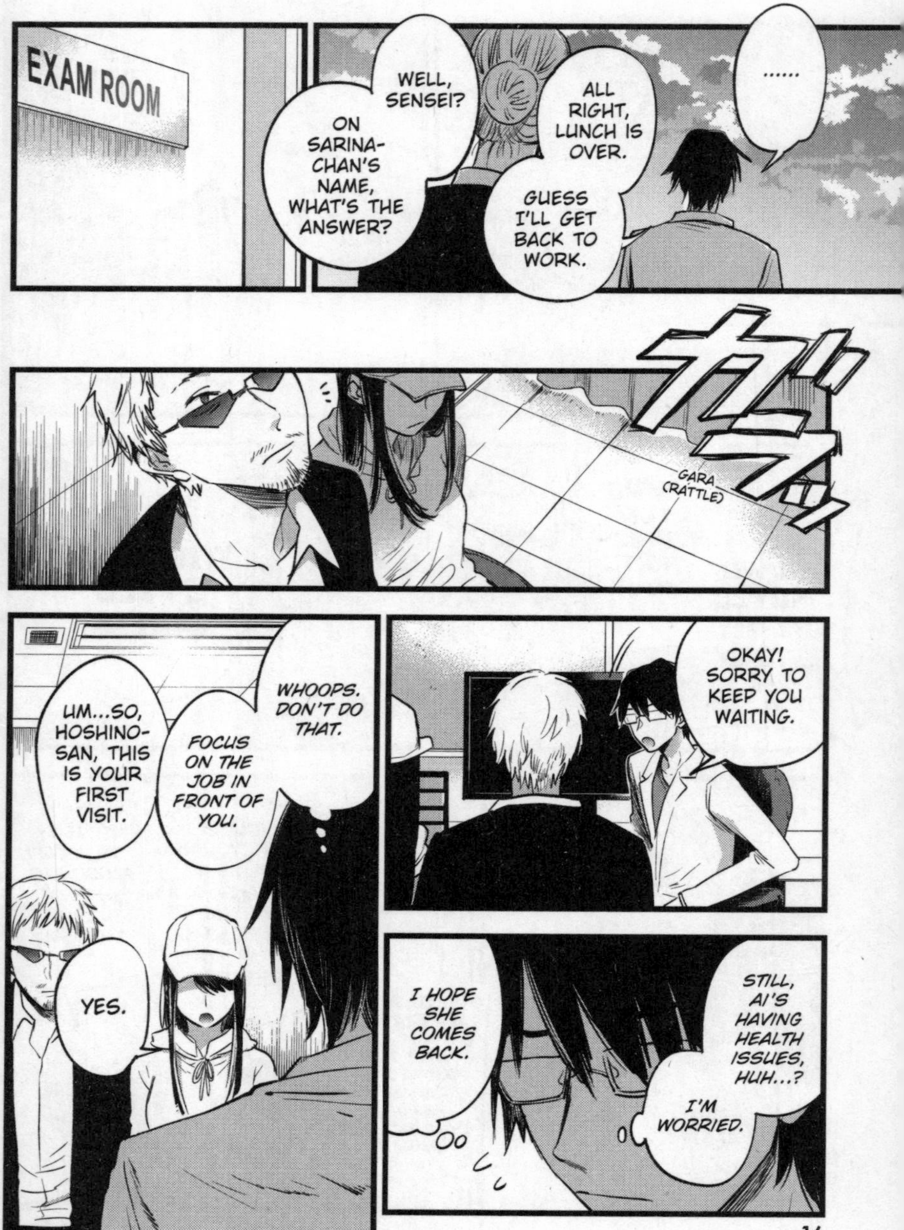
......
ALL RIGHT, LUNCH IS OVER.
GUESS I'LL GET BACK TO WORK.
WELL, SENSEI?
ON SARINA-CHAN'S NAME, WHAT'S THE ANSWER?
EXAM ROOM
GARA (RATTLE)
OKAY! SORRY TO KEEP YOU WAITING.
STILL, AI'S HAVING HEALTH ISSUES, HUH...?
I'M WORRIED.
I HOPE SHE COMES BACK.
WHOOPS. DON'T DO THAT.
FOCUS ON THE JOB IN FRONT OF YOU.
UM...SO, HOSHINO-SAN, THIS IS YOUR FIRST VISIT.
YES.

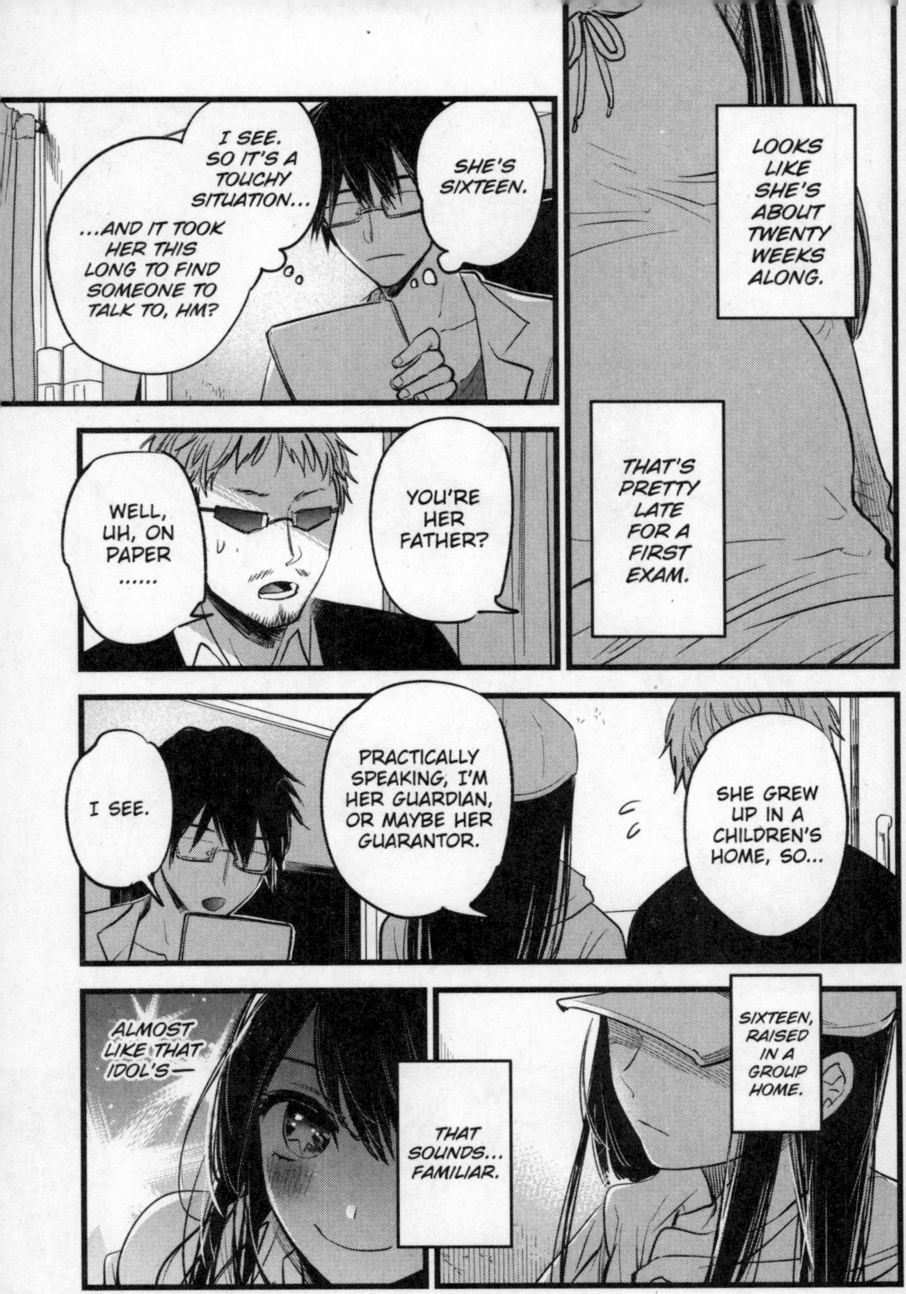
LOOKS LIKE SHE'S ABOUT TWENTY WEEKS ALONG.
THAT'S PRETTY LATE FOR A FIRST EXAM.
SHE'S SIXTEEN.
I SEE. SO IT'S A TOUCHY SITUATION...
...AND IT TOOK HER THIS LONG TO FIND SOMEONE TO TALK TO, HM?
YOU'RE HER FATHER?
WELL, UH, ON PAPER......
SHE GREW UP IN A CHILDREN'S HOME, SO...
PRACTICALLY SPEAKING, I'M HER GUARDIAN, OR MAYBE HER GUARANTOR.
I SEE.
SIXTEEN, RAISED IN A GROUP HOME.
THAT SOUNDS... FAMILIAR.
ALMOST LIKE THAT IDOL'S—

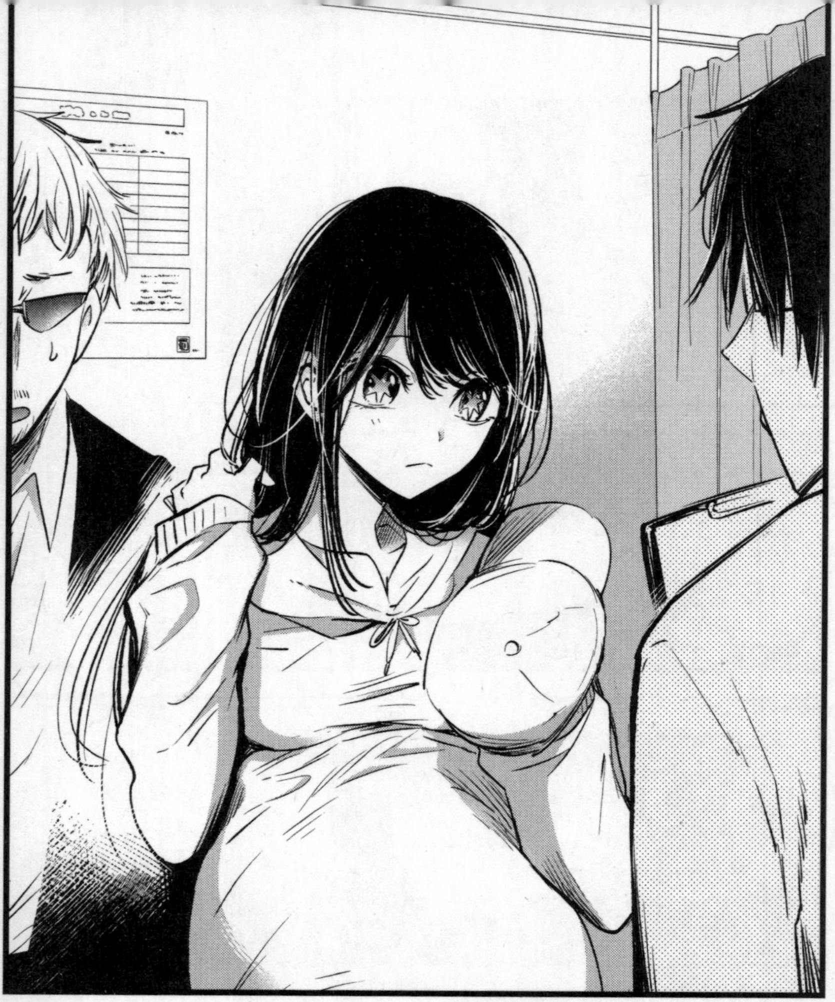

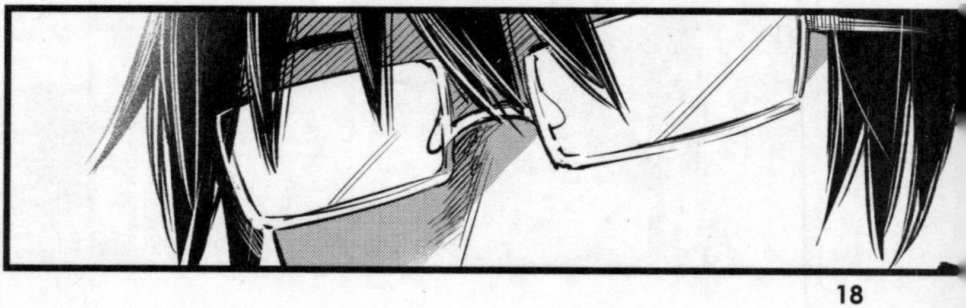

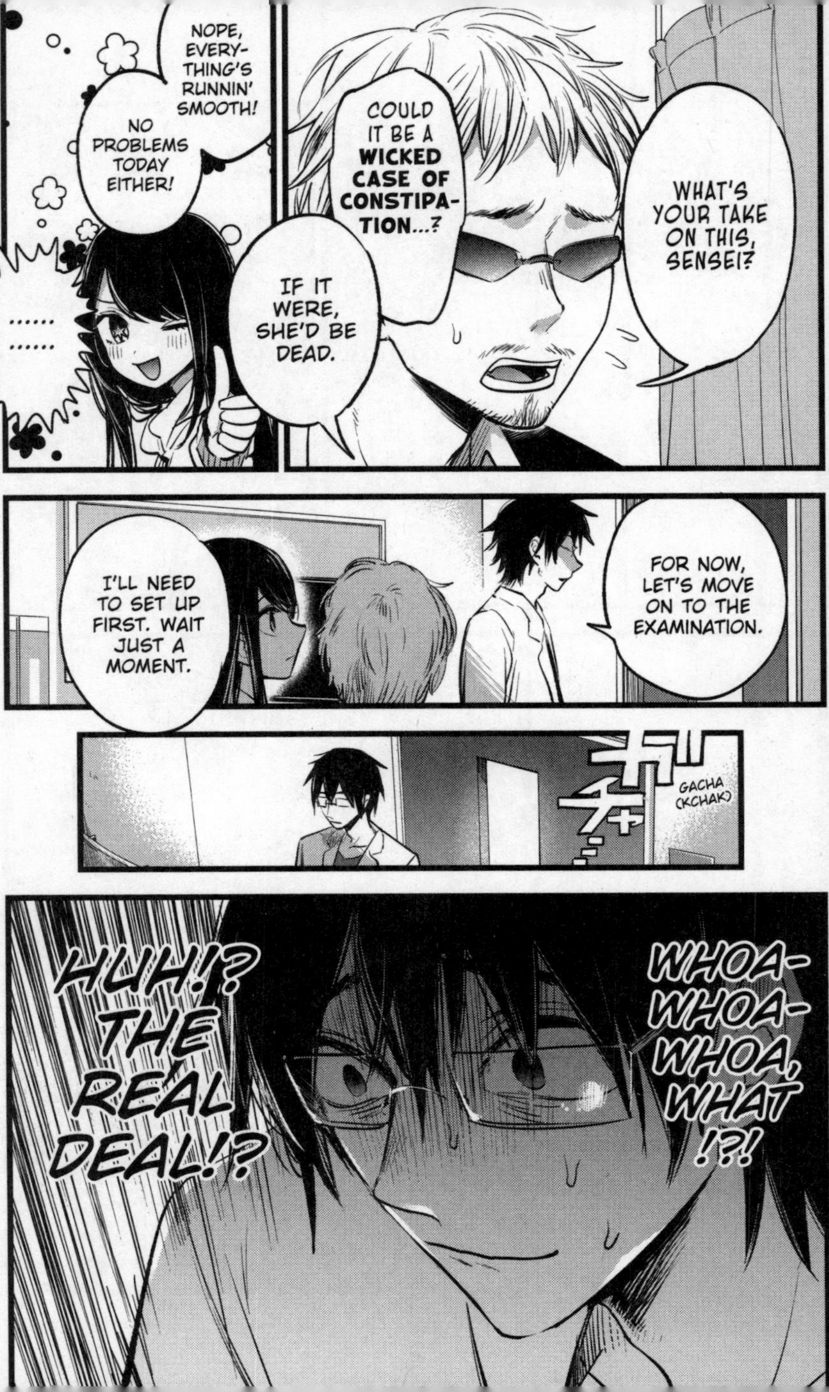
WHAT'S YOUR TAKE ON THIS, SENSEI!?
COULD IT BE A **WICKED CASE OF CONSTIPATION...?**
IF IT WERE, SHE'D BE DEAD.
NOPE, EVERYTHING'S RUNNIN' SMOOTH!
NO PROBLEMS TODAY EITHER!
......
......
FOR NOW, LET'S MOVE ON TO THE EXAMINATION.
I'LL NEED TO SET UP FIRST. WAIT JUST A MOMENT.
ガチャ
GACHA (KCHAK)
WHOA-WHOA-WHOA, WHAT!?!
HUH!? THE REAL DEAL!?

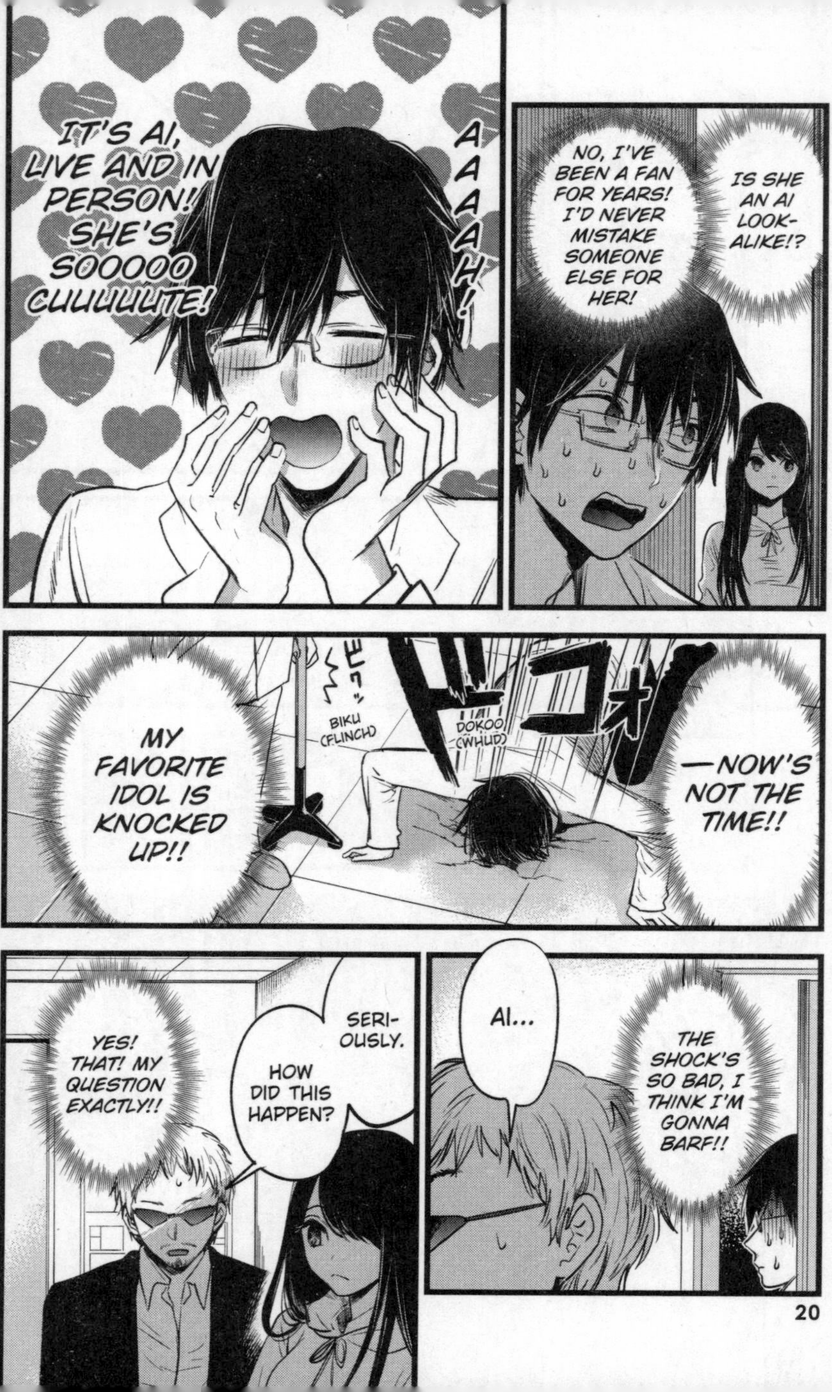
IS SHE AN AI LOOK-ALIKE!?
NO, I'VE BEEN A FAN FOR YEARS! I'D NEVER MISTAKE SOMEONE ELSE FOR HER!
AAAAAH!
IT'S AI, LIVE AND IN PERSON!! SHE'S SOOOOO CUUUUUUTE!
—NOW'S NOT THE TIME!!
DOKOO (WHUD)
BIKU (FLINCH)
MY FAVORITE IDOL IS KNOCKED UP!!
THE SHOCK'S SO BAD, I THINK I'M GONNA BARF!!
AI...
SERI-OUSLY.
HOW DID THIS HAPPEN?
YES! THAT! MY QUESTION EXACTLY!!

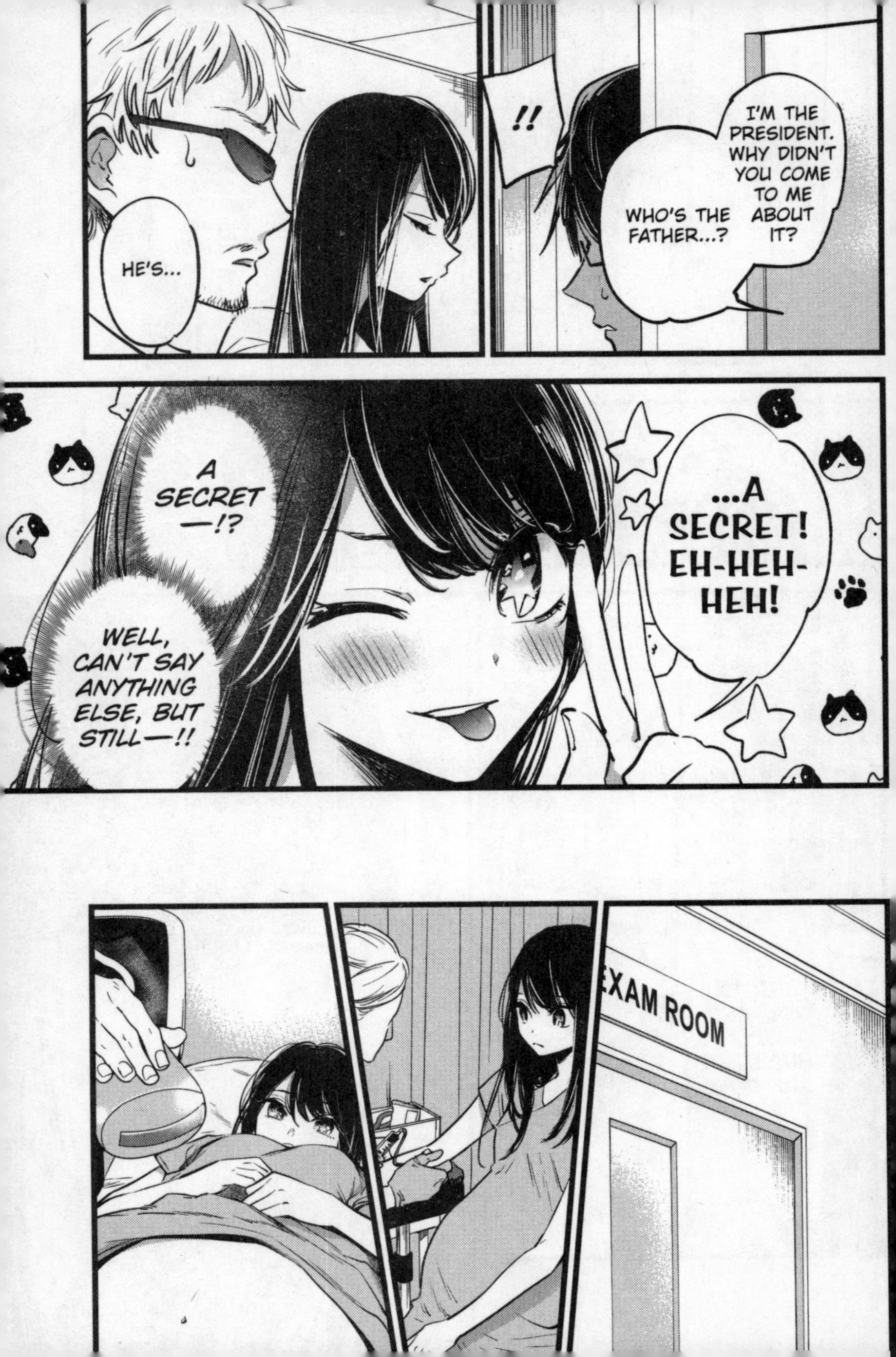
I'M THE PRESIDENT. WHY DIDN'T YOU COME TO ME ABOUT IT?
WHO'S THE FATHER...?
!!
HE'S...
...A SECRET! EH-HEH-HEH!
A SECRET—!?
WELL, CAN'T SAY ANYTHING ELSE, BUT STILL—!!
EXAM ROOM

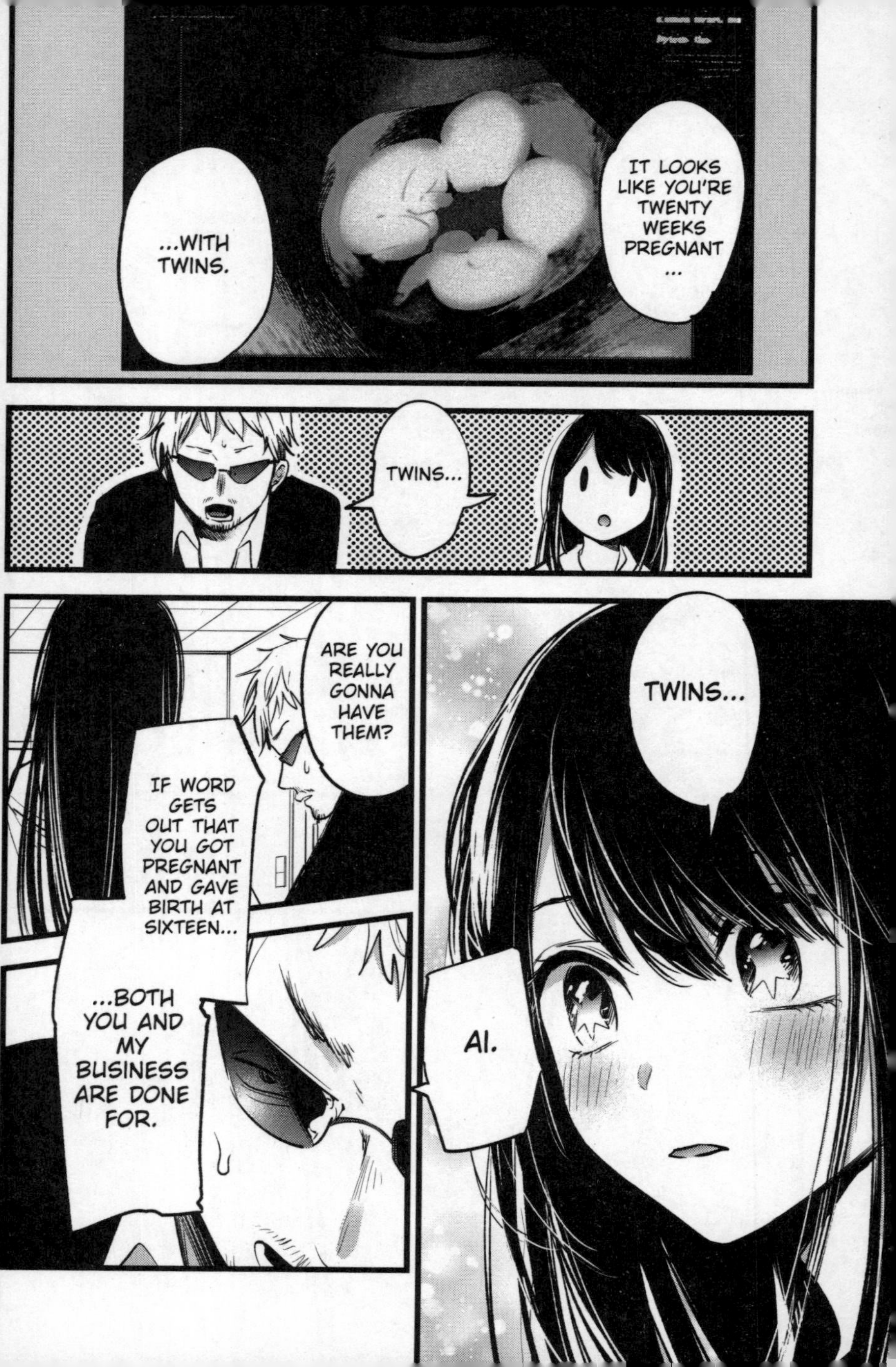
IT LOOKS LIKE YOU'RE TWENTY WEEKS PREGNANT...
...WITH TWINS.
TWINS...
TWINS...
AI.
ARE YOU REALLY GONNA HAVE THEM?
IF WORD GETS OUT THAT YOU GOT PREGNANT AND GAVE BIRTH AT SIXTEEN...
...BOTH YOU AND MY BUSINESS ARE DONE FOR.

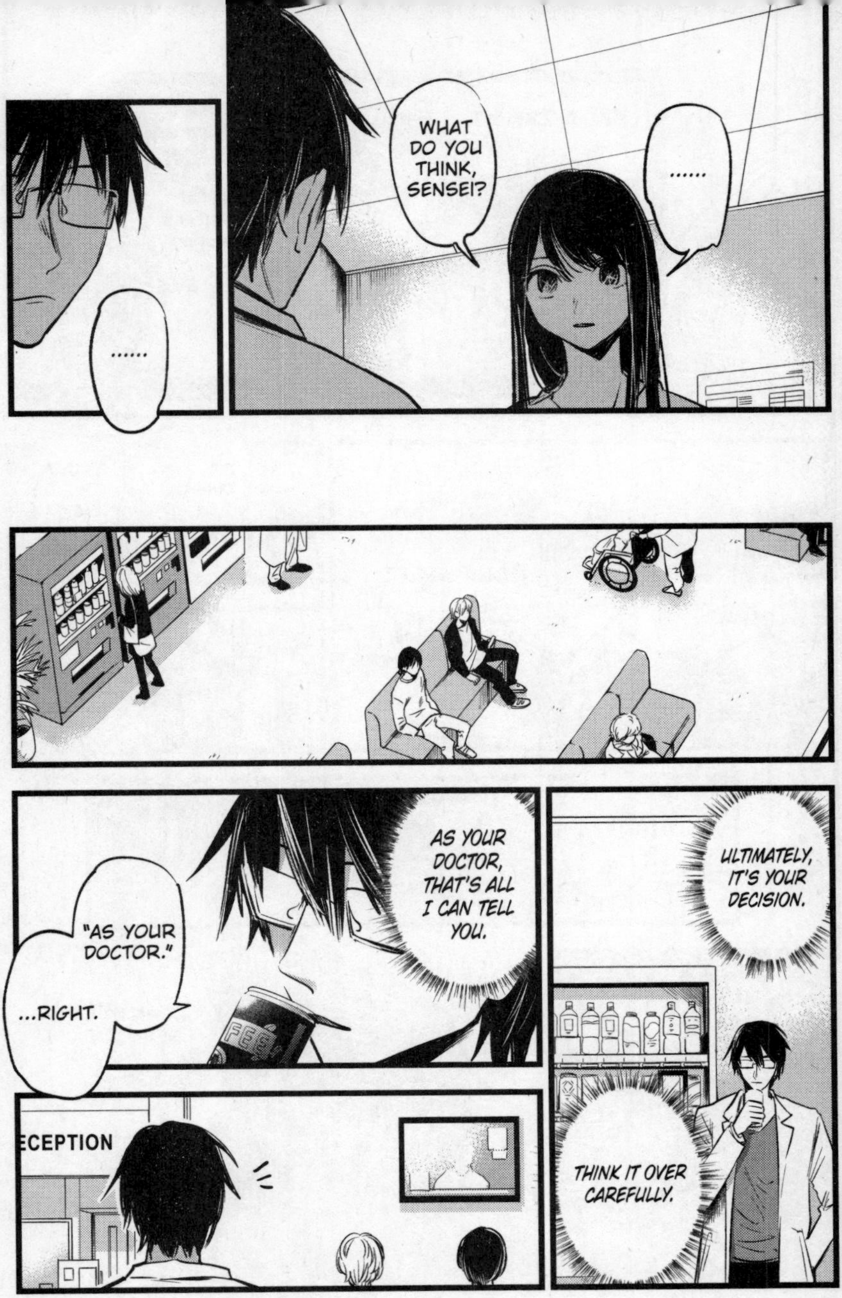
......
WHAT DO YOU THINK, SENSEI?
......
ULTIMATELY, IT'S YOUR DECISION.
THINK IT OVER CAREFULLY.
AS YOUR DOCTOR, THAT'S ALL I CAN TELL YOU.
"AS YOUR DOCTOR."
...RIGHT.
ECEPTION

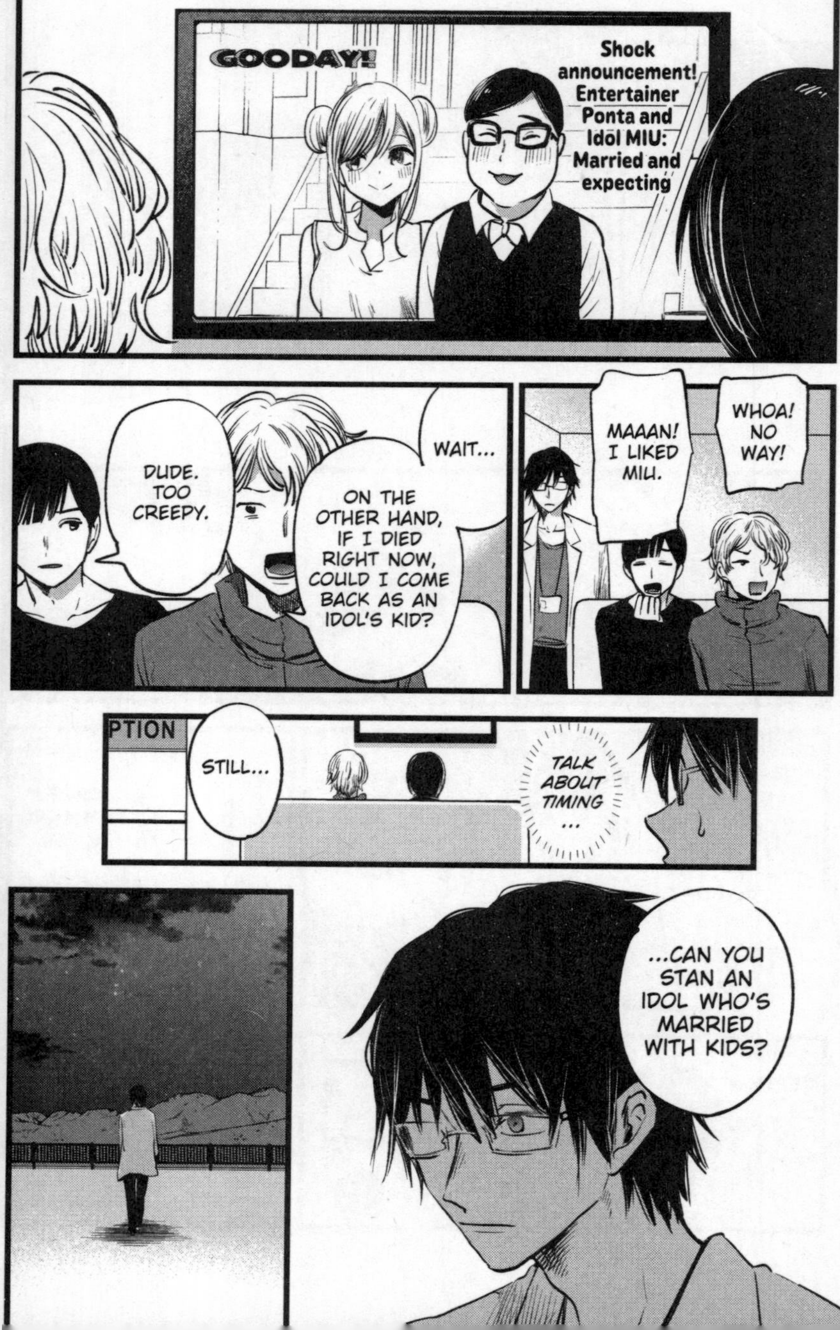
Shock announcement! Entertainer Ponta and Idol MIU: Married and expecting
GOODAY!
WHOA! NO WAY!
MAAAN! I LIKED MIU.
WAIT...
ON THE OTHER HAND, IF I DIED RIGHT NOW, COULD I COME BACK AS AN IDOL'S KID?
DUDE. TOO CREEPY.
TALK ABOUT TIMING ...
STILL...
PTION
...CAN YOU STAN AN IDOL WHO'S MARRIED WITH KIDS?

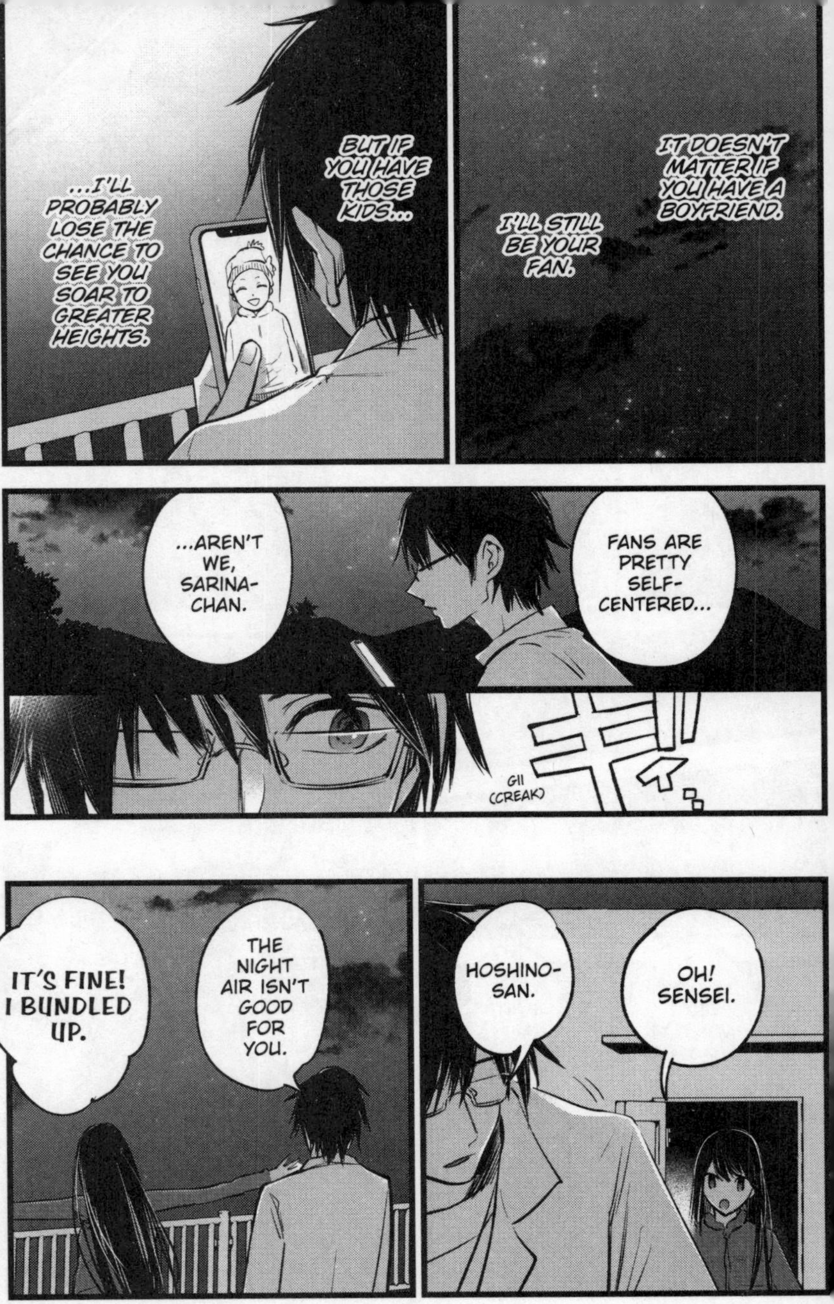
IT DOESN'T MATTER IF YOU HAVE A BOYFRIEND.
I'LL STILL BE YOUR FAN.
BUT IF YOU HAVE THOSE KIDS...
...I'LL PROBABLY LOSE THE CHANCE TO SEE YOU SOAR TO GREATER HEIGHTS.
FANS ARE PRETTY SELF-CENTERED...
...AREN'T WE, SARINA-CHAN.
GII (CREAK)
OH! SENSEI.
HOSHINO-SAN.
THE NIGHT AIR ISN'T GOOD FOR YOU.
IT'S FINE! I BUNDLED UP.

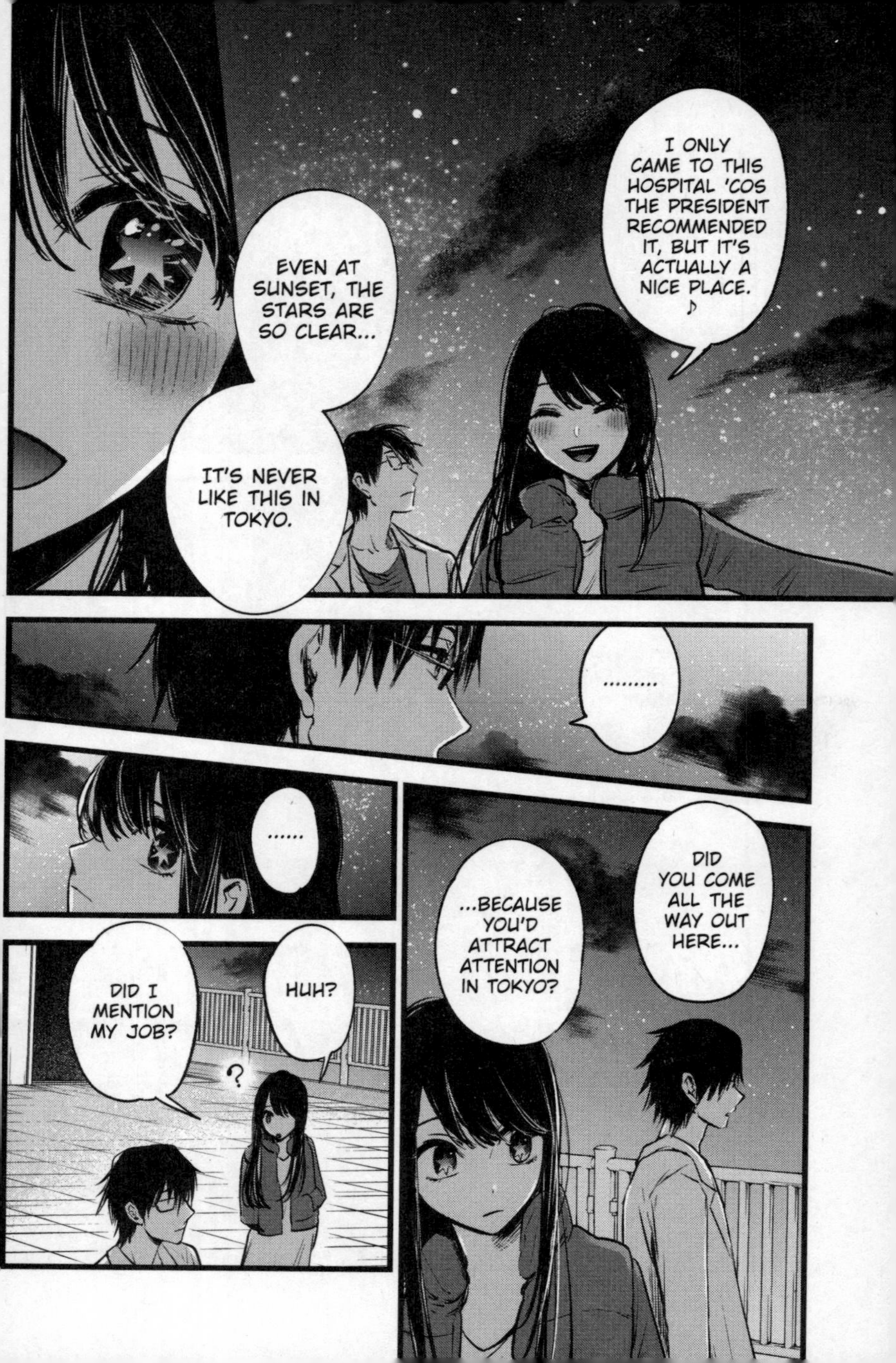
I ONLY CAME TO THIS HOSPITAL 'COS THE PRESIDENT RECOMMENDED IT, BUT IT'S ACTUALLY A NICE PLACE. ♪
EVEN AT SUNSET, THE STARS ARE SO CLEAR...
IT'S NEVER LIKE THIS IN TOKYO.
....
DID YOU COME ALL THE WAY OUT HERE...
...BECAUSE YOU'D ATTRACT ATTENTION IN TOKYO?
......
HUH?
DID I MENTION MY JOB?

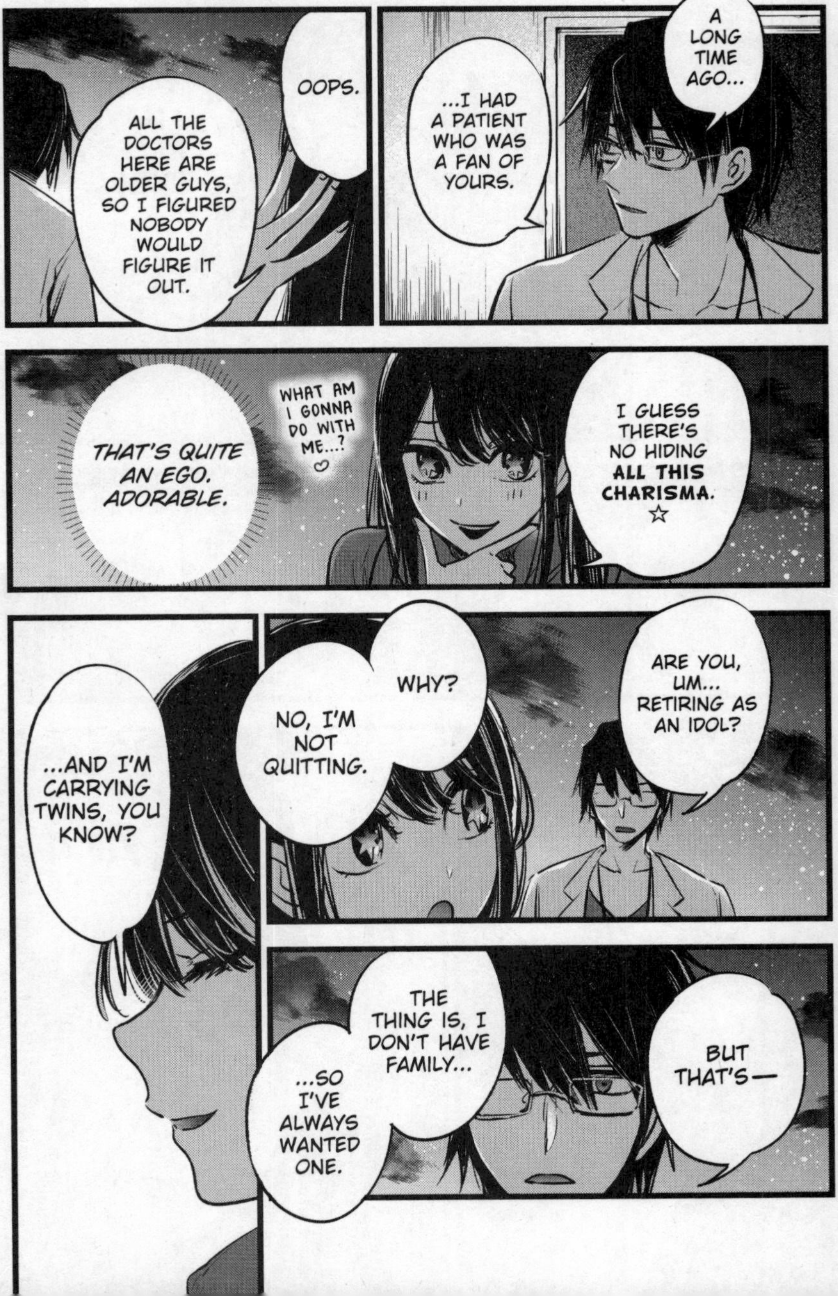
A LONG TIME AGO...
...I HAD A PATIENT WHO WAS A FAN OF YOURS.
OOPS.
ALL THE DOCTORS HERE ARE OLDER GUYS, SO I FIGURED NOBODY WOULD FIGURE IT OUT.
I GUESS THERE'S NO HIDING **ALL THIS CHARISMA.** ☆
WHAT AM I GONNA DO WITH ME...? ♡
THAT'S QUITE AN EGO. ADORABLE.
ARE YOU, UM... RETIRING AS AN IDOL?
WHY?
NO, I'M NOT QUITTING.
...AND I'M CARRYING TWINS, YOU KNOW?
BUT THAT'S—
THE THING IS, I DON'T HAVE FAMILY...
...SO I'VE ALWAYS WANTED ONE.

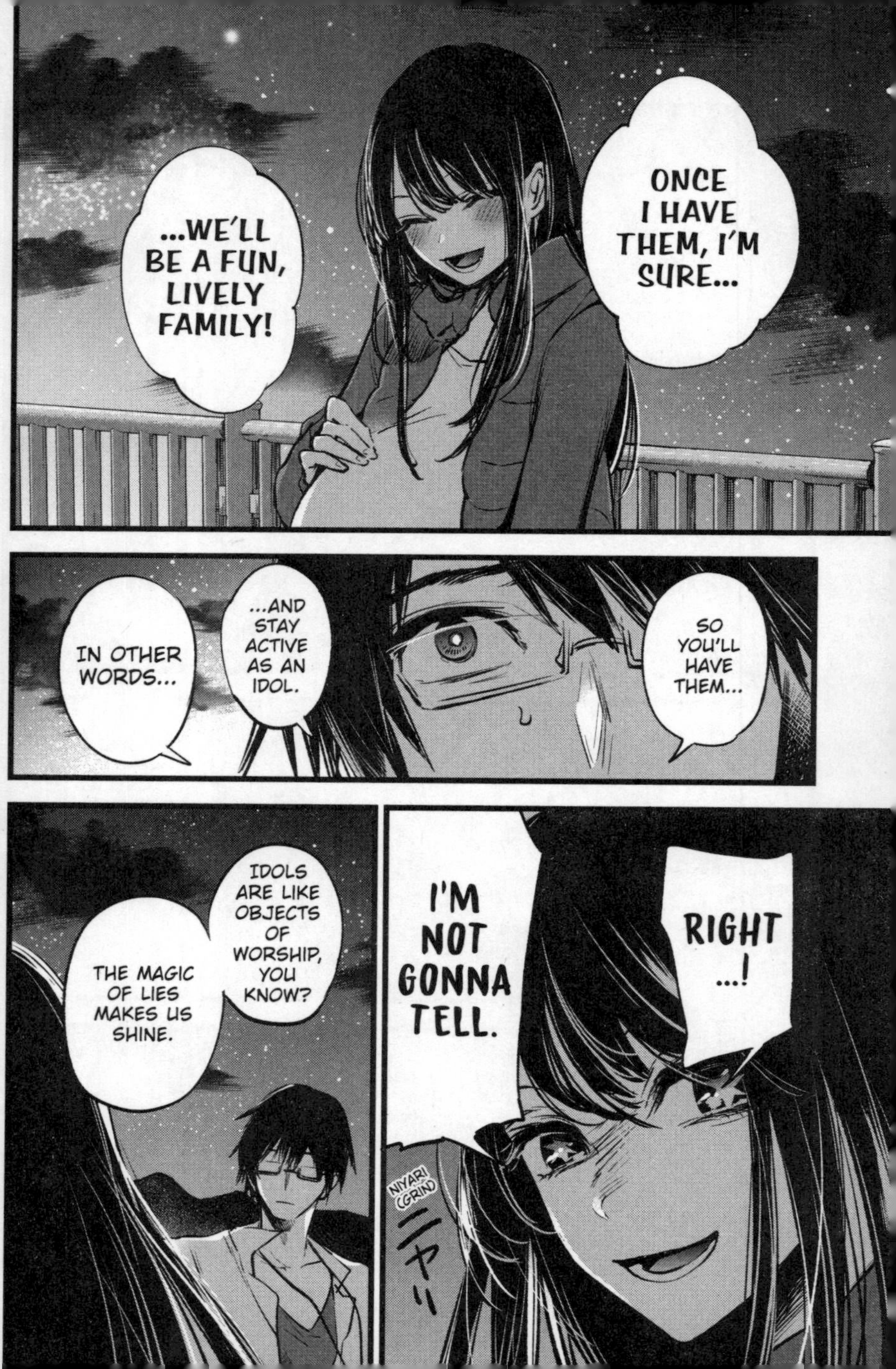
ONCE I HAVE THEM, I'M SURE...
...WE'LL BE A FUN, LIVELY FAMILY!
SO YOU'LL HAVE THEM...
...AND STAY ACTIVE AS AN IDOL.
IN OTHER WORDS...
RIGHT ...!
I'M NOT GONNA TELL.
NIYARI (GRIN)
ニヤリ
IDOLS ARE LIKE OBJECTS OF WORSHIP, YOU KNOW?
THE MAGIC OF LIES MAKES US SHINE.

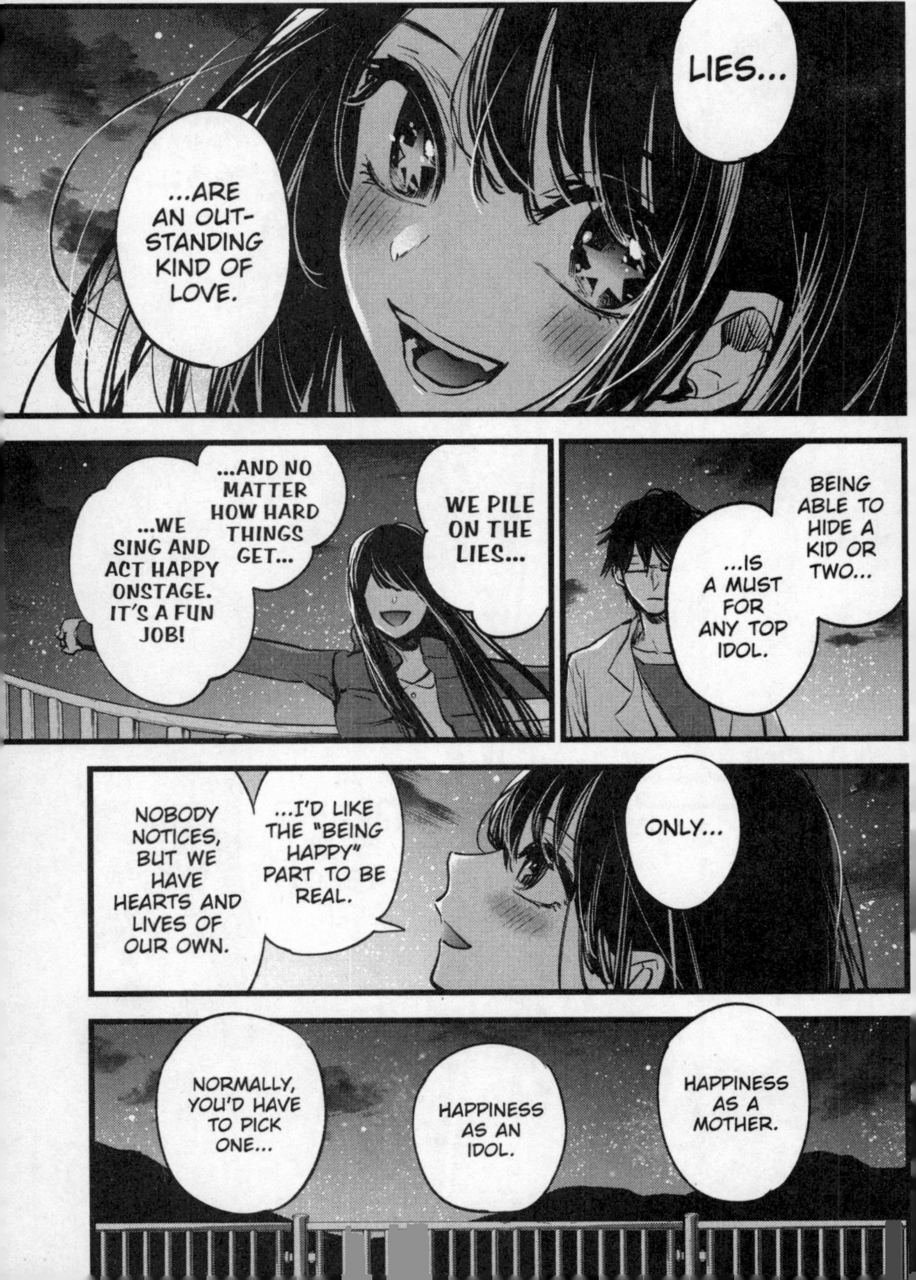
LIES...
...ARE AN OUT-STANDING KIND OF LOVE.
BEING ABLE TO HIDE A KID OR TWO...
...IS A MUST FOR ANY TOP IDOL.
WE PILE ON THE LIES...
...AND NO MATTER HOW HARD THINGS GET...
...WE SING AND ACT HAPPY ONSTAGE. IT'S A FUN JOB!
ONLY...
...I'D LIKE THE "BEING HAPPY" PART TO BE REAL.
NOBODY NOTICES, BUT WE HAVE HEARTS AND LIVES OF OUR OWN.
HAPPINESS AS A MOTHER.
HAPPINESS AS AN IDOL.
NORMALLY, YOU'D HAVE TO PICK ONE...

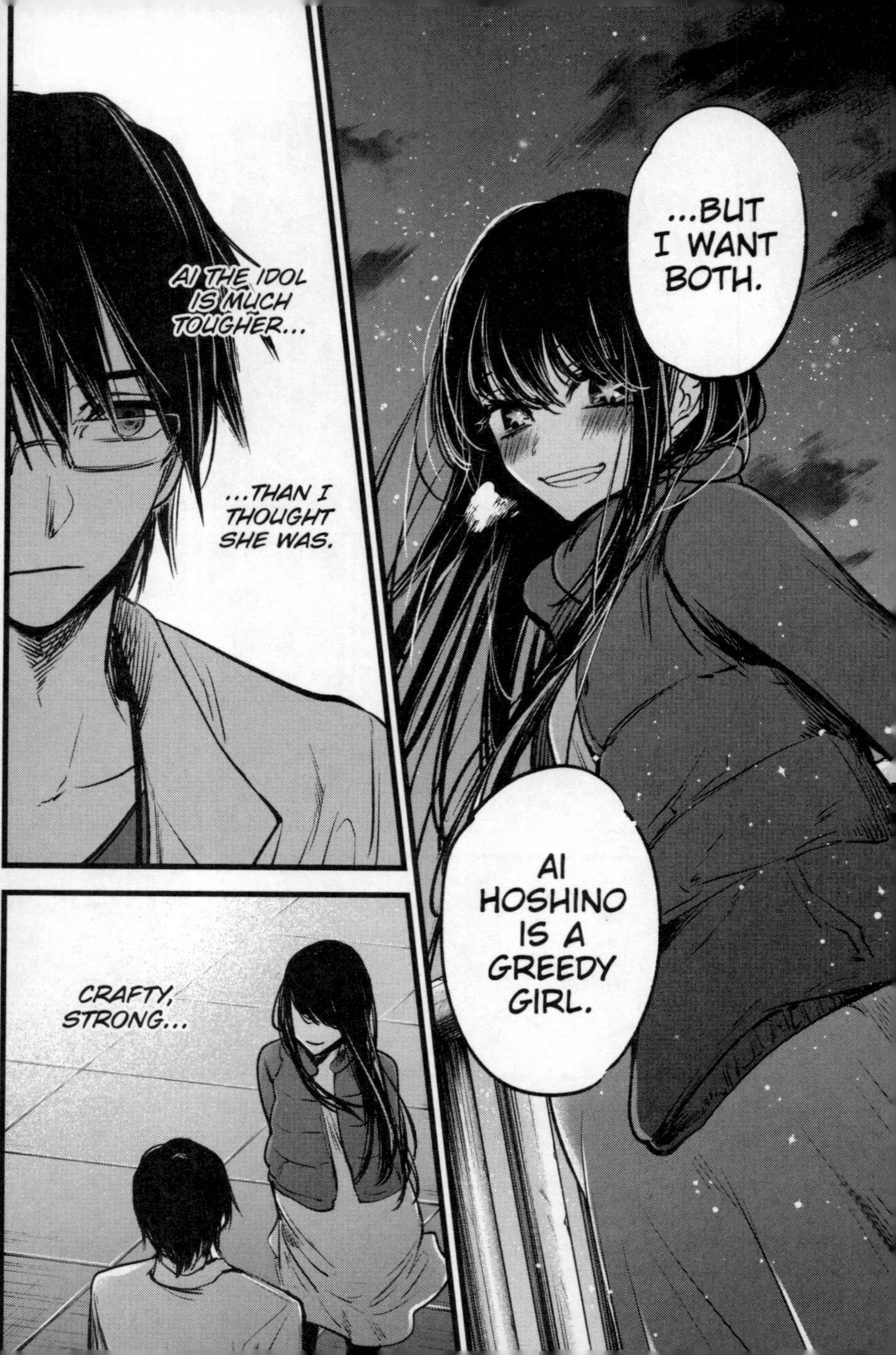
...BUT I WANT BOTH.
AI HOSHINO IS A GREEDY GIRL.
AI THE IDOL IS MUCH TOUGHER...
...THAN I THOUGHT SHE WAS.
CRAFTY, STRONG...

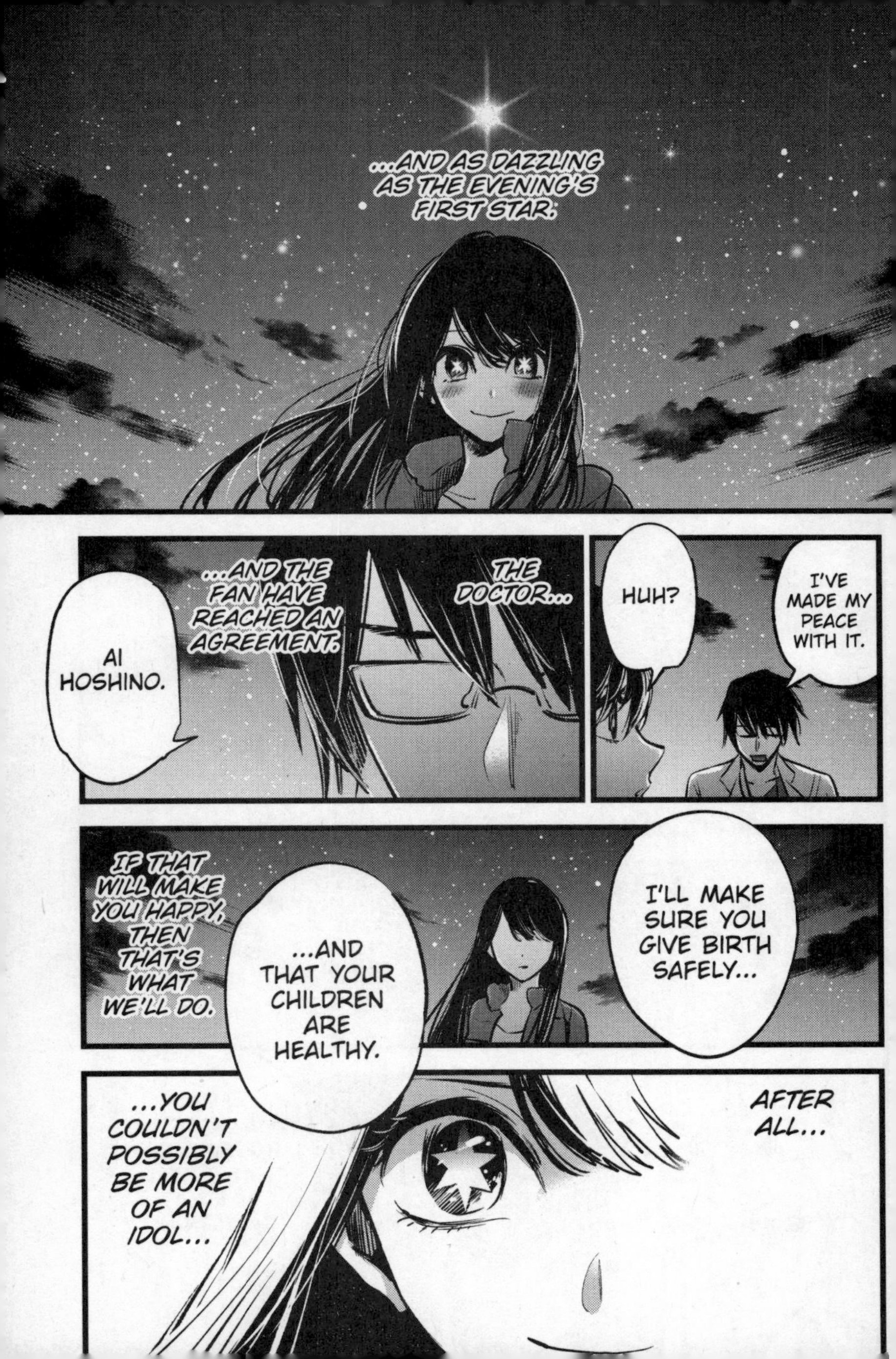
...AND AS DAZZLING AS THE EVENING'S FIRST STAR.
I'VE MADE MY PEACE WITH IT.
HUH?
THE DOCTOR...
...AND THE FAN HAVE REACHED AN AGREEMENT.
AI HOSHINO.
I'LL MAKE SURE YOU GIVE BIRTH SAFELY...
...AND THAT YOUR CHILDREN ARE HEALTHY.
IF THAT WILL MAKE YOU HAPPY, THEN THAT'S WHAT WE'LL DO.
AFTER ALL...
...YOU COULDN'T POSSIBLY BE MORE OF AN IDOL...

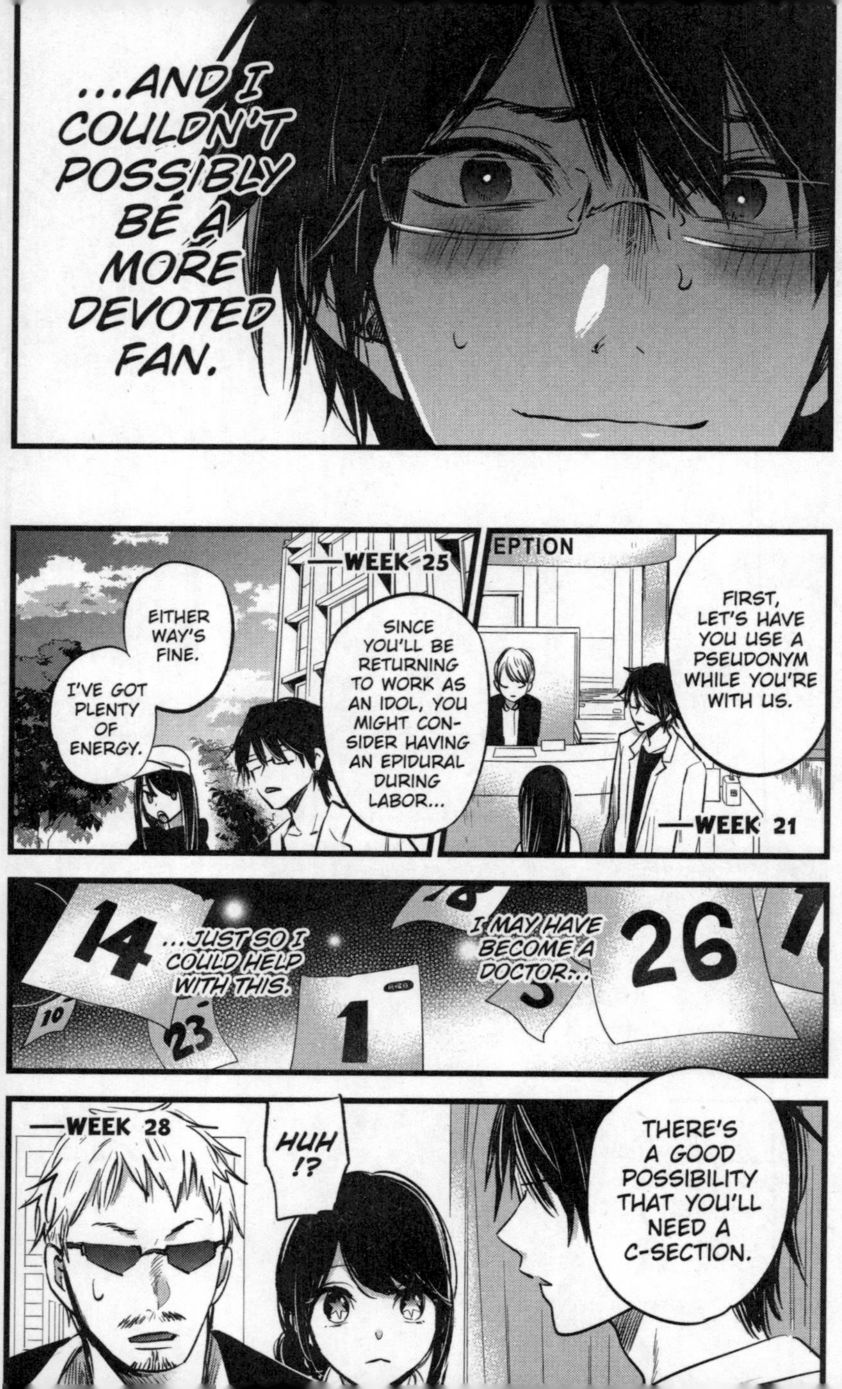
...AND I COULDN'T POSSIBLY BE A MORE DEVOTED FAN.
EPTION
FIRST, LET'S HAVE YOU USE A PSEUDONYM WHILE YOU'RE WITH US.
—WEEK 21
—WEEK 25
SINCE YOU'LL BE RETURNING TO WORK AS AN IDOL, YOU MIGHT CONSIDER HAVING AN EPIDURAL DURING LABOR...
EITHER WAY'S FINE.
I'VE GOT PLENTY OF ENERGY.
I MAY HAVE BECOME A DOCTOR...
...JUST SO I COULD HELP WITH THIS.
THERE'S A GOOD POSSIBILITY THAT YOU'LL NEED A C-SECTION.
HUH!?
—WEEK 28

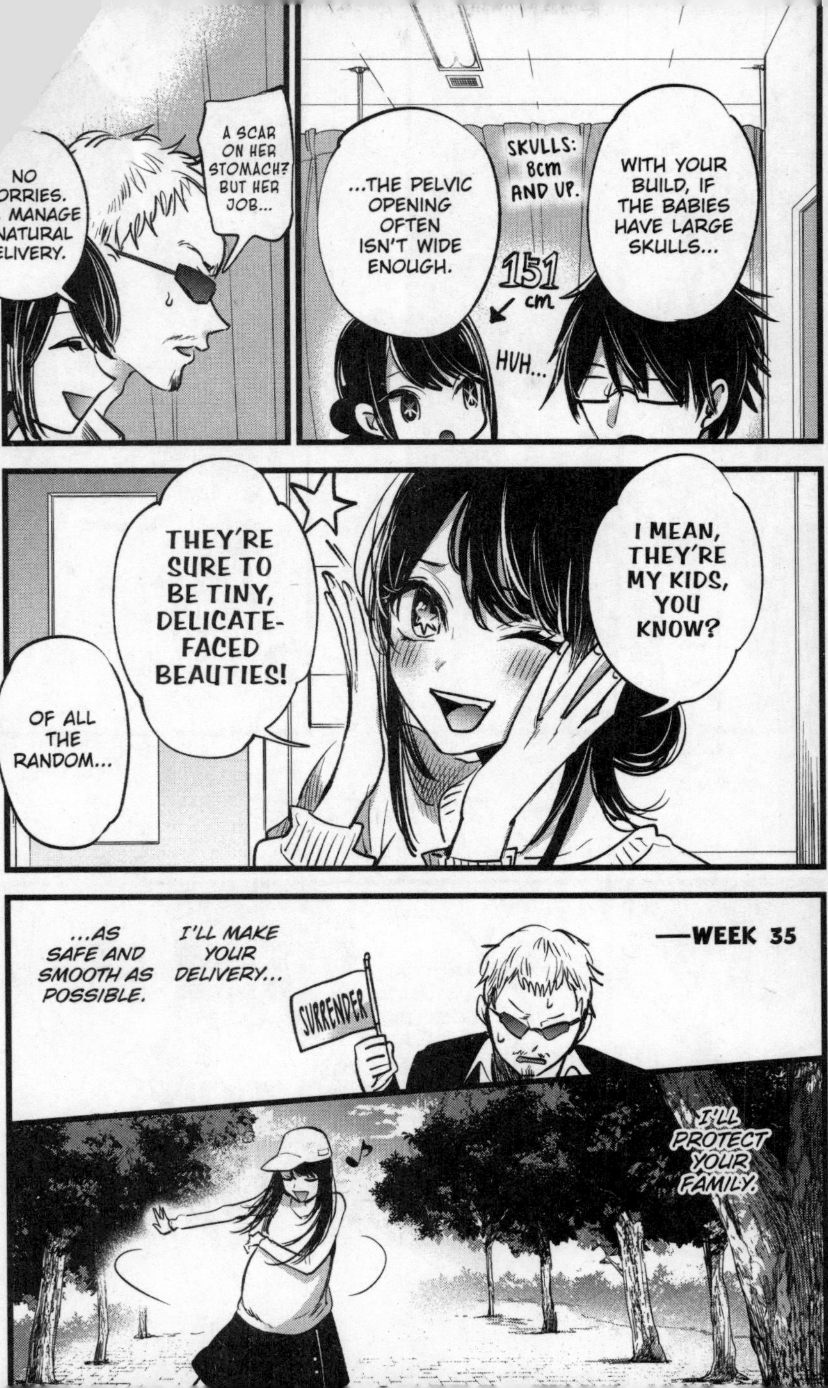
WITH YOUR BUILD, IF THE BABIES HAVE LARGE SKULLS...
SKULLS: 8cm AND UP.
...THE PELVIC OPENING OFTEN ISN'T WIDE ENOUGH.
151 cm
HUH...
A SCAR ON HER STOMACH? BUT HER JOB...
NO WORRIES. I'LL MANAGE A NATURAL DELIVERY.
I MEAN, THEY'RE MY KIDS, YOU KNOW?
THEY'RE SURE TO BE TINY, DELICATE-FACED BEAUTIES!
OF ALL THE RANDOM...
—WEEK 35
SURRENDER
I'LL MAKE YOUR DELIVERY...
...AS SAFE AND SMOOTH AS POSSIBLE.
I'LL PROTECT YOUR FAMILY.

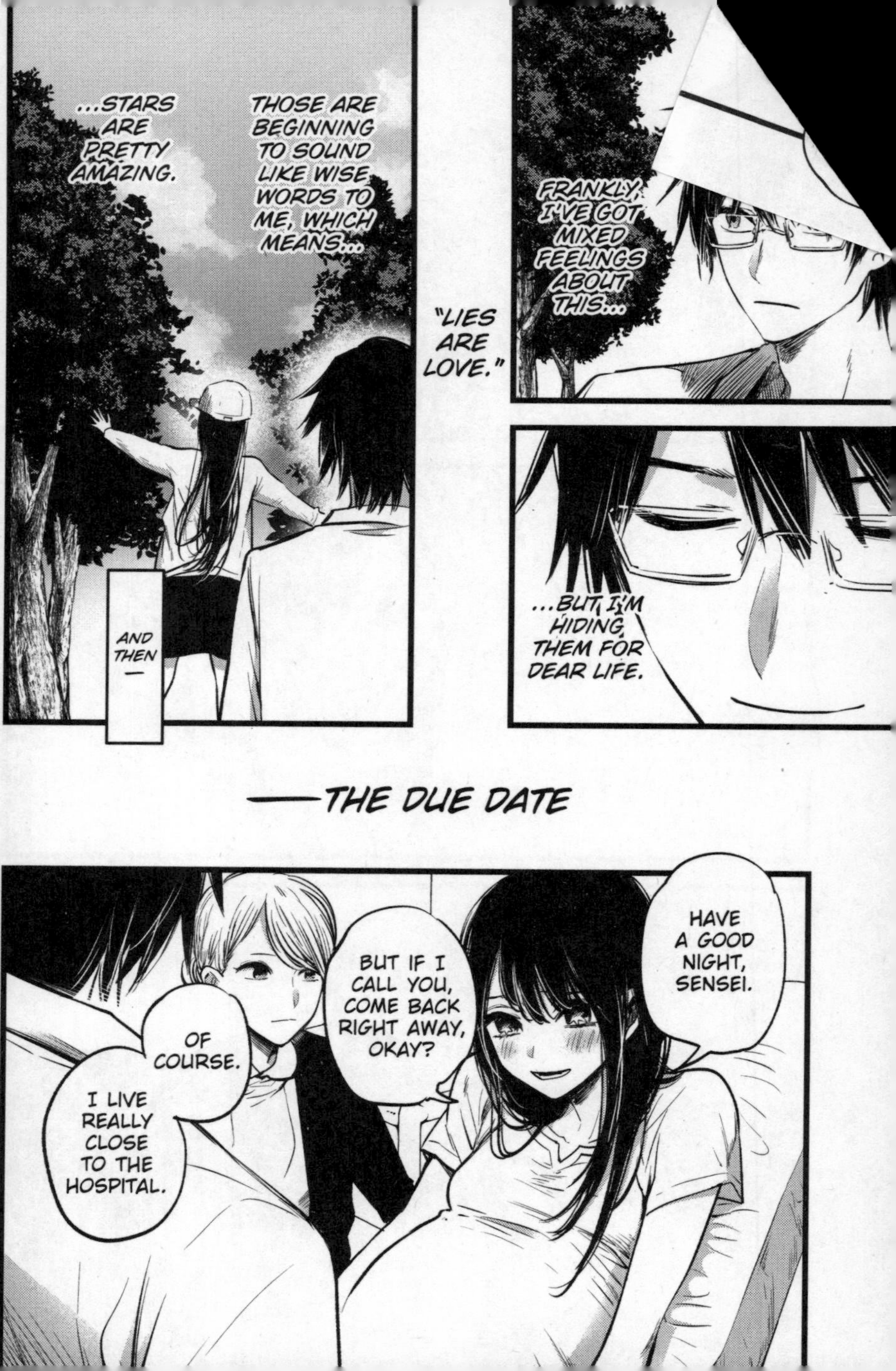
FRANKLY, I'VE GOT MIXED FEELINGS ABOUT THIS...
...BUT I'M HIDING THEM FOR DEAR LIFE.
"LIES ARE LOVE."
THOSE ARE BEGINNING TO SOUND LIKE WISE WORDS TO ME, WHICH MEANS...
...STARS ARE PRETTY AMAZING.
AND THEN—
—THE DUE DATE
HAVE A GOOD NIGHT, SENSEI.
BUT IF I CALL YOU, COME BACK RIGHT AWAY, OKAY?
OF COURSE.
I LIVE REALLY CLOSE TO THE HOSPITAL.

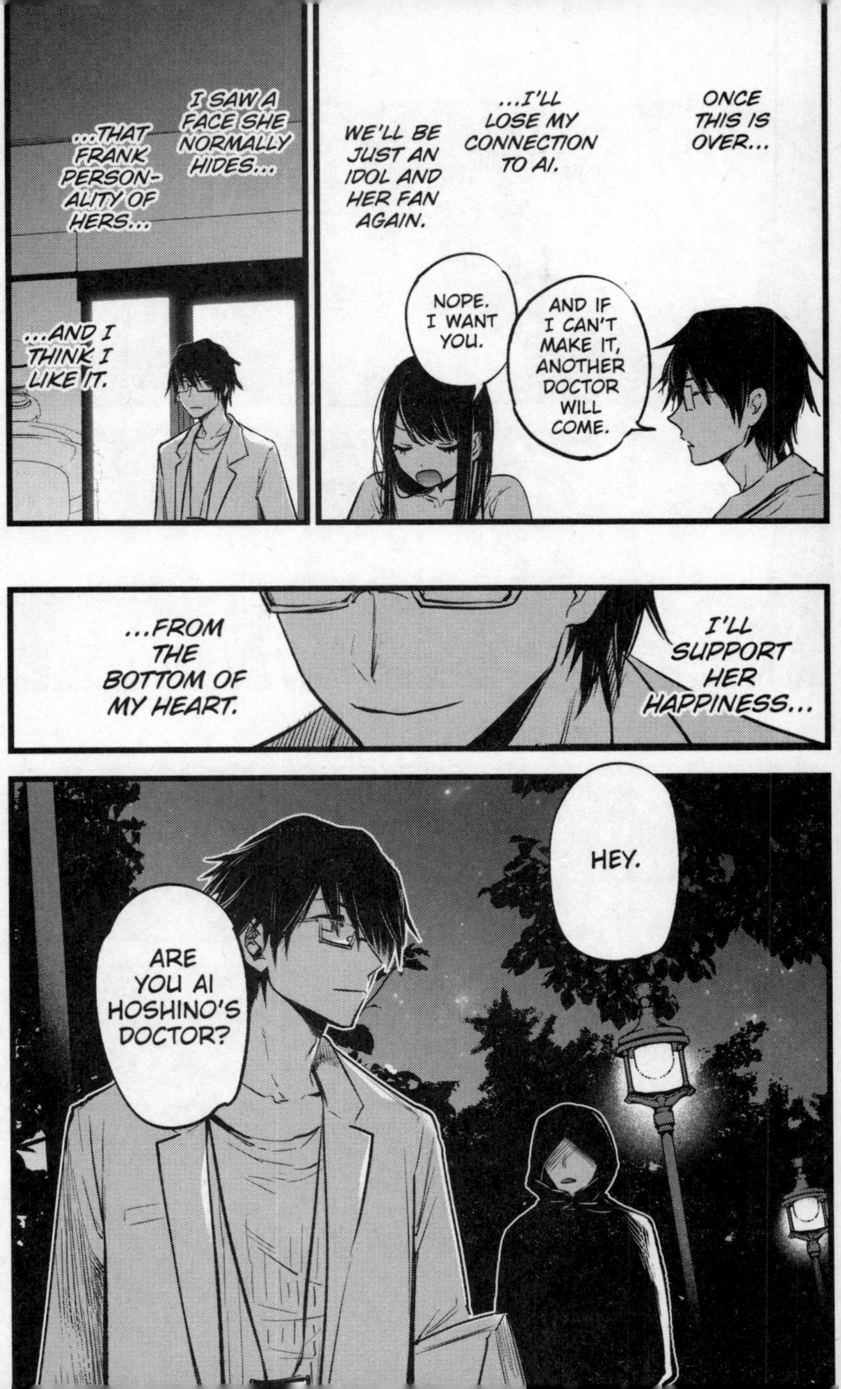
ONCE THIS IS OVER...
...I'LL LOSE MY CONNECTION TO AI.
WE'LL BE JUST AN IDOL AND HER FAN AGAIN.
AND IF I CAN'T MAKE IT, ANOTHER DOCTOR WILL COME.
NOPE. I WANT YOU.
I SAW A FACE SHE NORMALLY HIDES...
...THAT FRANK PERSONALITY OF HERS...
...AND I THINK I LIKE IT.
I'LL SUPPORT HER HAPPINESS...
...FROM THE BOTTOM OF MY HEART.
HEY.
ARE YOU AI HOSHINO'S DOCTOR?

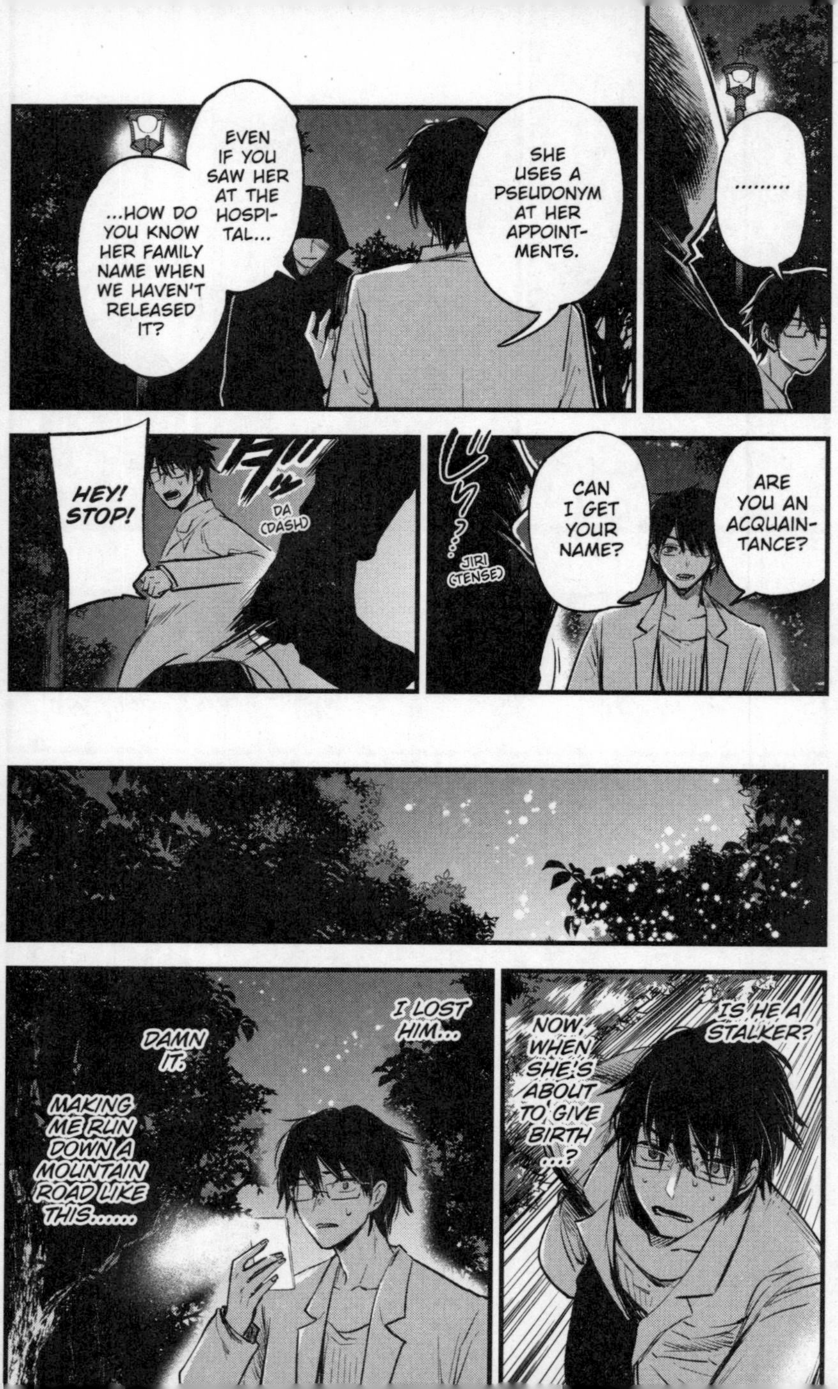
....
SHE USES A PSEUDONYM AT HER APPOINTMENTS.
EVEN IF YOU SAW HER AT THE HOSPITAL...
...HOW DO YOU KNOW HER FAMILY NAME WHEN WE HAVEN'T RELEASED IT?
ARE YOU AN ACQUAINTANCE?
CAN I GET YOUR NAME?
JIRI (TENSE)
DA (DASH)
HEY! STOP!
IS HE A STALKER?
NOW, WHEN SHE'S ABOUT TO GIVE BIRTH...?
I LOST HIM...
DAMN IT.
MAKING ME RUN DOWN A MOUNTAIN ROAD LIKE THIS......

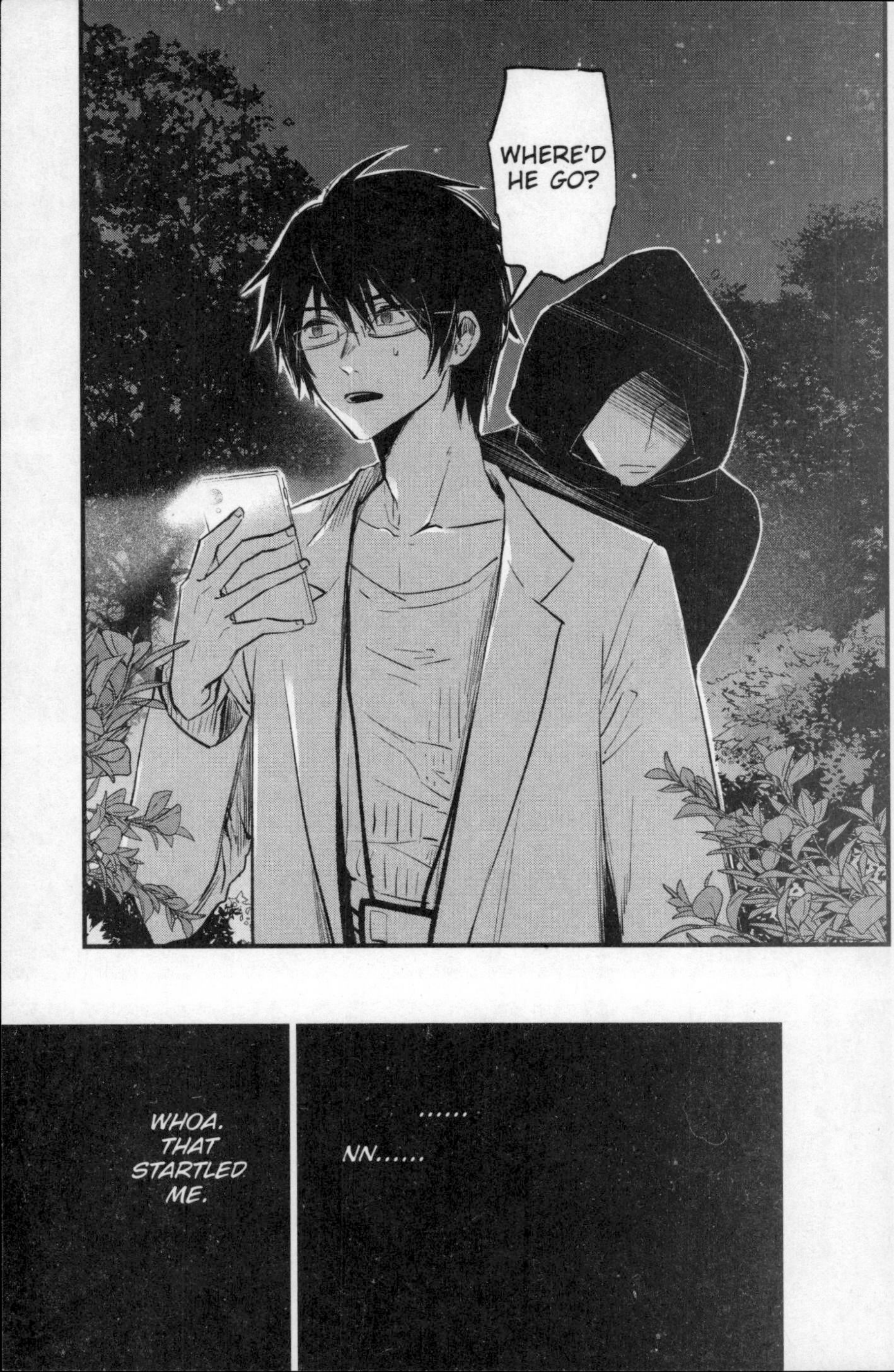
WHERE'D HE GO?
......
NN......
WHOA. THAT STARTLED ME.

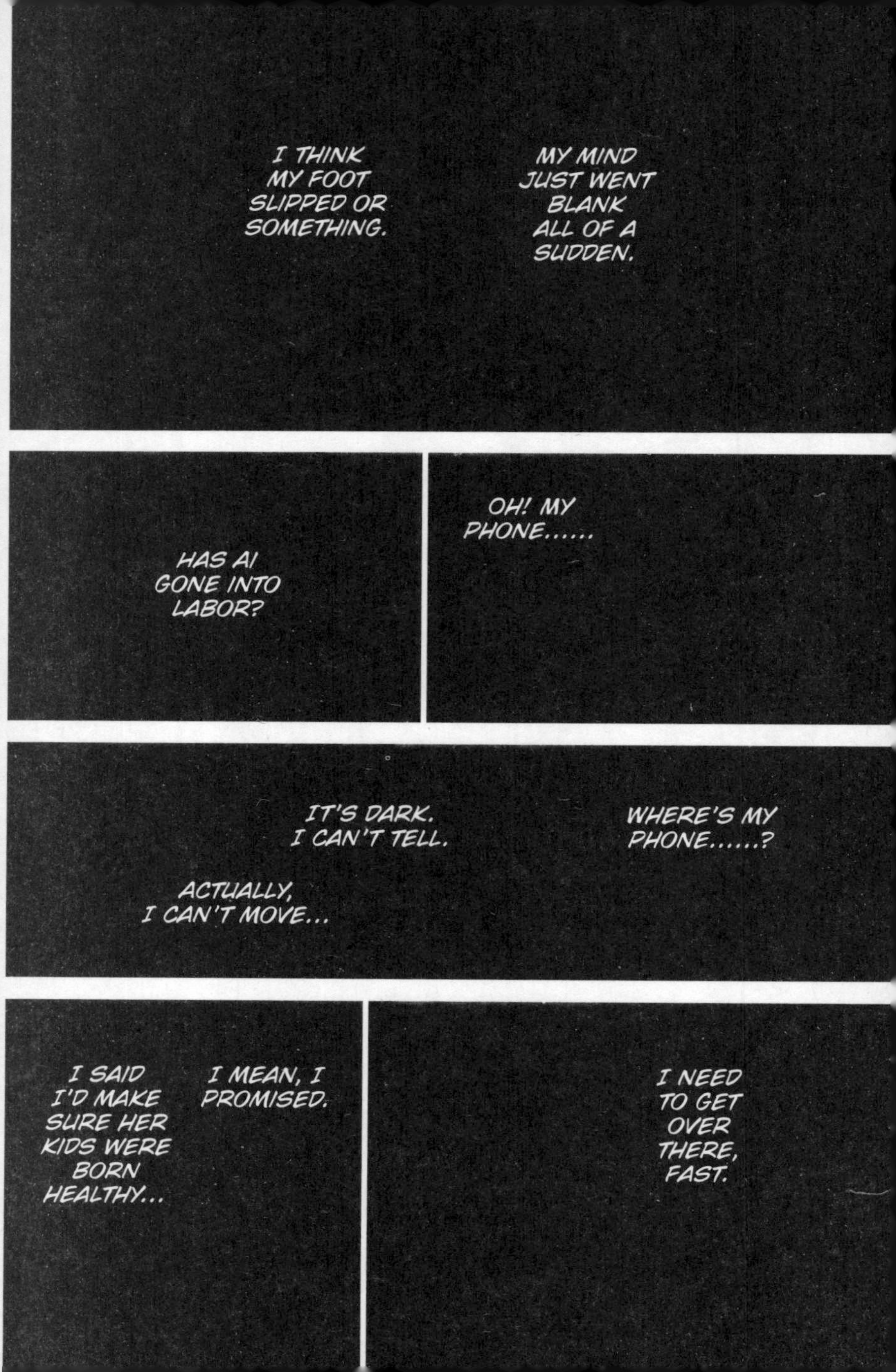
MY MIND JUST WENT BLANK ALL OF A SUDDEN.
I THINK MY FOOT SLIPPED OR SOMETHING.
OH! MY PHONE......
HAS AI GONE INTO LABOR?
WHERE'S MY PHONE......?
IT'S DARK. I CAN'T TELL.
ACTUALLY, I CAN'T MOVE...
I NEED TO GET OVER THERE, FAST.
I SAID I'D MAKE SURE HER KIDS WERE BORN HEALTHY...
I MEAN, I PROMISED.

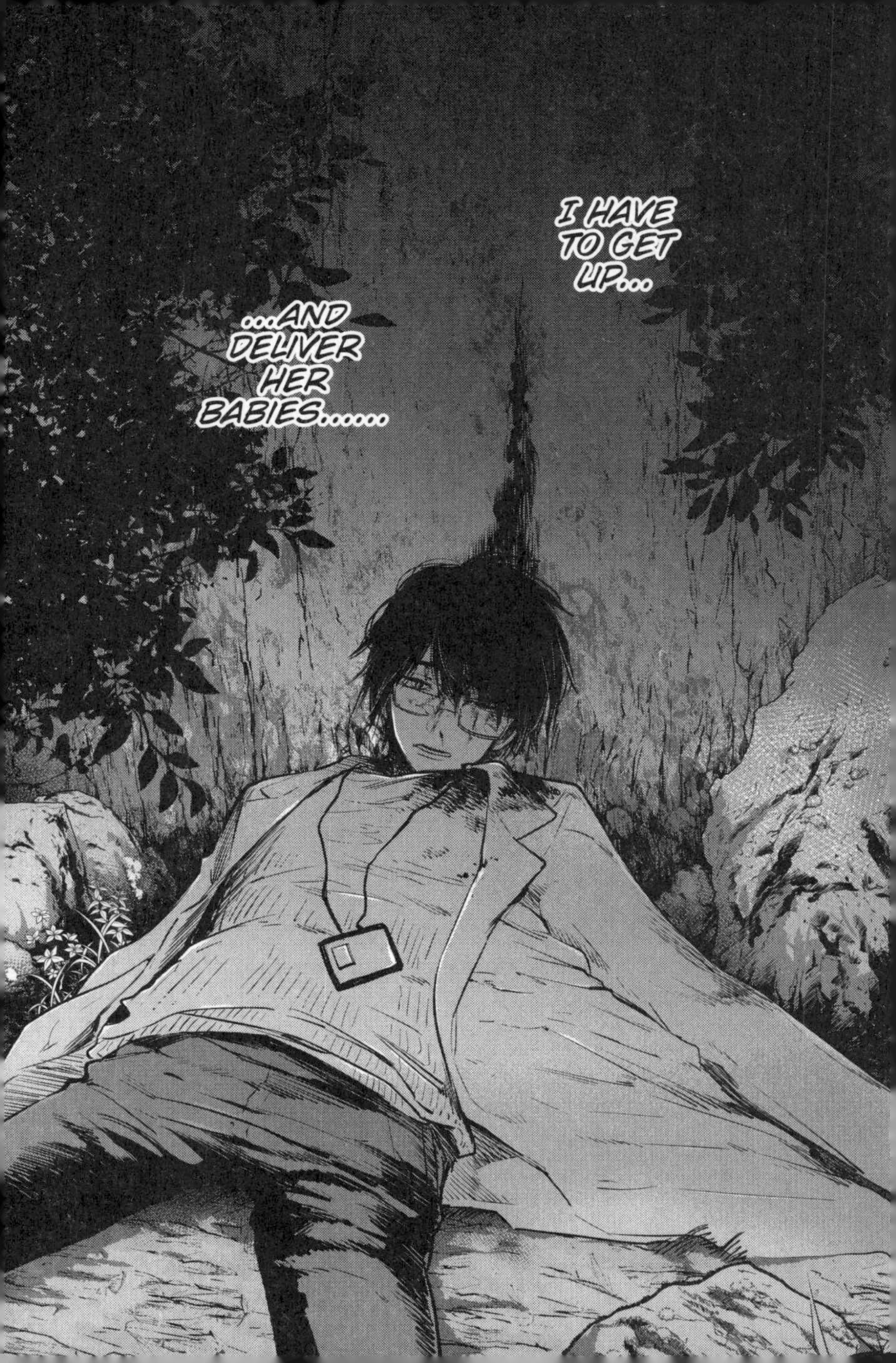
I HAVE TO GET UP...
...AND DELIVER HER BABIES......

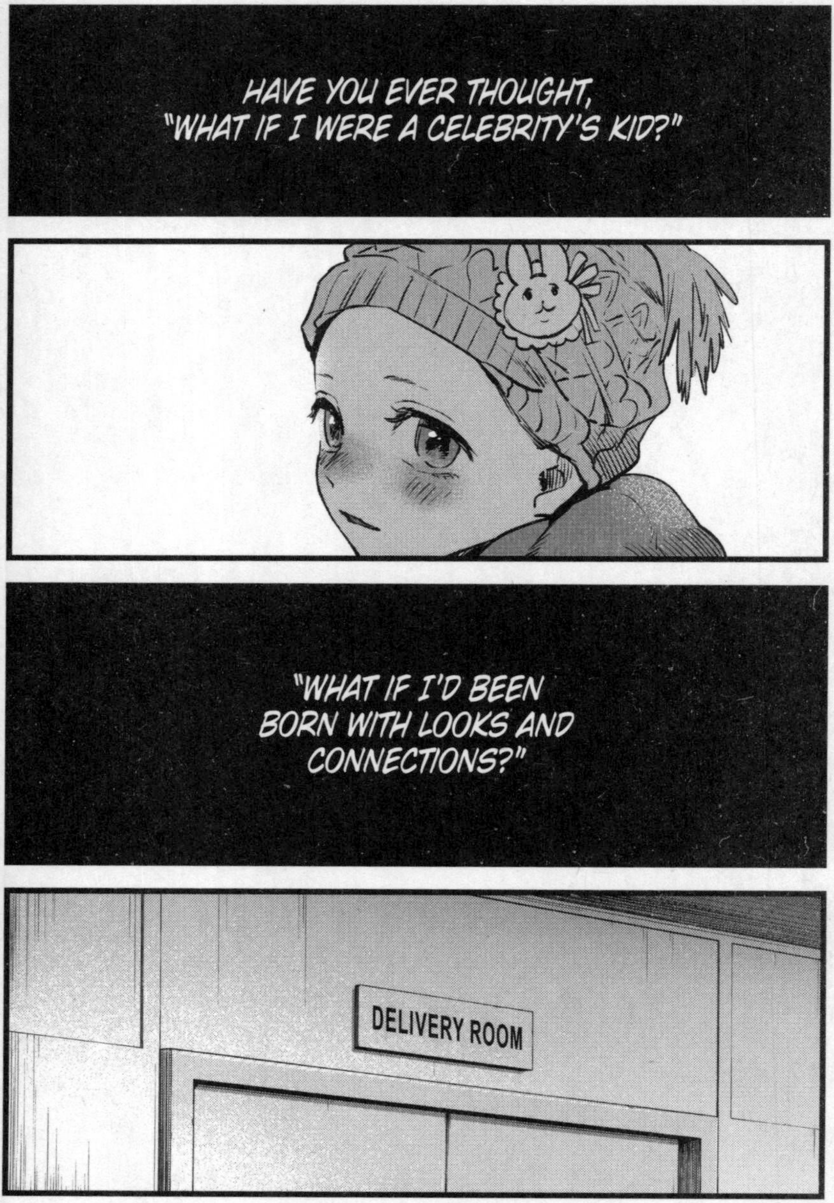
HAVE YOU EVER THOUGHT, "WHAT IF I WERE A CELEBRITY'S KID?"
"WHAT IF I'D BEEN BORN WITH LOOKS AND CONNECTIONS?"
DELIVERY ROOM

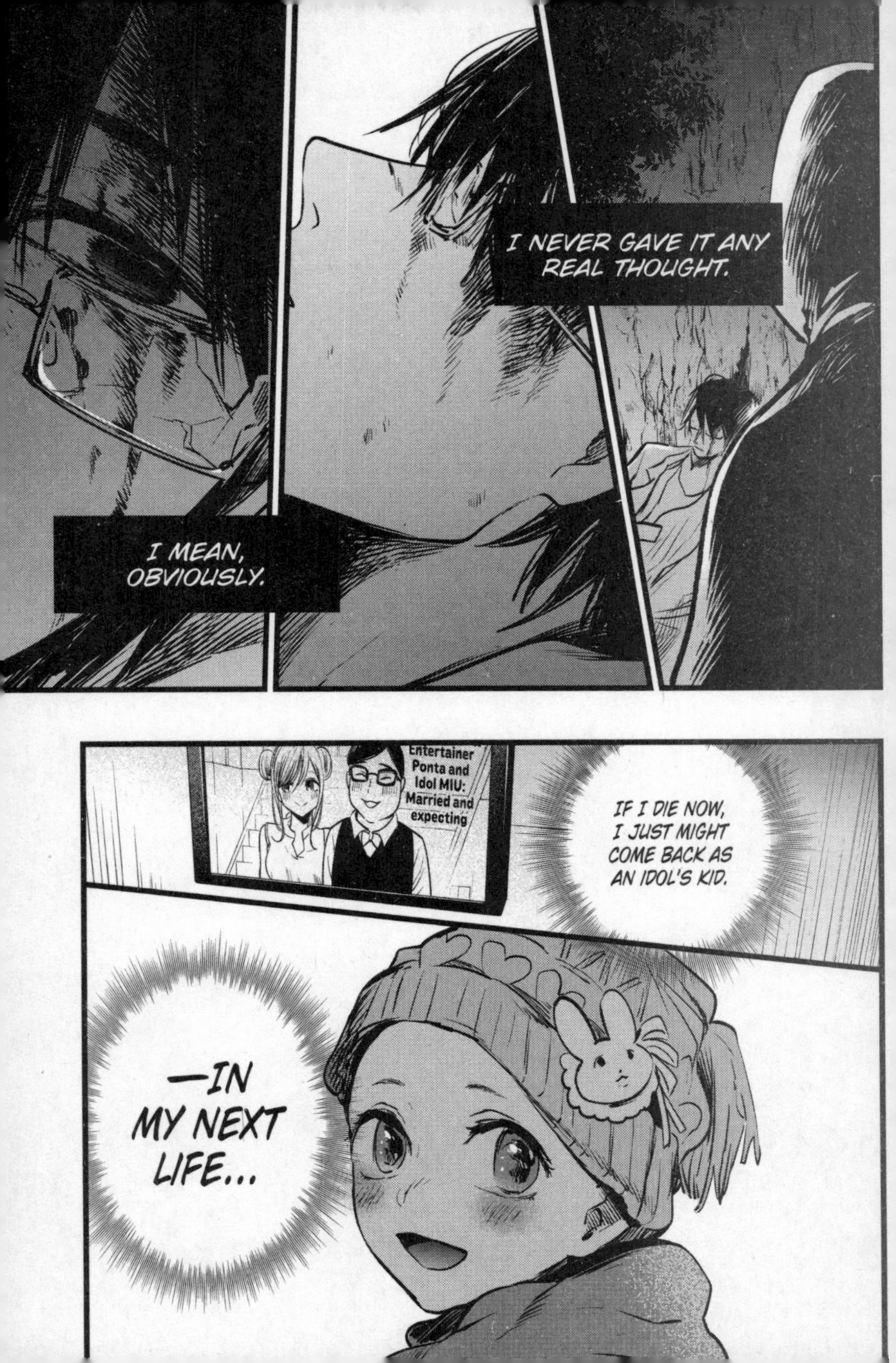
I NEVER GAVE IT ANY REAL THOUGHT.
I MEAN, OBVIOUSLY.
Entertainer Ponta and Idol MIU: Married and expecting
IF I DIE NOW, I JUST MIGHT COME BACK AS AN IDOL'S KID.
—IN MY NEXT LIFE...

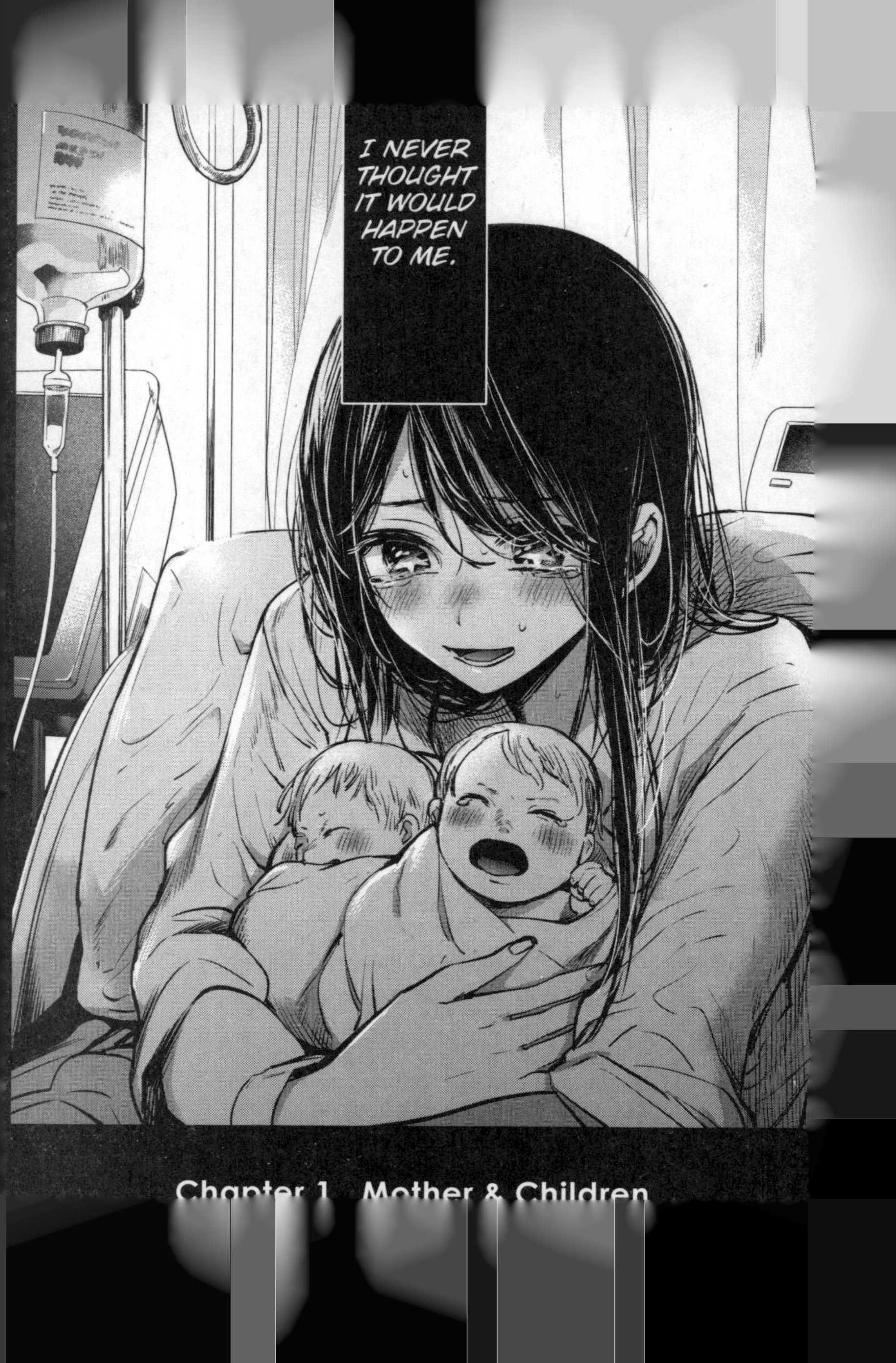
I NEVER THOUGHT IT WOULD HAPPEN TO ME.

Chapter 1 Mother & Children

【OSHI NO KO】

【Chapter 2】

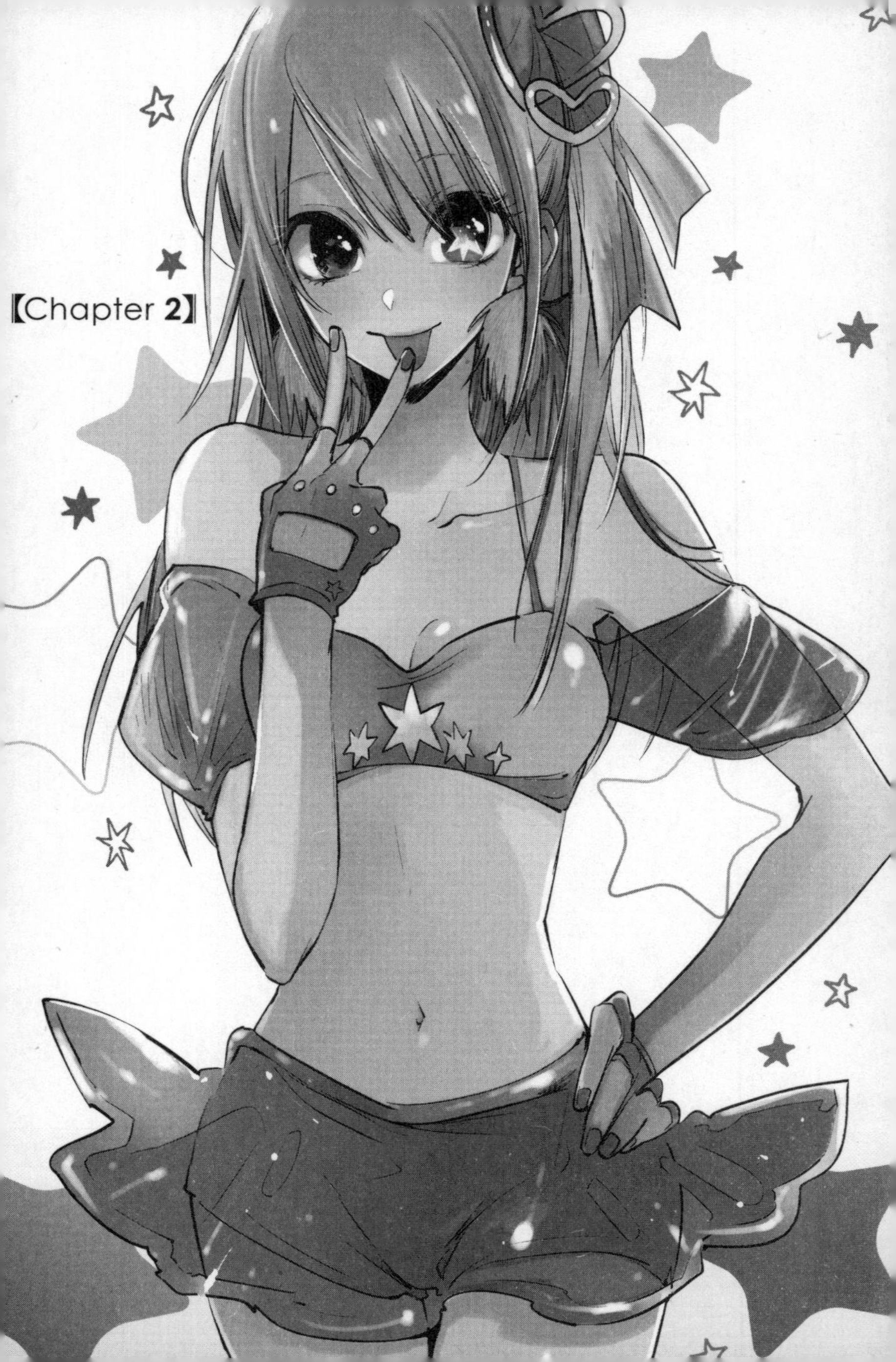

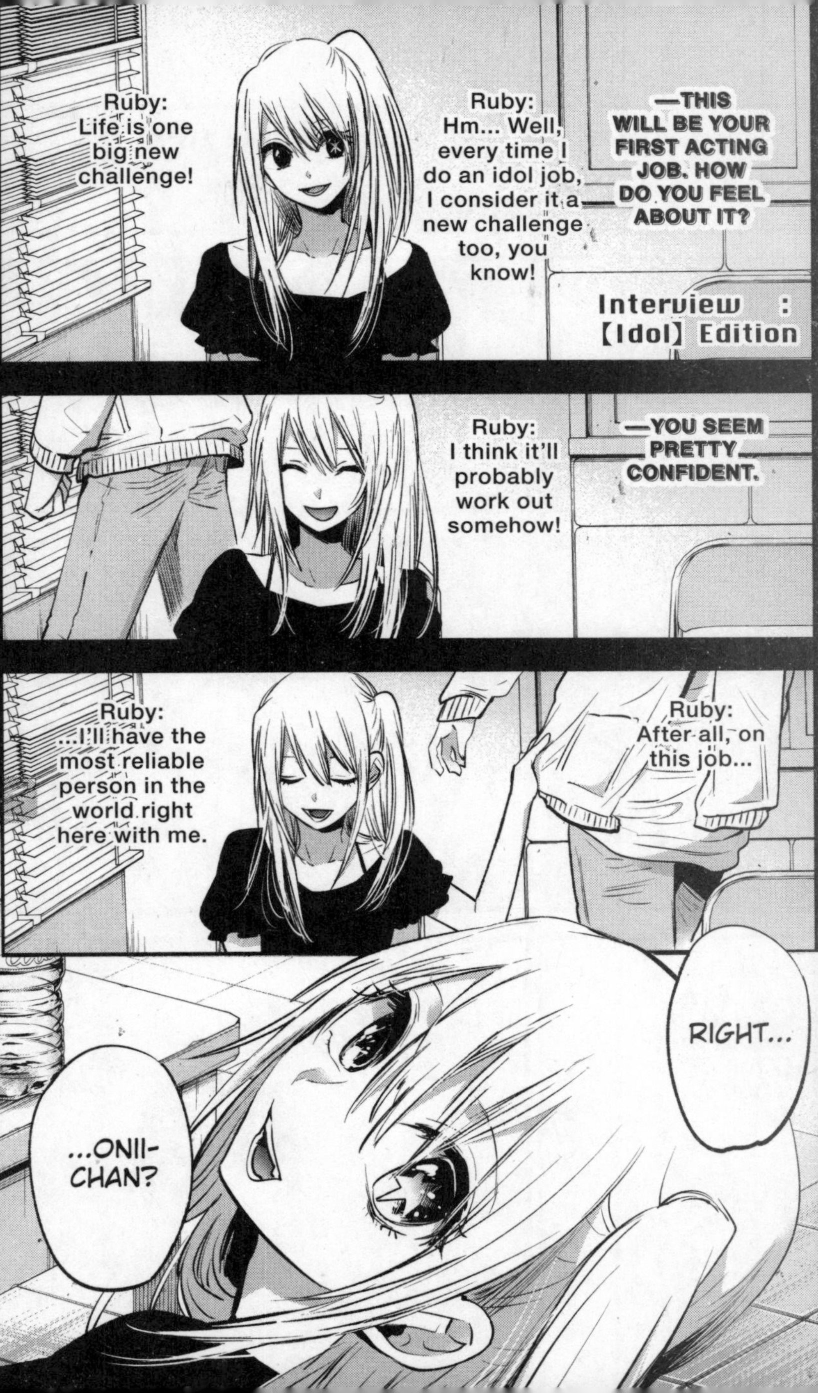
—THIS WILL BE YOUR FIRST ACTING JOB. HOW DO YOU FEEL ABOUT IT?
Interview : 【Idol】 Edition
Ruby: Hm... Well, every time I do an idol job, I consider it a new challenge too, you know!
Ruby: Life is one big new challenge!
—YOU SEEM PRETTY CONFIDENT.
Ruby: I think it'll probably work out somehow!
Ruby: After all, on this job...
Ruby: ...I'll have the most reliable person in the world right here with me.
RIGHT...
...ONII-CHAN?

Chapter 2 Big Brother & Little Sister

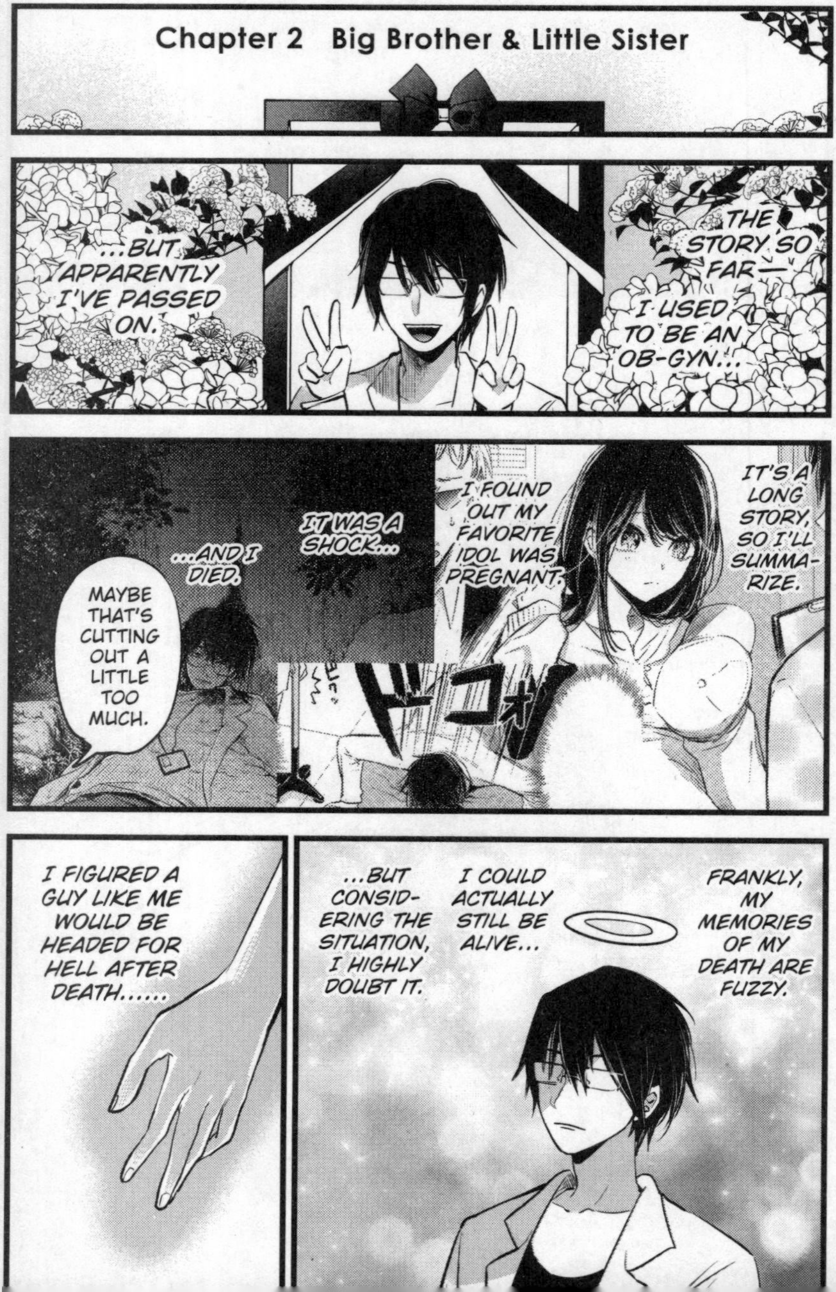
THE STORY SO FAR— I USED TO BE AN OB-GYN...
...BUT APPARENTLY I'VE PASSED ON.
IT'S A LONG STORY, SO I'LL SUMMA-RIZE.
I FOUND OUT MY FAVORITE IDOL WAS PREGNANT.
IT WAS A SHOCK...
...AND I DIED.
MAYBE THAT'S CUTTING OUT A LITTLE TOO MUCH.
FRANKLY, MY MEMORIES OF MY DEATH ARE FUZZY.
I COULD ACTUALLY STILL BE ALIVE...
...BUT CONSID-ERING THE SITUATION, I HIGHLY DOUBT IT.
I FIGURED A GUY LIKE ME WOULD BE HEADED FOR HELL AFTER DEATH......

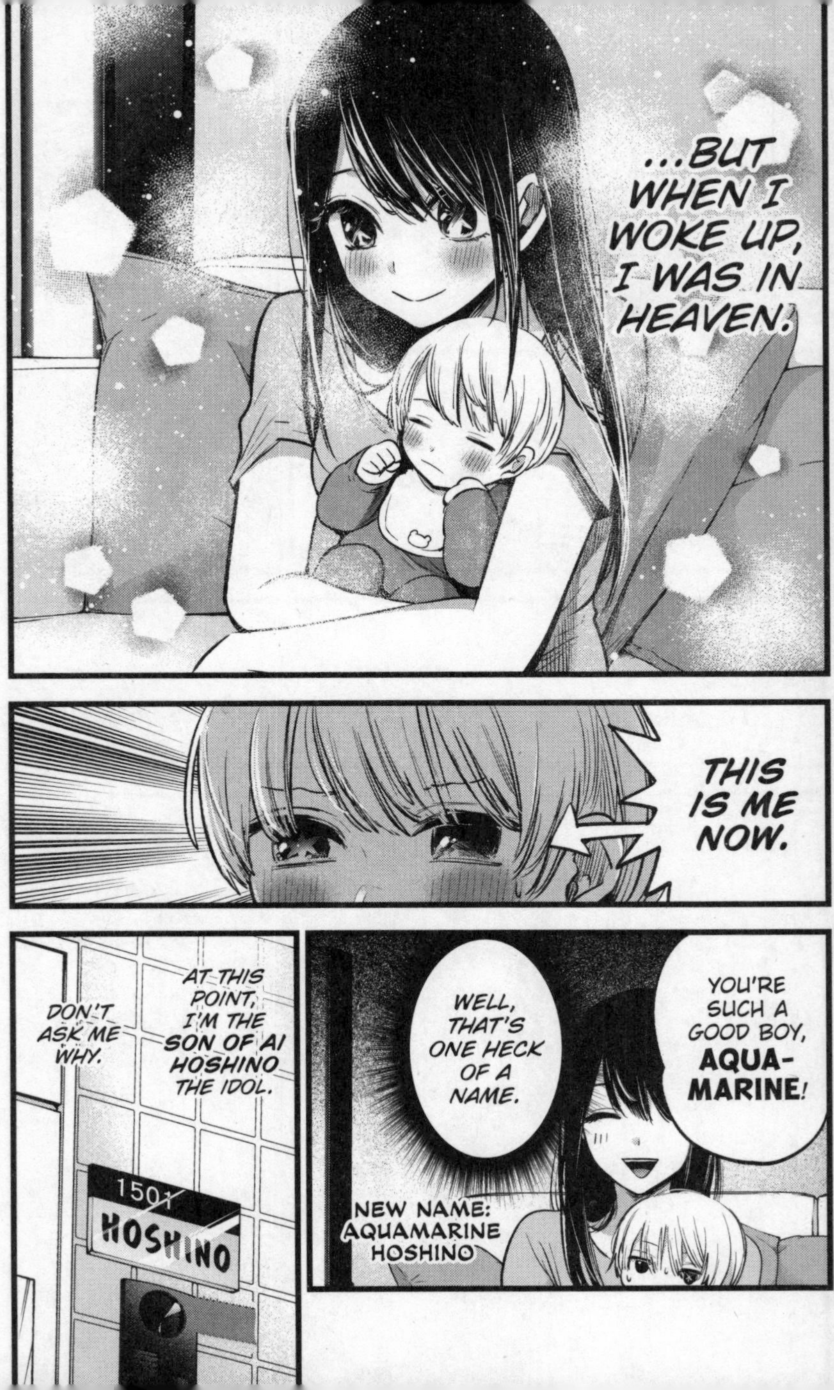
...BUT WHEN I WOKE UP, I WAS IN HEAVEN.
THIS IS ME NOW.
YOU'RE SUCH A GOOD BOY, AQUA-MARINE!
WELL, THAT'S ONE HECK OF A NAME.
NEW NAME: AQUAMARINE HOSHINO
AT THIS POINT, I'M THE SON OF AI HOSHINO THE IDOL.
DON'T ASK ME WHY.
1501
HOSHINO

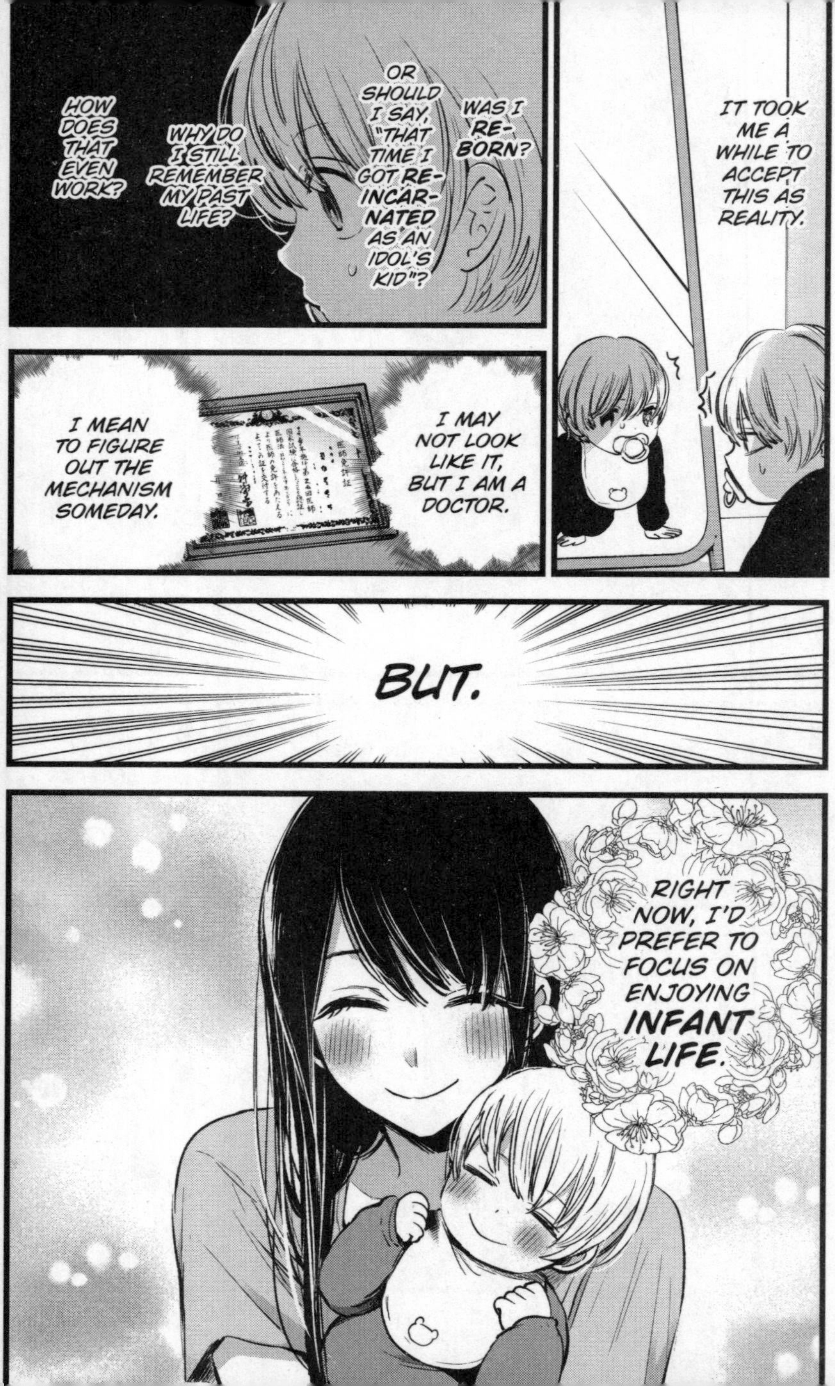
IT TOOK ME A WHILE TO ACCEPT THIS AS REALITY.
WAS I RE-BORN?
OR SHOULD I SAY, "THAT TIME I GOT RE-INCAR-NATED AS AN IDOL'S KID"?
WHY DO I STILL REMEMBER MY PAST LIFE?
HOW DOES THAT EVEN WORK?
I MAY NOT LOOK LIKE IT, BUT I AM A DOCTOR.
I MEAN TO FIGURE OUT THE MECHANISM SOMEDAY.
BUT.
RIGHT NOW, I'D PREFER TO FOCUS ON ENJOYING INFANT LIFE.

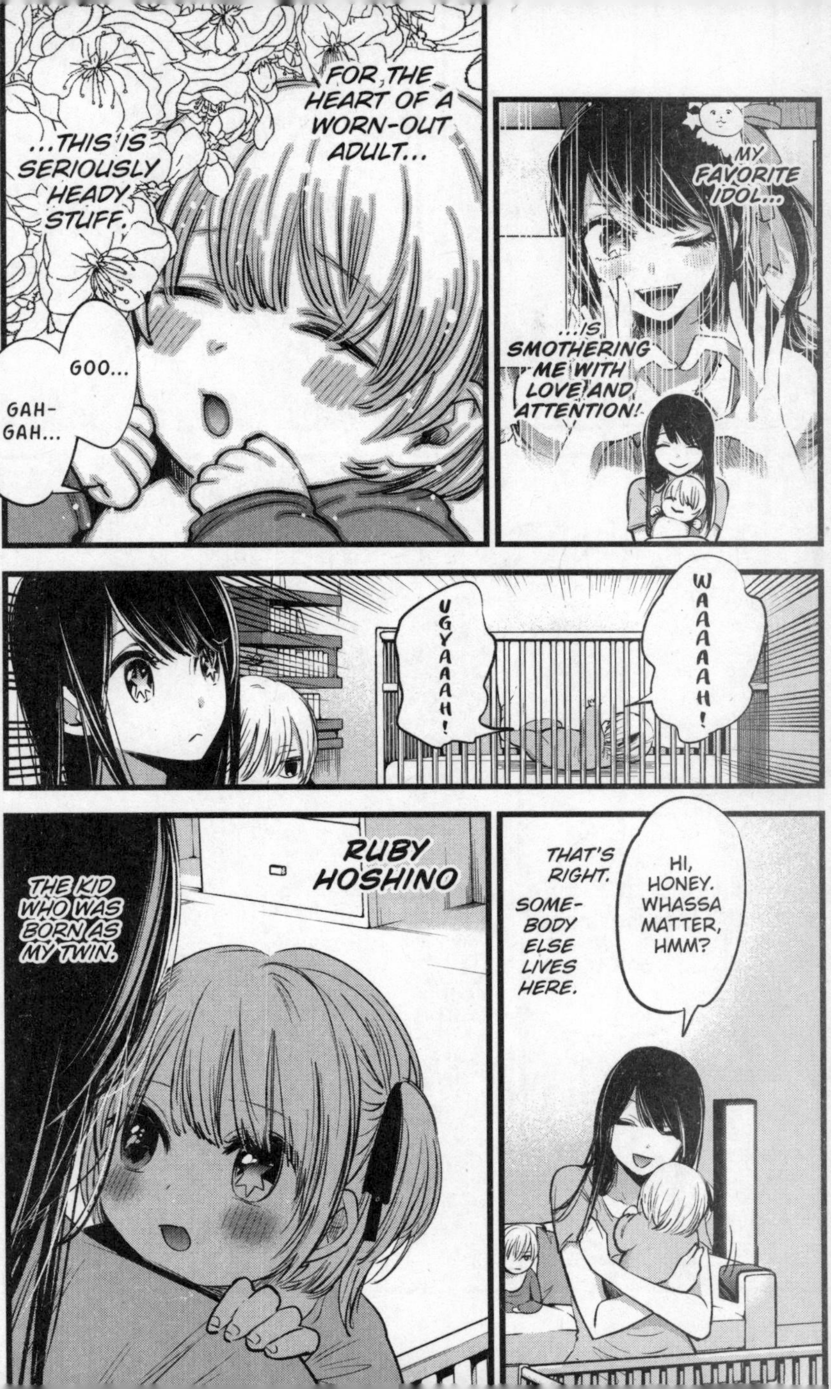
MY FAVORITE IDOL...
...IS SMOTHERING ME WITH LOVE AND ATTENTION!
FOR THE HEART OF A WORN-OUT ADULT...
...THIS IS SERIOUSLY HEADY STUFF.
GOO... GAH-GAH...
WAAAAAAH!
UGYAAAAH!
HI, HONEY. WHASSA MATTER, HMM?
THAT'S RIGHT.
SOMEBODY ELSE LIVES HERE.
RUBY HOSHINO
THE KID WHO WAS BORN AS MY TWIN.

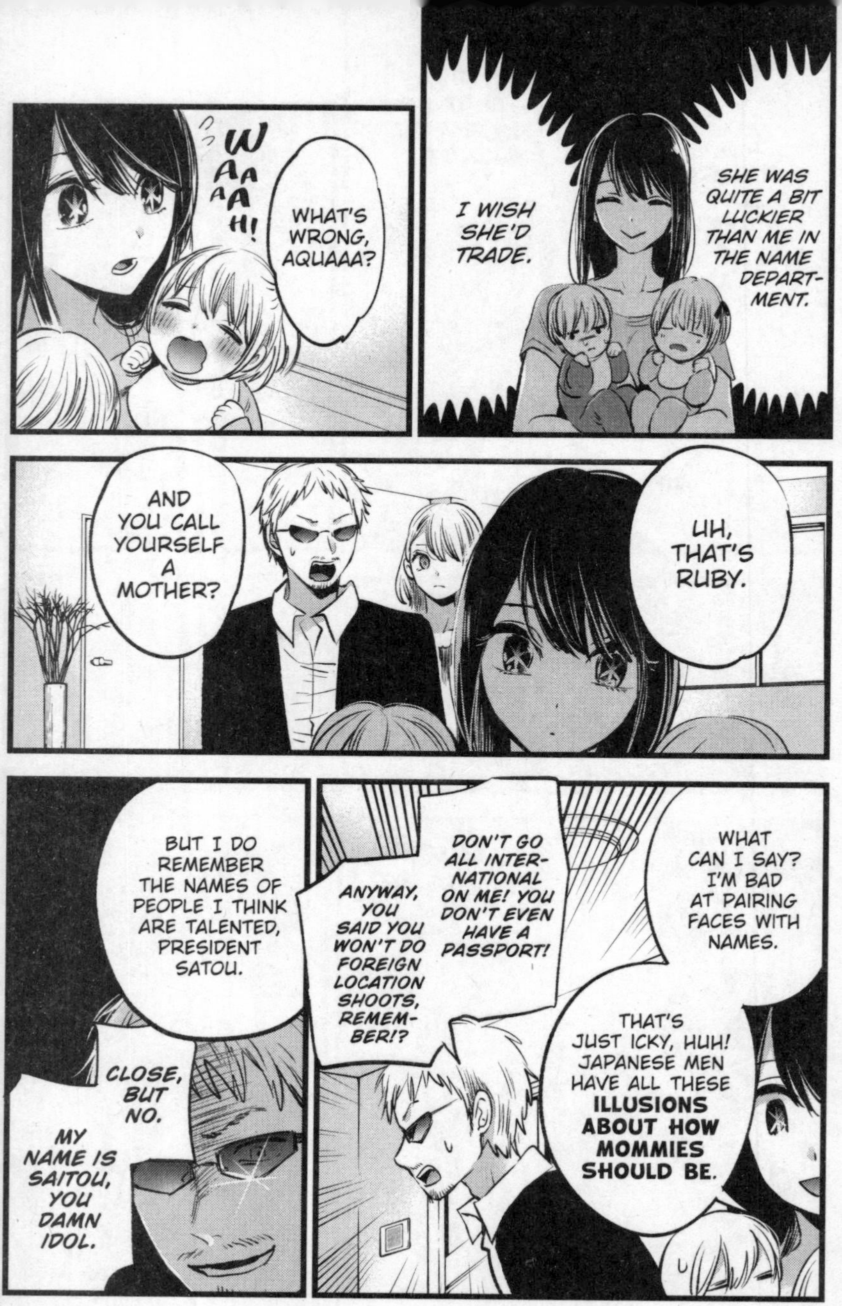
SHE WAS QUITE A BIT LUCKIER THAN ME IN THE NAME DEPARTMENT.
I WISH SHE'D TRADE.
WHAT'S WRONG, AQUAAA?
WAAAAAH!
UH, THAT'S RUBY.
AND YOU CALL YOURSELF A MOTHER?
WHAT CAN I SAY? I'M BAD AT PAIRING FACES WITH NAMES.
THAT'S JUST ICKY, HUH! JAPANESE MEN HAVE ALL THESE **ILLUSIONS ABOUT HOW MOMMIES SHOULD BE.**
DON'T GO ALL INTERNATIONAL ON ME! YOU DON'T EVEN HAVE A PASSPORT!
ANYWAY, YOU SAID YOU WON'T DO FOREIGN LOCATION SHOOTS, REMEMBER!?
BUT I DO REMEMBER THE NAMES OF PEOPLE I THINK ARE TALENTED, PRESIDENT SATOU.
CLOSE, BUT NO.
MY NAME IS SAITOU, YOU DAMN IDOL.

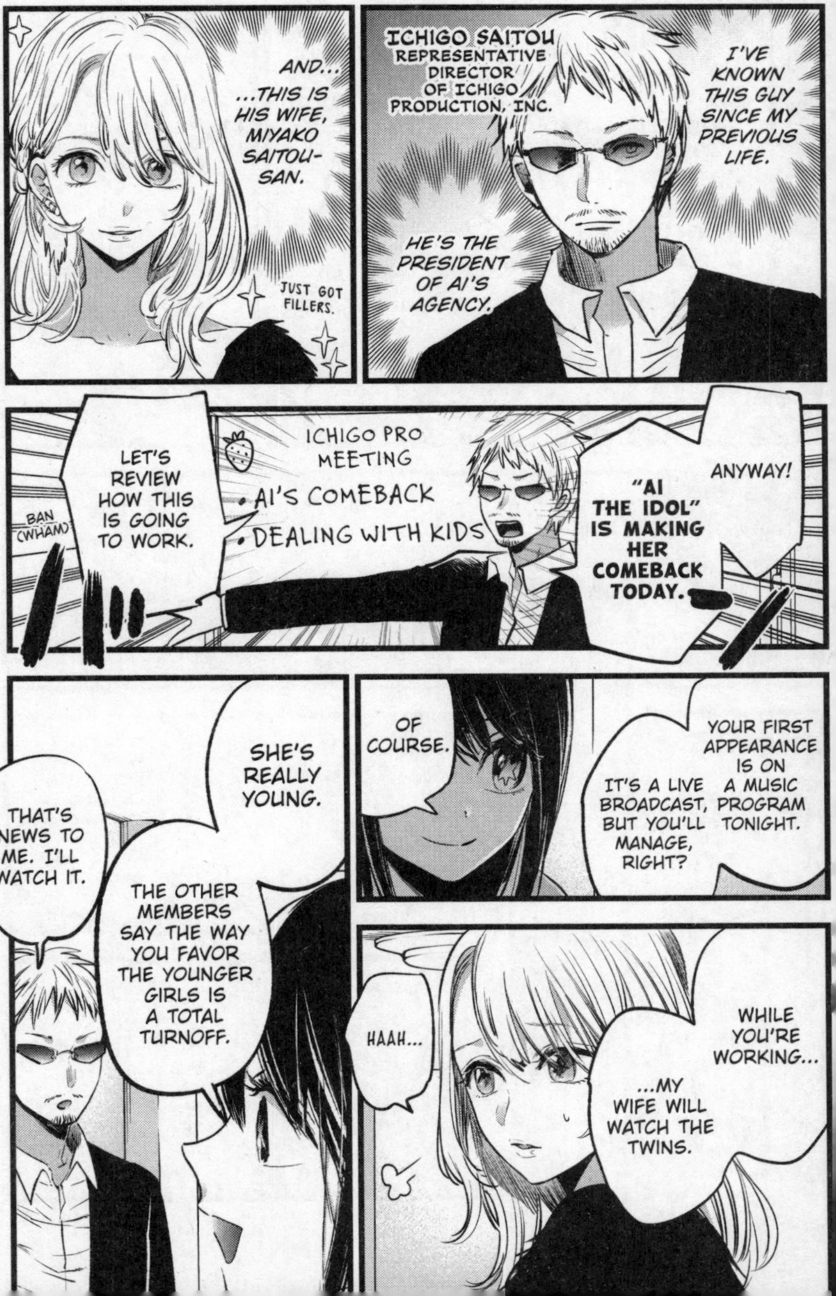
I'VE KNOWN THIS GUY SINCE MY PREVIOUS LIFE.
ICHIGO SAITOU
REPRESENTATIVE DIRECTOR OF ICHIGO PRODUCTION, INC.
HE'S THE PRESIDENT OF AI'S AGENCY.
AND... ...THIS IS HIS WIFE, MIYAKO SAITOU-SAN.
JUST GOT FILLERS.
ANYWAY!
"AI THE IDOL" IS MAKING HER COMEBACK TODAY.
ICHIGO PRO MEETING
• AI'S COMEBACK
• DEALING WITH KIDS
LET'S REVIEW HOW THIS IS GOING TO WORK.
BAN (WHAM)
YOUR FIRST APPEARANCE IS ON A MUSIC PROGRAM TONIGHT.
IT'S A LIVE BROADCAST, BUT YOU'LL MANAGE, RIGHT?
OF COURSE.
WHILE YOU'RE WORKING...
...MY WIFE WILL WATCH THE TWINS.
HAAH...
SHE'S REALLY YOUNG.
THAT'S NEWS TO ME. I'LL WATCH IT.
THE OTHER MEMBERS SAY THE WAY YOU FAVOR THE YOUNGER GIRLS IS A TOTAL TURNOFF.

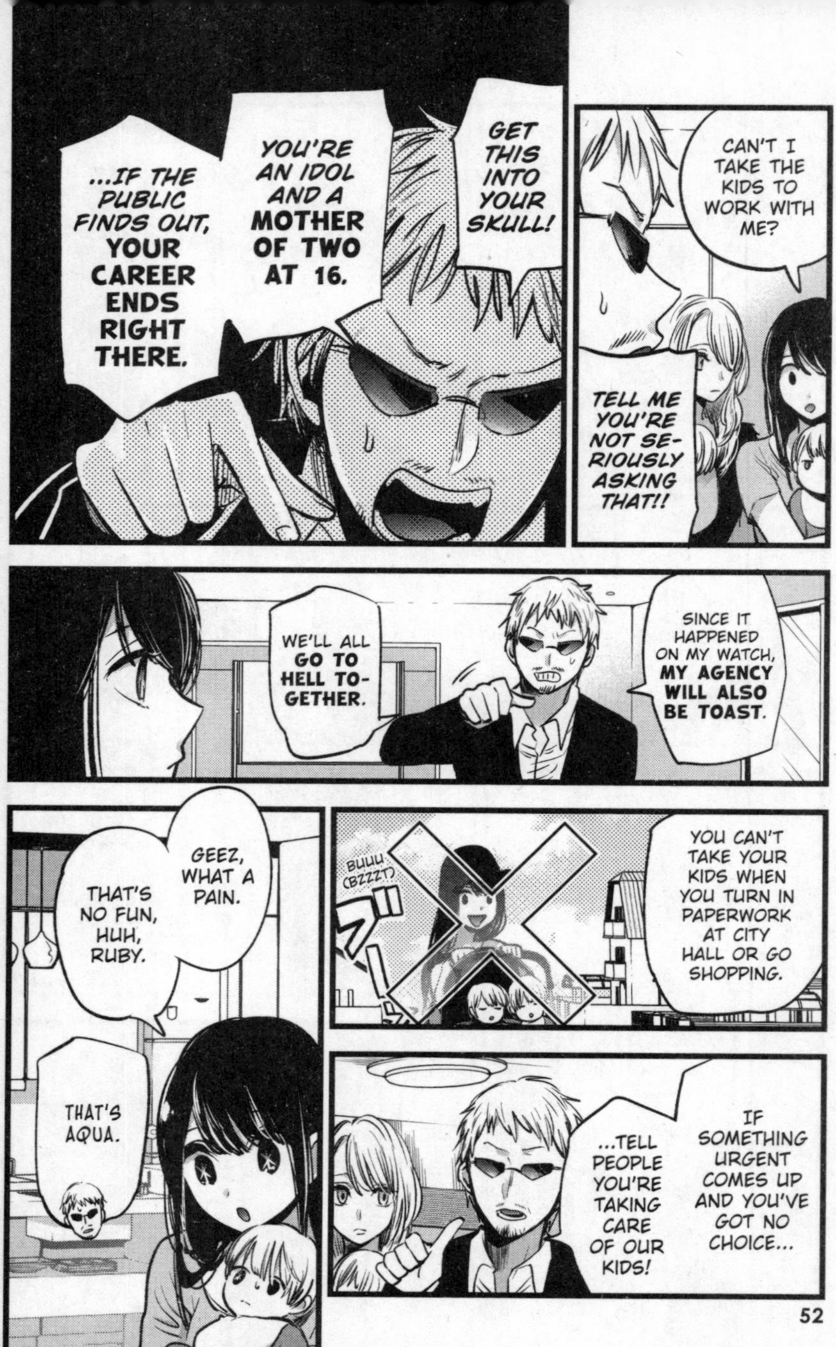
CAN'T I TAKE THE KIDS TO WORK WITH ME?
TELL ME YOU'RE NOT SE-RIOUSLY ASKING THAT!!
GET THIS INTO YOUR SKULL!
YOU'RE AN IDOL AND A MOTHER OF TWO AT 16.
...IF THE PUBLIC FINDS OUT, YOUR CAREER ENDS RIGHT THERE.
SINCE IT HAPPENED ON MY WATCH, MY AGENCY WILL ALSO BE TOAST.
WE'LL ALL GO TO HELL TO-GETHER.
YOU CAN'T TAKE YOUR KIDS WHEN YOU TURN IN PAPERWORK AT CITY HALL OR GO SHOPPING.
BUUU (BZZZT)
IF SOMETHING URGENT COMES UP AND YOU'VE GOT NO CHOICE...
...TELL PEOPLE YOU'RE TAKING CARE OF OUR KIDS!
GEEZ, WHAT A PAIN.
THAT'S NO FUN, HUH, RUBY.
THAT'S AQUA.

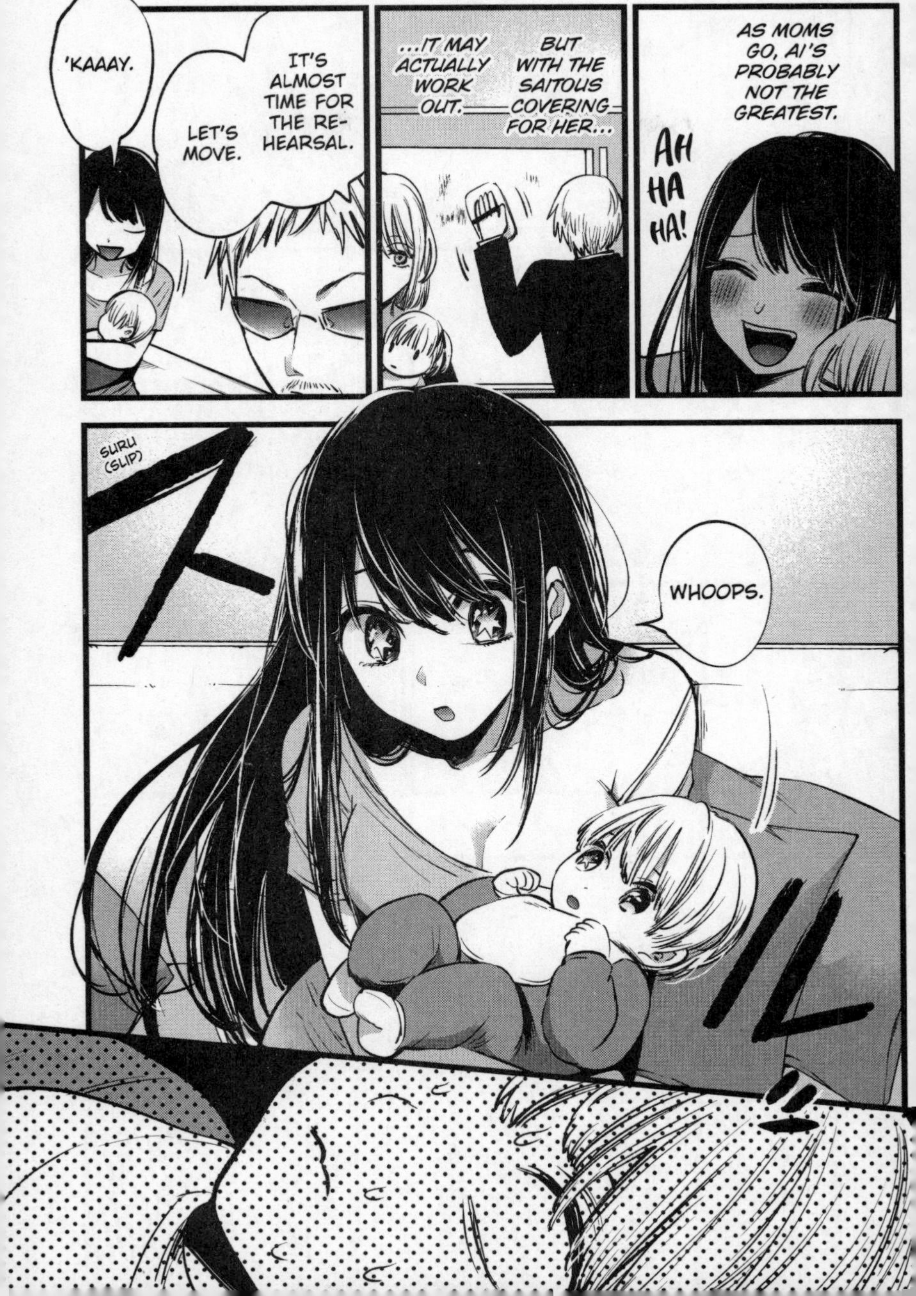
AS MOMS GO, AI'S PROBABLY NOT THE GREATEST.
AH HA HA!
BUT WITH THE SAITOUS COVERING FOR HER...
...IT MAY ACTUALLY WORK OUT.
IT'S ALMOST TIME FOR THE RE-HEARSAL.
LET'S MOVE.
'KAAAY.
WHOOPS.
SURU (SLIP)

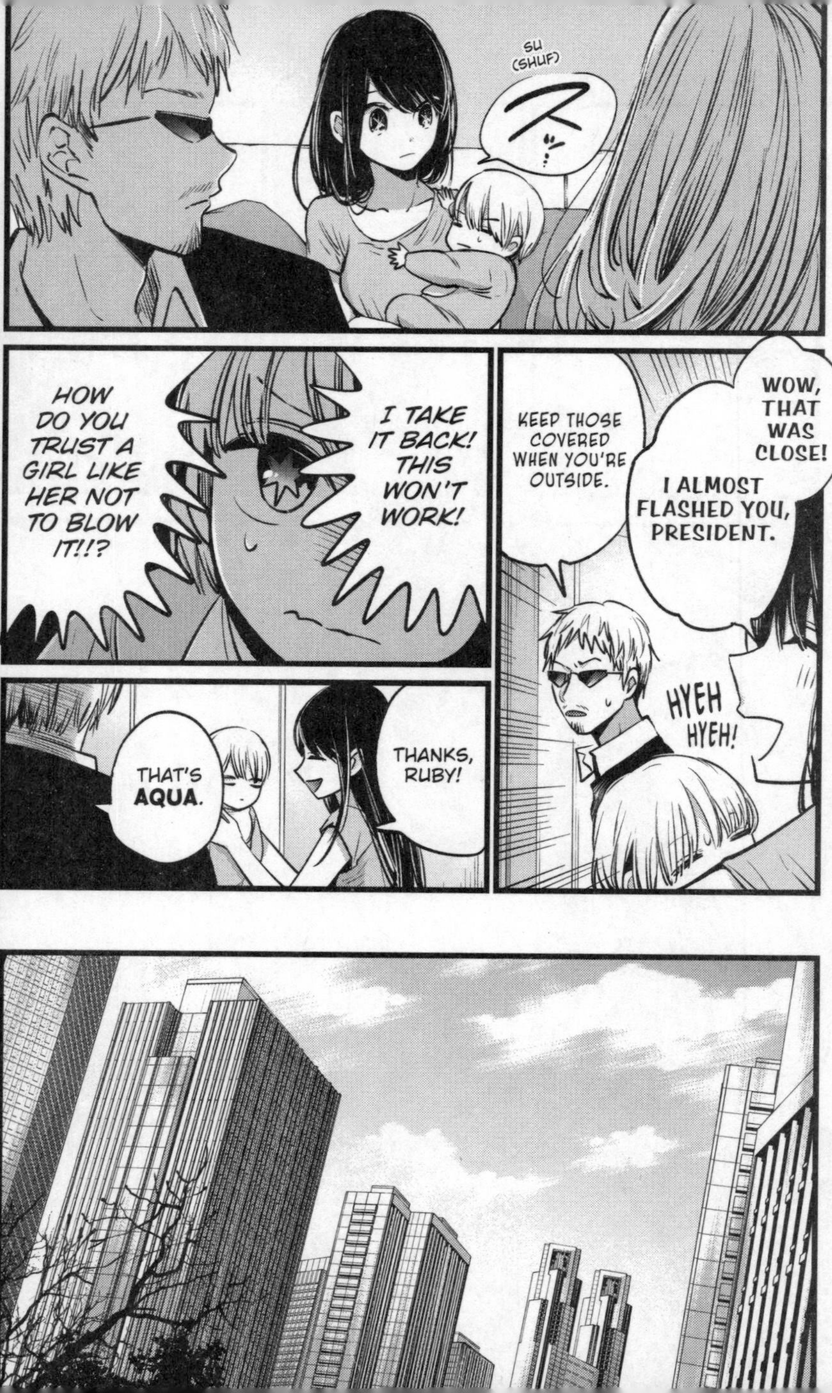
SU (SHUF)
WOW, THAT WAS CLOSE!
I ALMOST FLASHED YOU, PRESIDENT.
KEEP THOSE COVERED WHEN YOU'RE OUTSIDE.
HYEH HYEH!
I TAKE IT BACK! THIS WON'T WORK!
HOW DO YOU TRUST A GIRL LIKE HER NOT TO BLOW IT!!?
THANKS, RUBY!
THAT'S AQUA.

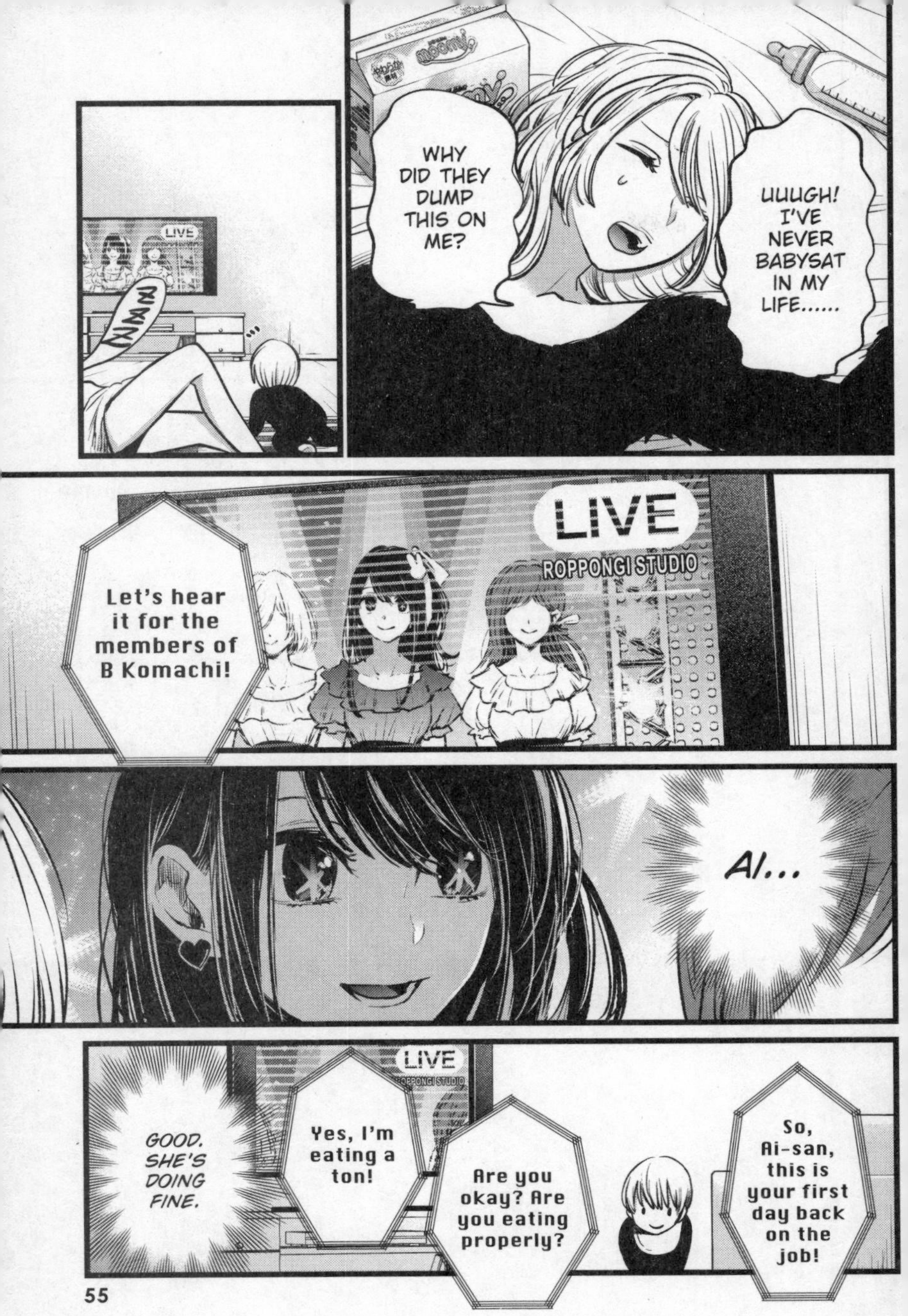
UUUGH! I'VE NEVER BABYSAT IN MY LIFE......
WHY DID THEY DUMP THIS ON ME?
LIVE
LIVE
ROPPONGI STUDIO
Let's hear it for the members of B Komachi!
AI...
So, Ai-san, this is your first day back on the job!
Are you okay? Are you eating properly?
Yes, I'm eating a ton!
LIVE
ROPPONGI STUDIO
GOOD. SHE'S DOING FINE.

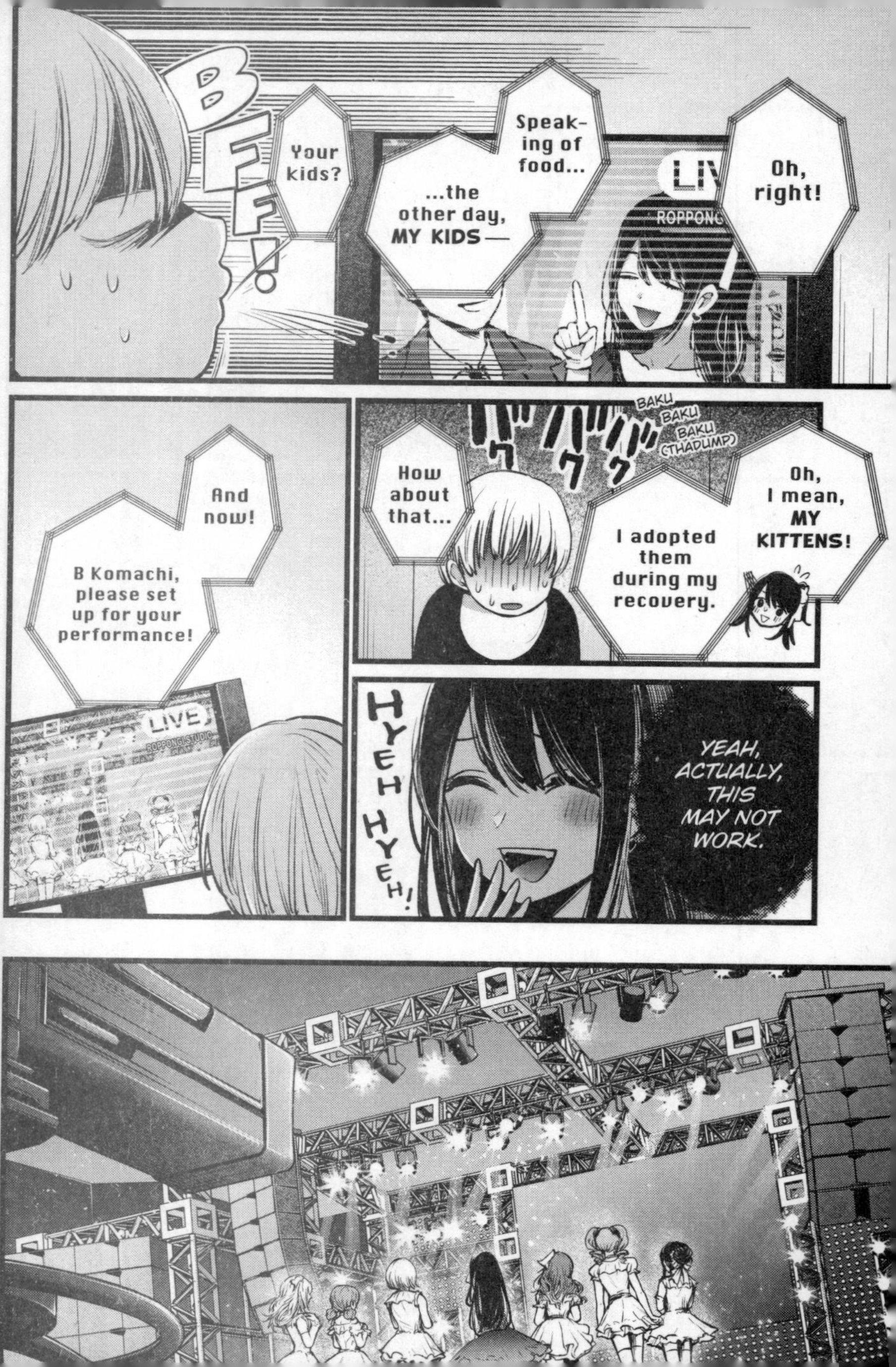
Oh, right!
Speak-ing of food...
...the other day, MY KIDS—
Your kids?
BFF!
BAKU BAKU BAKU (THADUMP)
Oh, I mean, MY KITTENS!
I adopted them during my recovery.
How about that...
HYEH HYEH!
YEAH, ACTUALLY, THIS MAY NOT WORK.
And now!
B Komachi, please set up for your performance!
LIVE
ROPPONGI STUDIO

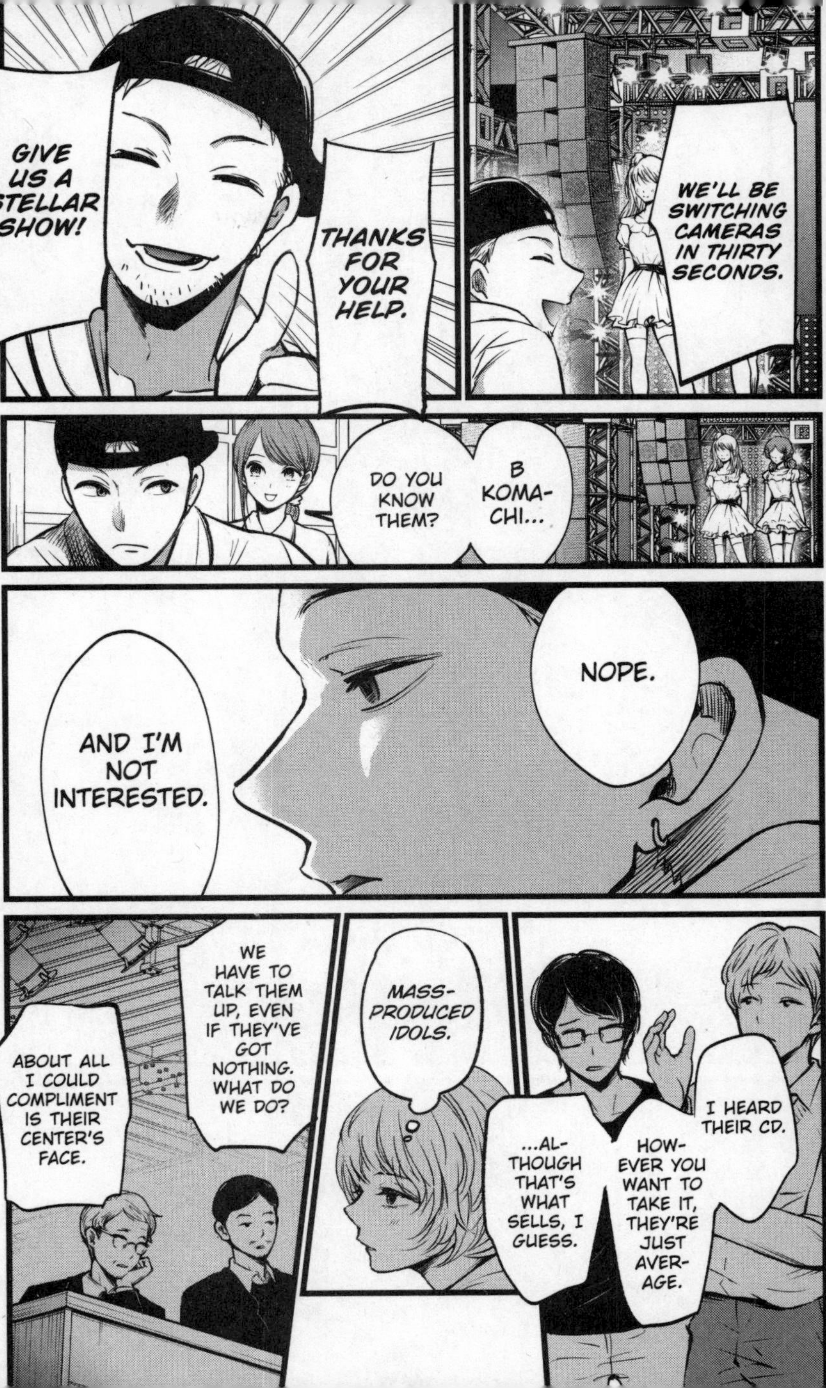
WE'LL BE SWITCHING CAMERAS IN THIRTY SECONDS.
THANKS FOR YOUR HELP.
GIVE US A STELLAR SHOW!
B KOMACHI...
DO YOU KNOW THEM?
NOPE.
AND I'M NOT INTERESTED.
I HEARD THEIR CD.
HOWEVER YOU WANT TO TAKE IT, THEY'RE JUST AVERAGE.
...ALTHOUGH THAT'S WHAT SELLS, I GUESS.
MASS-PRODUCED IDOLS.
WE HAVE TO TALK THEM UP, EVEN IF THEY'VE GOT NOTHING. WHAT DO WE DO?
ABOUT ALL I COULD COMPLIMENT IS THEIR CENTER'S FACE.

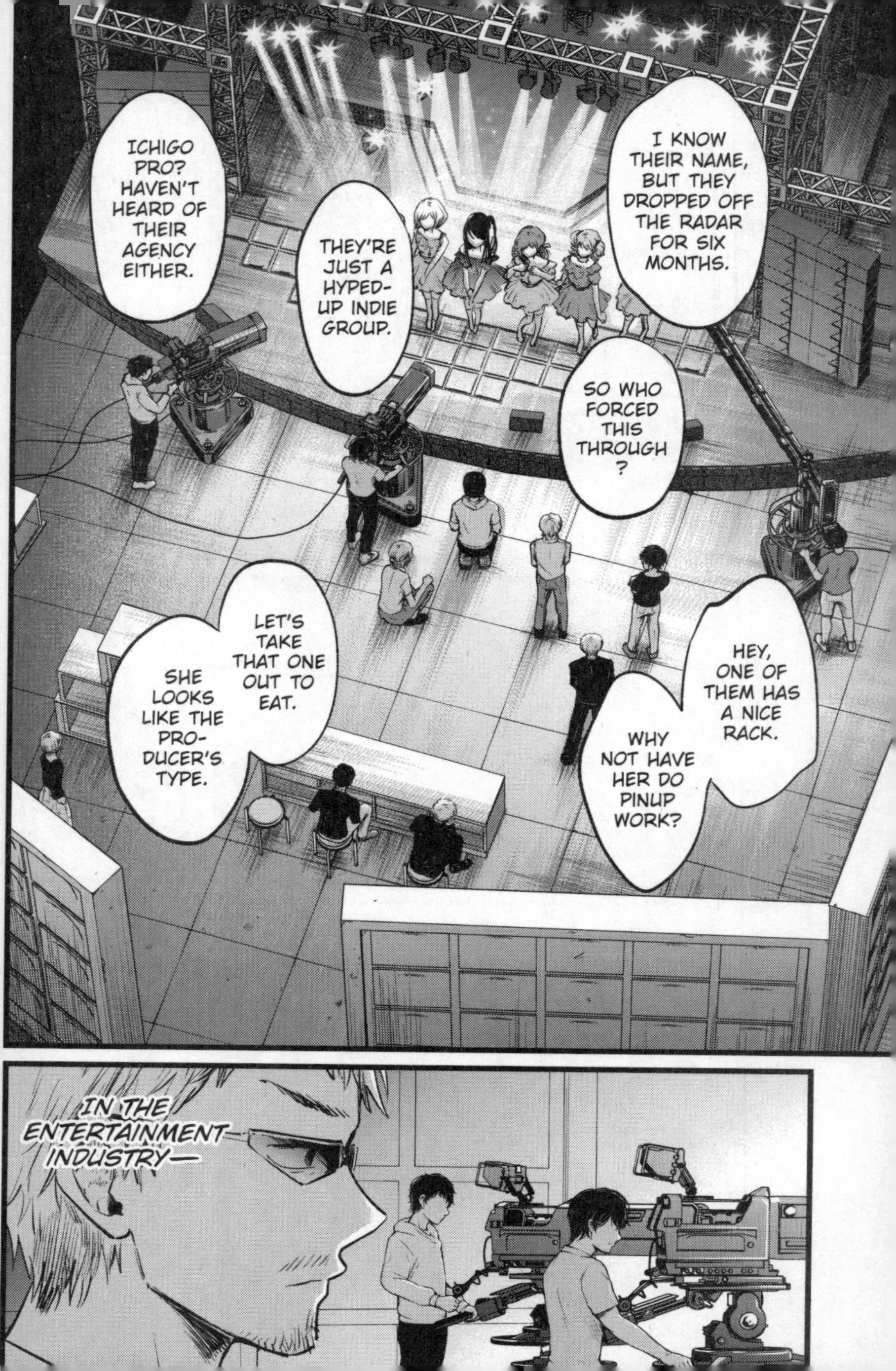
I KNOW THEIR NAME, BUT THEY DROPPED OFF THE RADAR FOR SIX MONTHS.
ICHIGO PRO? HAVEN'T HEARD OF THEIR AGENCY EITHER.
THEY'RE JUST A HYPED-UP INDIE GROUP.
SO WHO FORCED THIS THROUGH?
HEY, ONE OF THEM HAS A NICE RACK.
WHY NOT HAVE HER DO PINUP WORK?
LET'S TAKE THAT ONE OUT TO EAT.
SHE LOOKS LIKE THE PRODUCER'S TYPE.
IN THE ENTERTAINMENT INDUSTRY—

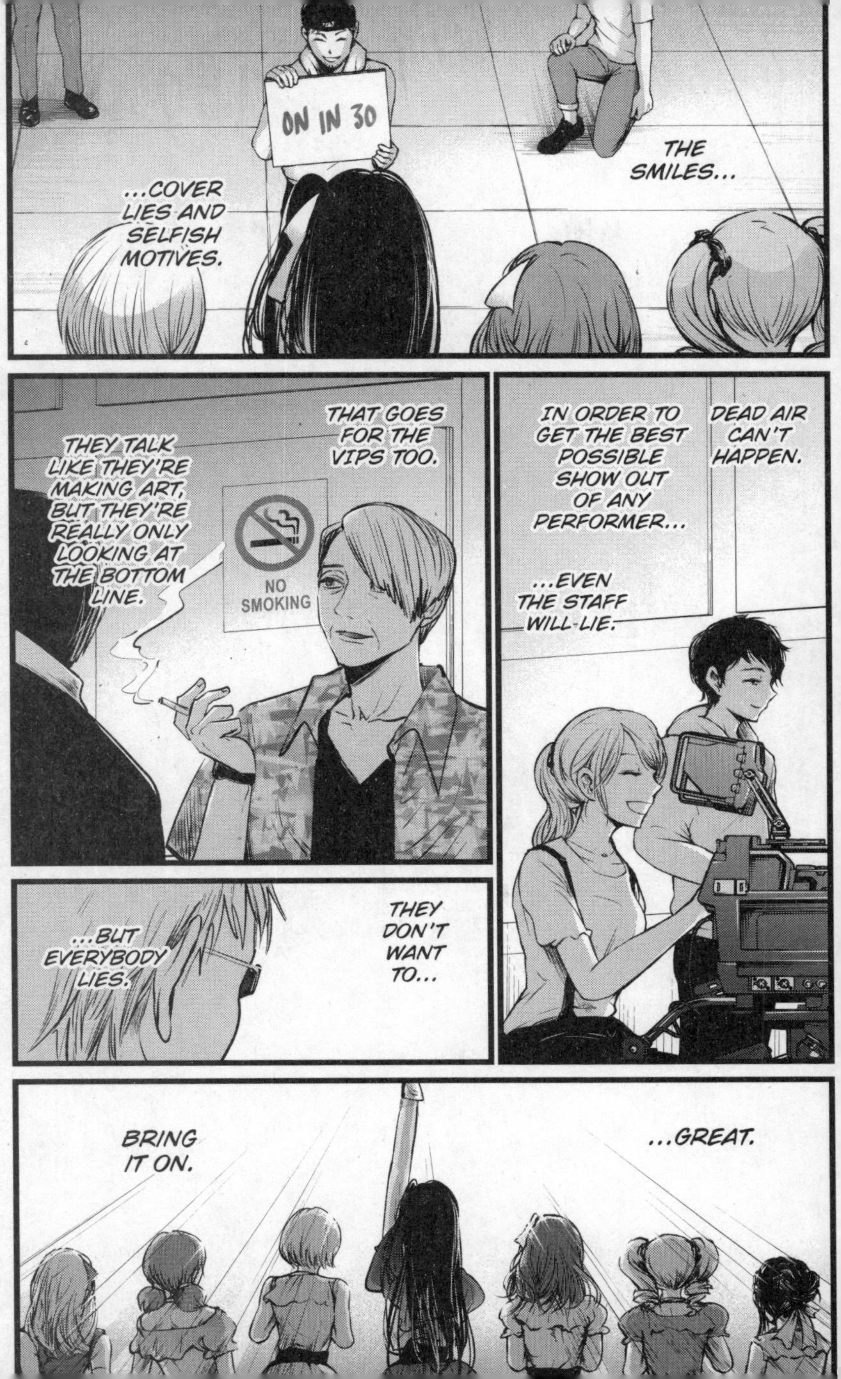
ON IN 30
THE SMILES...
...COVER LIES AND SELFISH MOTIVES.
DEAD AIR CAN'T HAPPEN.
IN ORDER TO GET THE BEST POSSIBLE SHOW OUT OF ANY PERFORMER...
...EVEN THE STAFF WILL LIE.
THAT GOES FOR THE VIPS TOO.
THEY TALK LIKE THEY'RE MAKING ART, BUT THEY'RE REALLY ONLY LOOKING AT THE BOTTOM LINE.
NO SMOKING
THEY DON'T WANT TO...
...BUT EVERYBODY LIES.
...GREAT.
BRING IT ON.

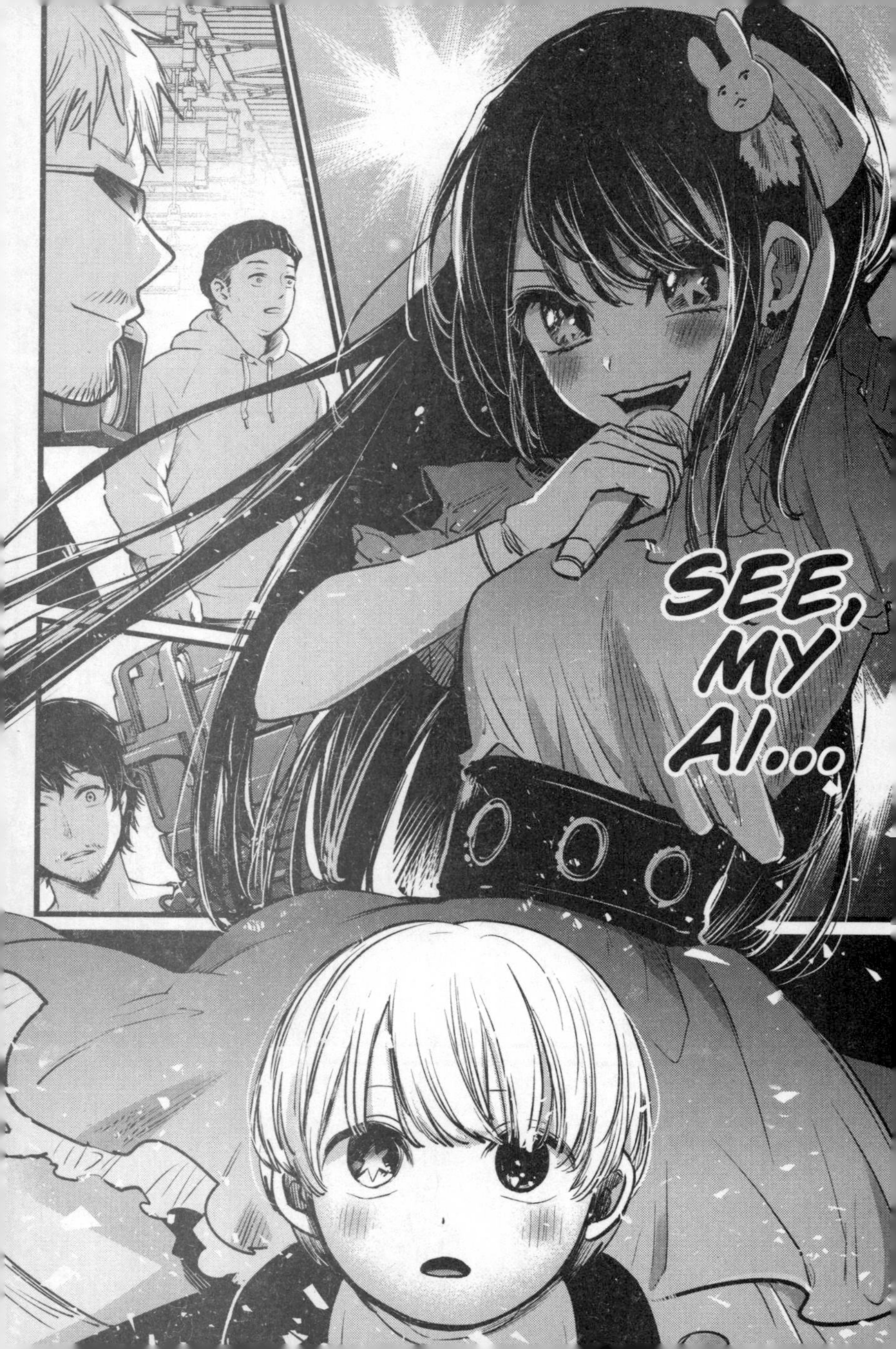
SEE, MY AI...

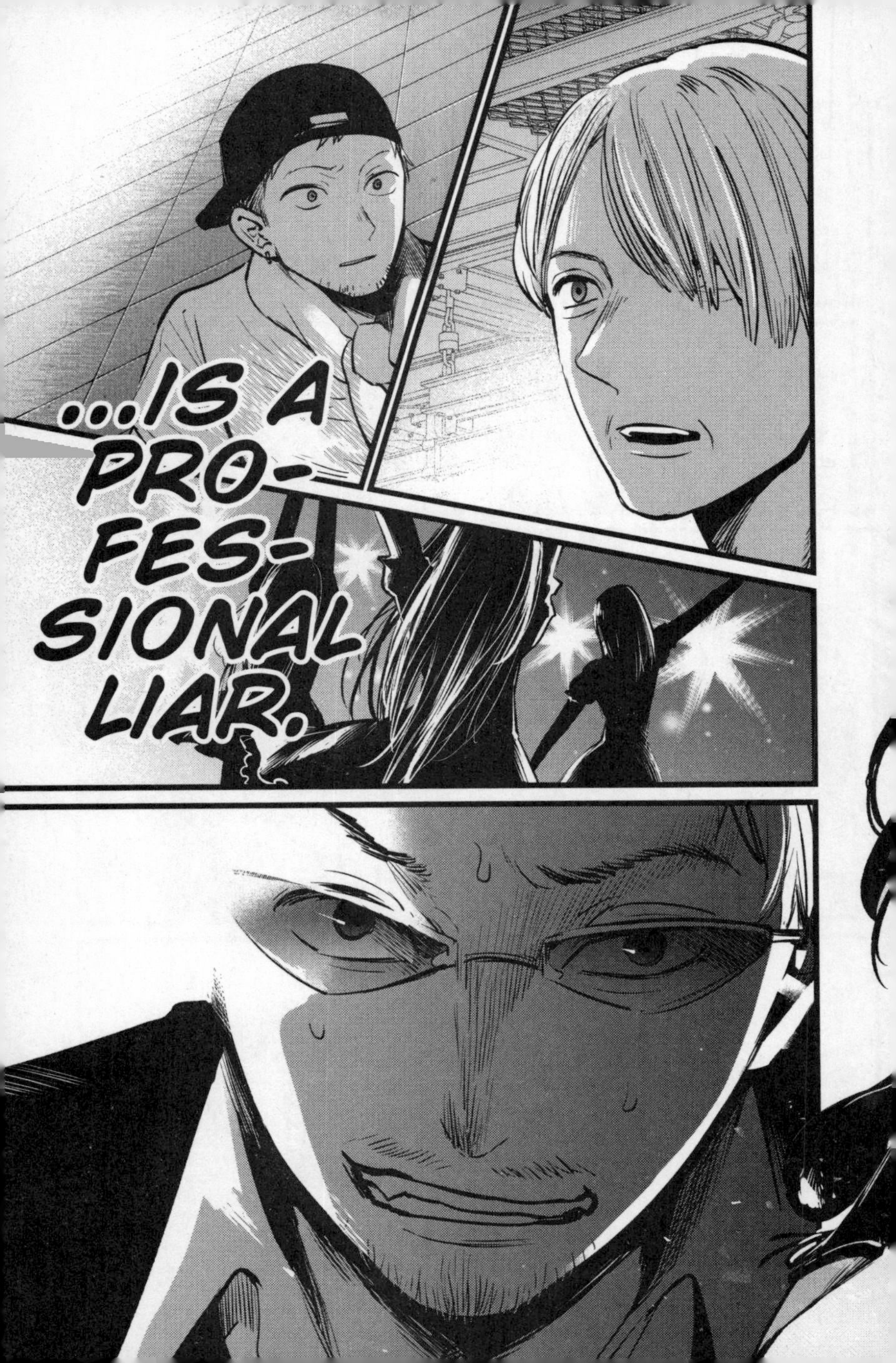
...IS A PRO-FES-SIONAL LIAR.

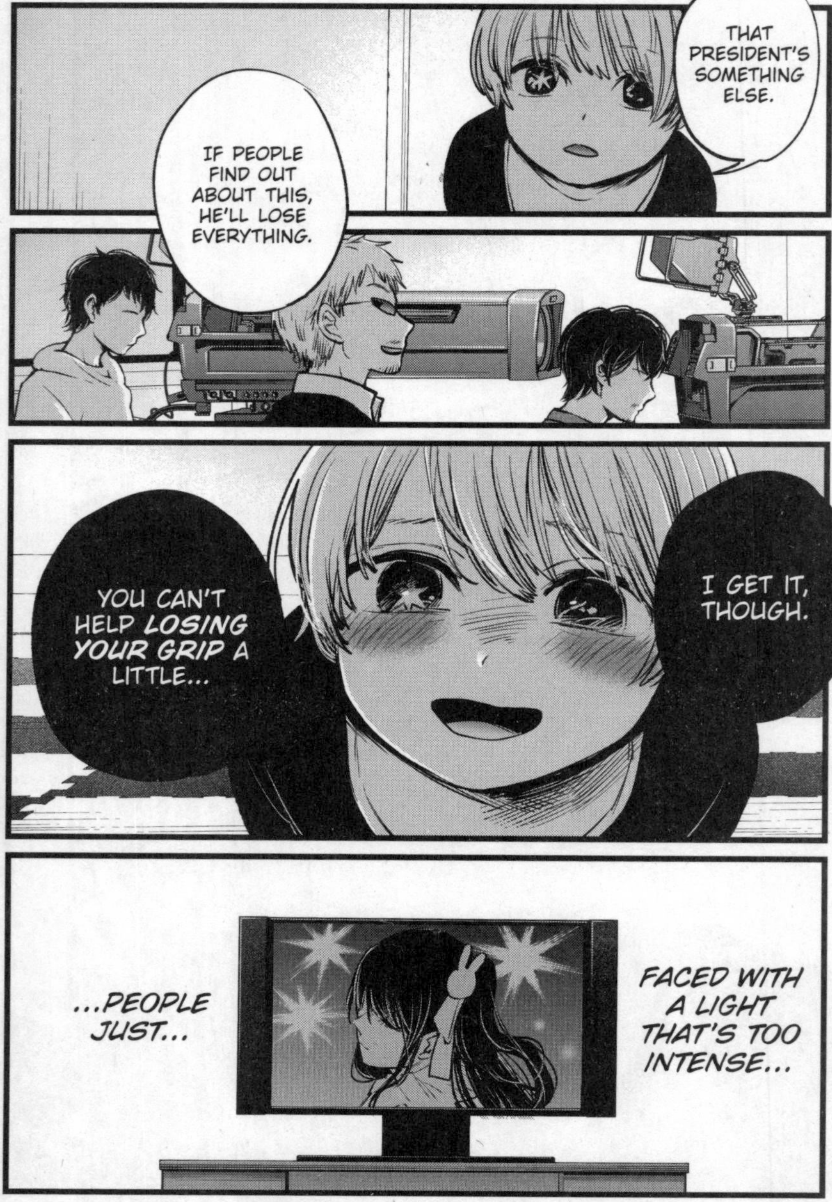
THAT PRESIDENT'S SOMETHING ELSE.
IF PEOPLE FIND OUT ABOUT THIS, HE'LL LOSE EVERYTHING.
I GET IT, THOUGH.
YOU CAN'T HELP *LOSING YOUR GRIP* A LITTLE...
FACED WITH A LIGHT THAT'S TOO INTENSE...
...PEOPLE JUST...

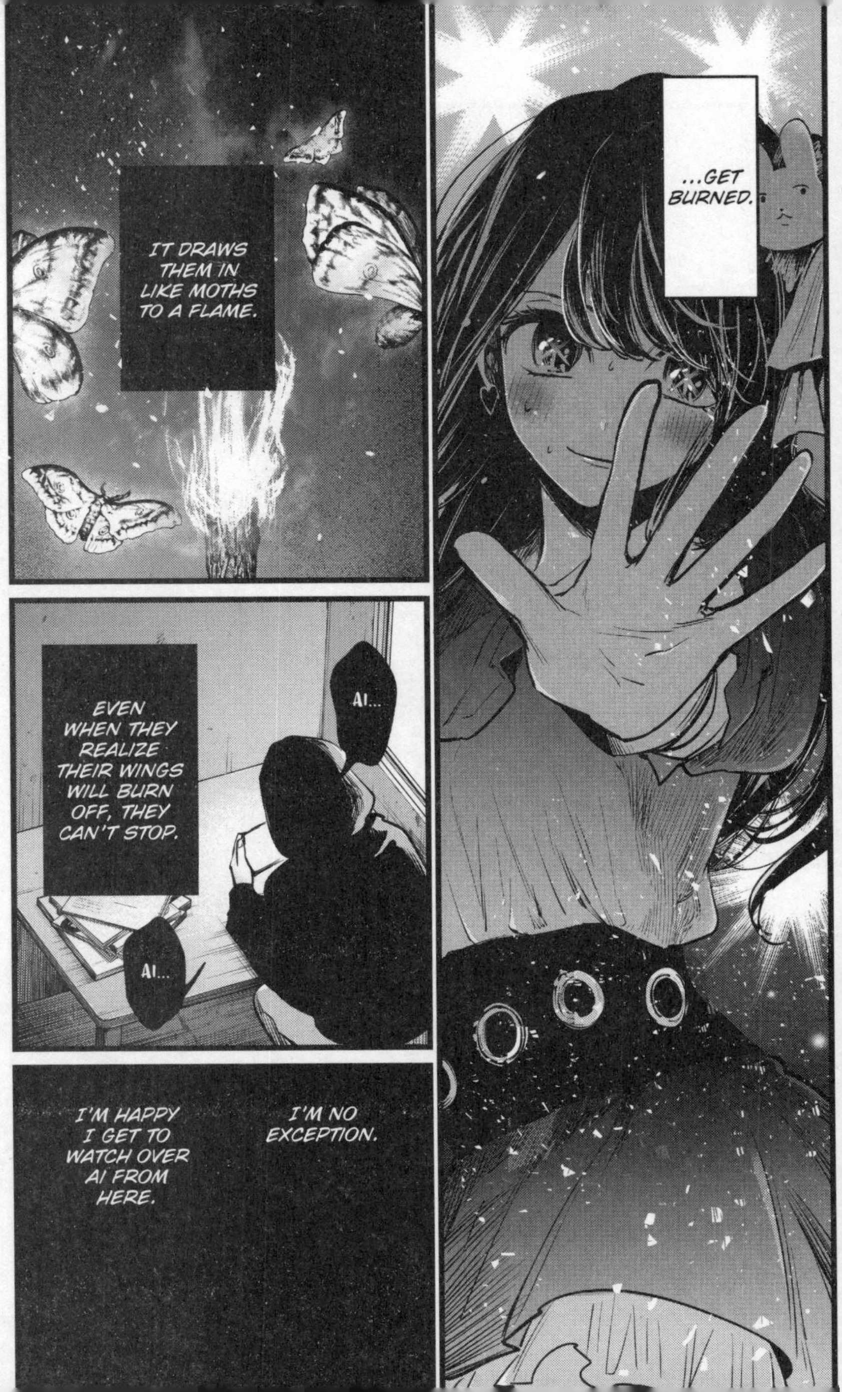
...GET BURNED.
IT DRAWS THEM IN LIKE MOTHS TO A FLAME.
EVEN WHEN THEY REALIZE THEIR WINGS WILL BURN OFF, THEY CAN'T STOP.
AI...
AI...
I'M NO EXCEPTION.
I'M HAPPY I GET TO WATCH OVER AI FROM HERE.

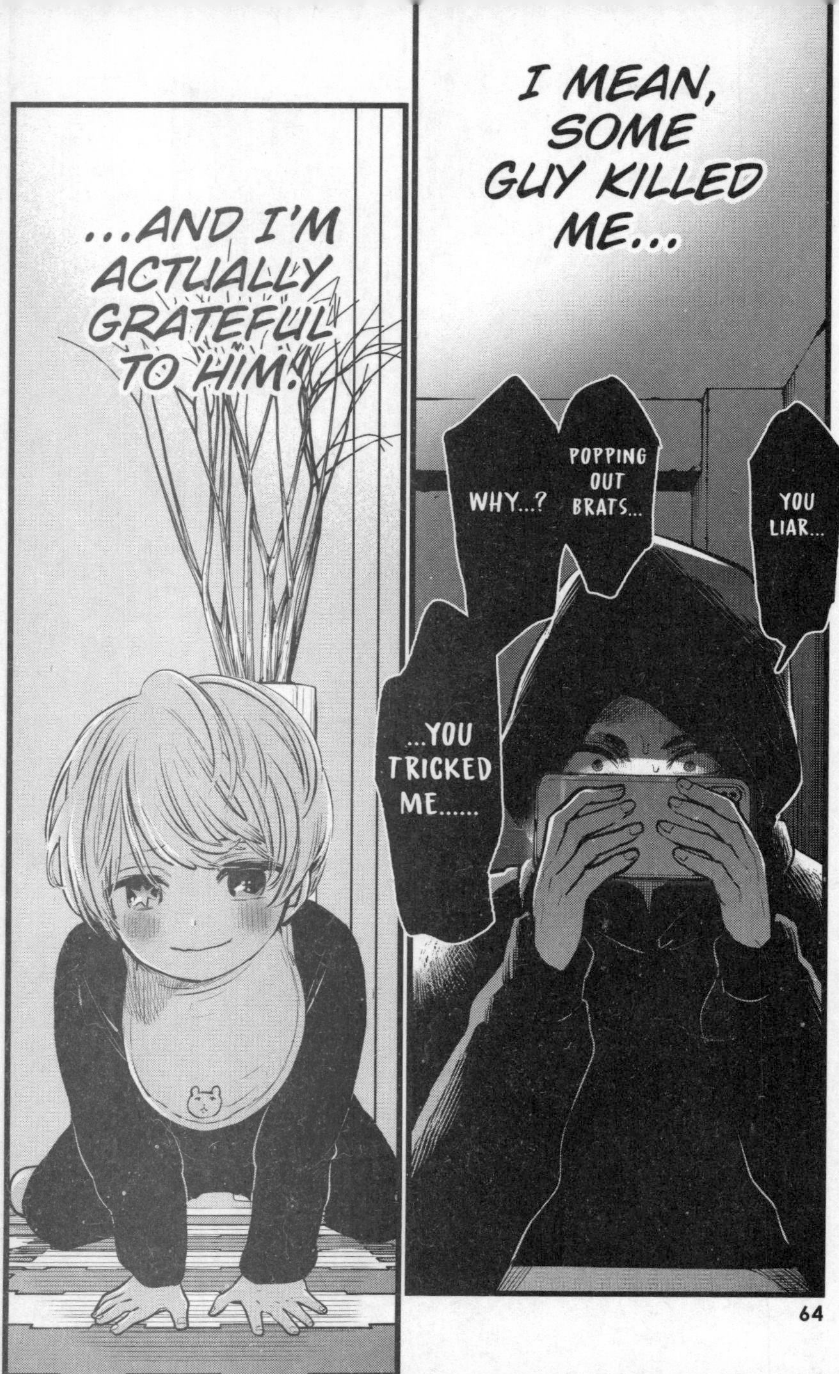
I MEAN, SOME GUY KILLED ME...
YOU LIAR...
POPPING OUT BRATS...
WHY...?
...YOU TRICKED ME......
...AND I'M ACTUALLY GRATEFUL TO HIM!

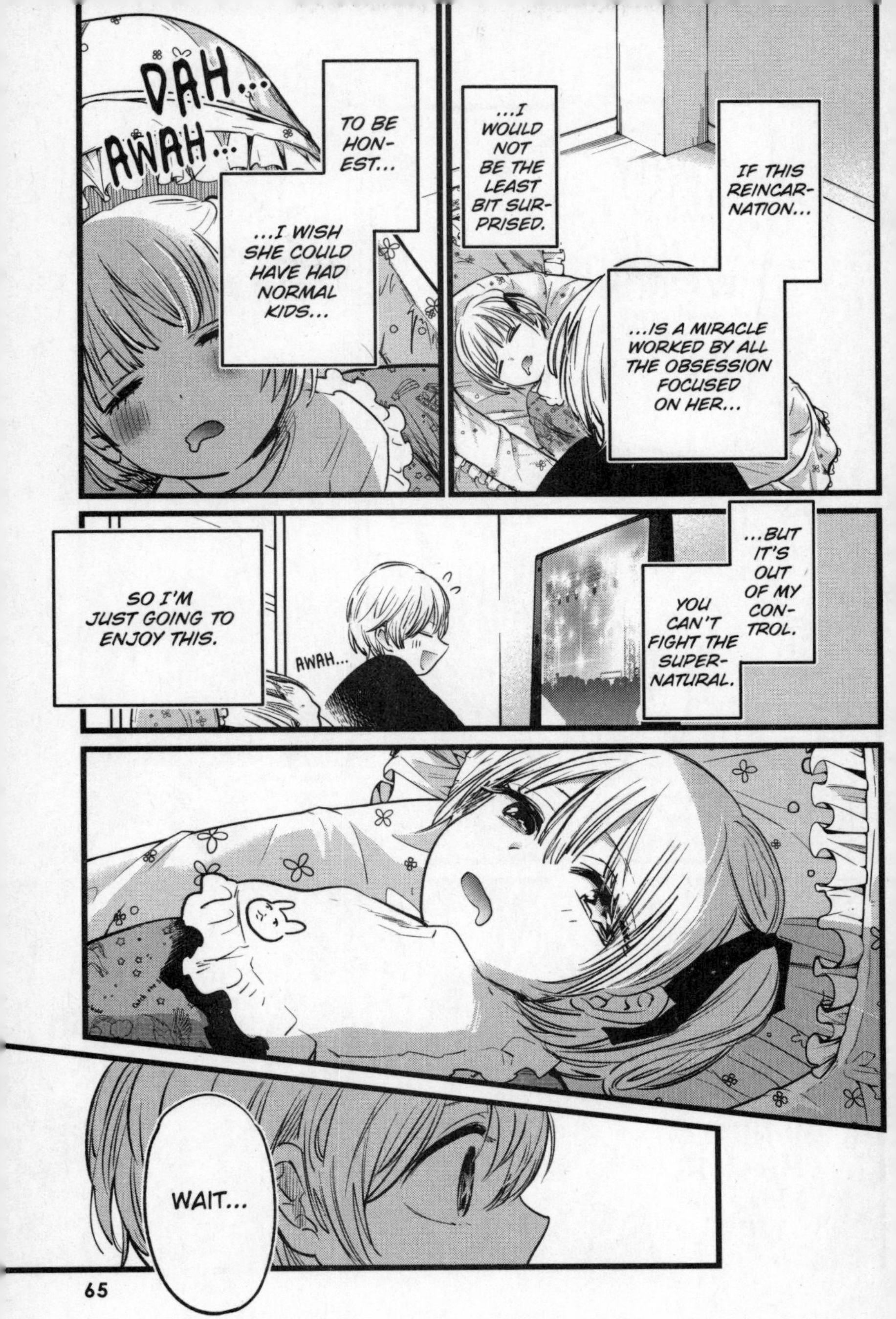
IF THIS REINCARNATION...
...IS A MIRACLE WORKED BY ALL THE OBSESSION FOCUSED ON HER...
...I WOULD NOT BE THE LEAST BIT SURPRISED.
TO BE HONEST...
...I WISH SHE COULD HAVE HAD NORMAL KIDS...
DAH...
AWAH...
...BUT IT'S OUT OF MY CONTROL.
YOU CAN'T FIGHT THE SUPERNATURAL.
AWAH...
SO I'M JUST GOING TO ENJOY THIS.
WAIT...

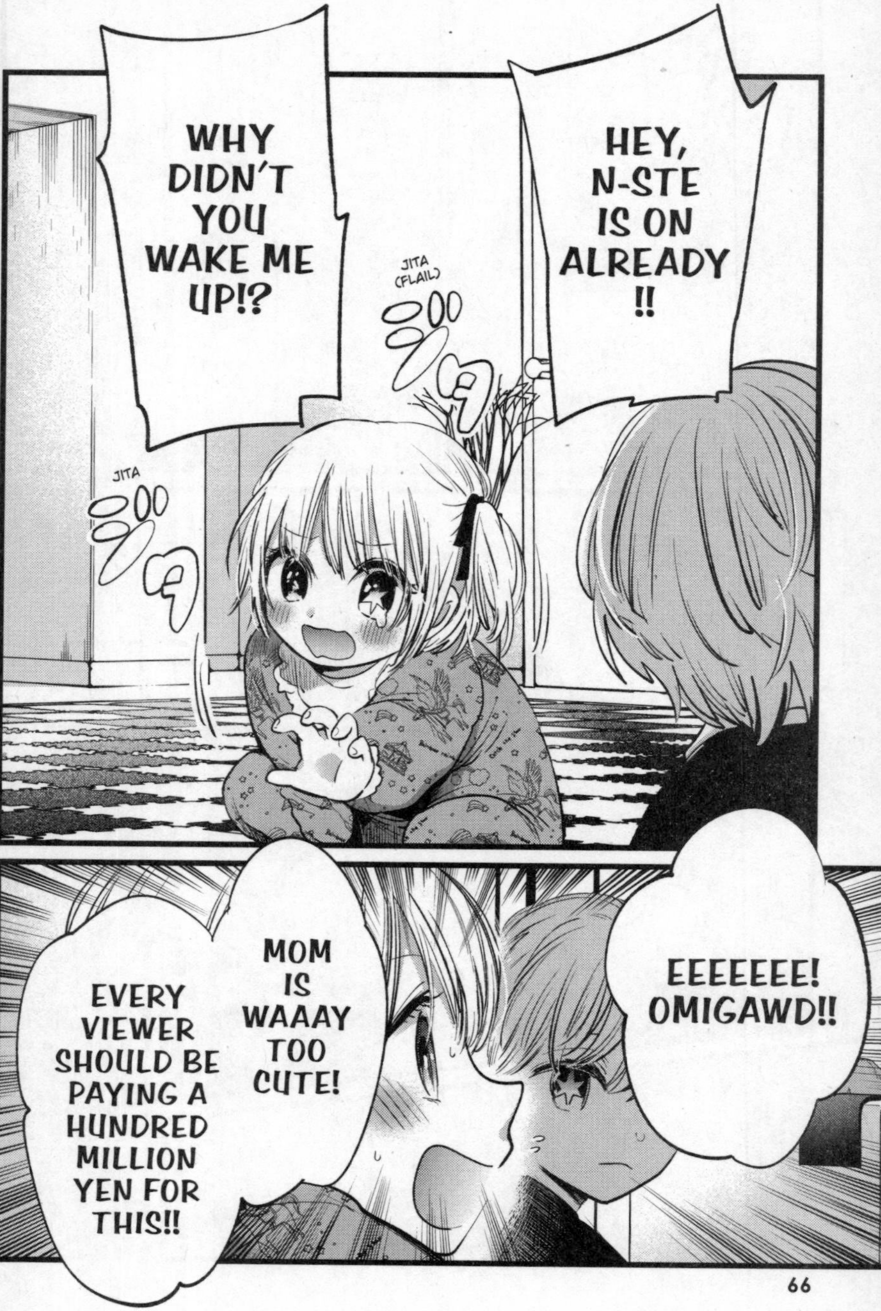
HEY, N-STE IS ON ALREADY!!
WHY DIDN'T YOU WAKE ME UP!?
JITA (FLAIL)
JITA
EEEEEEE! OMIGAWD!!
MOM IS WAAAY TOO CUTE!
EVERY VIEWER SHOULD BE PAYING A HUNDRED MILLION YEN FOR THIS!!

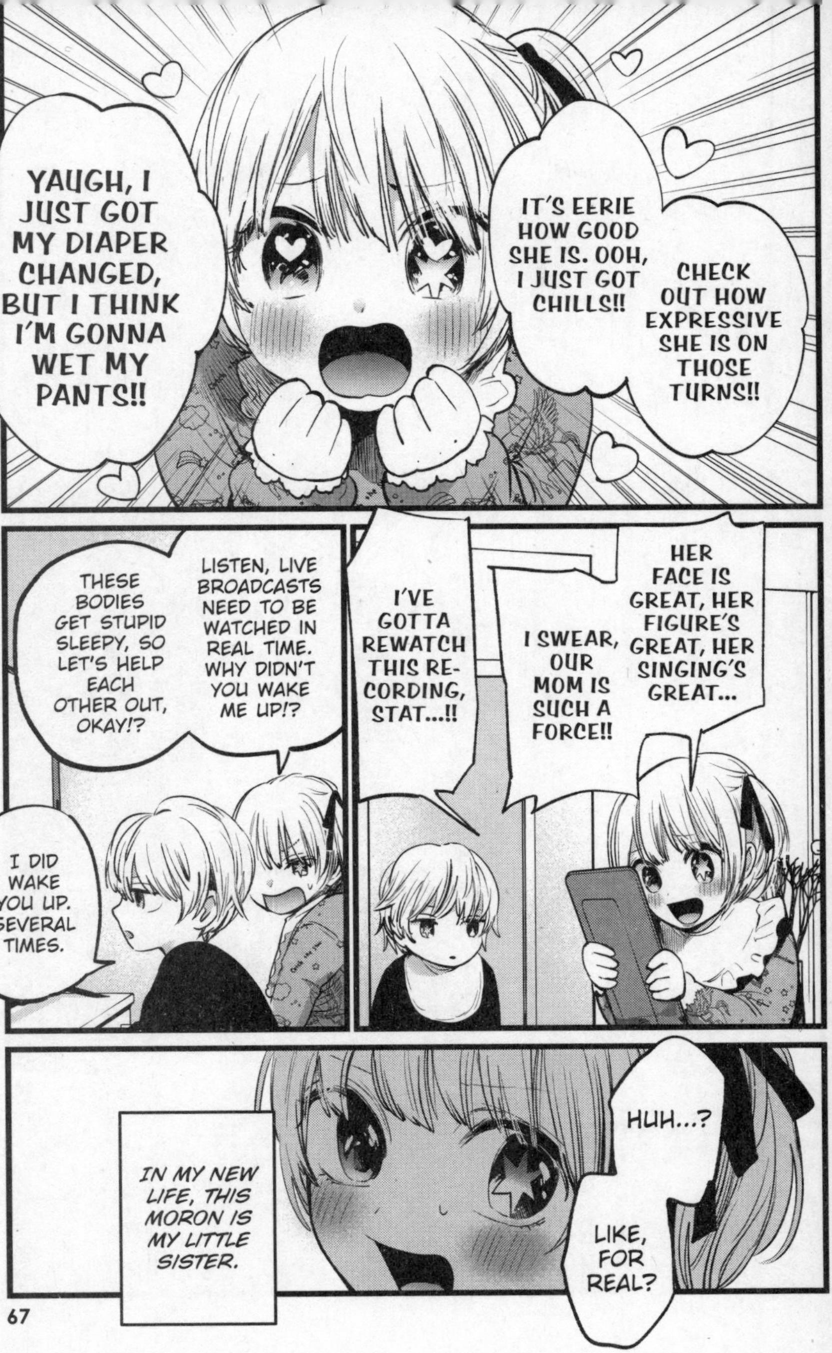
CHECK OUT HOW EXPRESSIVE SHE IS ON THOSE TURNS!!
IT'S EERIE HOW GOOD SHE IS. OOH, I JUST GOT CHILLS!!
YAUGH, I JUST GOT MY DIAPER CHANGED, BUT I THINK I'M GONNA WET MY PANTS!!
HER FACE IS GREAT, HER FIGURE'S GREAT, HER SINGING'S GREAT...
I SWEAR, OUR MOM IS SUCH A FORCE!!
I'VE GOTTA REWATCH THIS RE-CORDING, STAT...!!
LISTEN, LIVE BROADCASTS NEED TO BE WATCHED IN REAL TIME. WHY DIDN'T YOU WAKE ME UP!?
THESE BODIES GET STUPID SLEEPY, SO LET'S HELP EACH OTHER OUT, OKAY!?
I DID WAKE YOU UP. SEVERAL TIMES.
HUH...?
LIKE, FOR REAL?
IN MY NEW LIFE, THIS MORON IS MY LITTLE SISTER.

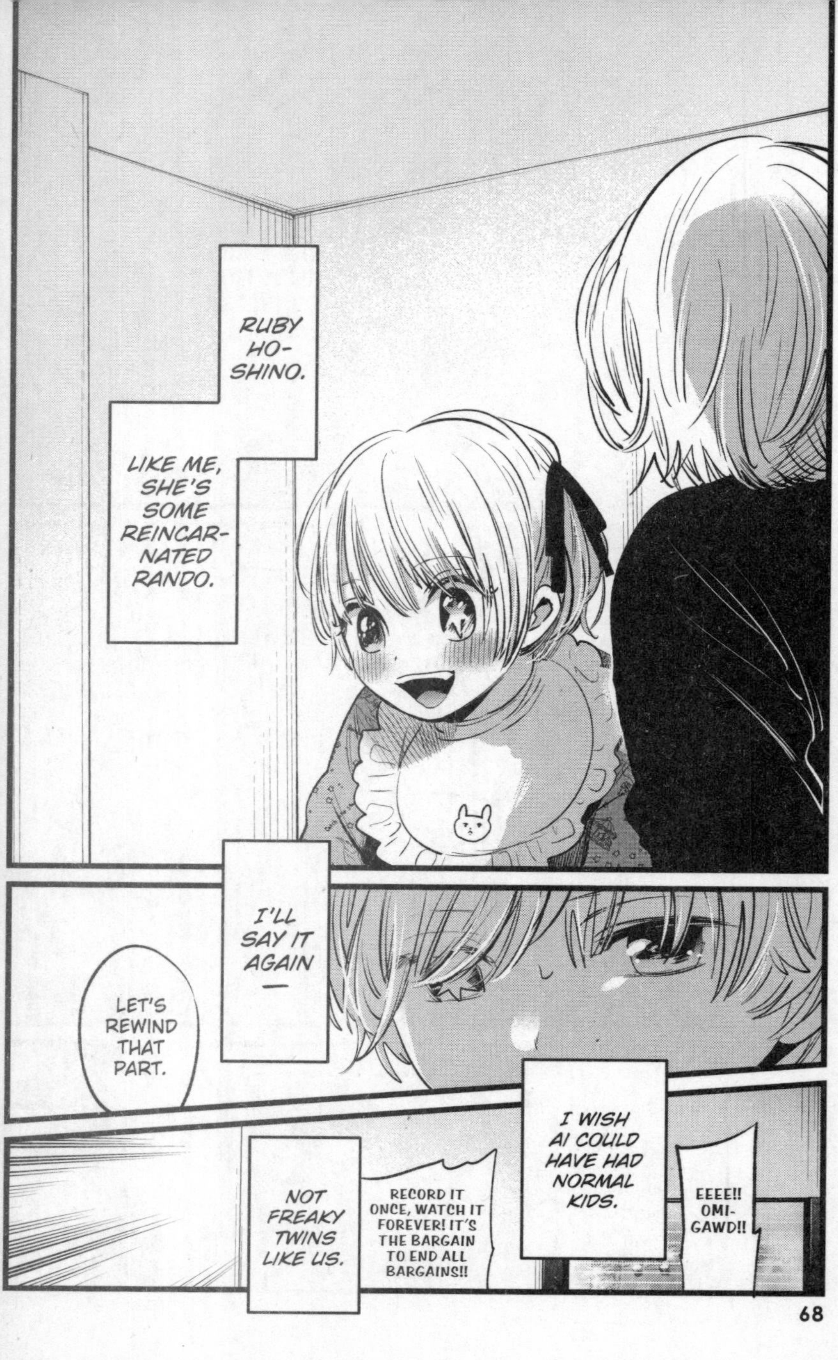
RUBY HO-SHINO.
LIKE ME, SHE'S SOME REINCAR-NATED RANDO.
I'LL SAY IT AGAIN—
LET'S REWIND THAT PART.
EEEE!! OMI-GAWD!!
I WISH AI COULD HAVE HAD NORMAL KIDS.
RECORD IT ONCE, WATCH IT FOREVER! IT'S THE BARGAIN TO END ALL BARGAINS!!
NOT FREAKY TWINS LIKE US.

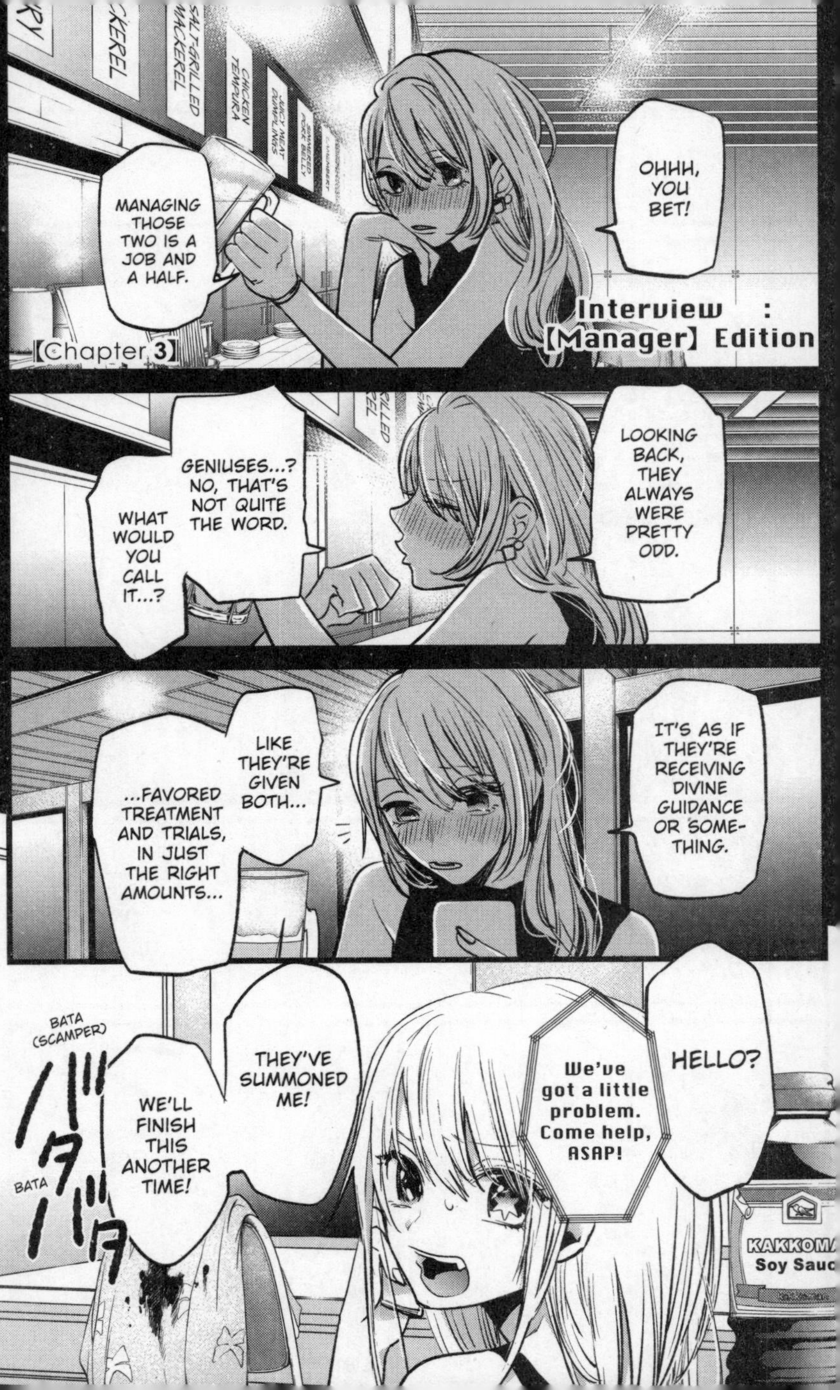
Interview : 【Manager】 Edition
【Chapter 3】
SALT-GRILLED MACKEREL
MACKEREL
CHICKEN TEMPURA
JUICY MEAT DUMPLINGS
SIMMERED PORK BELLY
OHHH, YOU BET!
MANAGING THOSE TWO IS A JOB AND A HALF.
LOOKING BACK, THEY ALWAYS WERE PRETTY ODD.
GENIUSES...? NO, THAT'S NOT QUITE THE WORD.
WHAT WOULD YOU CALL IT...?
IT'S AS IF THEY'RE RECEIVING DIVINE GUIDANCE OR SOME-THING.
LIKE THEY'RE GIVEN BOTH...
...FAVORED TREATMENT AND TRIALS, IN JUST THE RIGHT AMOUNTS...
HELLO?
We've got a little problem. Come help, ASAP!
THEY'VE SUMMONED ME!
WE'LL FINISH THIS ANOTHER TIME!
BATA (SCAMPER)
BATA

Chapter 3 Babysitter

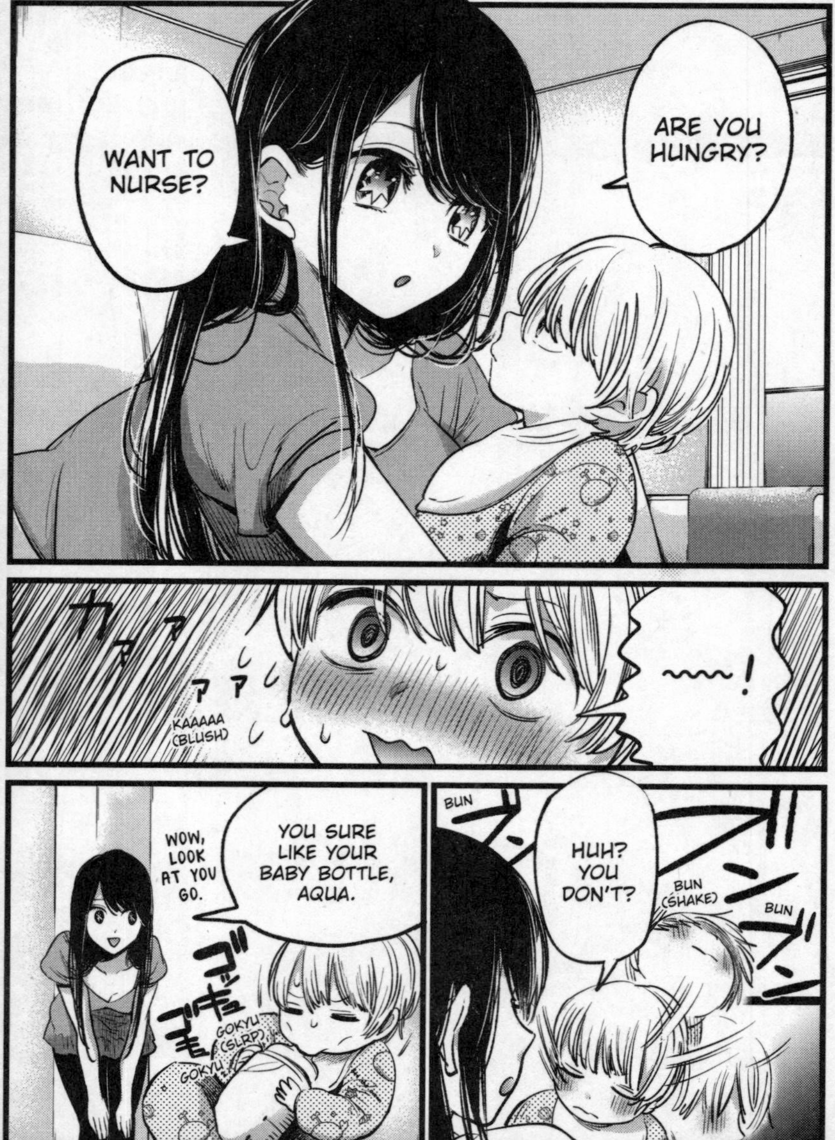
ARE YOU HUNGRY?
WANT TO NURSE?
~~~~!
KAAAAA (BLUSH)
BUN
HUH? YOU DON'T?
BUN (SHAKE)
BUN
YOU SURE LIKE YOUR BABY BOTTLE, AQUA.
WOW, LOOK AT YOU GO.
GOKYU (SLRP)
GOKYU
~~~~

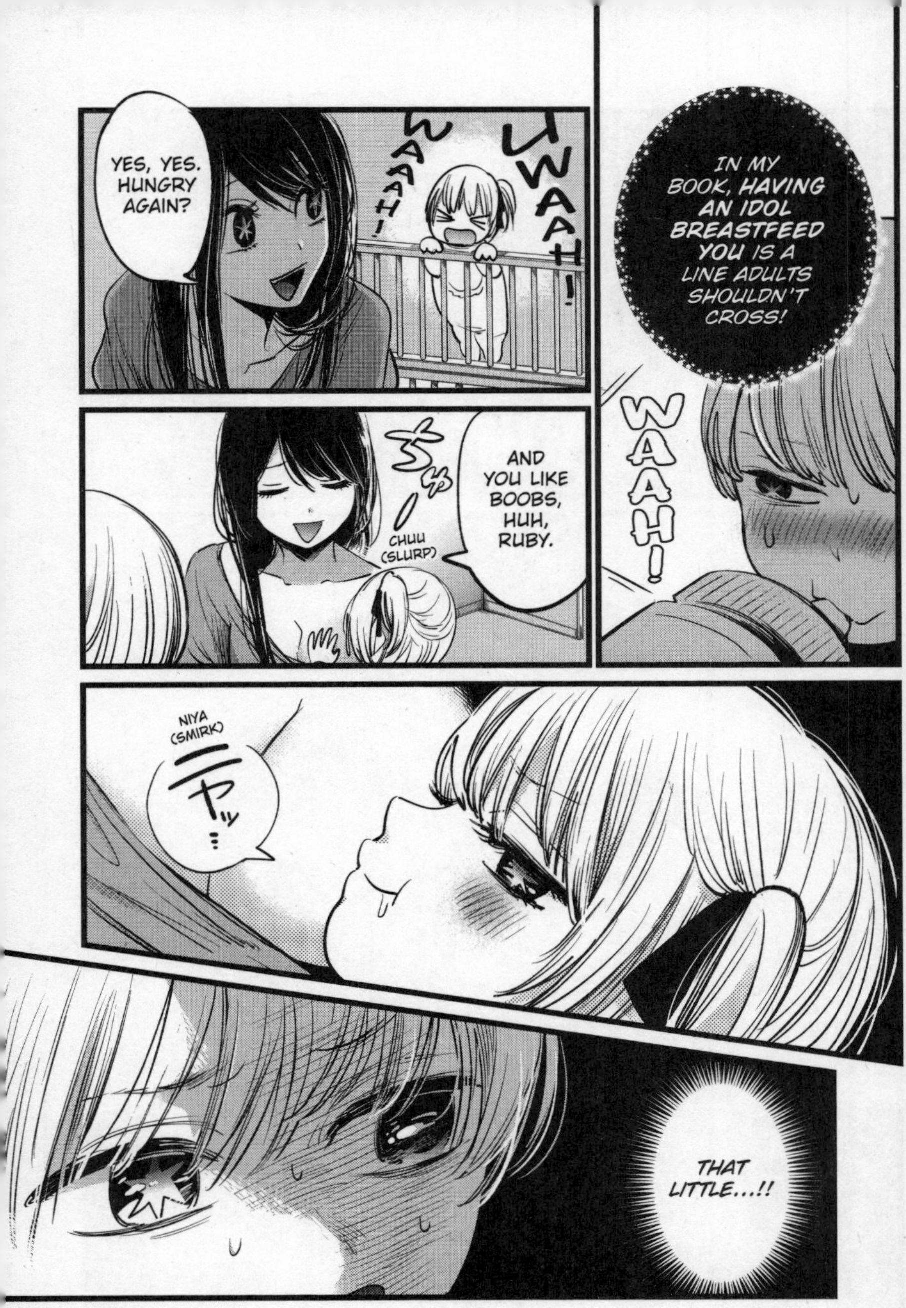
IN MY BOOK, HAVING AN IDOL BREASTFEED YOU IS A LINE ADULTS SHOULDN'T CROSS!
WAAAH!
UWAAAH!
WAAAH!
YES, YES. HUNGRY AGAIN?
AND YOU LIKE BOOBS, HUH, RUBY.
CHUU (SLURP)
NIYA (SMIRK)
THAT LITTLE...!!

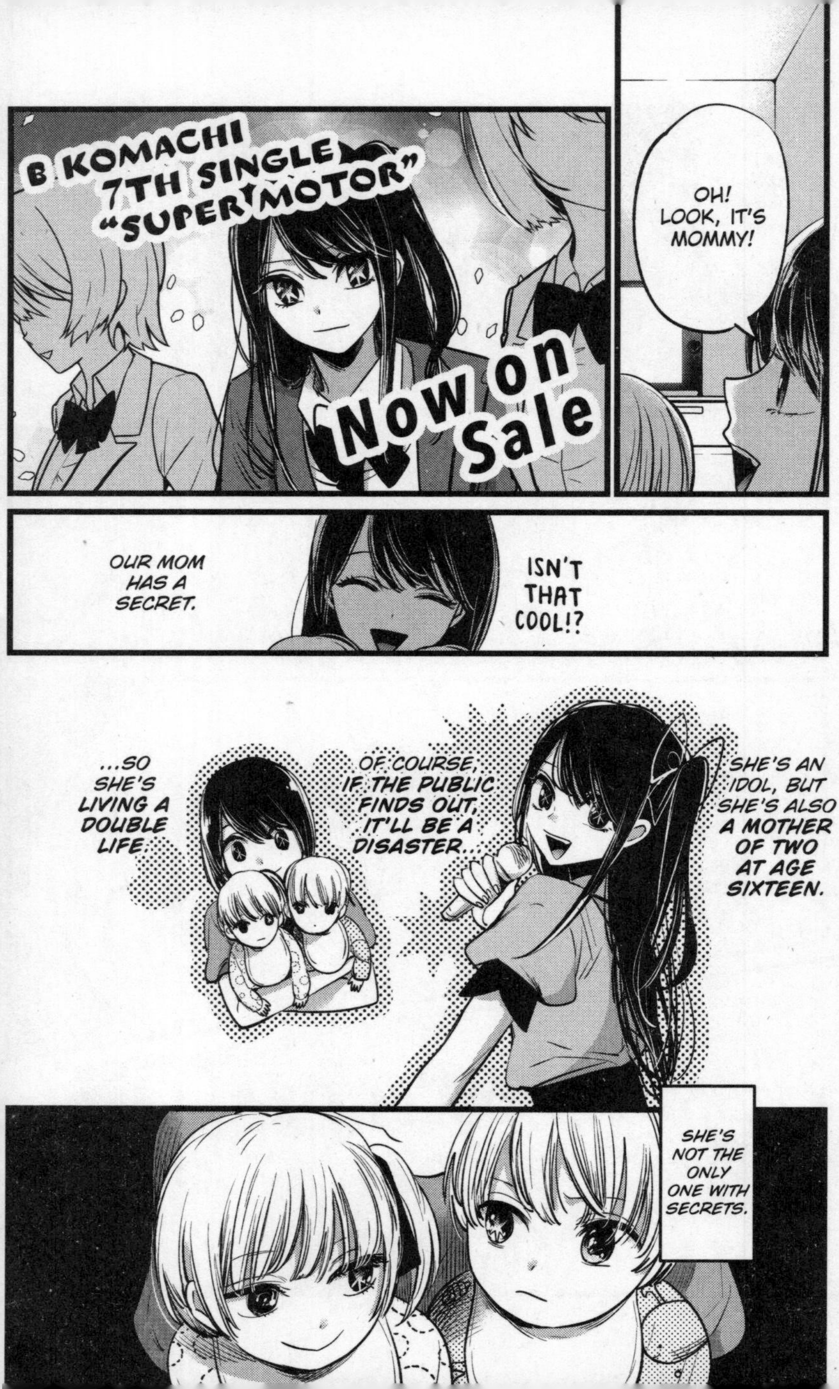
OH! LOOK, IT'S MOMMY!
B KOMACHI 7TH SINGLE "SUPER MOTOR"
Now on Sale
ISN'T THAT COOL!?
OUR MOM HAS A SECRET.
SHE'S AN IDOL, BUT SHE'S ALSO A MOTHER OF TWO AT AGE SIXTEEN.
OF COURSE, IF THE PUBLIC FINDS OUT, IT'LL BE A DISASTER...
...SO SHE'S LIVING A DOUBLE LIFE.
SHE'S NOT THE ONLY ONE WITH SECRETS.

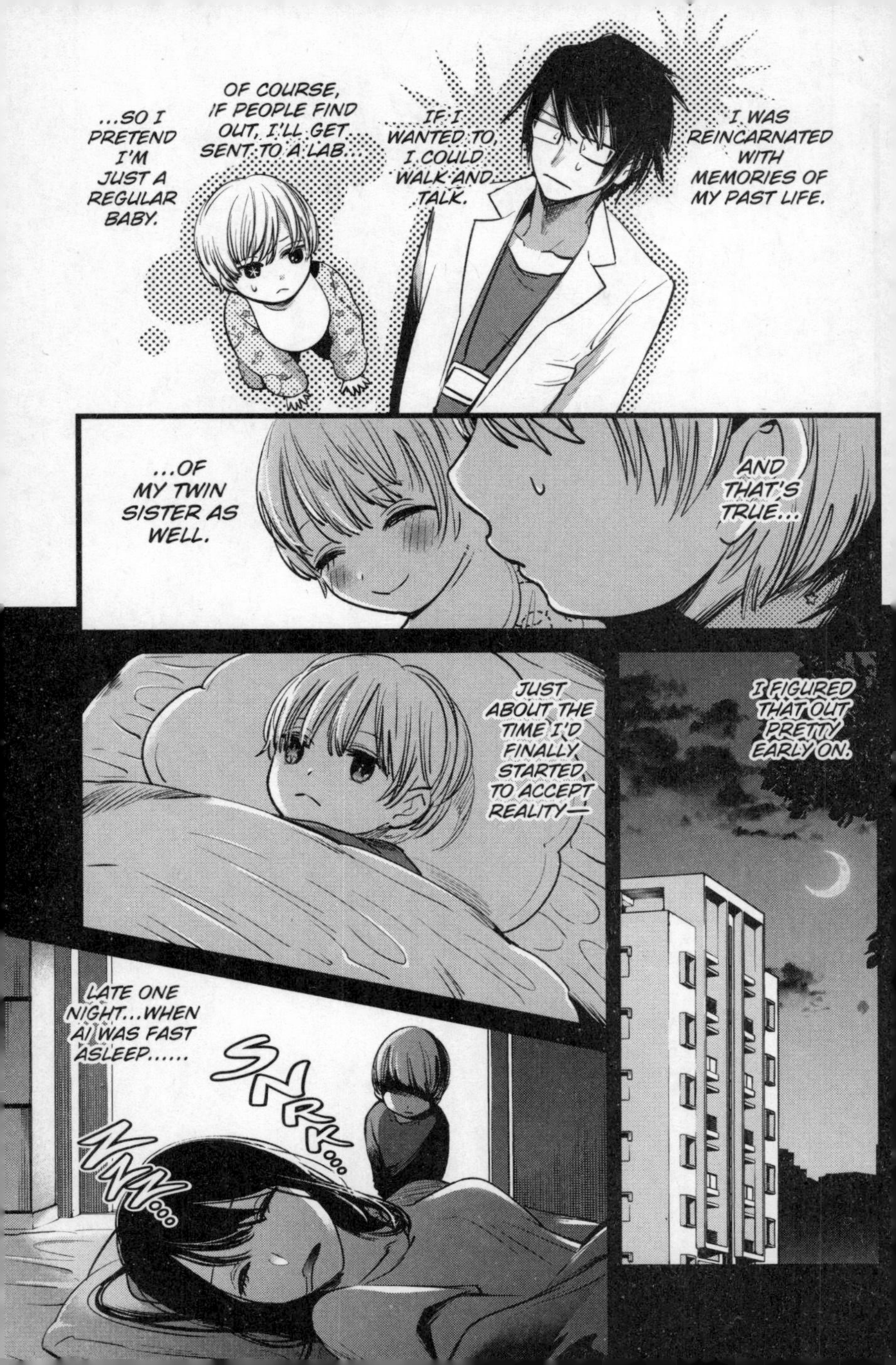
I WAS REINCARNATED WITH MEMORIES OF MY PAST LIFE.
IF I WANTED TO, I COULD WALK AND TALK.
OF COURSE, IF PEOPLE FIND OUT, I'LL GET SENT TO A LAB...
...SO I PRETEND I'M JUST A REGULAR BABY.
AND THAT'S TRUE...
...OF MY TWIN SISTER AS WELL.
I FIGURED THAT OUT PRETTY EARLY ON.
JUST ABOUT THE TIME I'D FINALLY STARTED TO ACCEPT REALITY—
LATE ONE NIGHT...WHEN AI WAS FAST ASLEEP......
SNRK...
NNN...

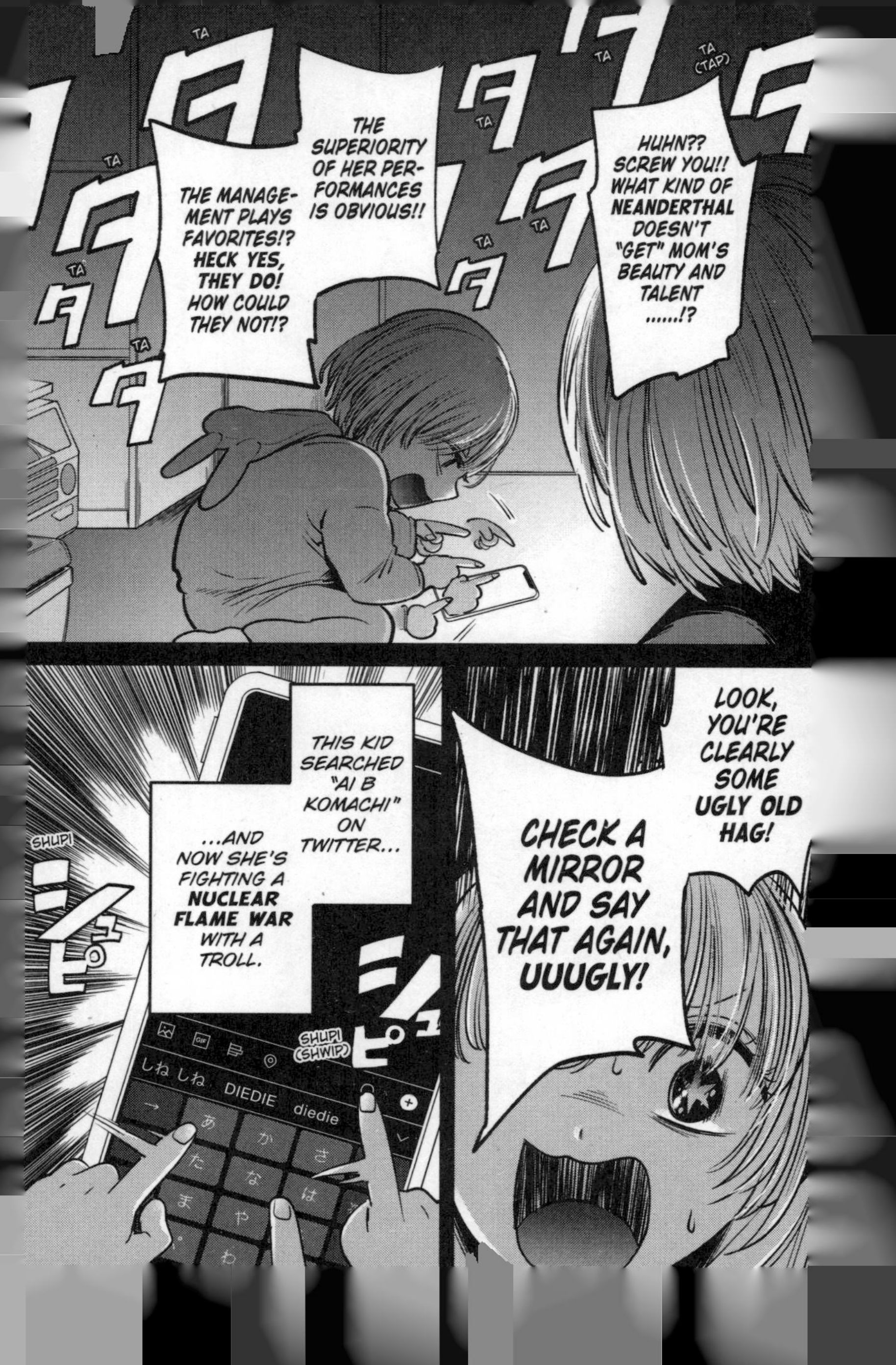
TA (TAP)
TA
TA
HUHN?? SCREW YOU!! WHAT KIND OF NEANDERTHAL DOESN'T "GET" MOM'S BEAUTY AND TALENT ......!?
TA
TA
TA
THE SUPERIORITY OF HER PER-FORMANCES IS OBVIOUS!!
THE MANAGE-MENT PLAYS FAVORITES!? HECK YES, THEY DO! HOW COULD THEY NOT!?
TA
TA
TA
LOOK, YOU'RE CLEARLY SOME UGLY OLD HAG!
CHECK A MIRROR AND SAY THAT AGAIN, UUUGLY!
THIS KID SEARCHED "AI B KOMACHI" ON TWITTER...
...AND NOW SHE'S FIGHTING A NUCLEAR FLAME WAR WITH A TROLL.
SHUPI (SHWIP)
しねしね DIEDIE diedie
SHUPI

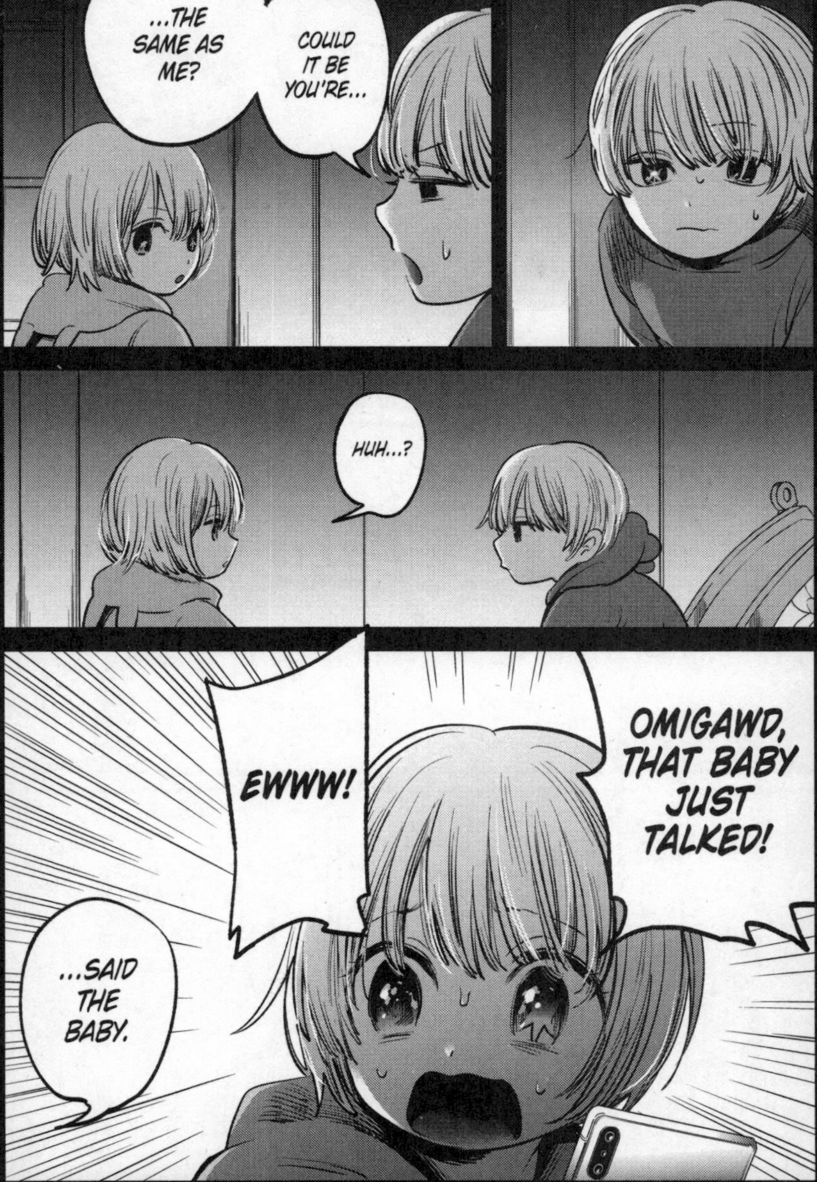
COULD IT BE YOU'RE...
...THE SAME AS ME?
HUH...?
OMIGAWD, THAT BABY JUST TALKED!
EWWW!
...SAID THE BABY.

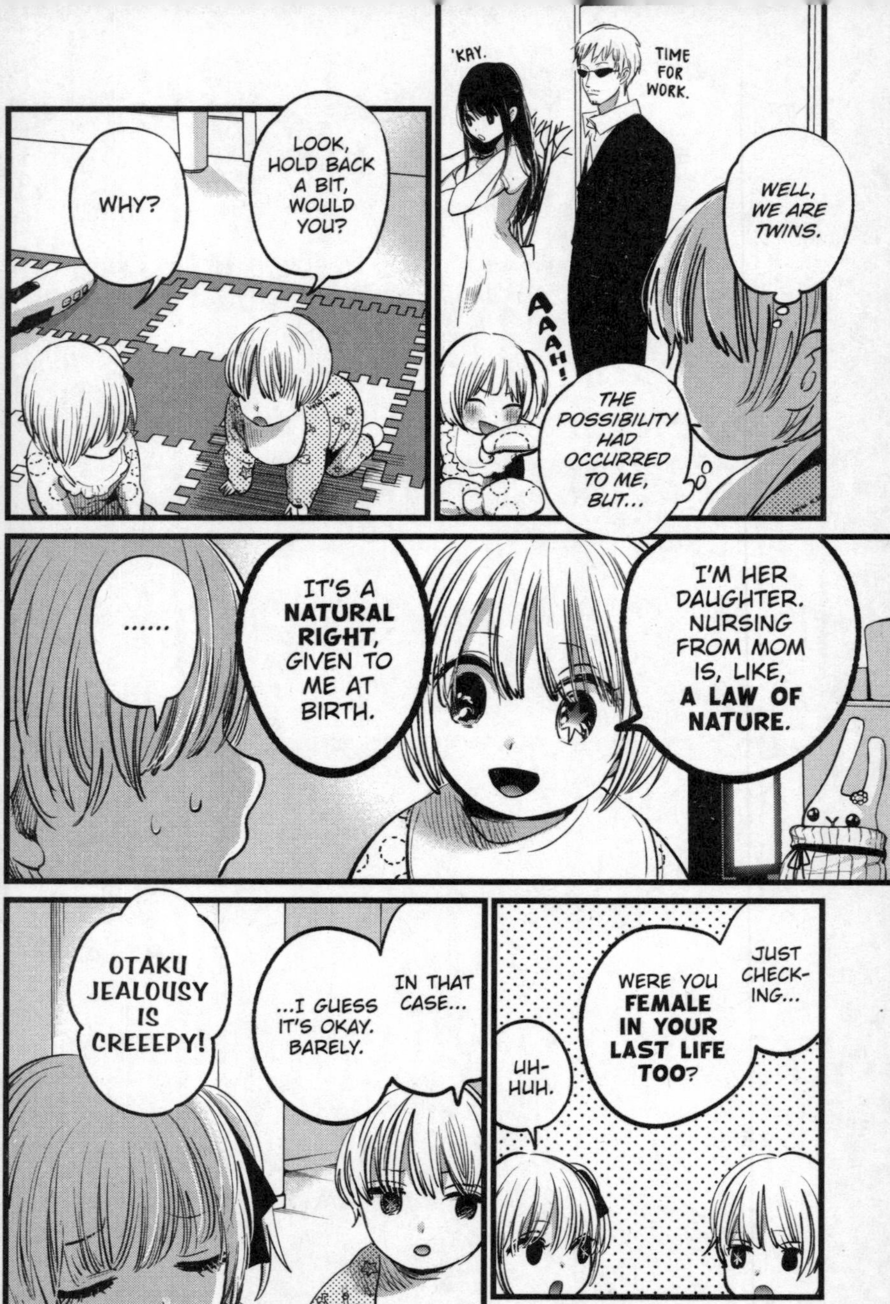
TIME FOR WORK.
'KAY.
WELL, WE ARE TWINS.
AAAH!
THE POSSIBILITY HAD OCCURRED TO ME, BUT...
LOOK, HOLD BACK A BIT, WOULD YOU?
WHY?
I'M HER DAUGHTER. NURSING FROM MOM IS, LIKE, **A LAW OF NATURE.**
IT'S A **NATURAL RIGHT,** GIVEN TO ME AT BIRTH.
......
JUST CHECKING...
WERE YOU **FEMALE IN YOUR LAST LIFE TOO**?
UH-HUH.
IN THAT CASE...
...I GUESS IT'S OKAY. BARELY.
OTAKU JEALOUSY IS CREEEPY!

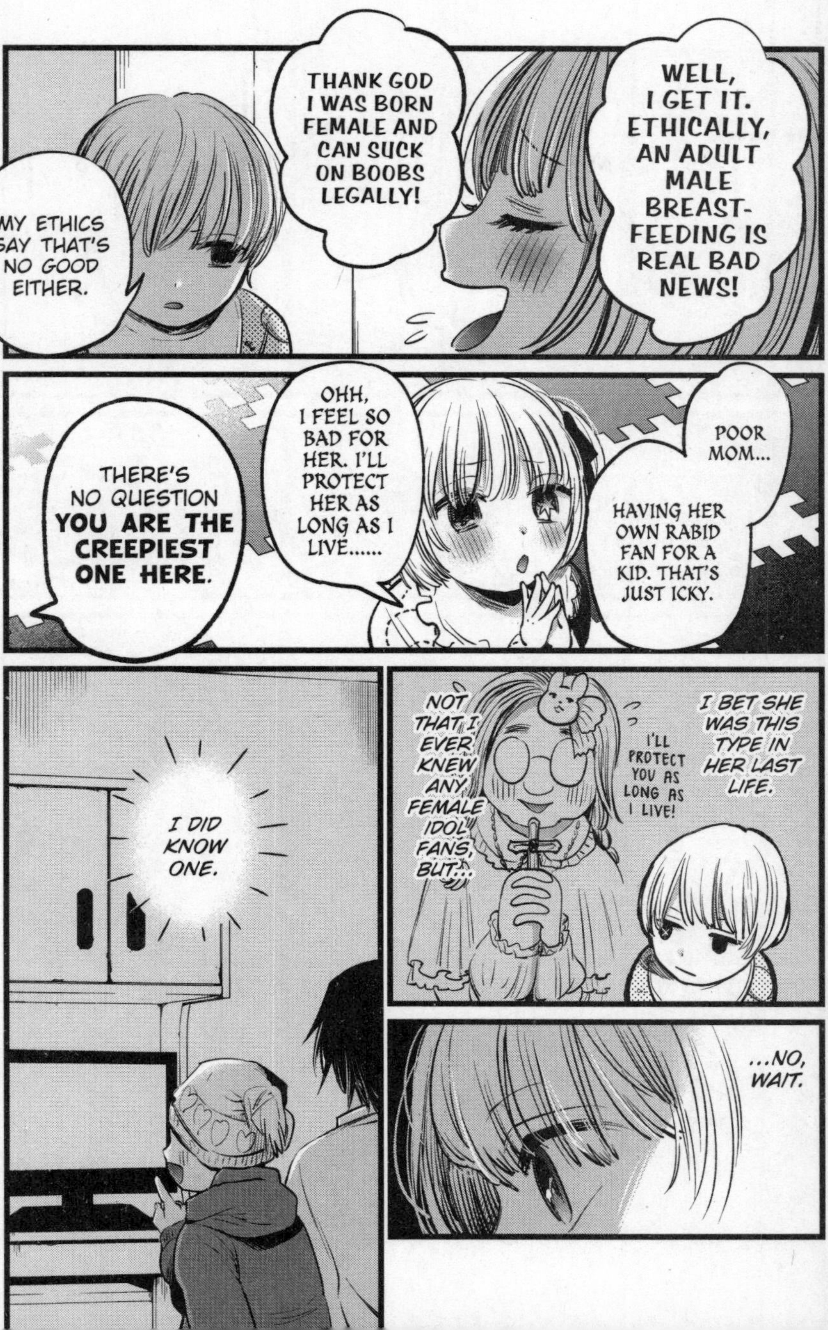
WELL, I GET IT. ETHICALLY, AN ADULT MALE BREAST-FEEDING IS REAL BAD NEWS!
THANK GOD I WAS BORN FEMALE AND CAN SUCK ON BOOBS LEGALLY!
MY ETHICS SAY THAT'S NO GOOD EITHER.
POOR MOM...
HAVING HER OWN RABID FAN FOR A KID. THAT'S JUST ICKY.
OHH, I FEEL SO BAD FOR HER. I'LL PROTECT HER AS LONG AS I LIVE......
THERE'S NO QUESTION YOU ARE THE CREEPIEST ONE HERE.
I BET SHE WAS THIS TYPE IN HER LAST LIFE.
I'LL PROTECT YOU AS LONG AS I LIVE!
NOT THAT I EVER KNEW ANY FEMALE IDOL FANS, BUT...
...NO, WAIT.
I DID KNOW ONE.

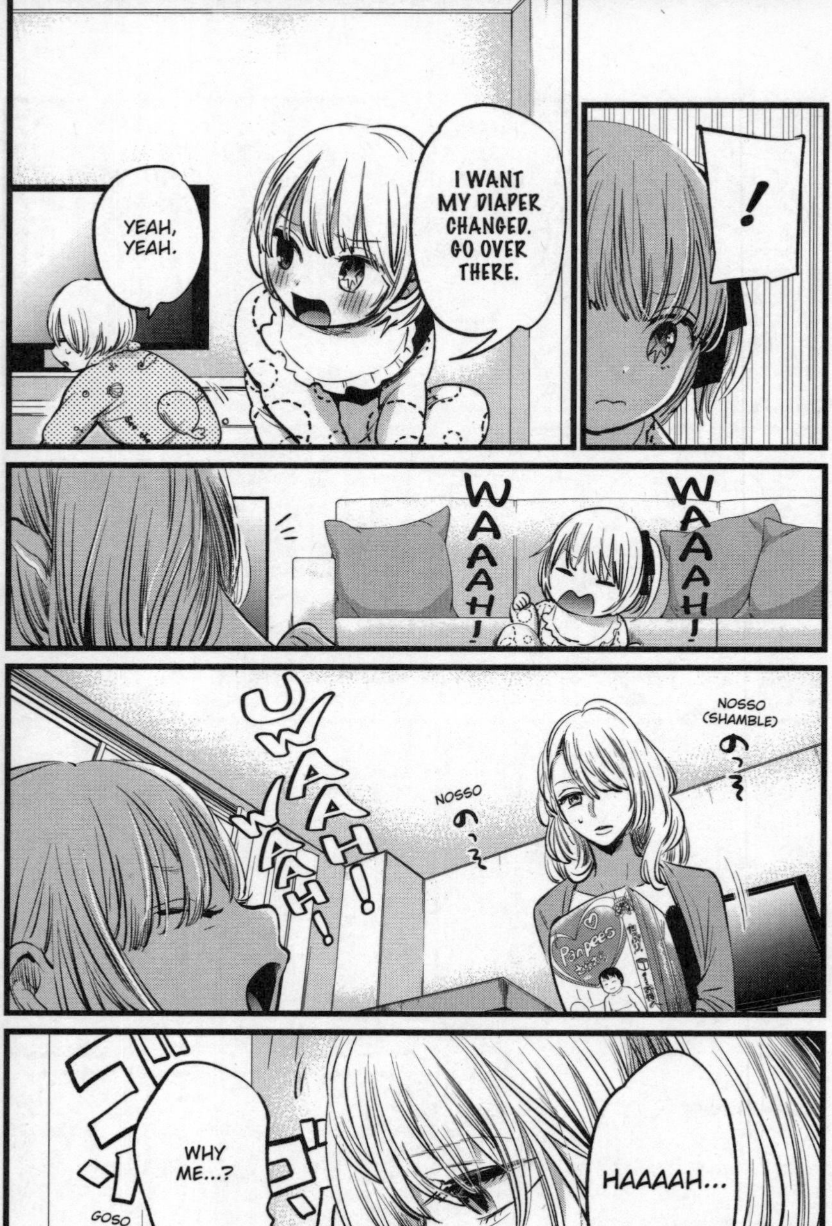
I WANT MY DIAPER CHANGED. GO OVER THERE.
YEAH, YEAH.
!
WAAAH!
WAAAH!
NOSSO (SHAMBLE)
NOSSO
UWAAAH!
WAAAH!
HAAAAH...
WHY ME...?
GOSO (RUSTLE)
GOSO

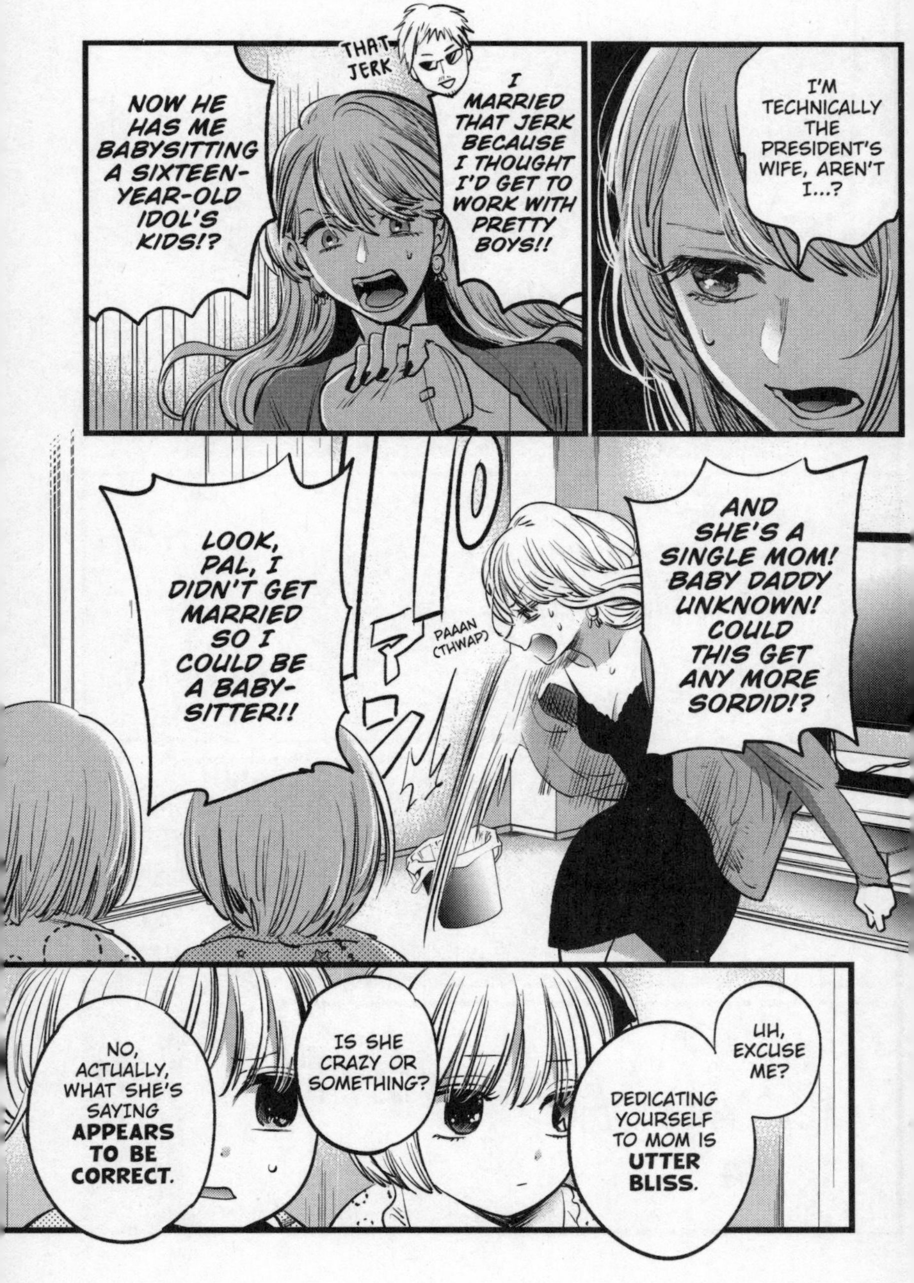
I'M TECHNICALLY THE PRESIDENT'S WIFE, AREN'T I...?
THAT JERK
I MARRIED THAT JERK BECAUSE I THOUGHT I'D GET TO WORK WITH PRETTY BOYS!!
NOW HE HAS ME BABYSITTING A SIXTEEN-YEAR-OLD IDOL'S KIDS!?
AND SHE'S A SINGLE MOM! BABY DADDY UNKNOWN! COULD THIS GET ANY MORE SORDID!?
PAAAN (THWAP)
LOOK, PAL, I DIDN'T GET MARRIED SO I COULD BE A BABY-SITTER!!
UH, EXCUSE ME?
DEDICATING YOURSELF TO MOM IS UTTER BLISS.
IS SHE CRAZY OR SOMETHING?
NO, ACTUALLY, WHAT SHE'S SAYING APPEARS TO BE CORRECT.

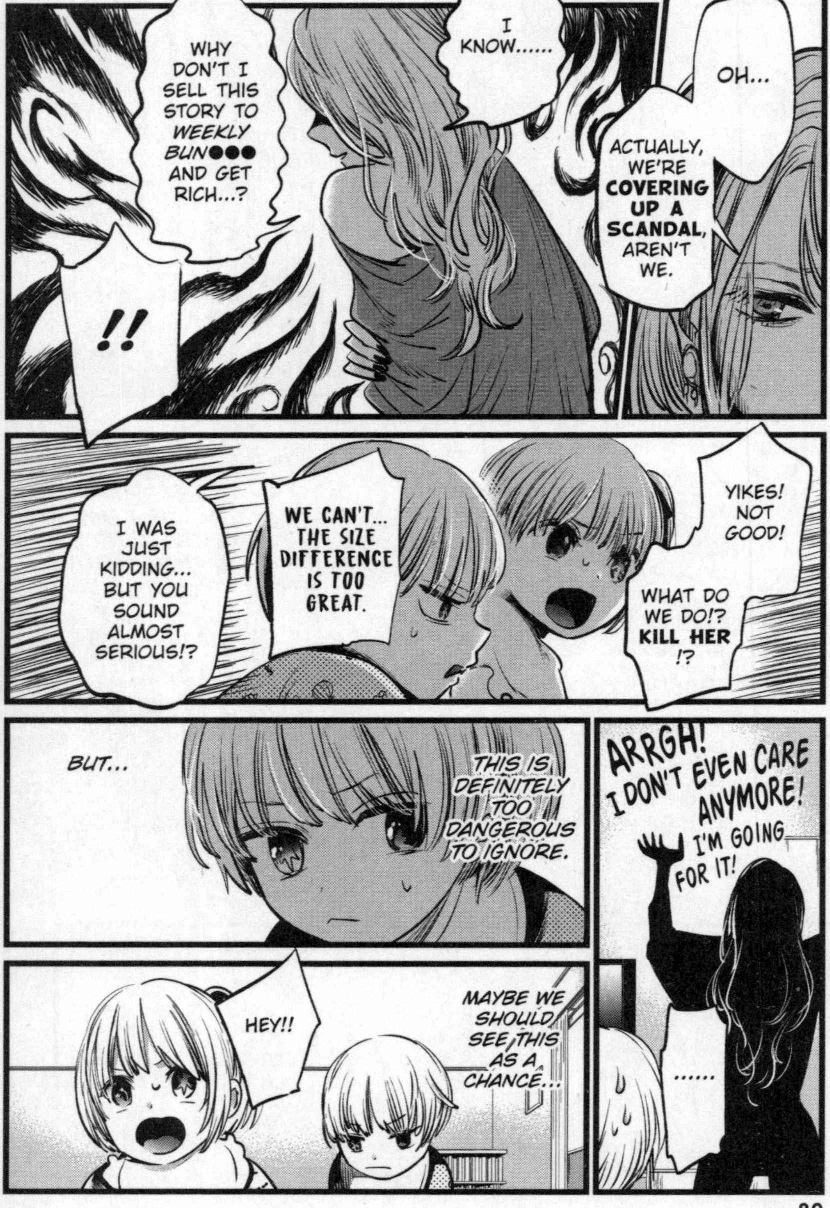

OH...
ACTUALLY, WE'RE **COVERING UP A SCANDAL,** AREN'T WE.
I KNOW......
WHY DON'T I SELL THIS STORY TO *WEEKLY BUN●●●* AND GET RICH...?
!!
YIKES! NOT GOOD!
WHAT DO WE DO!? **KILL HER**!?
WE CAN'T... THE SIZE DIFFERENCE IS TOO GREAT.
I WAS JUST KIDDING... BUT YOU SOUND ALMOST SERIOUS!?
ARRGH! I DON'T EVEN CARE ANYMORE!
I'M GOING FOR IT!
......
THIS IS DEFINITELY TOO DANGEROUS TO IGNORE.
BUT...
MAYBE WE SHOULD SEE THIS AS A CHANCE...
HEY!!

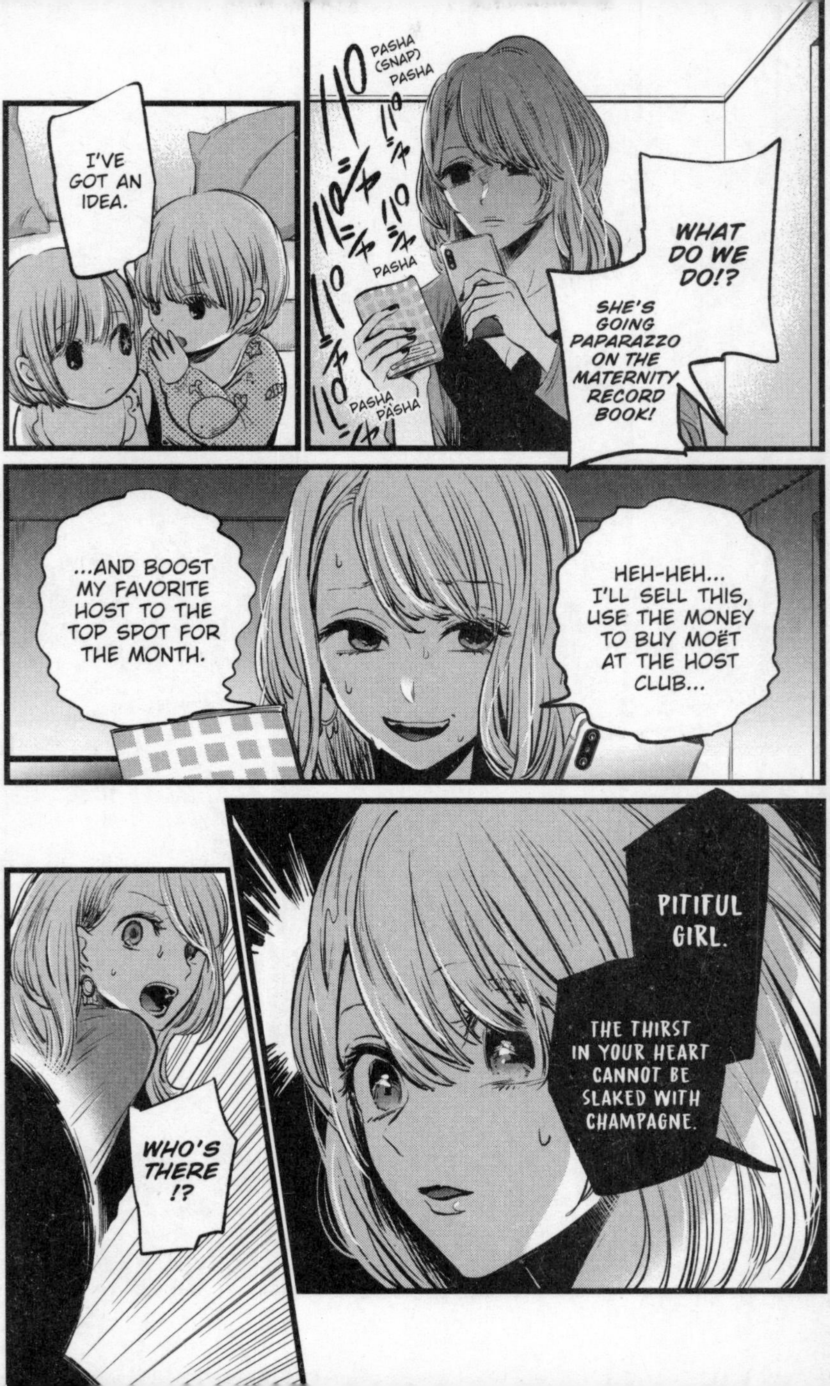
PASHA (SNAP)
PASHA
PASHA
PASHA
PASHA
WHAT DO WE DO!?
SHE'S GOING PAPARAZZO ON THE MATERNITY RECORD BOOK!
I'VE GOT AN IDEA.
HEH-HEH... I'LL SELL THIS, USE THE MONEY TO BUY MOËT AT THE HOST CLUB...
...AND BOOST MY FAVORITE HOST TO THE TOP SPOT FOR THE MONTH.
PITIFUL GIRL.
THE THIRST IN YOUR HEART CANNOT BE SLAKED WITH CHAMPAGNE.
WHO'S THERE !?

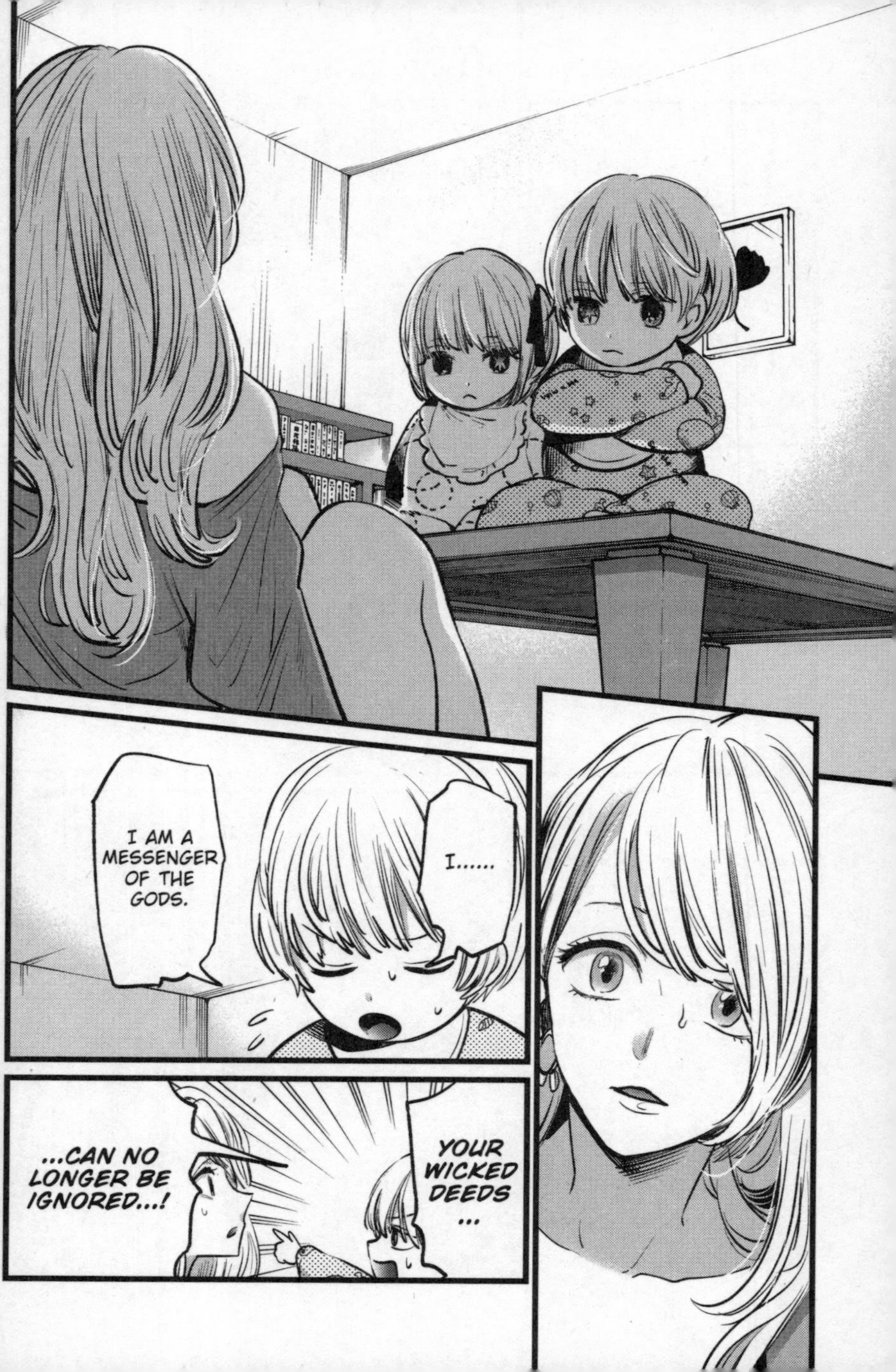
I......
I AM A MESSENGER OF THE GODS.
YOUR WICKED DEEDS ...
...CAN NO LONGER BE IGNORED...!

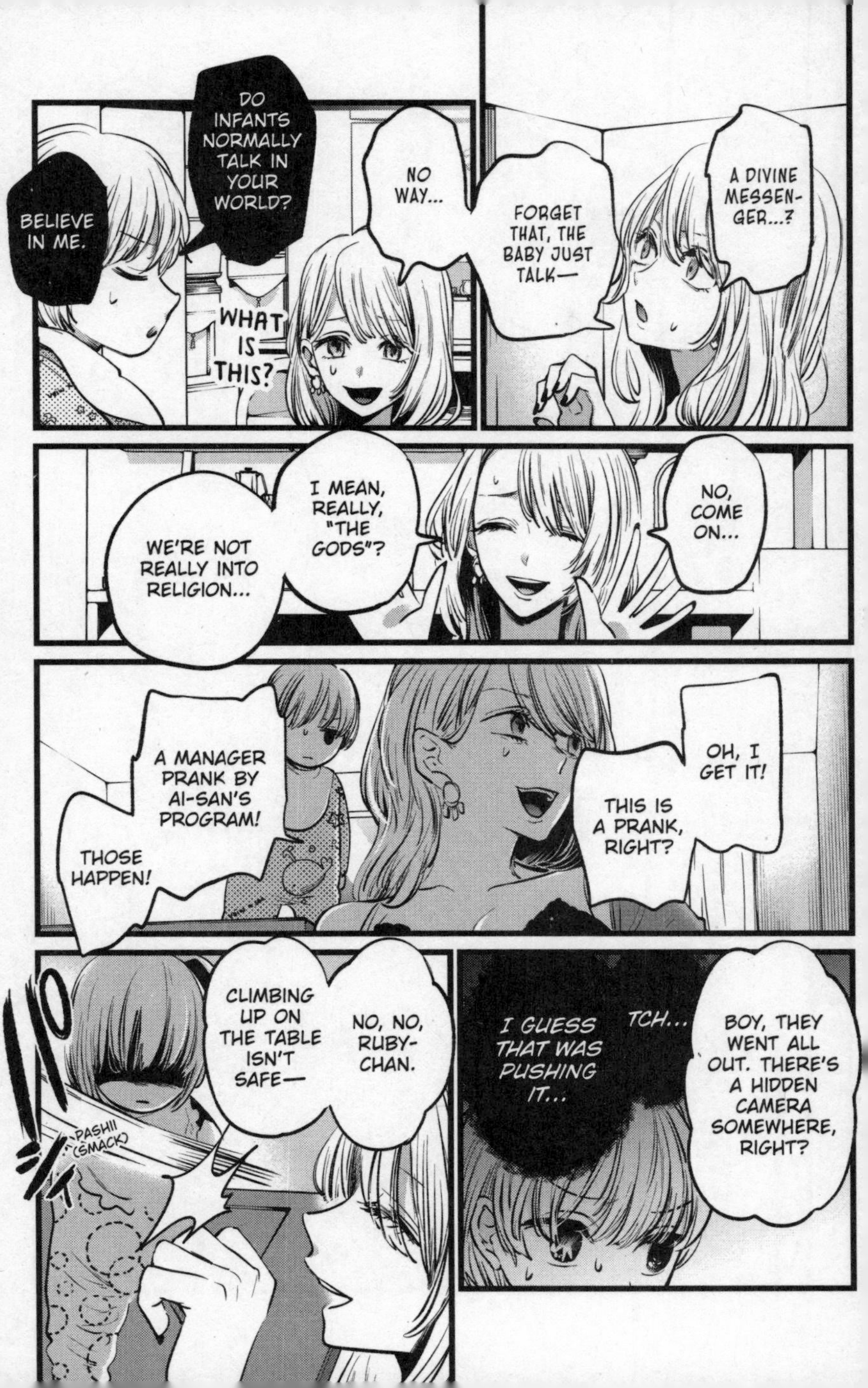
A DIVINE MESSENGER...?
FORGET THAT, THE BABY JUST TALK—
NO WAY...
DO INFANTS NORMALLY TALK IN YOUR WORLD?
BELIEVE IN ME.
WHAT IS THIS?
NO, COME ON...
I MEAN, REALLY, "THE GODS"?
WE'RE NOT REALLY INTO RELIGION...
OH, I GET IT!
THIS IS A PRANK, RIGHT?
A MANAGER PRANK BY AI-SAN'S PROGRAM!
THOSE HAPPEN!
BOY, THEY WENT ALL OUT. THERE'S A HIDDEN CAMERA SOMEWHERE, RIGHT?
TCH...
I GUESS THAT WAS PUSHING IT...
NO, NO, RUBY-CHAN.
CLIMBING UP ON THE TABLE ISN'T SAFE—
PASHII (SMACK)

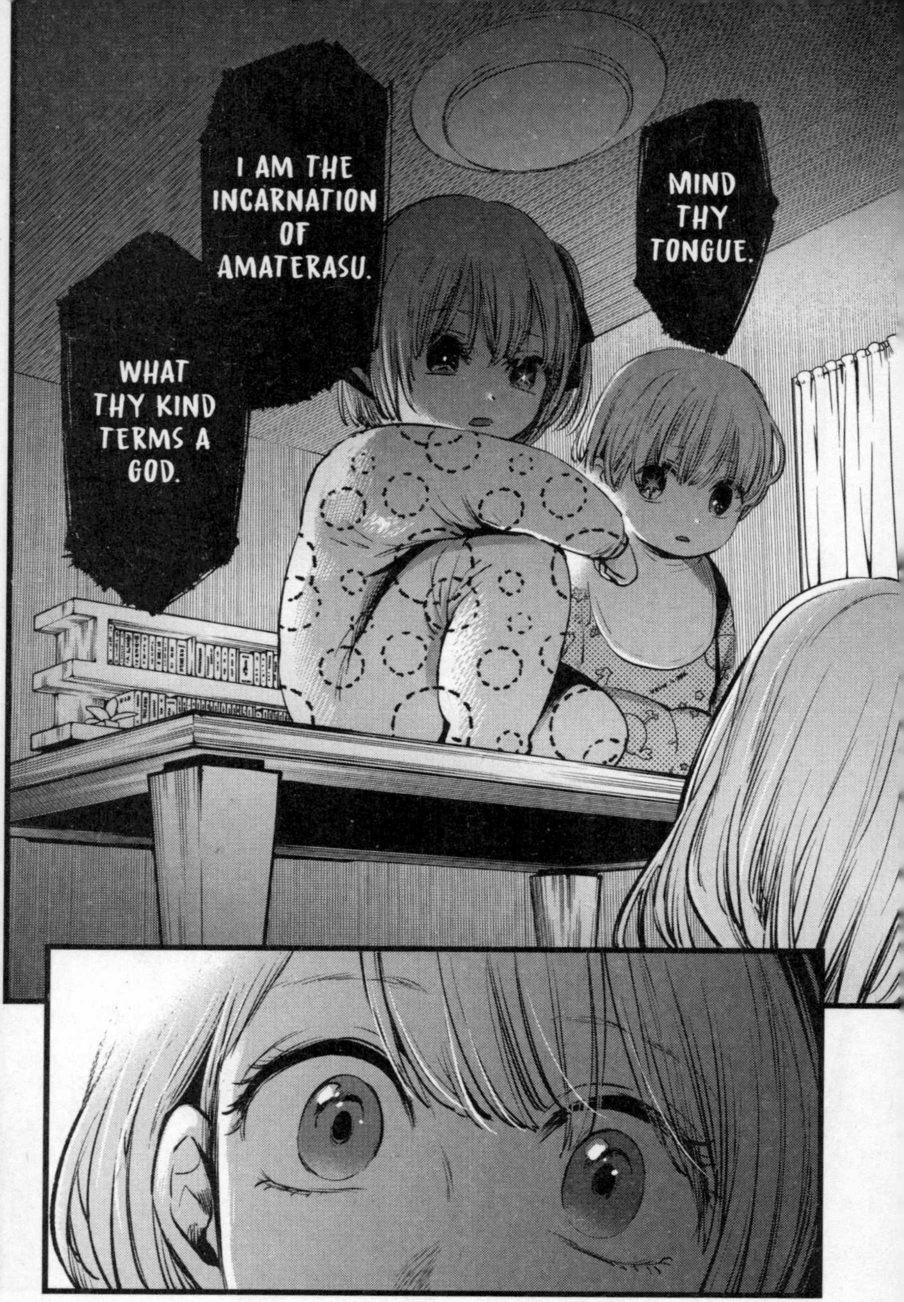
MIND THY TONGUE.
I AM THE INCARNATION OF AMATERASU.
WHAT THY KIND TERMS A GOD.

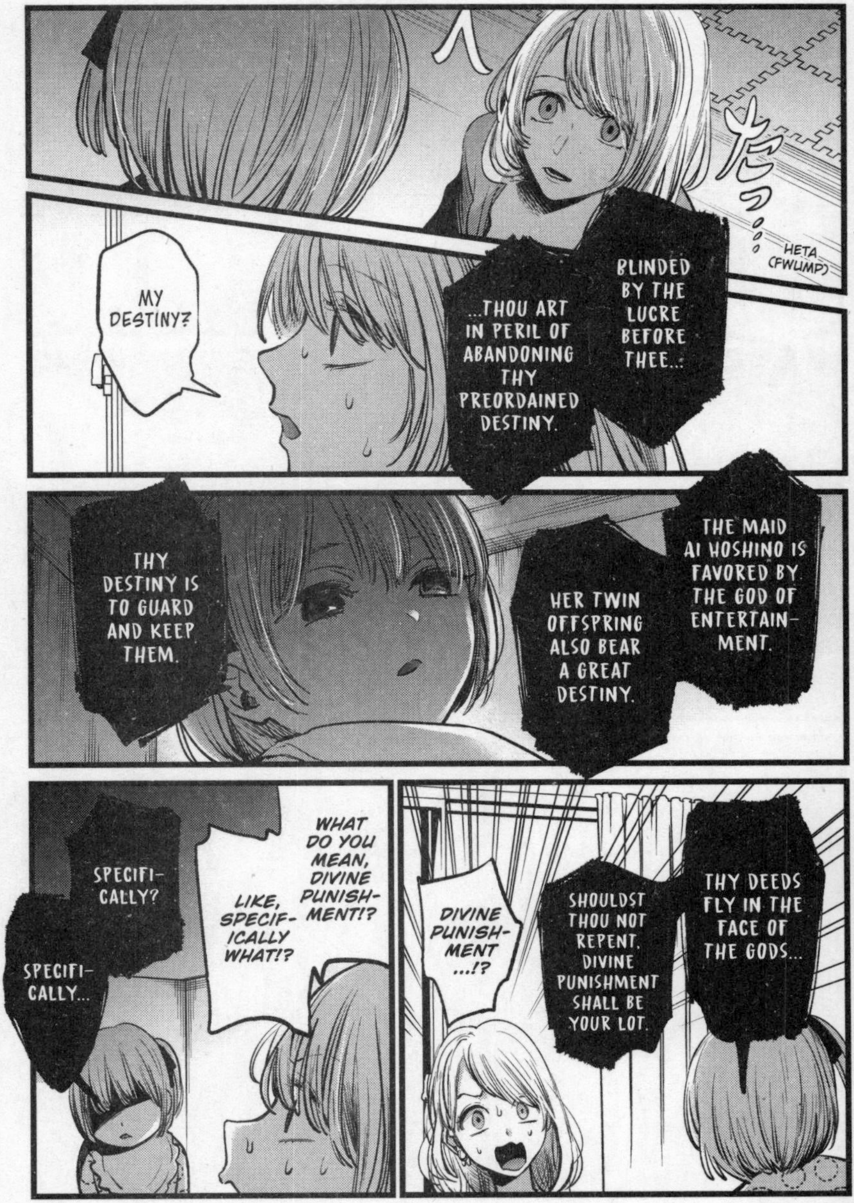
HETA (FWUMP)
BLINDED BY THE LUCRE BEFORE THEE...
...THOU ART IN PERIL OF ABANDONING THY PREORDAINED DESTINY.
MY DESTINY?
THE MAID AI HOSHINO IS FAVORED BY THE GOD OF ENTERTAINMENT.
HER TWIN OFFSPRING ALSO BEAR A GREAT DESTINY.
THY DESTINY IS TO GUARD AND KEEP THEM.
THY DEEDS FLY IN THE FACE OF THE GODS...
SHOULDST THOU NOT REPENT, DIVINE PUNISHMENT SHALL BE YOUR LOT.
DIVINE PUNISHMENT ...!?
WHAT DO YOU MEAN, DIVINE PUNISHMENT!?
LIKE, SPECIFICALLY WHAT!?
SPECIFICALLY?
SPECIFICALLY...

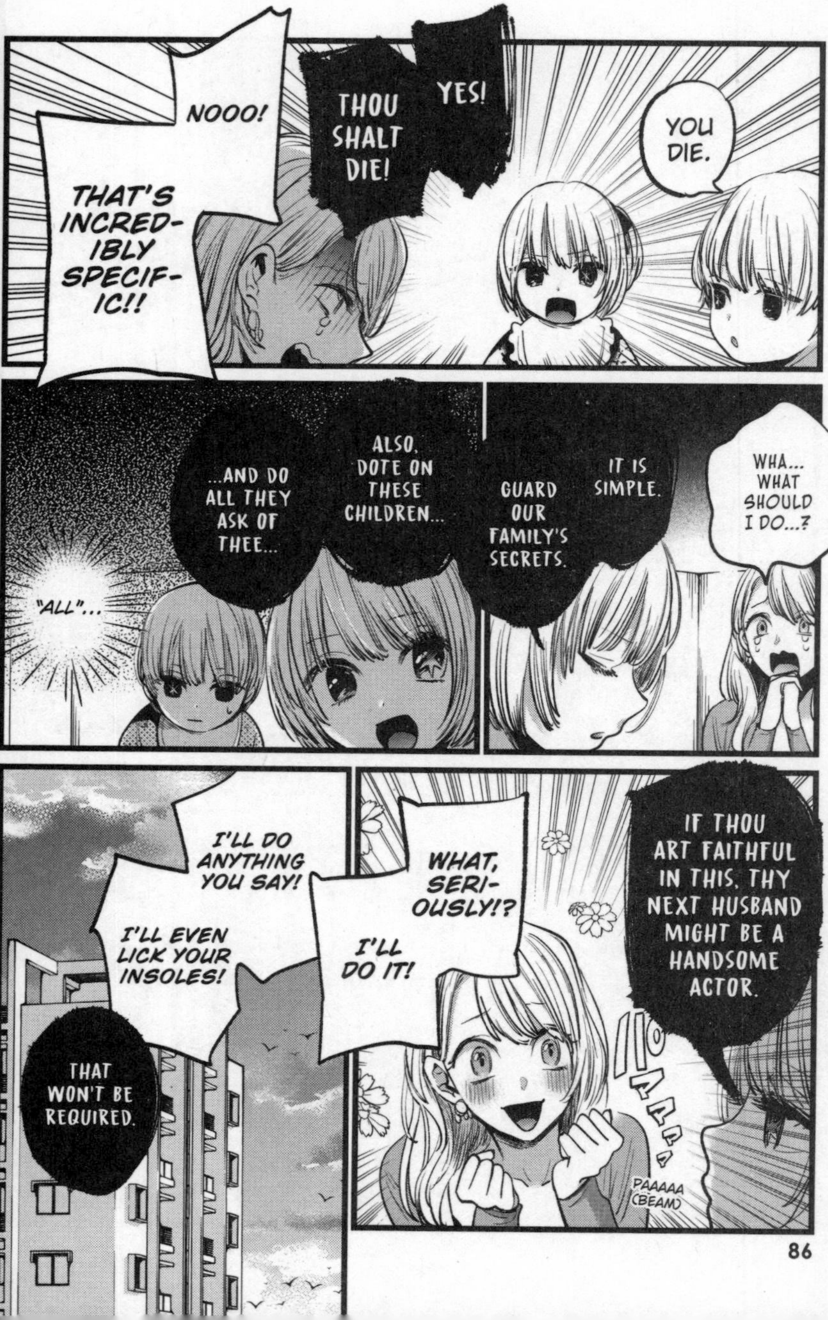
YOU DIE.
YES!
THOU SHALT DIE!
NOOO!
THAT'S INCRED-IBLY SPECIF-IC!!
WHA... WHAT SHOULD I DO...?
IT IS SIMPLE.
GUARD OUR FAMILY'S SECRETS.
ALSO, DOTE ON THESE CHILDREN...
...AND DO ALL THEY ASK OF THEE...
"ALL"...
IF THOU ART FAITHFUL IN THIS, THY NEXT HUSBAND MIGHT BE A HANDSOME ACTOR.
WHAT, SERI-OUSLY!?
I'LL DO IT!
PAAAAA (BEAM)
I'LL DO ANYTHING YOU SAY!
I'LL EVEN LICK YOUR INSOLES!
THAT WON'T BE REQUIRED.

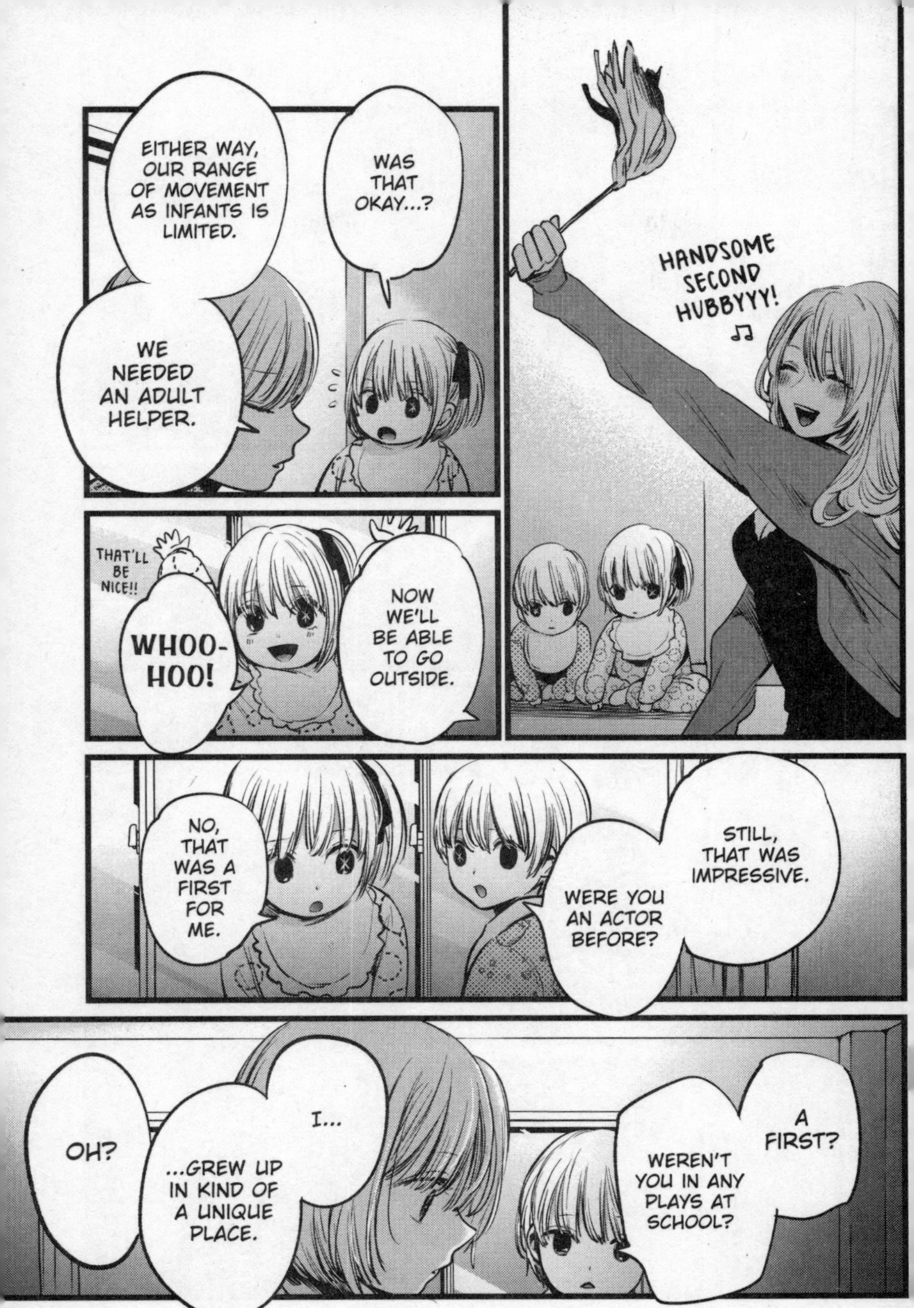
HANDSOME SECOND HUBBYYY! ♫
WAS THAT OKAY...?
EITHER WAY, OUR RANGE OF MOVEMENT AS INFANTS IS LIMITED.
WE NEEDED AN ADULT HELPER.
NOW WE'LL BE ABLE TO GO OUTSIDE.
THAT'LL BE NICE!!
WHOO-HOO!
STILL, THAT WAS IMPRESSIVE.
WERE YOU AN ACTOR BEFORE?
NO, THAT WAS A FIRST FOR ME.
A FIRST?
WEREN'T YOU IN ANY PLAYS AT SCHOOL?
I...
...GREW UP IN KIND OF A UNIQUE PLACE.
OH?

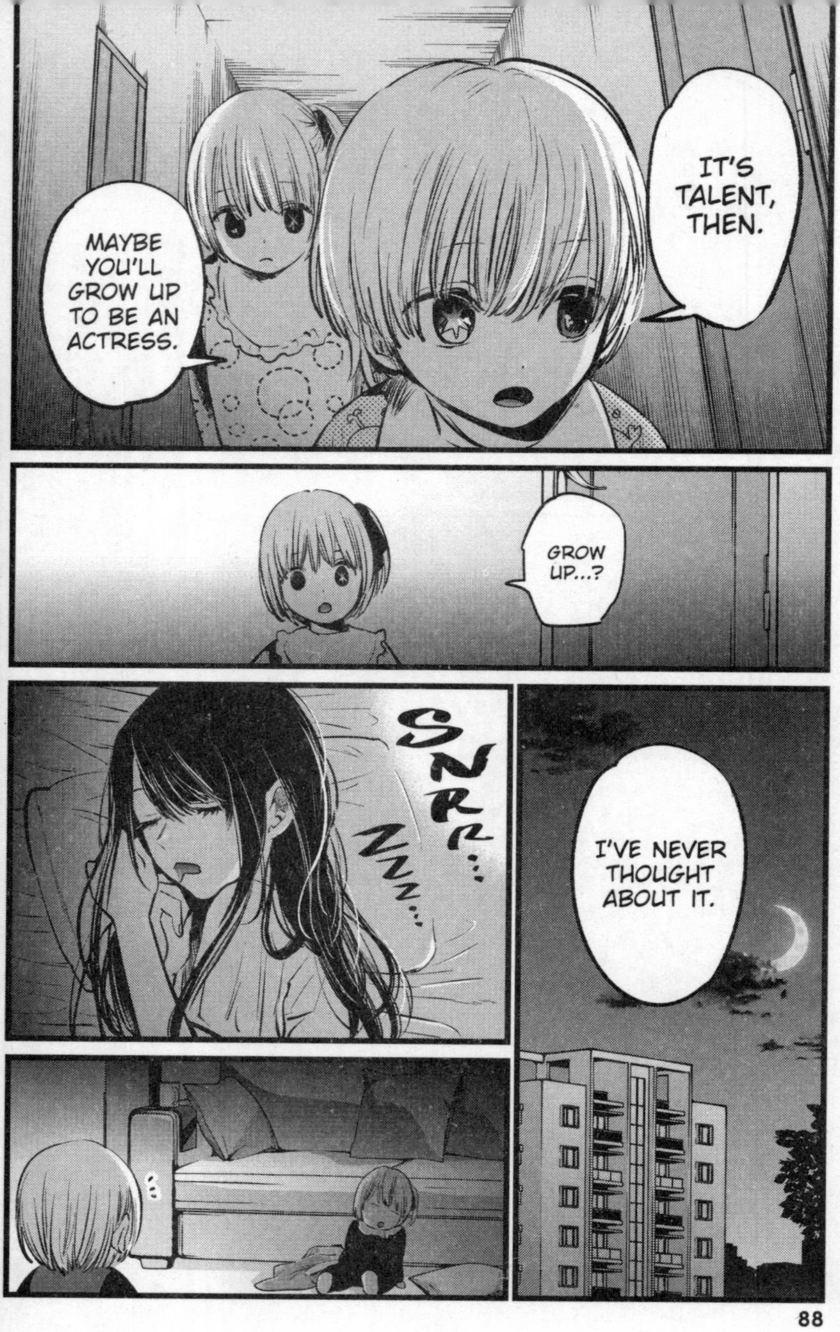
IT'S TALENT, THEN.
MAYBE YOU'LL GROW UP TO BE AN ACTRESS.
GROW UP...?
I'VE NEVER THOUGHT ABOUT IT.
SNRR... ZZZ...
...

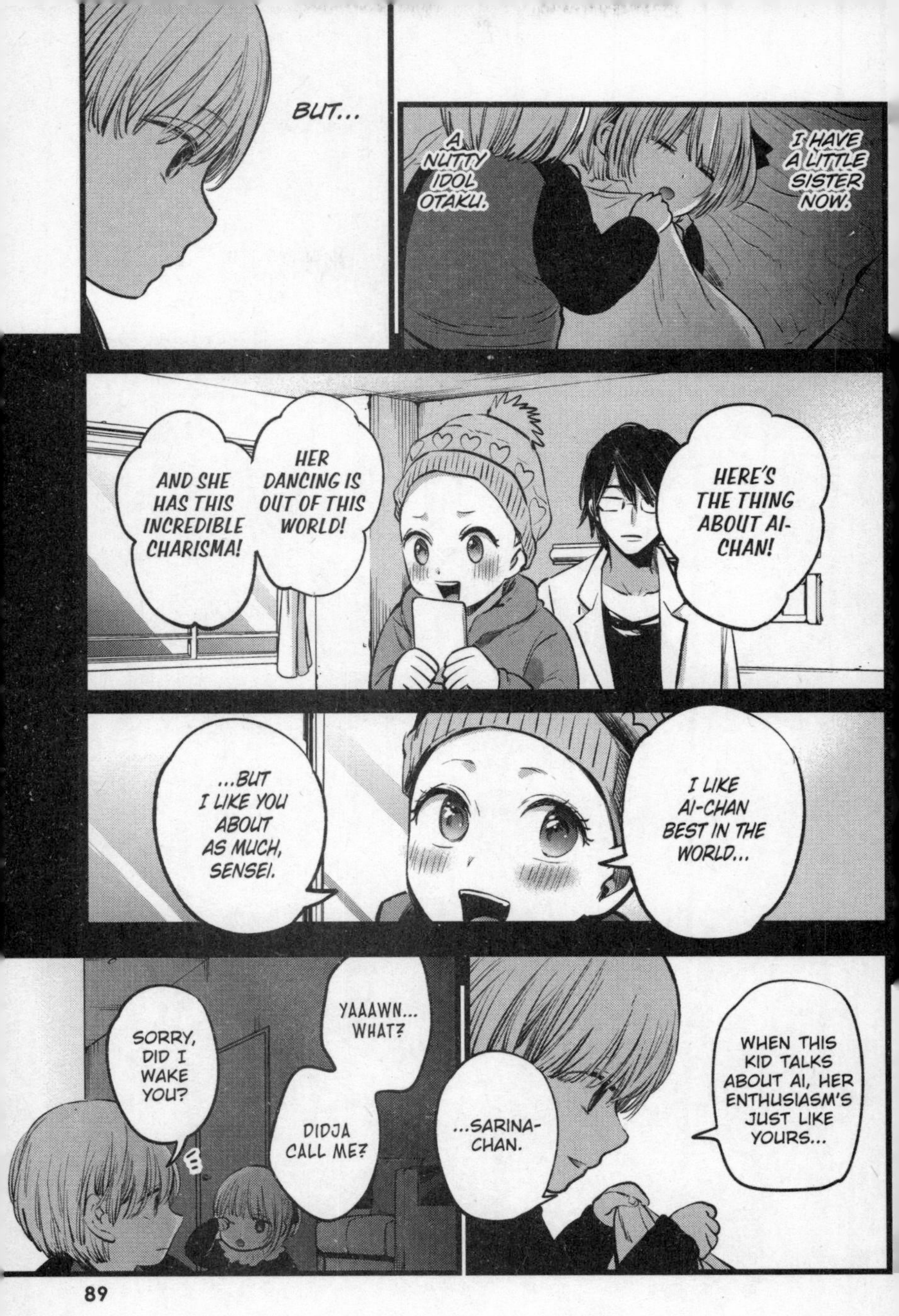
I HAVE A LITTLE SISTER NOW.
A NUTTY IDOL OTAKU.
BUT...
HERE'S THE THING ABOUT AI-CHAN!
HER DANCING IS OUT OF THIS WORLD!
AND SHE HAS THIS INCREDIBLE CHARISMA!
I LIKE AI-CHAN BEST IN THE WORLD...
...BUT I LIKE YOU ABOUT AS MUCH, SENSEI.
WHEN THIS KID TALKS ABOUT AI, HER ENTHUSIASM'S JUST LIKE YOURS...
...SARINA-CHAN.
YAAAWN... WHAT?
DIDJA CALL ME?
SORRY, DID I WAKE YOU?

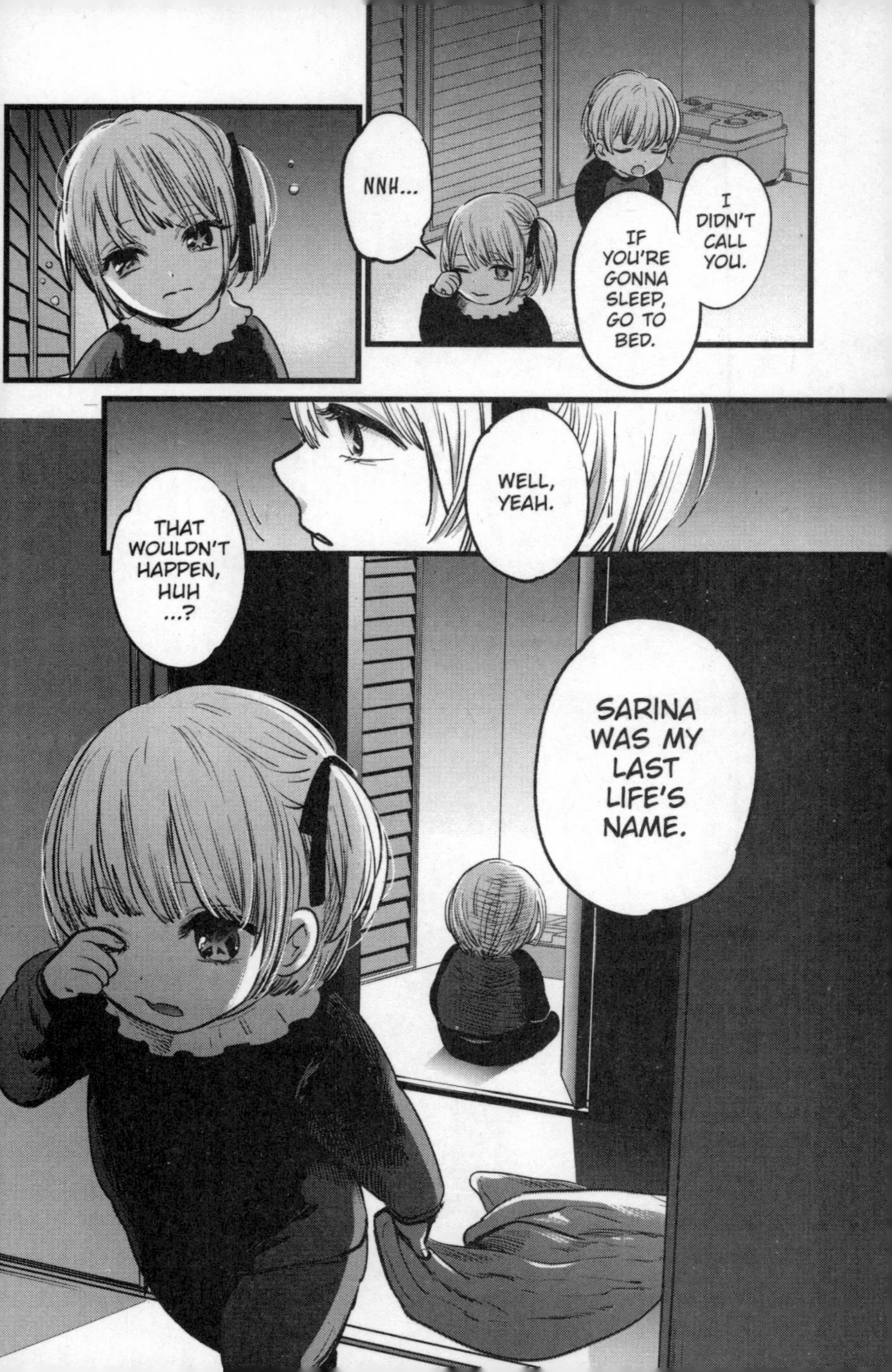
I DIDN'T CALL YOU.
IF YOU'RE GONNA SLEEP, GO TO BED.
NNH...
WELL, YEAH.
THAT WOULDN'T HAPPEN, HUH ...?
SARINA WAS MY LAST LIFE'S NAME.

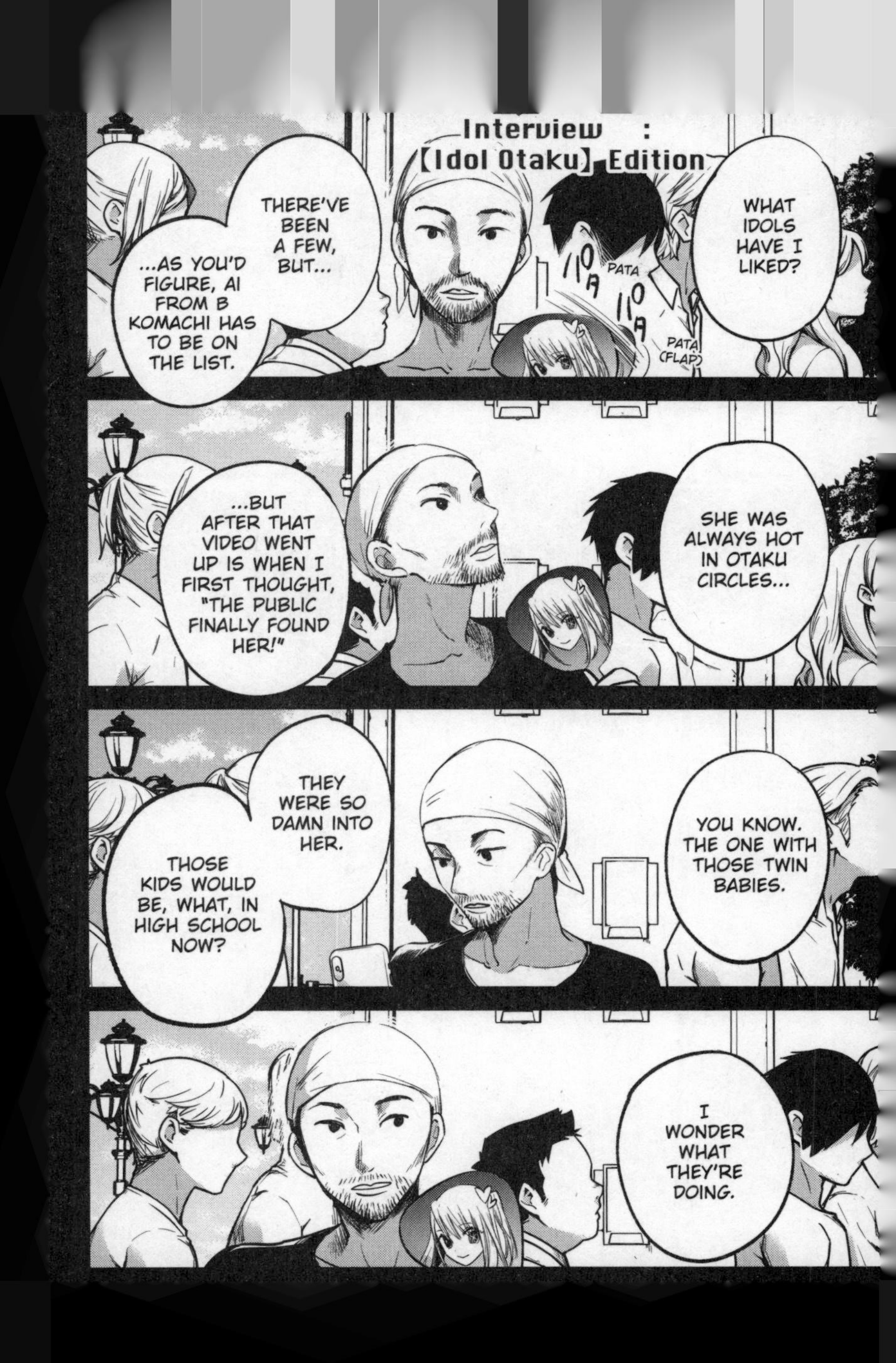
Interview : 【Idol Otaku】 Edition
WHAT IDOLS HAVE I LIKED?
PATA PATA (FLAP)
THERE'VE BEEN A FEW, BUT...
...AS YOU'D FIGURE, AI FROM B KOMACHI HAS TO BE ON THE LIST.
SHE WAS ALWAYS HOT IN OTAKU CIRCLES...
...BUT AFTER THAT VIDEO WENT UP IS WHEN I FIRST THOUGHT, "THE PUBLIC FINALLY FOUND HER!"
YOU KNOW. THE ONE WITH THOSE TWIN BABIES.
THEY WERE SO DAMN INTO HER.
THOSE KIDS WOULD BE, WHAT, IN HIGH SCHOOL NOW?
I WONDER WHAT THEY'RE DOING.

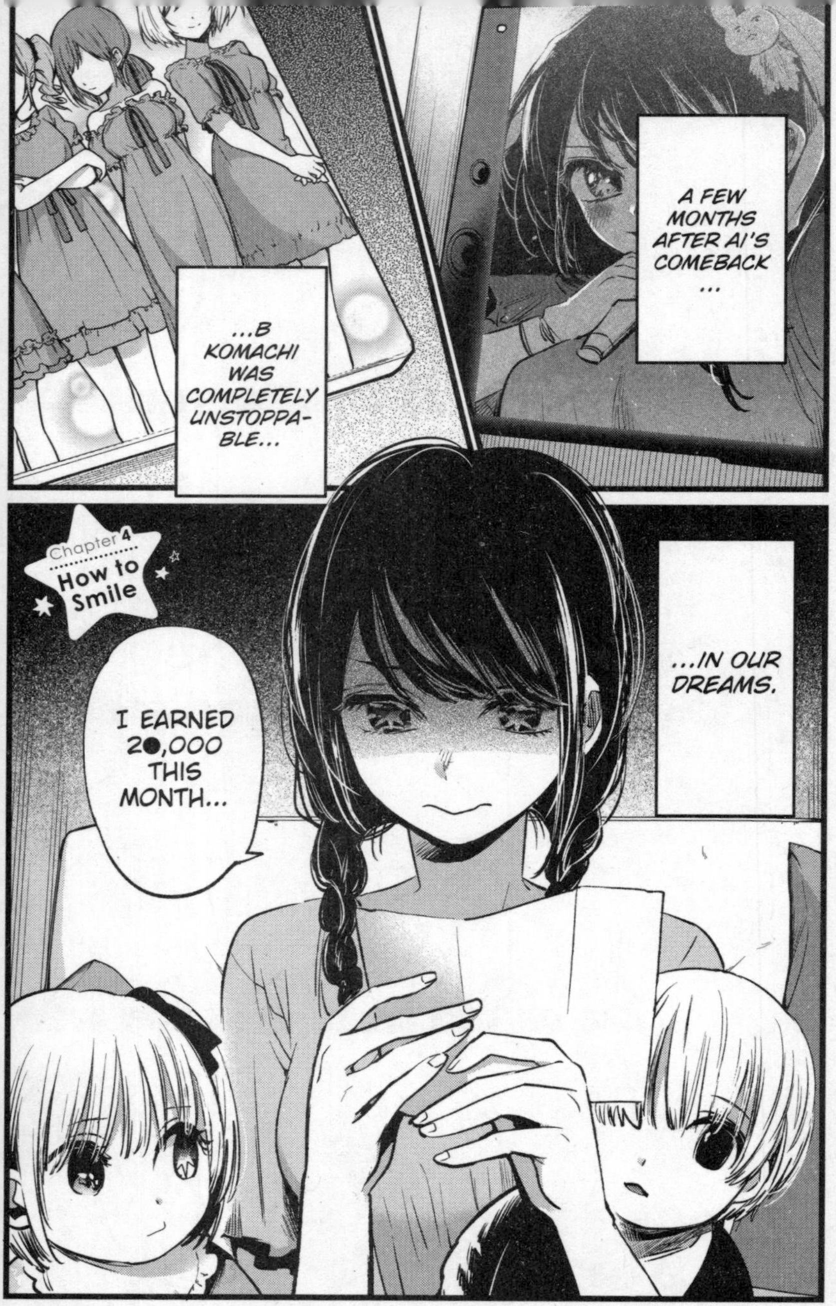
A FEW MONTHS AFTER AI'S COMEBACK ...
...B KOMACHI WAS COMPLETELY UNSTOPPA-BLE...
...IN OUR DREAMS.
Chapter 4
How to Smile
I EARNED 2●,000 THIS MONTH...

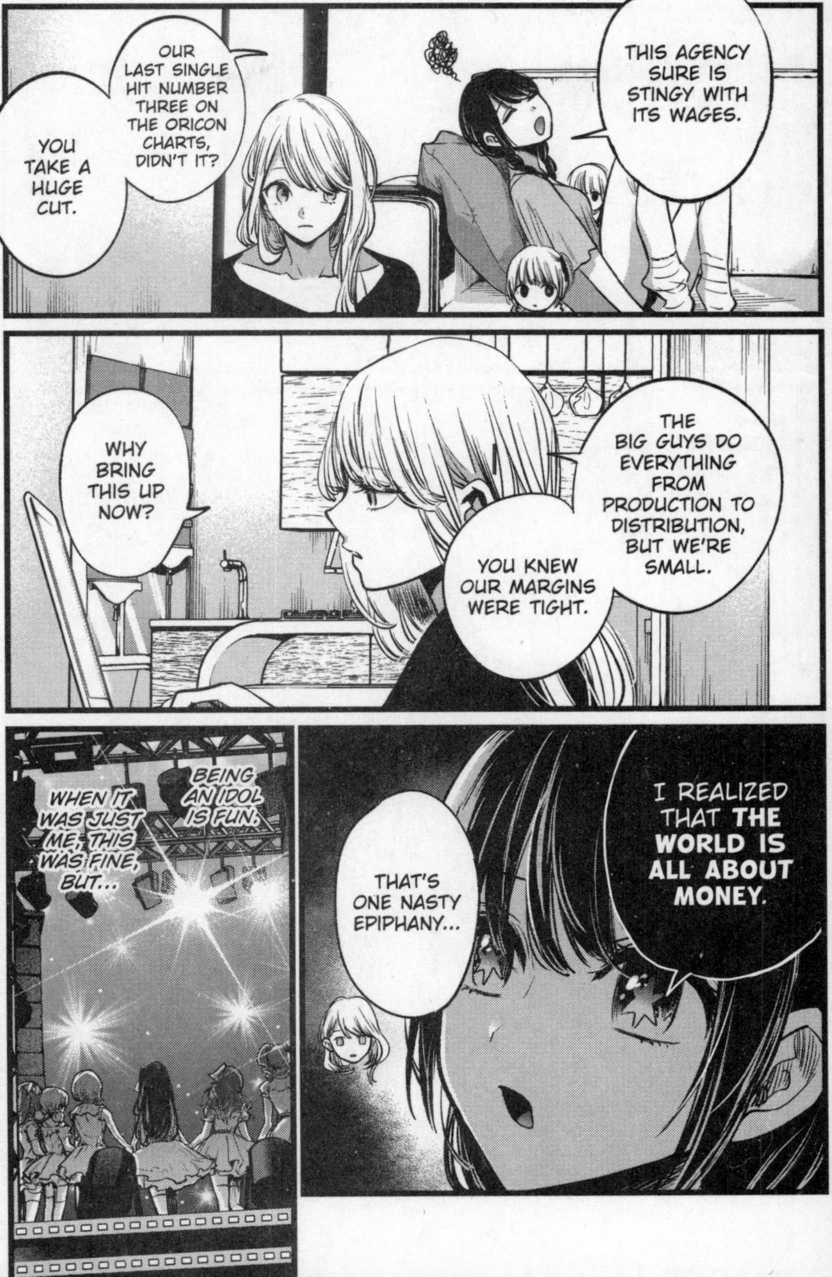
THIS AGENCY SURE IS STINGY WITH ITS WAGES.
OUR LAST SINGLE HIT NUMBER THREE ON THE ORICON CHARTS, DIDN'T IT?
YOU TAKE A HUGE CUT.
THE BIG GUYS DO EVERYTHING FROM PRODUCTION TO DISTRIBUTION, BUT WE'RE SMALL.
YOU KNEW OUR MARGINS WERE TIGHT.
WHY BRING THIS UP NOW?
I REALIZED THAT **THE WORLD IS ALL ABOUT MONEY**.
THAT'S ONE NASTY EPIPHANY...
BEING AN IDOL IS FUN.
WHEN IT WAS JUST ME, THIS WAS FINE, BUT...

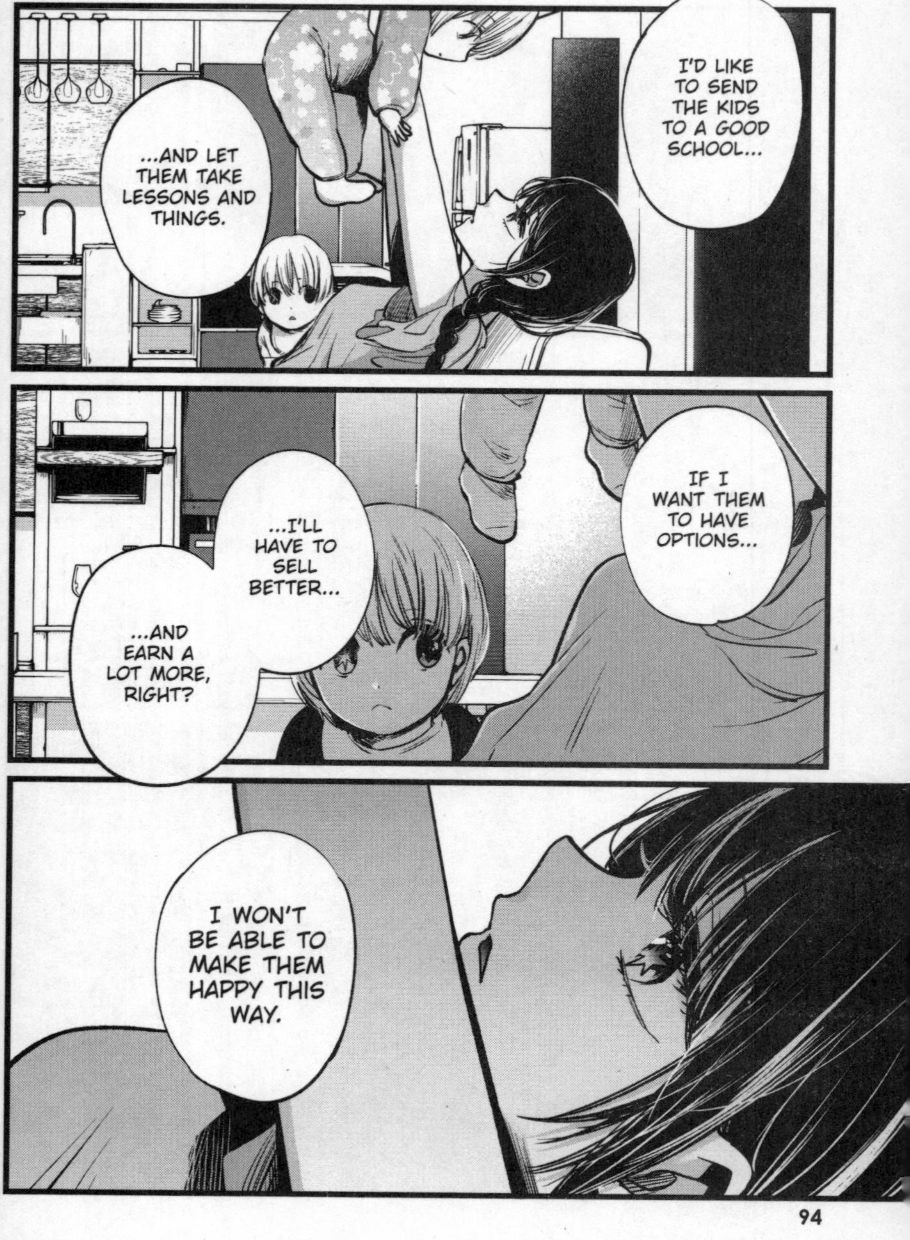
I'D LIKE TO SEND THE KIDS TO A GOOD SCHOOL...
...AND LET THEM TAKE LESSONS AND THINGS.
IF I WANT THEM TO HAVE OPTIONS...
...I'LL HAVE TO SELL BETTER...
...AND EARN A LOT MORE, RIGHT?
I WON'T BE ABLE TO MAKE THEM HAPPY THIS WAY.

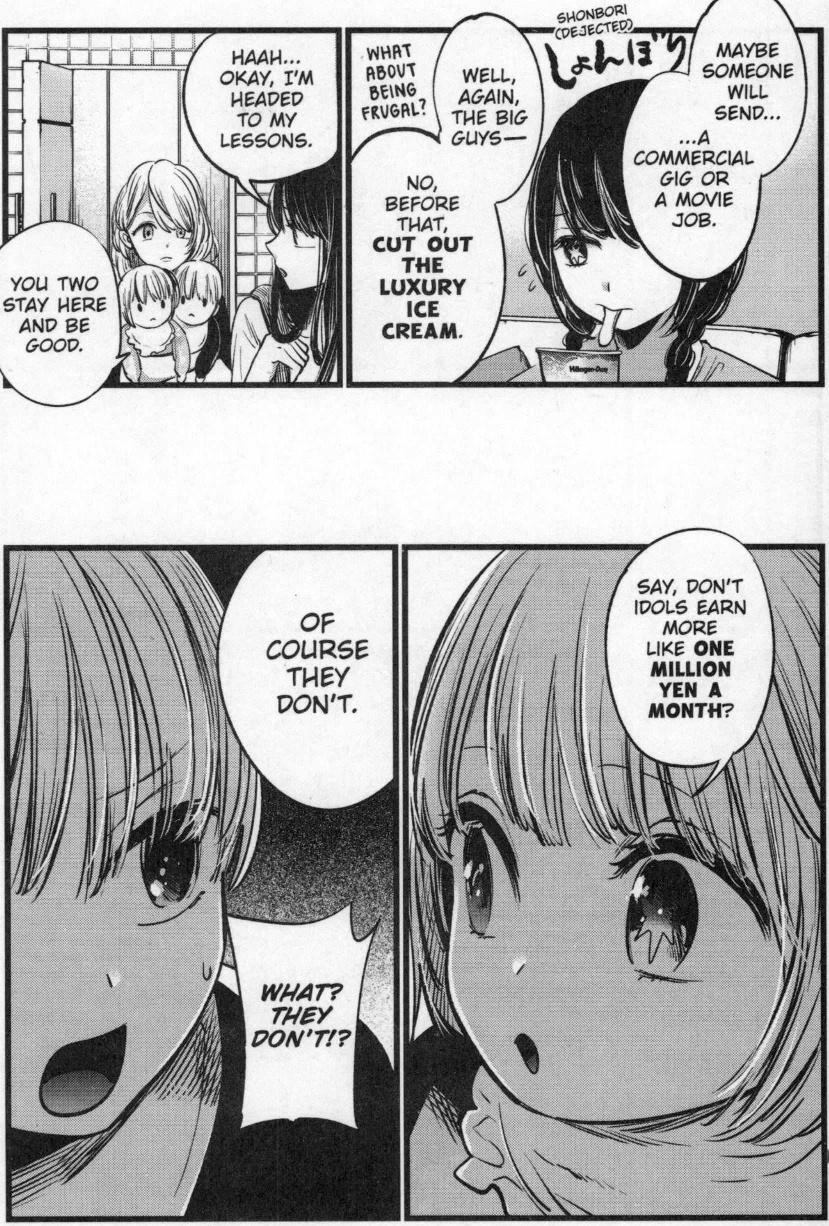
MAYBE SOMEONE WILL SEND...
...A COMMERCIAL GIG OR A MOVIE JOB.
SHONBORI (DEJECTED)
しょんぼり
WELL, AGAIN, THE BIG GUYS—
WHAT ABOUT BEING FRUGAL?
NO, BEFORE THAT, **CUT OUT THE LUXURY ICE CREAM.**
HAAH... OKAY, I'M HEADED TO MY LESSONS.
YOU TWO STAY HERE AND BE GOOD.
SAY, DON'T IDOLS EARN MORE LIKE **ONE MILLION YEN A MONTH**?
OF COURSE THEY DON'T.
WHAT? THEY DON'T!?

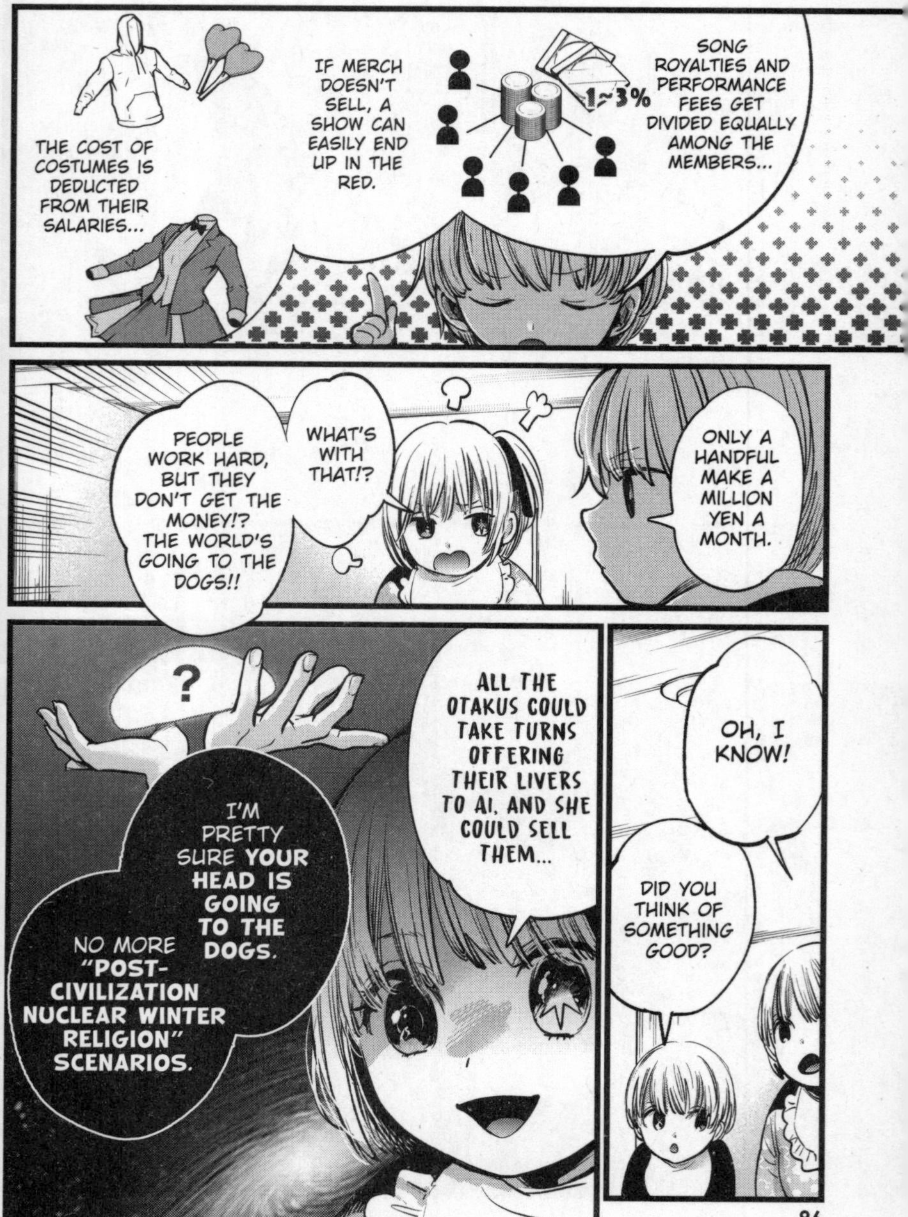
SONG ROYALTIES AND PERFORMANCE FEES GET DIVIDED EQUALLY AMONG THE MEMBERS...
1~3%
IF MERCH DOESN'T SELL, A SHOW CAN EASILY END UP IN THE RED.
THE COST OF COSTUMES IS DEDUCTED FROM THEIR SALARIES...
ONLY A HANDFUL MAKE A MILLION YEN A MONTH.
WHAT'S WITH THAT!?
PEOPLE WORK HARD, BUT THEY DON'T GET THE MONEY!? THE WORLD'S GOING TO THE DOGS!!
OH, I KNOW!
DID YOU THINK OF SOMETHING GOOD?
ALL THE OTAKUS COULD TAKE TURNS OFFERING THEIR LIVERS TO AI, AND SHE COULD SELL THEM...
?
I'M PRETTY SURE YOUR HEAD IS GOING TO THE DOGS.
NO MORE "POST-CIVILIZATION NUCLEAR WINTER RELIGION" SCENARIOS.

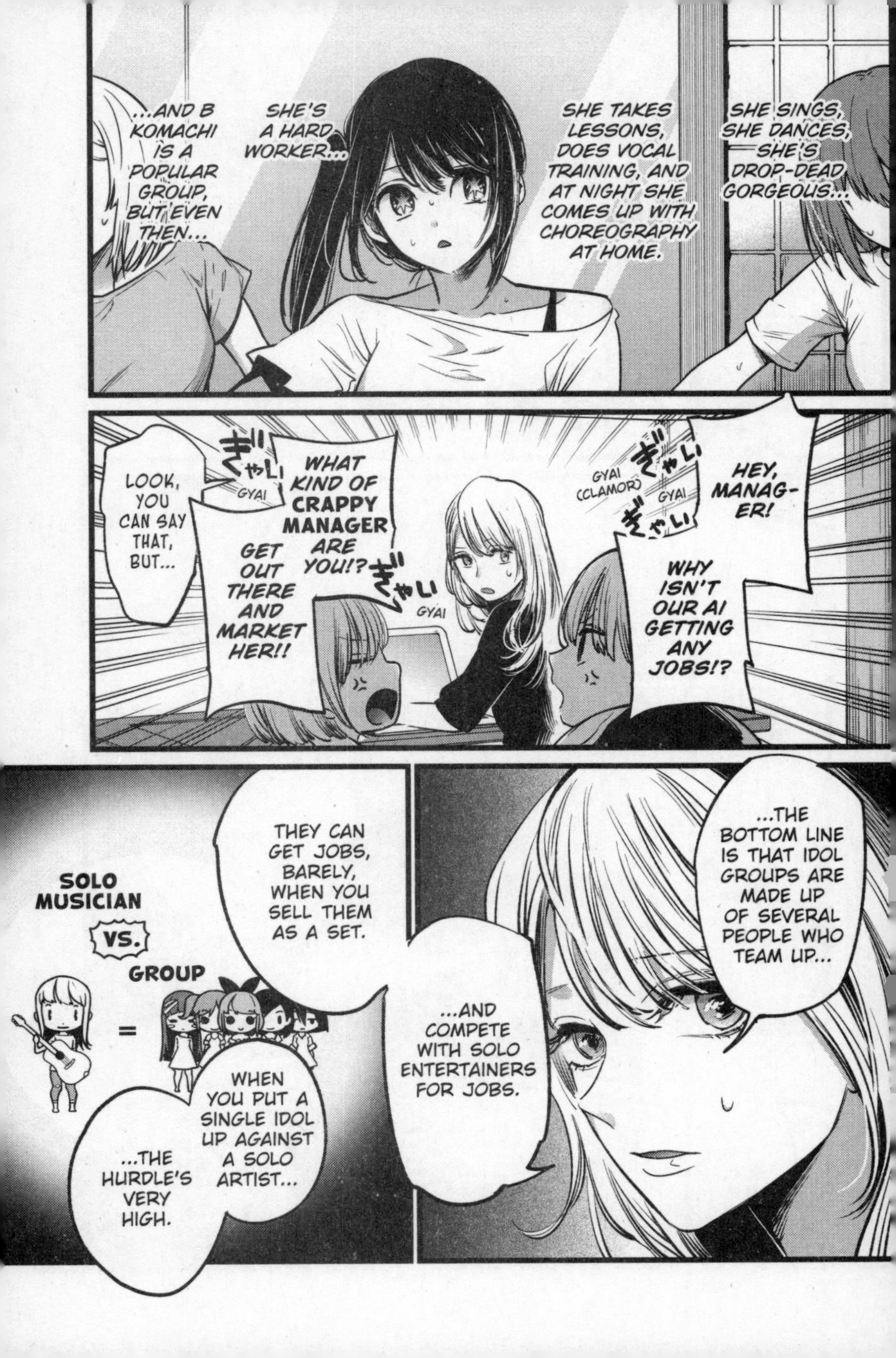
SHE SINGS, SHE DANCES, SHE'S DROP-DEAD GORGEOUS...
SHE TAKES LESSONS, DOES VOCAL TRAINING, AND AT NIGHT SHE COMES UP WITH CHOREOGRAPHY AT HOME.
SHE'S A HARD WORKER...
...AND B KOMACHI IS A POPULAR GROUP, BUT EVEN THEN...
HEY, MANAGER!
ぎゃい GYAI (CLAMOR)
ぎゃい GYAI
WHY ISN'T OUR AI GETTING ANY JOBS!?
WHAT KIND OF CRAPPY MANAGER ARE YOU!?
ぎゃい GYAI
GET OUT THERE AND MARKET HER!!
ぎゃい GYAI
LOOK, YOU CAN SAY THAT, BUT...
...THE BOTTOM LINE IS THAT IDOL GROUPS ARE MADE UP OF SEVERAL PEOPLE WHO TEAM UP...
...AND COMPETE WITH SOLO ENTERTAINERS FOR JOBS.
THEY CAN GET JOBS, BARELY, WHEN YOU SELL THEM AS A SET.
SOLO MUSICIAN
VS.
GROUP
=
WHEN YOU PUT A SINGLE IDOL UP AGAINST A SOLO ARTIST...
...THE HURDLE'S VERY HIGH.

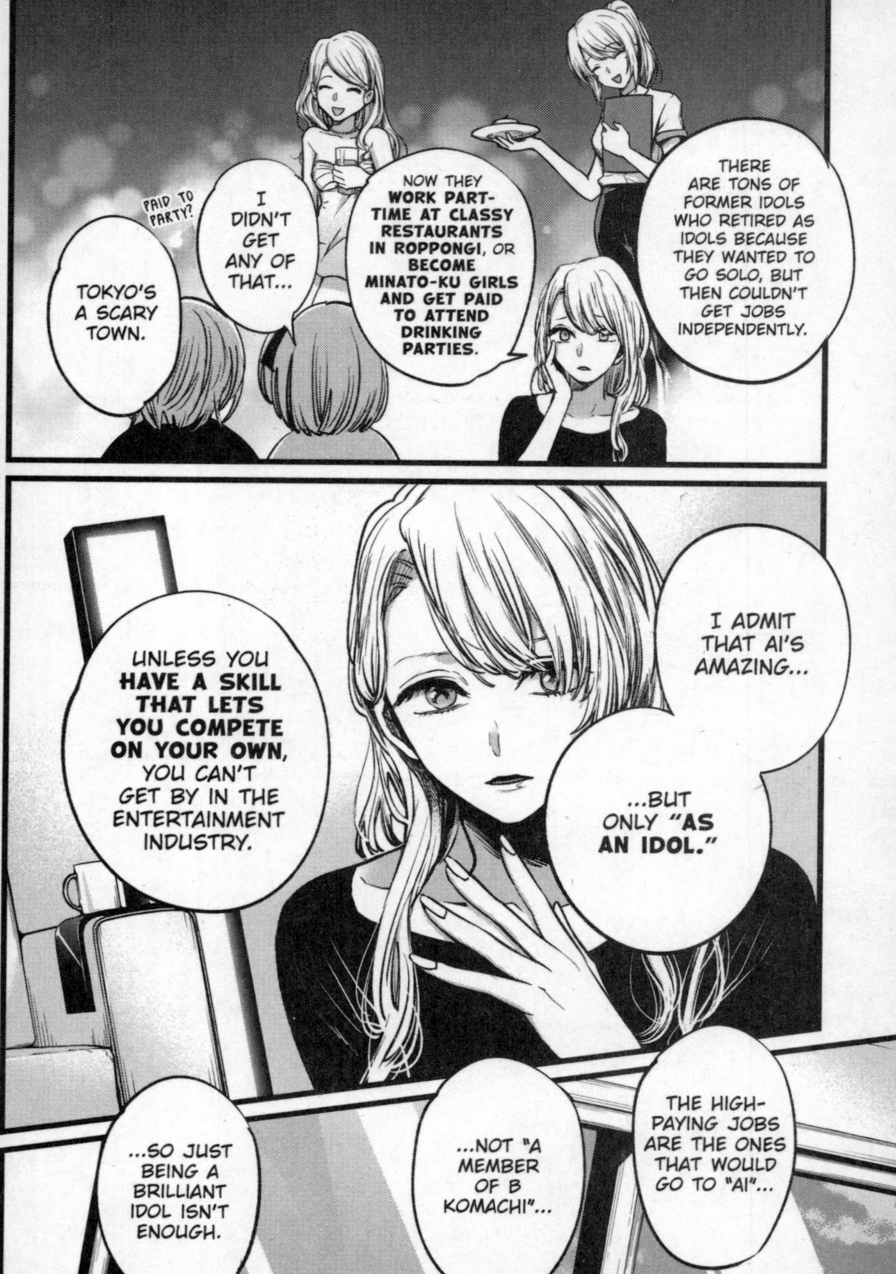
THERE ARE TONS OF FORMER IDOLS WHO RETIRED AS IDOLS BECAUSE THEY WANTED TO GO SOLO, BUT THEN COULDN'T GET JOBS INDEPENDENTLY.
NOW THEY **WORK PART-TIME AT CLASSY RESTAURANTS IN ROPPONGI**, OR **BECOME MINATO-KU GIRLS AND GET PAID TO ATTEND DRINKING PARTIES.**
I DIDN'T GET ANY OF THAT...
PAID TO PARTY?
TOKYO'S A SCARY TOWN.
I ADMIT THAT AI'S AMAZING...
...BUT ONLY **"AS AN IDOL."**
UNLESS YOU **HAVE A SKILL THAT LETS YOU COMPETE ON YOUR OWN,** YOU CAN'T GET BY IN THE ENTERTAINMENT INDUSTRY.
THE HIGH-PAYING JOBS ARE THE ONES THAT WOULD GO TO "AI"...
...NOT "A MEMBER OF B KOMACHI"...
...SO JUST BEING A BRILLIANT IDOL ISN'T ENOUGH.

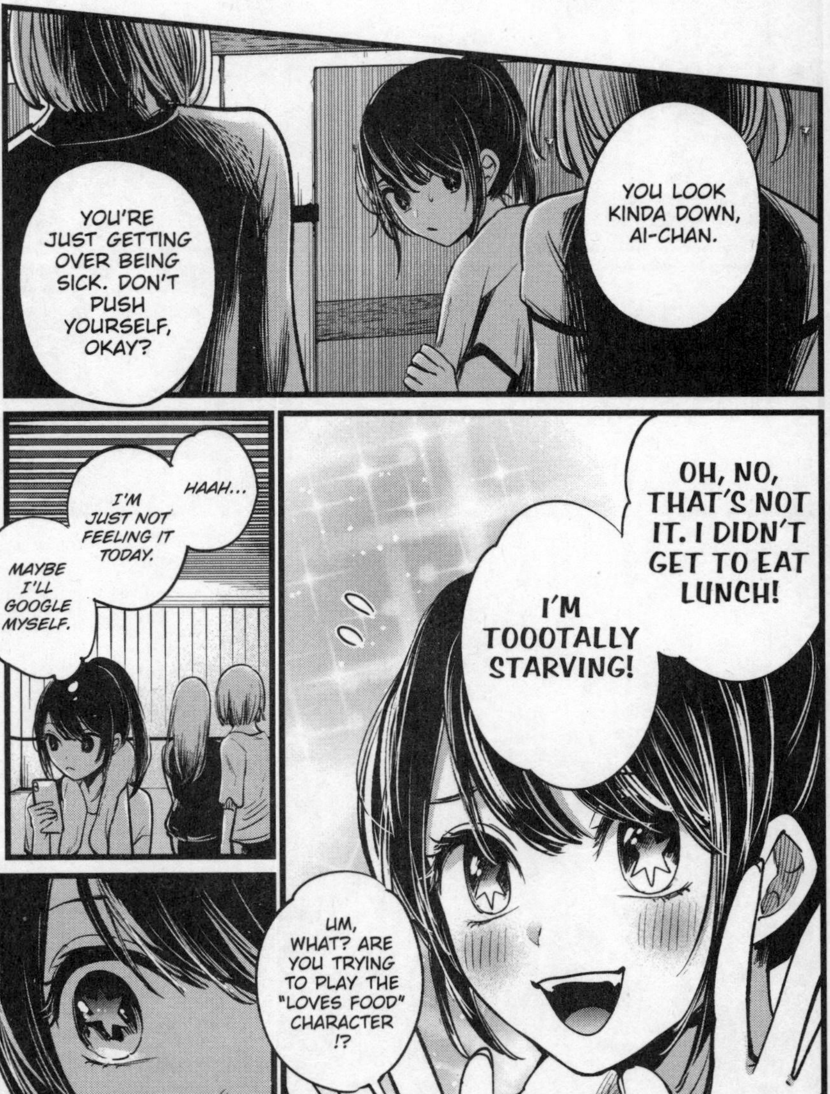
YOU LOOK KINDA DOWN, AI-CHAN.
YOU'RE JUST GETTING OVER BEING SICK. DON'T PUSH YOURSELF, OKAY?
OH, NO, THAT'S NOT IT. I DIDN'T GET TO EAT LUNCH!
I'M TOOOTALLY STARVING!
UM, WHAT? ARE YOU TRYING TO PLAY THE "LOVES FOOD" CHARACTER !?
HAAH...
I'M JUST NOT FEELING IT TODAY.
MAYBE I'LL GOOGLE MYSELF.

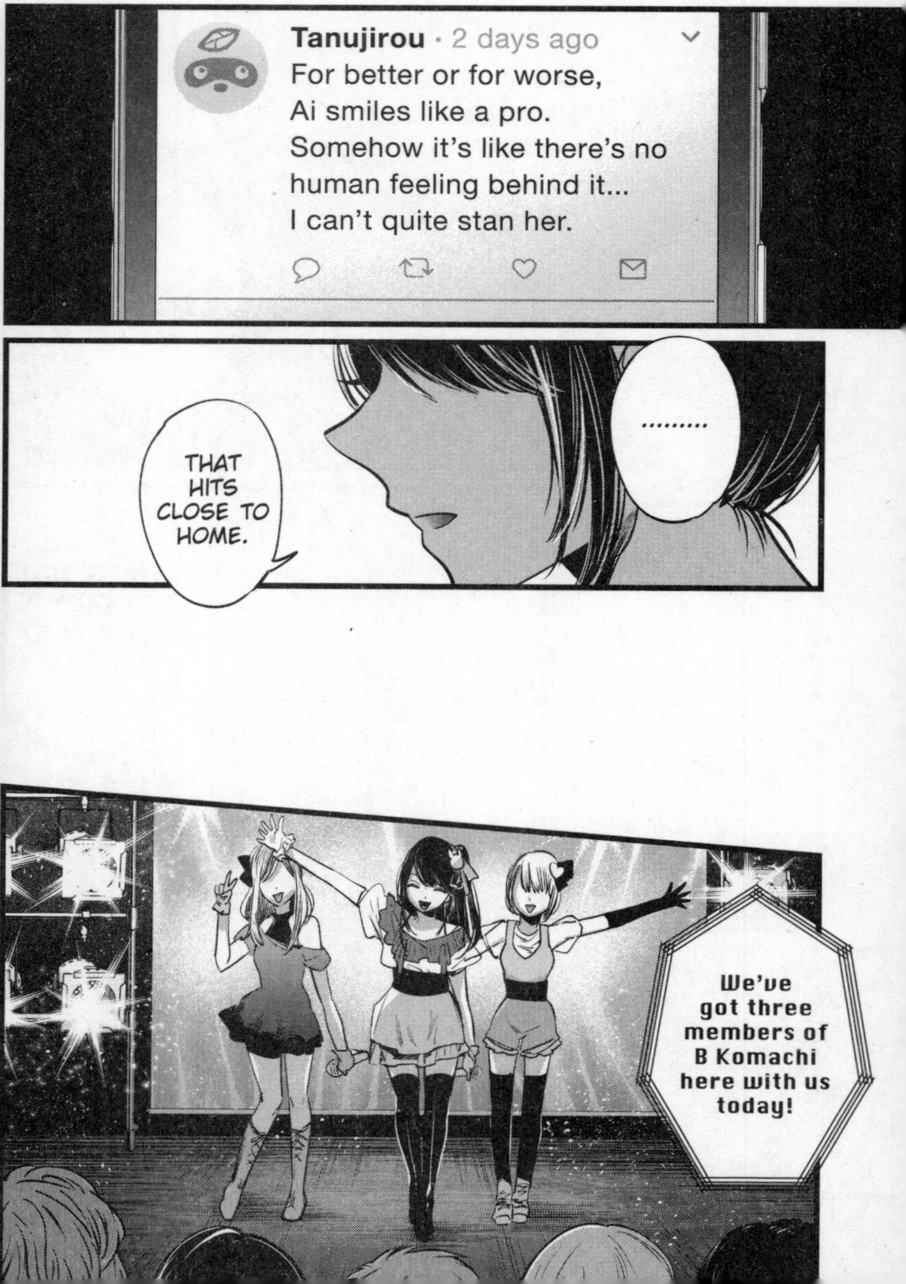
Tanujirou · 2 days ago
For better or for worse, Ai smiles like a pro. Somehow it's like there's no human feeling behind it... I can't quite stan her.
....
THAT HITS CLOSE TO HOME.
We've got three members of B Komachi here with us today!

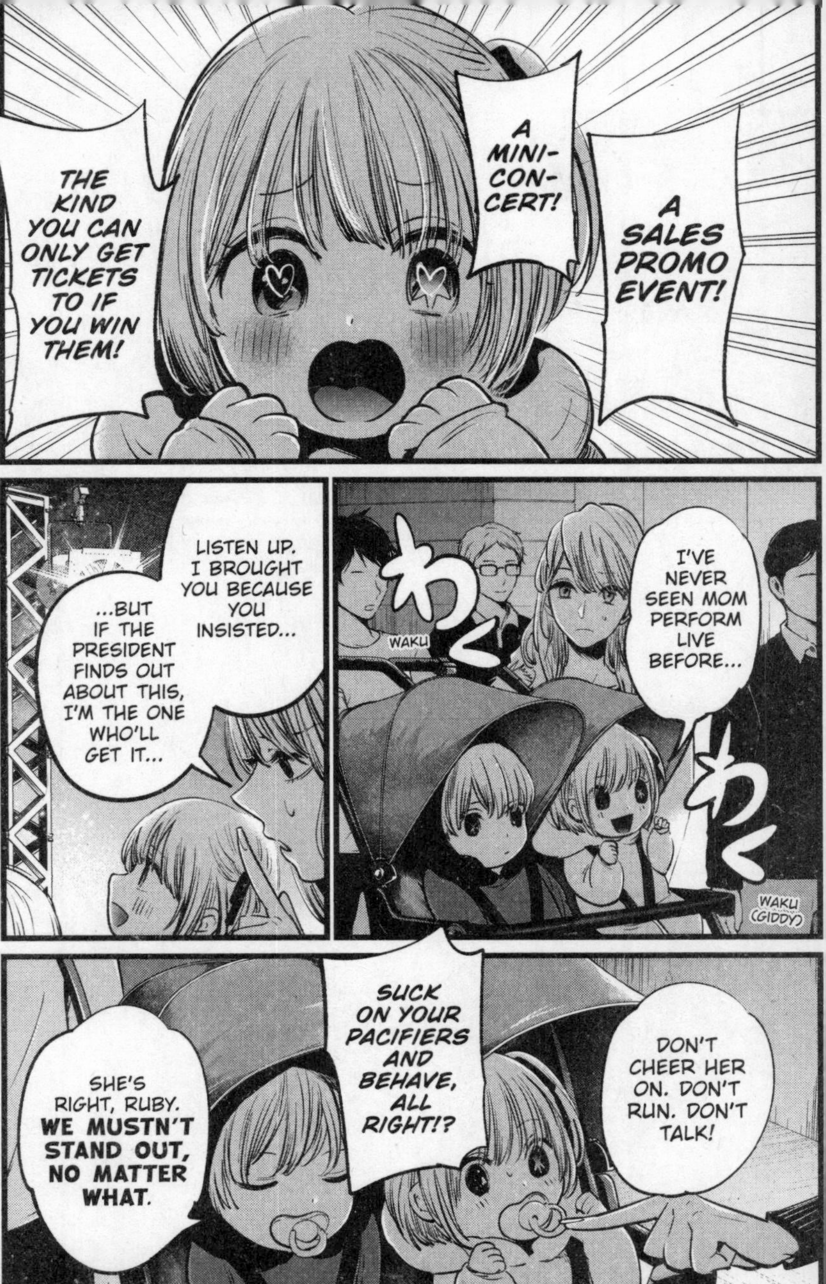
A SALES PROMO EVENT!
A MINI-CONCERT!
THE KIND YOU CAN ONLY GET TICKETS TO IF YOU WIN THEM!
I'VE NEVER SEEN MOM PERFORM LIVE BEFORE...
WAKU
WAKU (GIDDY)
LISTEN UP. I BROUGHT YOU BECAUSE YOU INSISTED...
...BUT IF THE PRESIDENT FINDS OUT ABOUT THIS, I'M THE ONE WHO'LL GET IT...
DON'T CHEER HER ON. DON'T RUN. DON'T TALK!
SUCK ON YOUR PACIFIERS AND BEHAVE, ALL RIGHT!?
SHE'S RIGHT, RUBY. WE MUSTN'T STAND OUT, NO MATTER WHAT.

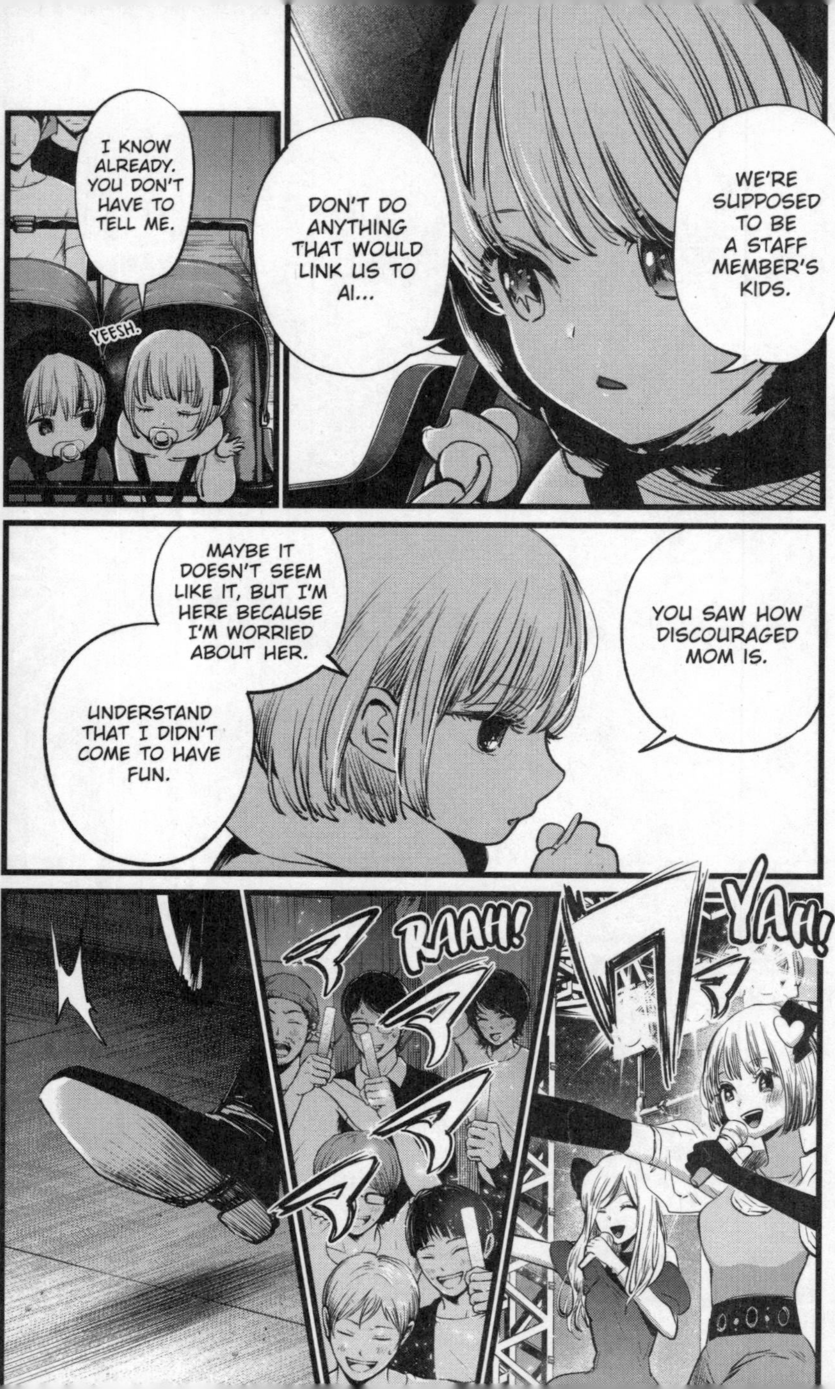
WE'RE SUPPOSED TO BE A STAFF MEMBER'S KIDS.
DON'T DO ANYTHING THAT WOULD LINK US TO AI...
I KNOW ALREADY. YOU DON'T HAVE TO TELL ME.
YEESH.
YOU SAW HOW DISCOURAGED MOM IS.
MAYBE IT DOESN'T SEEM LIKE IT, BUT I'M HERE BECAUSE I'M WORRIED ABOUT HER.
UNDERSTAND THAT I DIDN'T COME TO HAVE FUN.
YAH!
RAAH!

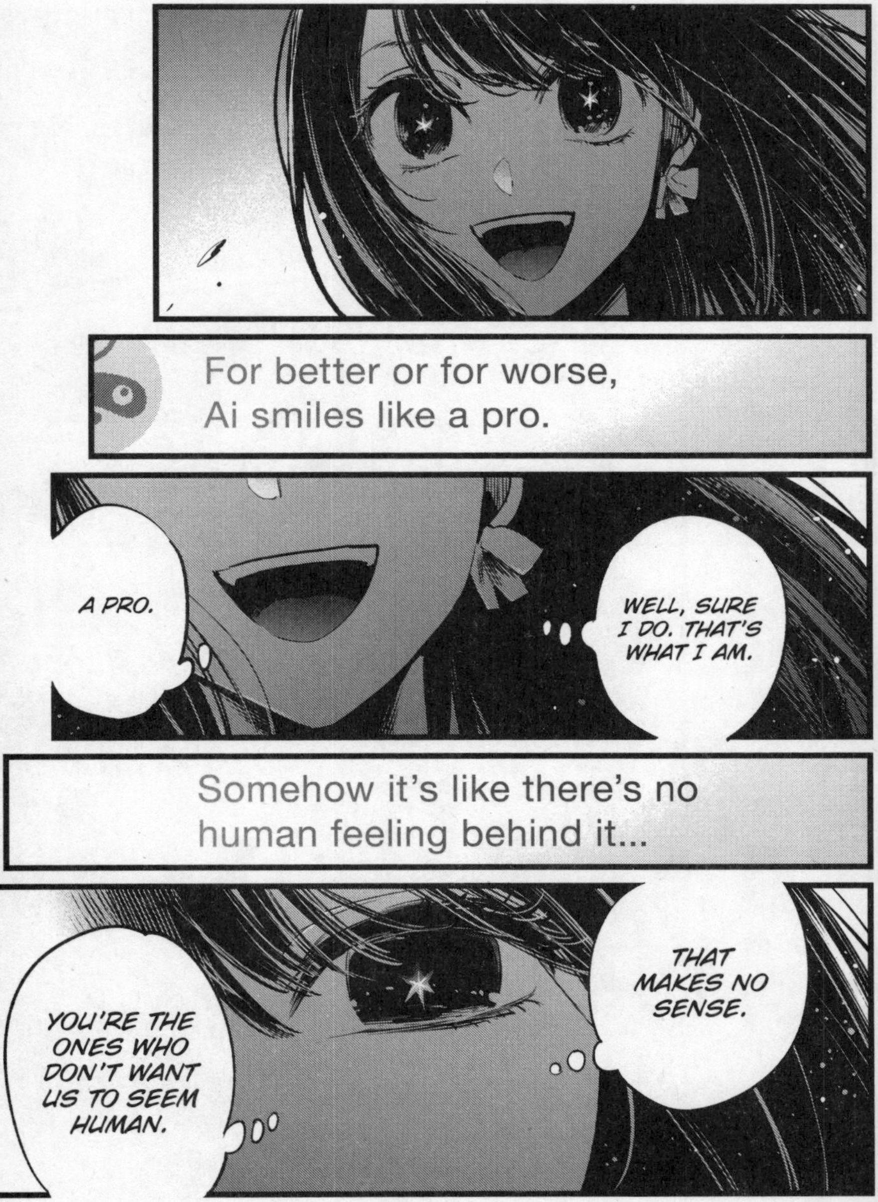
For better or for worse, Ai smiles like a pro.
WELL, SURE I DO. THAT'S WHAT I AM.
A PRO.
Somehow it's like there's no human feeling behind it...
THAT MAKES NO SENSE.
YOU'RE THE ONES WHO DON'T WANT US TO SEEM HUMAN.

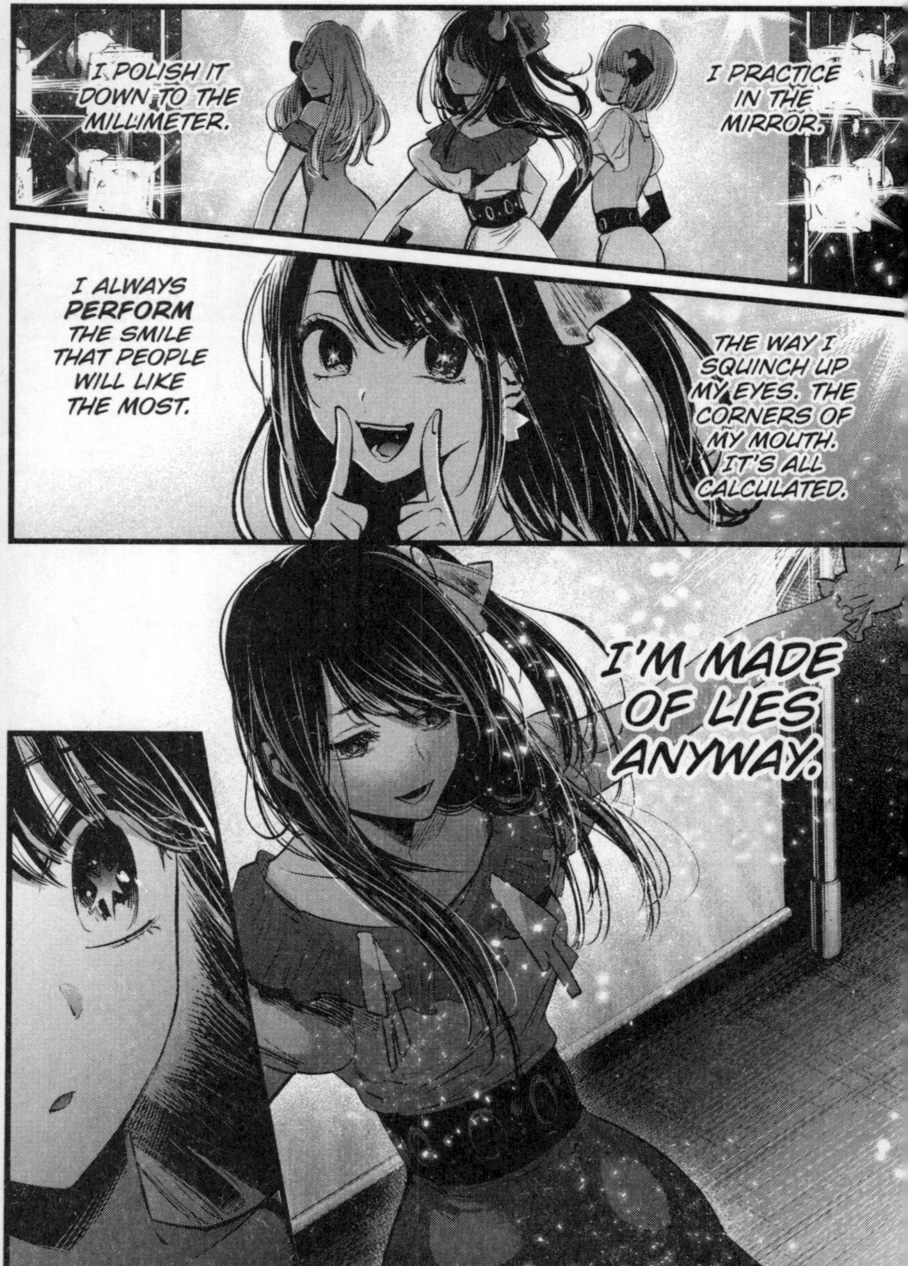
I PRACTICE IN THE MIRROR.
I POLISH IT DOWN TO THE MILLIMETER.
I ALWAYS PERFORM THE SMILE THAT PEOPLE WILL LIKE THE MOST.
THE WAY I SQUINCH UP MY EYES. THE CORNERS OF MY MOUTH. IT'S ALL CALCULATED.
I'M MADE OF LIES ANYWAY.

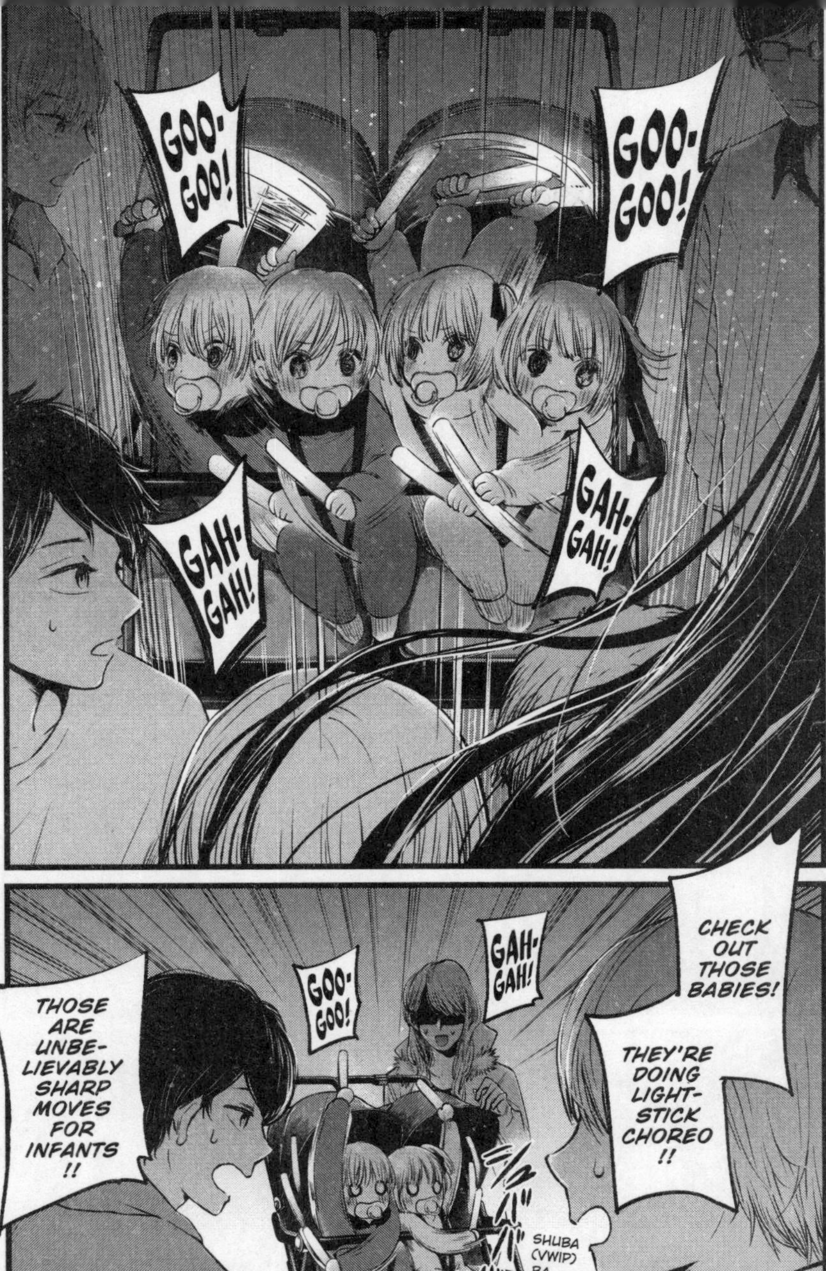
GOO-GOO!
GOO-GOO!
GAH-GAH!
GAH-GAH!
CHECK OUT THOSE BABIES!
THEY'RE DOING LIGHT-STICK CHOREO!!
GAH-GAH!
GOO-GOO!
THOSE ARE UNBELIEVABLY SHARP MOVES FOR INFANTS!!
SHUBA (VWIP) BA BA BA

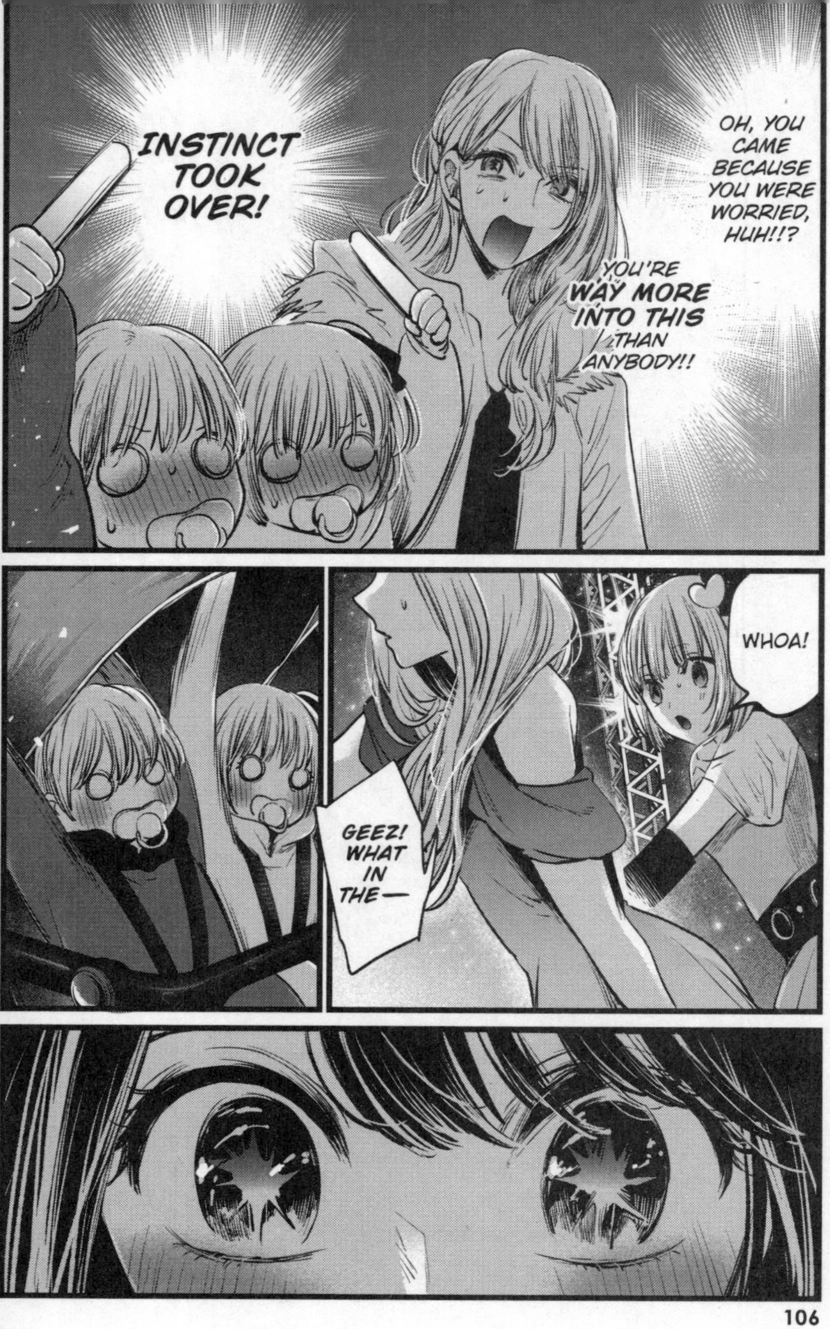
OH, YOU CAME BECAUSE YOU WERE WORRIED, HUH!!?
YOU'RE WAY MORE INTO THIS THAN ANYBODY!!
INSTINCT TOOK OVER!
WHOA!
GEEZ! WHAT IN THE—

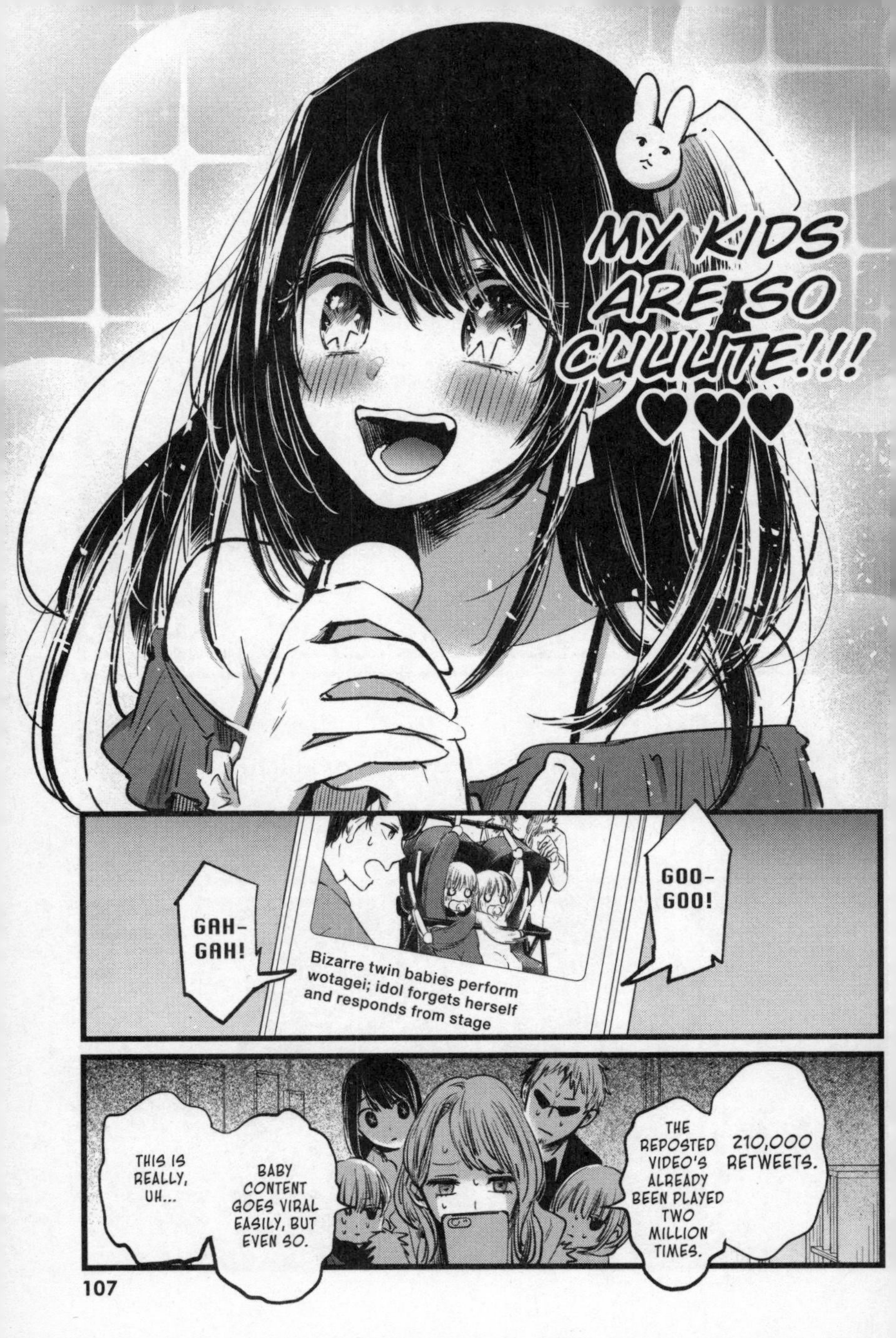

MY KIDS ARE SO CUUUTE!!! ♥♥♥
GOO-GOO!
Bizarre twin babies perform wotagei; idol forgets herself and responds from stage
GAH-GAH!
210,000 RETWEETS.
THE REPOSTED VIDEO'S ALREADY BEEN PLAYED TWO MILLION TIMES.
BABY CONTENT GOES VIRAL EASILY, BUT EVEN SO.
THIS IS REALLY, UH...

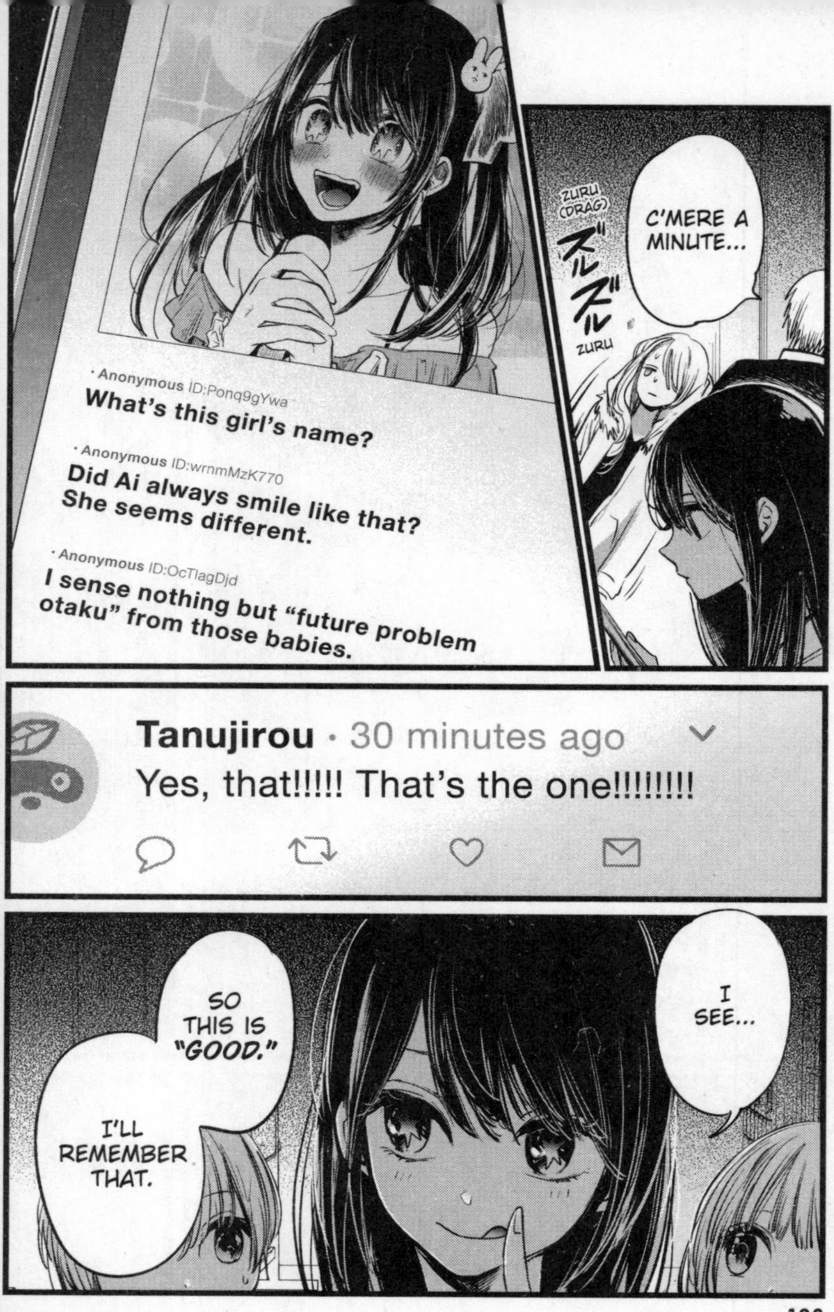
ZURU (DRAG)
ズルズル
ZURU
C'MERE A MINUTE...
・Anonymous ID:Ponq9gYwa
What's this girl's name?
・Anonymous ID:wrnmMzK770
Did Ai always smile like that? She seems different.
・Anonymous ID:OcTlagDjd
I sense nothing but "future problem otaku" from those babies.
Tanujirou · 30 minutes ago
Yes, that!!!!! That's the one!!!!!!!!
I SEE...
SO THIS IS "GOOD."
I'LL REMEMBER THAT.

Interview : 【Film Director】 Edition

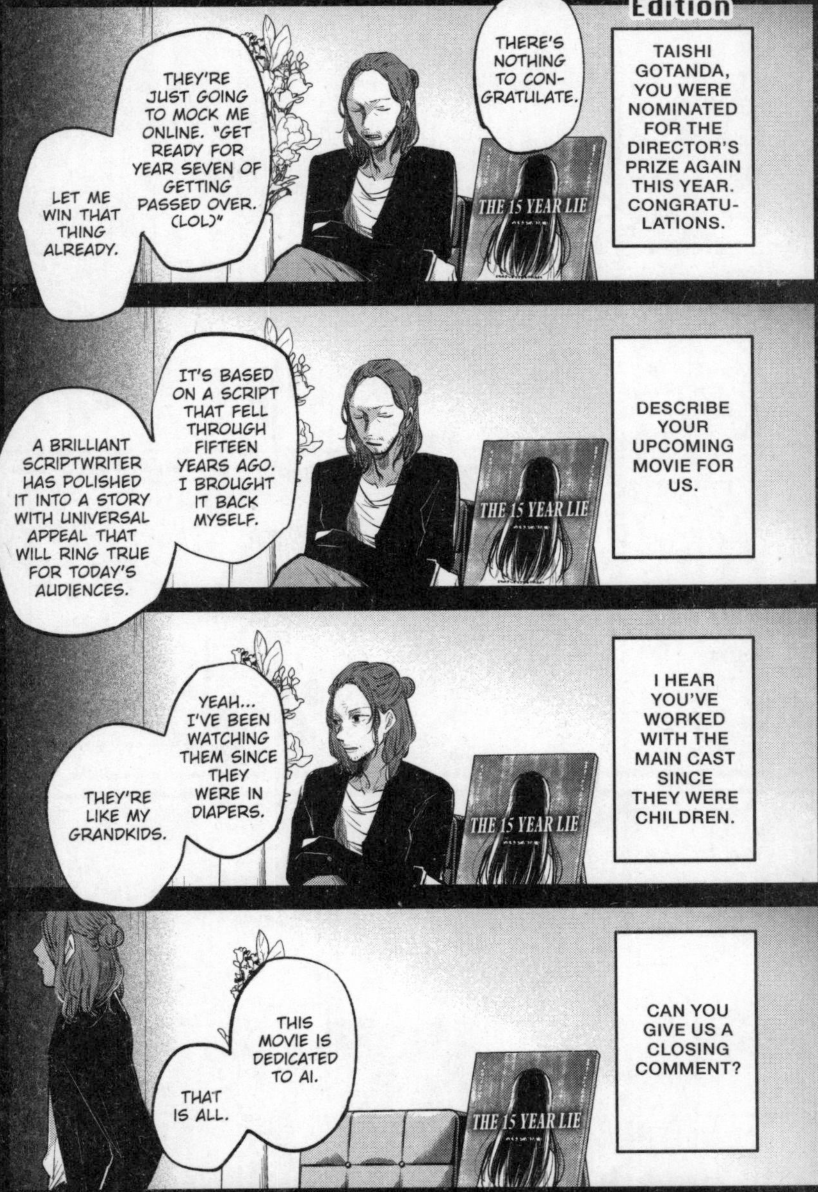
TAISHI GOTANDA, YOU WERE NOMINATED FOR THE DIRECTOR'S PRIZE AGAIN THIS YEAR. CONGRATULATIONS.
THERE'S NOTHING TO CON-GRATULATE.
THE 15 YEAR LIE
THEY'RE JUST GOING TO MOCK ME ONLINE. "GET READY FOR YEAR SEVEN OF GETTING PASSED OVER. (LOL)"
LET ME WIN THAT THING ALREADY.
DESCRIBE YOUR UPCOMING MOVIE FOR US.
THE 15 YEAR LIE
IT'S BASED ON A SCRIPT THAT FELL THROUGH FIFTEEN YEARS AGO. I BROUGHT IT BACK MYSELF.
A BRILLIANT SCRIPTWRITER HAS POLISHED IT INTO A STORY WITH UNIVERSAL APPEAL THAT WILL RING TRUE FOR TODAY'S AUDIENCES.
I HEAR YOU'VE WORKED WITH THE MAIN CAST SINCE THEY WERE CHILDREN.
THE 15 YEAR LIE
YEAH... I'VE BEEN WATCHING THEM SINCE THEY WERE IN DIAPERS.
THEY'RE LIKE MY GRANDKIDS.
CAN YOU GIVE US A CLOSING COMMENT?
THE 15 YEAR LIE
THIS MOVIE IS DEDICATED TO AI.
THAT IS ALL.

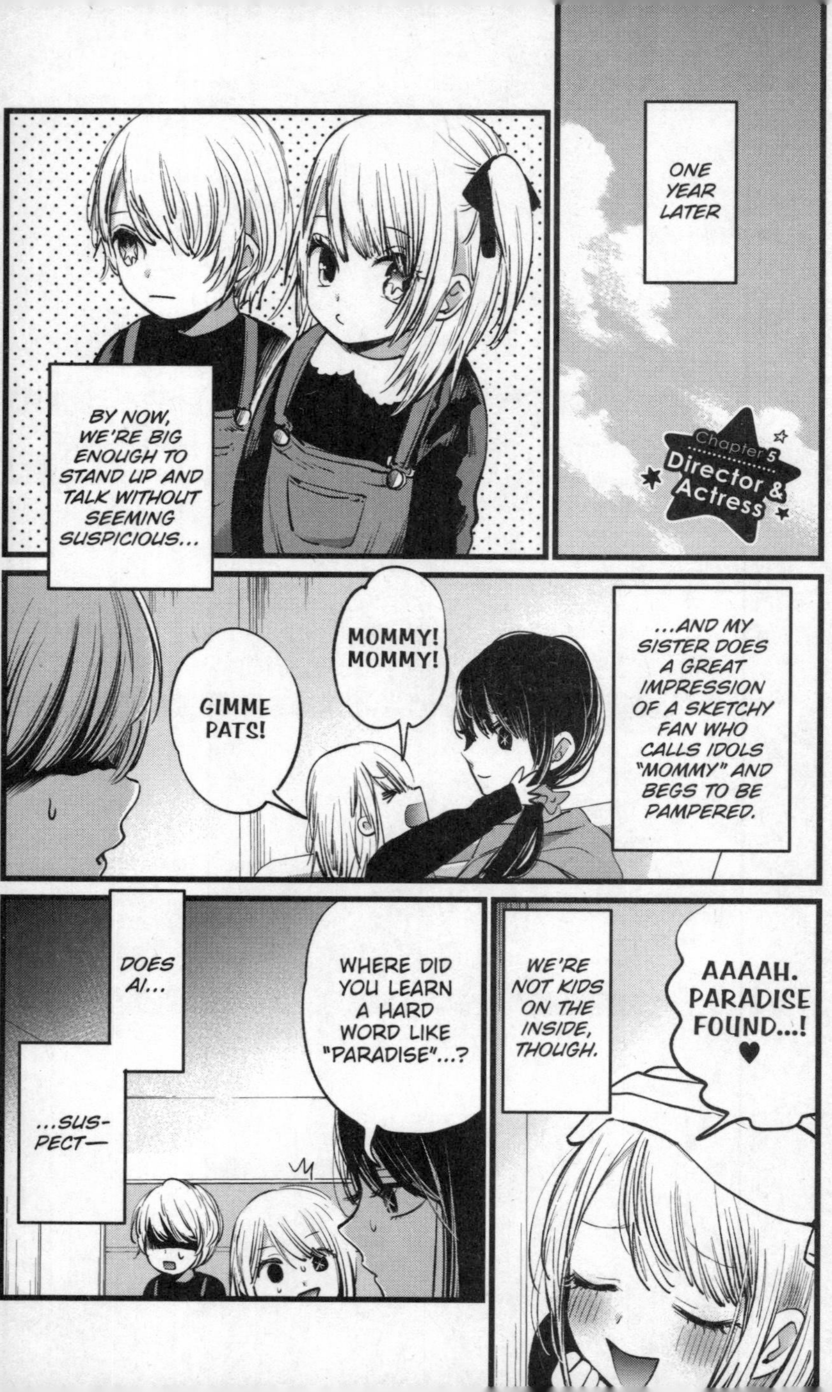
ONE YEAR LATER
Chapter 5
Director & Actress
BY NOW, WE'RE BIG ENOUGH TO STAND UP AND TALK WITHOUT SEEMING SUSPICIOUS...
...AND MY SISTER DOES A GREAT IMPRESSION OF A SKETCHY FAN WHO CALLS IDOLS "MOMMY" AND BEGS TO BE PAMPERED.
MOMMY! MOMMY!
GIMME PATS!
AAAAH. PARADISE FOUND...! ♥
WE'RE NOT KIDS ON THE INSIDE, THOUGH.
WHERE DID YOU LEARN A HARD WORD LIKE "PARADISE"...?
DOES AI...
...SUS-PECT—

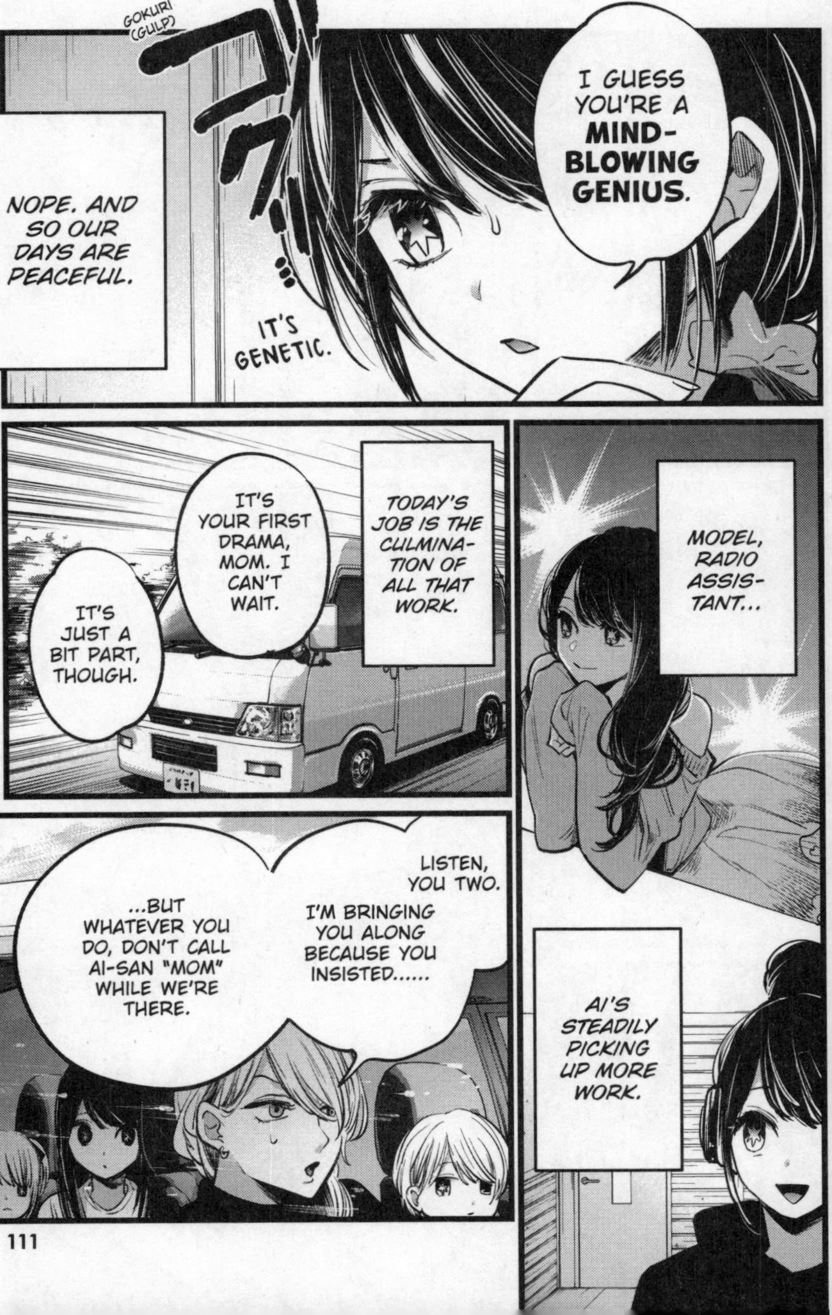
I GUESS YOU'RE A MIND-BLOWING GENIUS.
GOKURI (GULP)
IT'S GENETIC.
NOPE. AND SO OUR DAYS ARE PEACEFUL.
MODEL, RADIO ASSIS-TANT...
AI'S STEADILY PICKING UP MORE WORK.
TODAY'S JOB IS THE CULMINA-TION OF ALL THAT WORK.
IT'S YOUR FIRST DRAMA, MOM. I CAN'T WAIT.
IT'S JUST A BIT PART, THOUGH.
LISTEN, YOU TWO.
I'M BRINGING YOU ALONG BECAUSE YOU INSISTED......
...BUT WHATEVER YOU DO, DON'T CALL AI-SAN "MOM" WHILE WE'RE THERE.

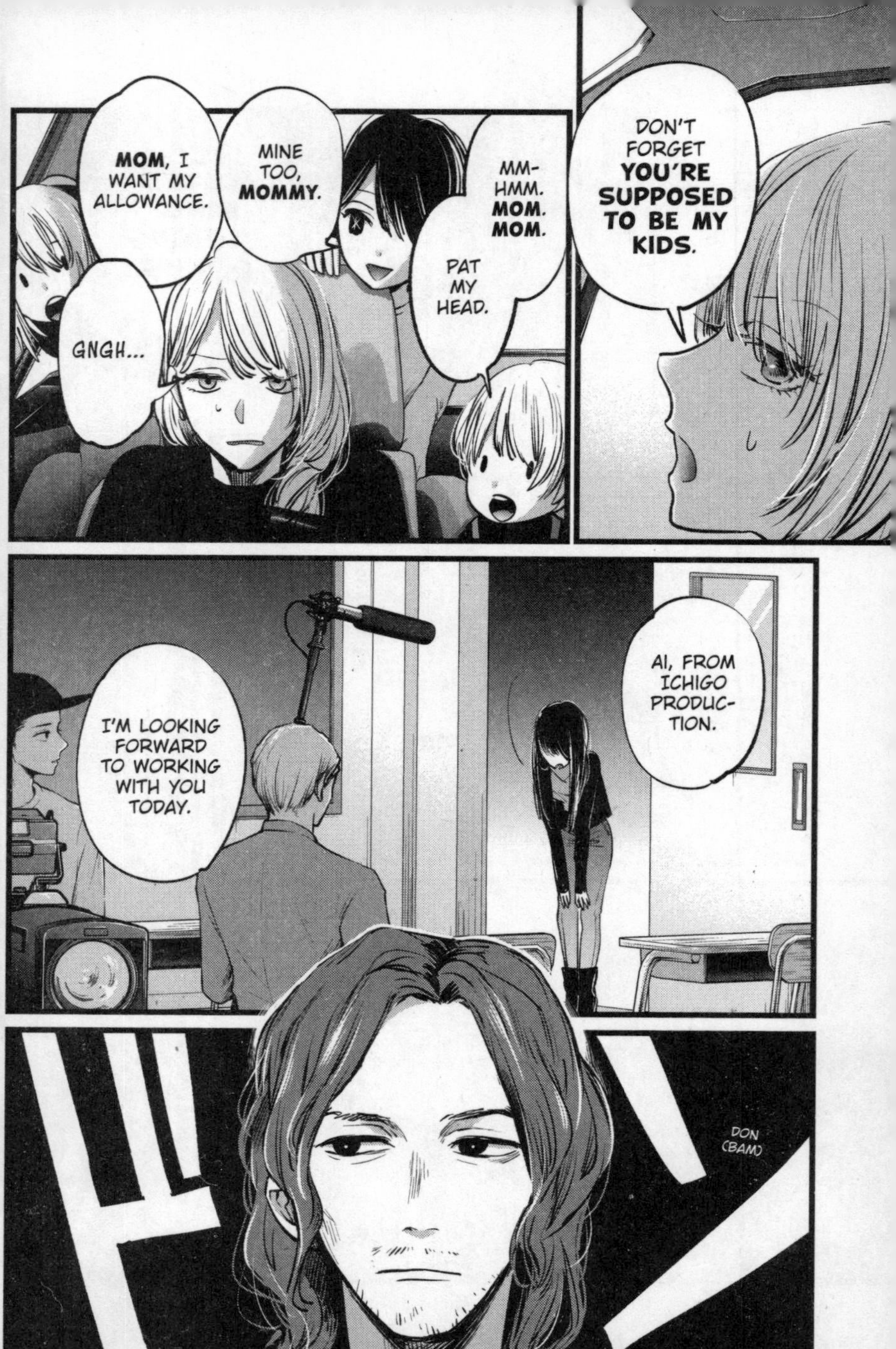
DON'T FORGET YOU'RE SUPPOSED TO BE MY KIDS.
MM-HMM. MOM. MOM.
PAT MY HEAD.
MINE TOO, MOMMY.
MOM, I WANT MY ALLOWANCE.
GNGH...
AI, FROM ICHIGO PRODUC-TION.
I'M LOOKING FORWARD TO WORKING WITH YOU TODAY.
DON (BAM)

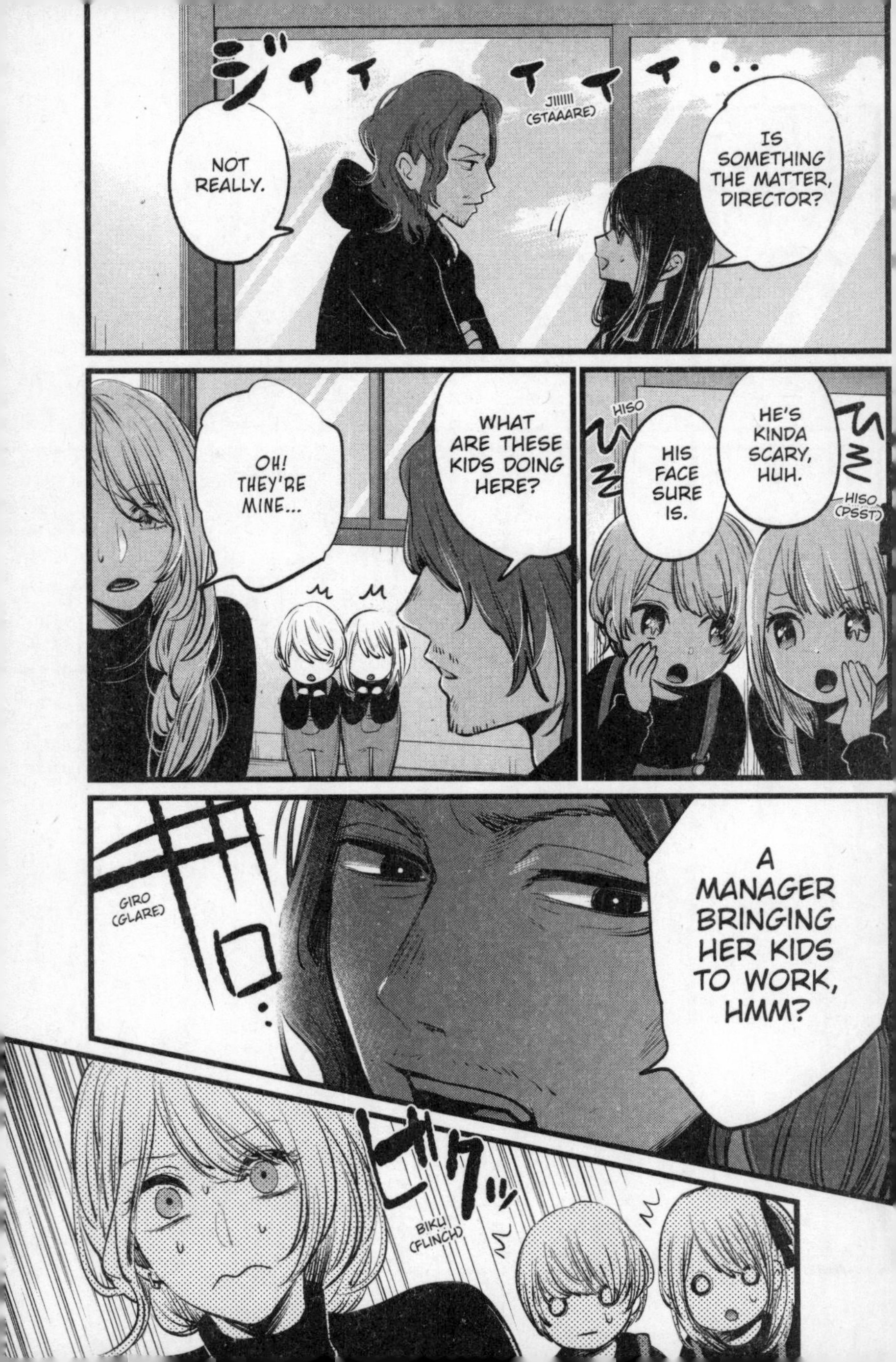
JIIIIII (STAAARE)
IS SOMETHING THE MATTER, DIRECTOR?
NOT REALLY.
HE'S KINDA SCARY, HUH.
HISO (PSST)
HIS FACE SURE IS.
HISO
WHAT ARE THESE KIDS DOING HERE?
OH! THEY'RE MINE...
A MANAGER BRINGING HER KIDS TO WORK, HMM?
GIRO (GLARE)
BIKU (FLINCH)

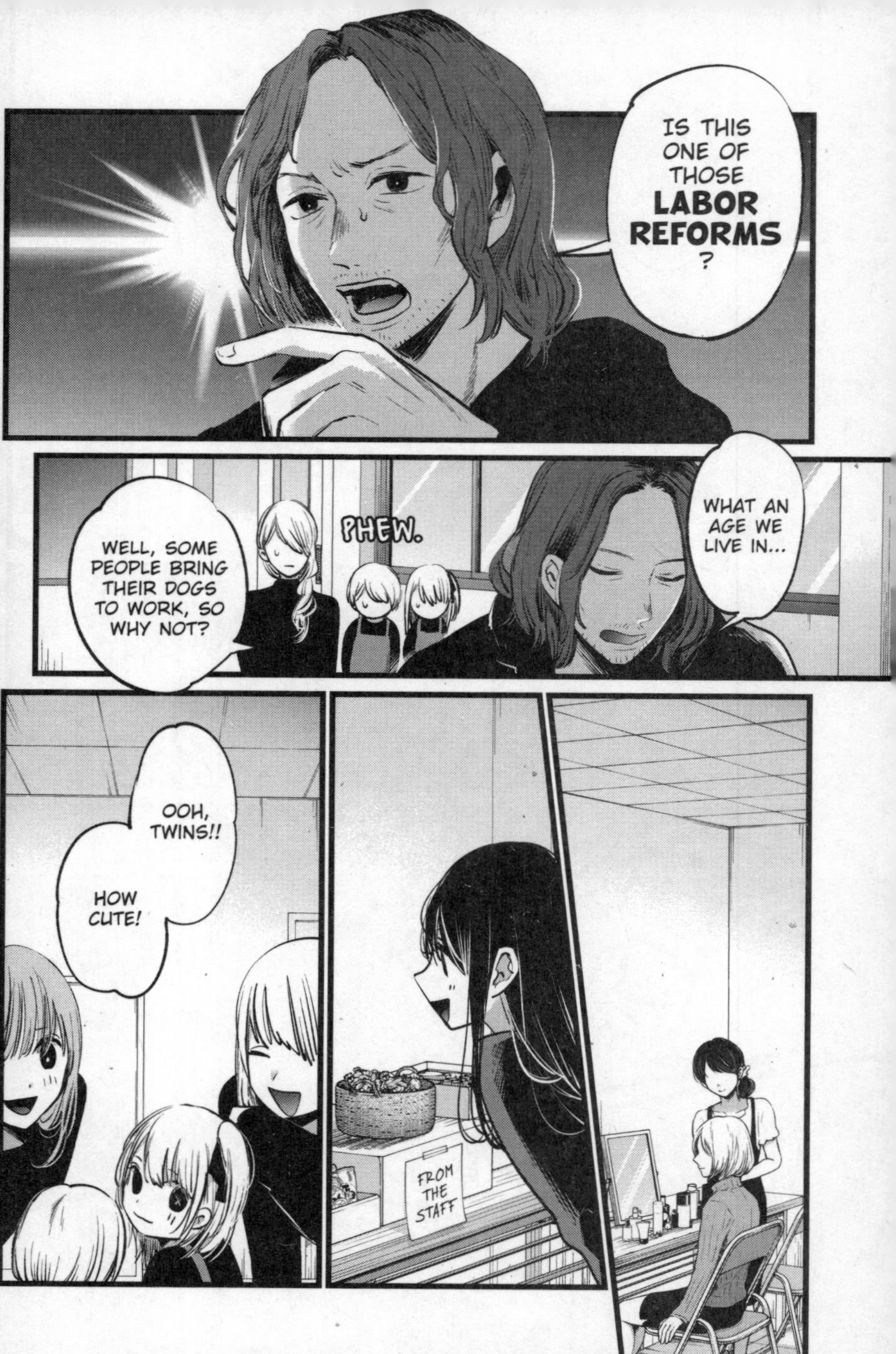
IS THIS ONE OF THOSE LABOR REFORMS?
WHAT AN AGE WE LIVE IN...
PHEW.
WELL, SOME PEOPLE BRING THEIR DOGS TO WORK, SO WHY NOT?
FROM THE STAFF
OOH, TWINS!!
HOW CUTE!

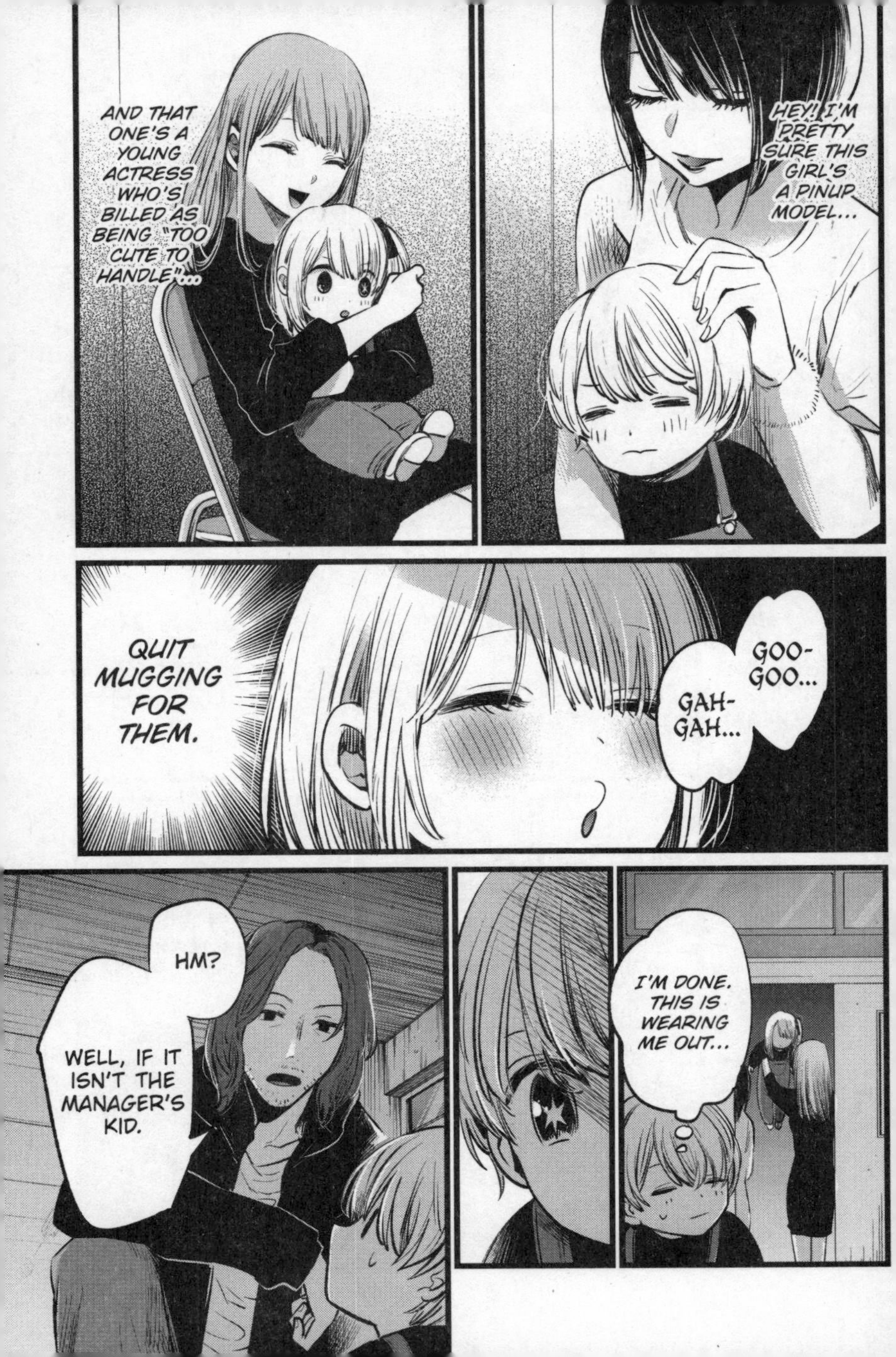
HEY! I'M PRETTY SURE THIS GIRL'S A PINUP MODEL...
AND THAT ONE'S A YOUNG ACTRESS WHO'S BILLED AS BEING "TOO CUTE TO HANDLE"...
GOO-GOO...
GAH-GAH...
QUIT MUGGING FOR THEM.
I'M DONE. THIS IS WEARING ME OUT...
HM?
WELL, IF IT ISN'T THE MANAGER'S KID.

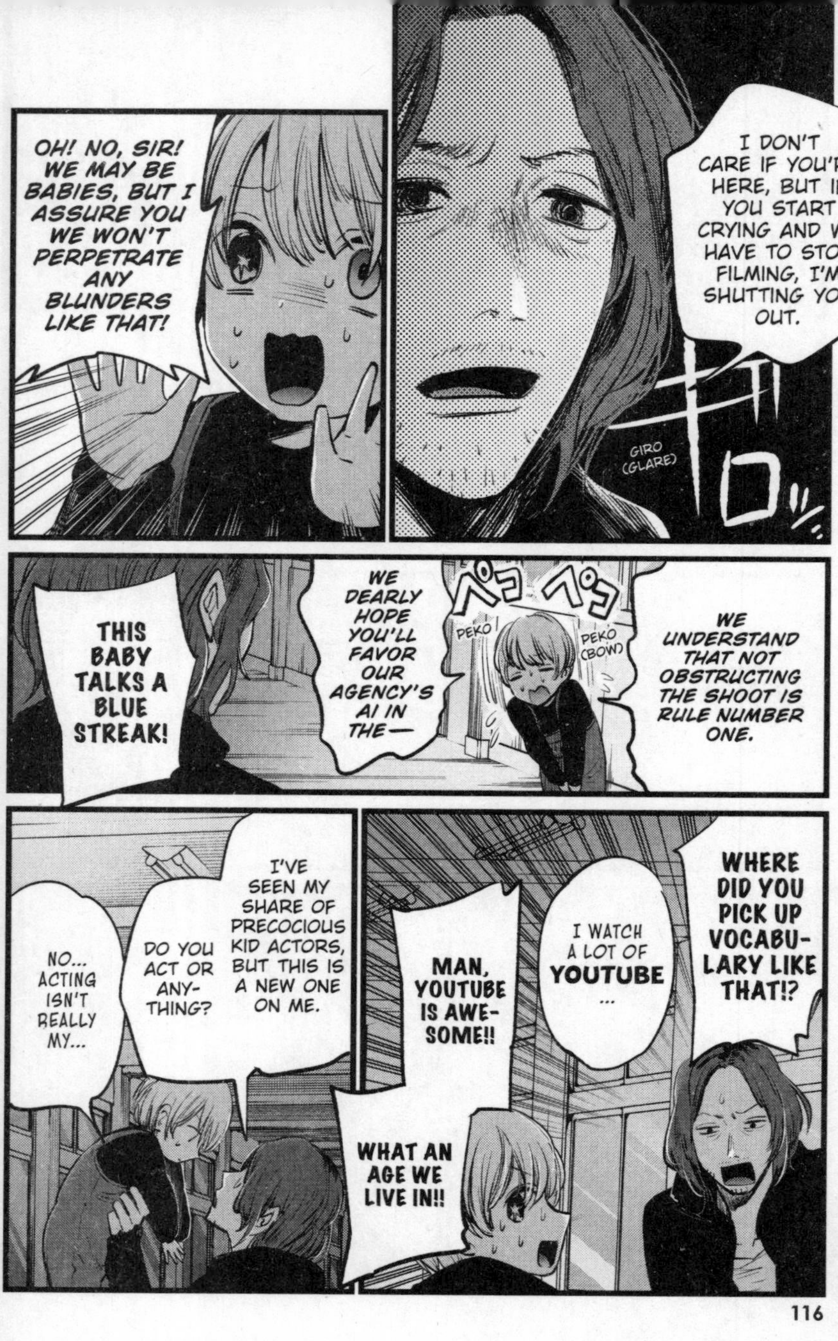
I DON'T CARE IF YOU'RE HERE, BUT IF YOU START CRYING AND WE HAVE TO STOP FILMING, I'M SHUTTING YOU OUT.
GIRO (GLARE)
OH! NO, SIR! WE MAY BE BABIES, BUT I ASSURE YOU WE WON'T PERPETRATE ANY BLUNDERS LIKE THAT!
WE UNDERSTAND THAT NOT OBSTRUCTING THE SHOOT IS RULE NUMBER ONE.
PEKO PEKO (BOW)
WE DEARLY HOPE YOU'LL FAVOR OUR AGENCY'S AI IN THE—
THIS BABY TALKS A BLUE STREAK!
WHERE DID YOU PICK UP VOCABU-LARY LIKE THAT!?
I WATCH A LOT OF YOUTUBE ...
MAN, YOUTUBE IS AWE-SOME!!
WHAT AN AGE WE LIVE IN!!
I'VE SEEN MY SHARE OF PRECOCIOUS KID ACTORS, BUT THIS IS A NEW ONE ON ME.
DO YOU ACT OR ANY-THING?
NO... ACTING ISN'T REALLY MY...

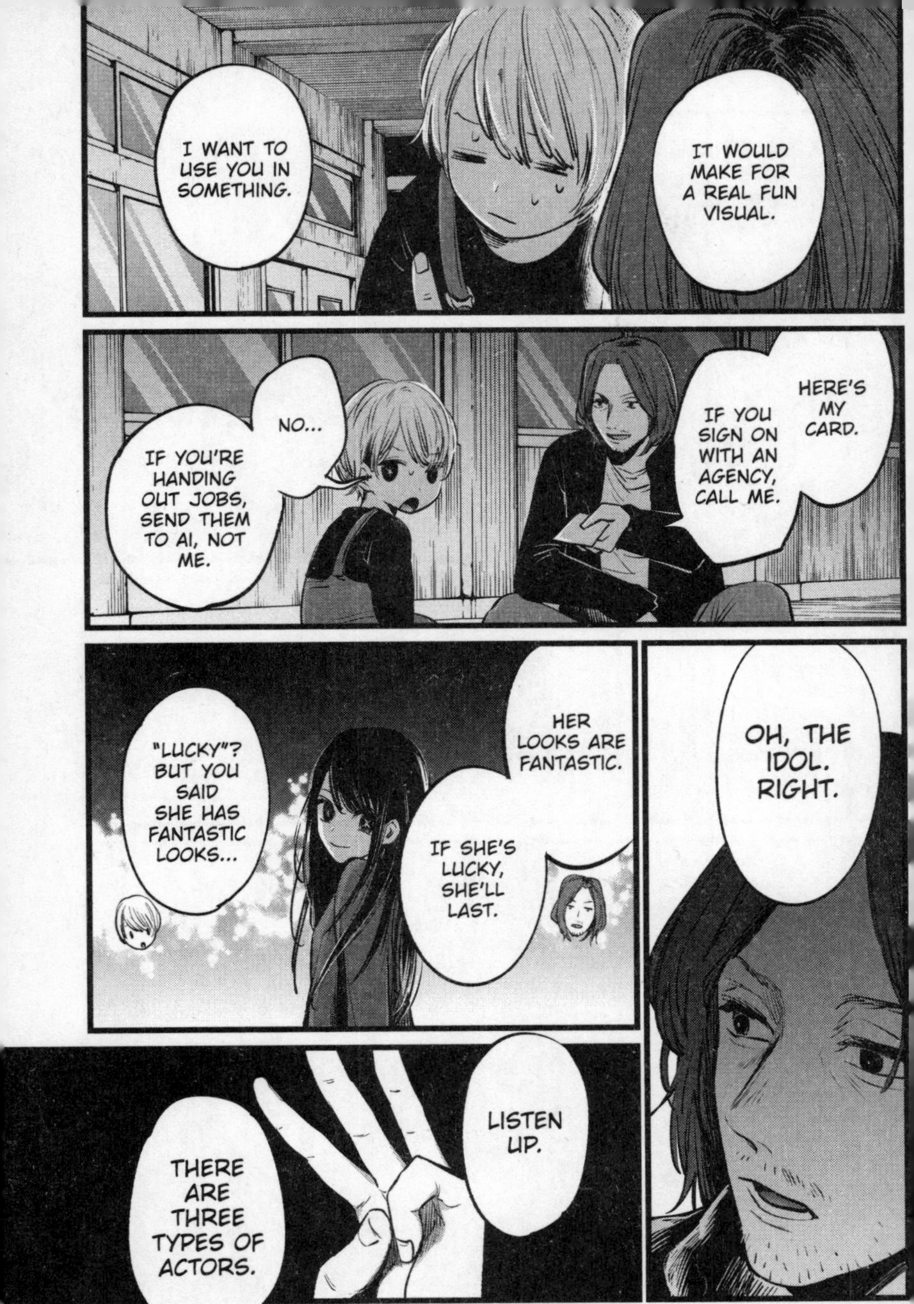
IT WOULD MAKE FOR A REAL FUN VISUAL.
I WANT TO USE YOU IN SOMETHING.
HERE'S MY CARD.
IF YOU SIGN ON WITH AN AGENCY, CALL ME.
NO...
IF YOU'RE HANDING OUT JOBS, SEND THEM TO AI, NOT ME.
OH, THE IDOL. RIGHT.
HER LOOKS ARE FANTASTIC.
IF SHE'S LUCKY, SHE'LL LAST.
"LUCKY"? BUT YOU SAID SHE HAS FANTASTIC LOOKS...
LISTEN UP.
THERE ARE THREE TYPES OF ACTORS.

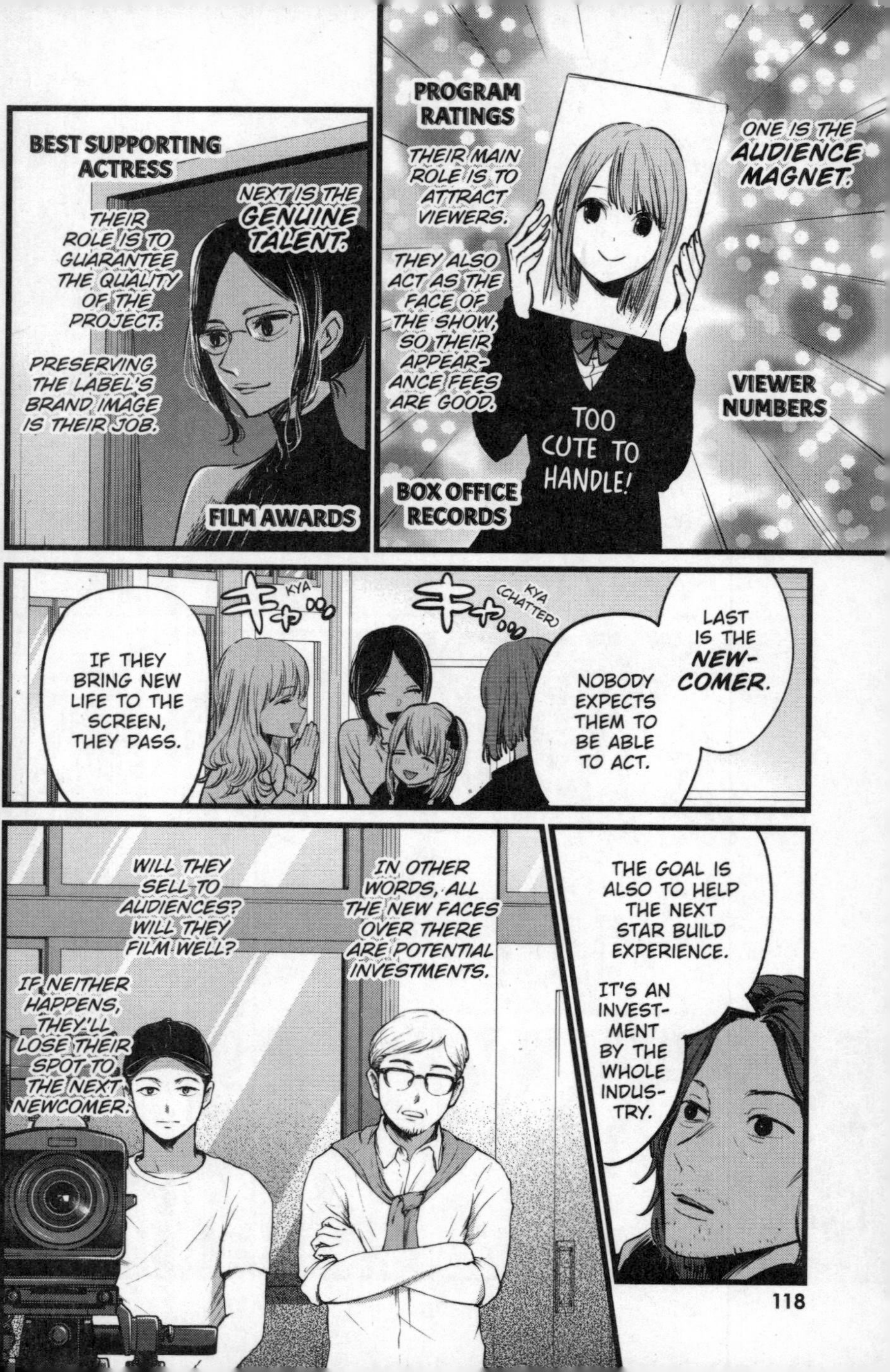

ONE IS THE AUDIENCE MAGNET.
PROGRAM RATINGS
THEIR MAIN ROLE IS TO ATTRACT VIEWERS.
THEY ALSO ACT AS THE FACE OF THE SHOW, SO THEIR APPEARANCE FEES ARE GOOD.
VIEWER NUMBERS
TOO CUTE TO HANDLE!
BOX OFFICE RECORDS
NEXT IS THE GENUINE TALENT.
BEST SUPPORTING ACTRESS
THEIR ROLE IS TO GUARANTEE THE QUALITY OF THE PROJECT.
PRESERVING THE LABEL'S BRAND IMAGE IS THEIR JOB.
FILM AWARDS
LAST IS THE NEWCOMER.
NOBODY EXPECTS THEM TO BE ABLE TO ACT.
KYA (CHATTER)
KYA
IF THEY BRING NEW LIFE TO THE SCREEN, THEY PASS.
THE GOAL IS ALSO TO HELP THE NEXT STAR BUILD EXPERIENCE.
IT'S AN INVESTMENT BY THE WHOLE INDUSTRY.
IN OTHER WORDS, ALL THE NEW FACES OVER THERE ARE POTENTIAL INVESTMENTS.
WILL THEY SELL TO AUDIENCES? WILL THEY FILM WELL?
IF NEITHER HAPPENS, THEY'LL LOSE THEIR SPOT TO THE NEXT NEWCOMER.

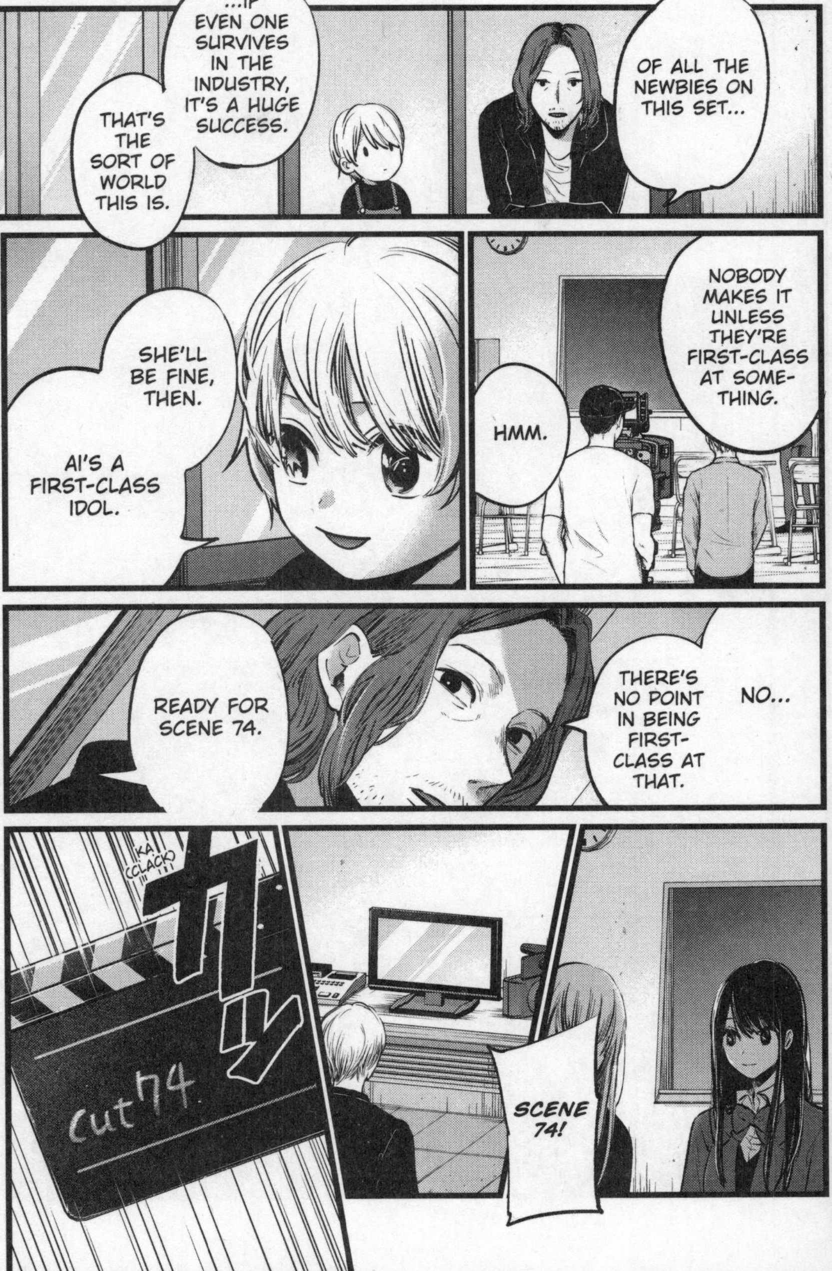
OF ALL THE NEWBIES ON THIS SET...
...IF EVEN ONE SURVIVES IN THE INDUSTRY, IT'S A HUGE SUCCESS.
THAT'S THE SORT OF WORLD THIS IS.
NOBODY MAKES IT UNLESS THEY'RE FIRST-CLASS AT SOME-THING.
HMM.
SHE'LL BE FINE, THEN.
AI'S A FIRST-CLASS IDOL.
NO...
THERE'S NO POINT IN BEING FIRST-CLASS AT THAT.
READY FOR SCENE 74.
SCENE 74!
KA (CLACK)
Cut 74

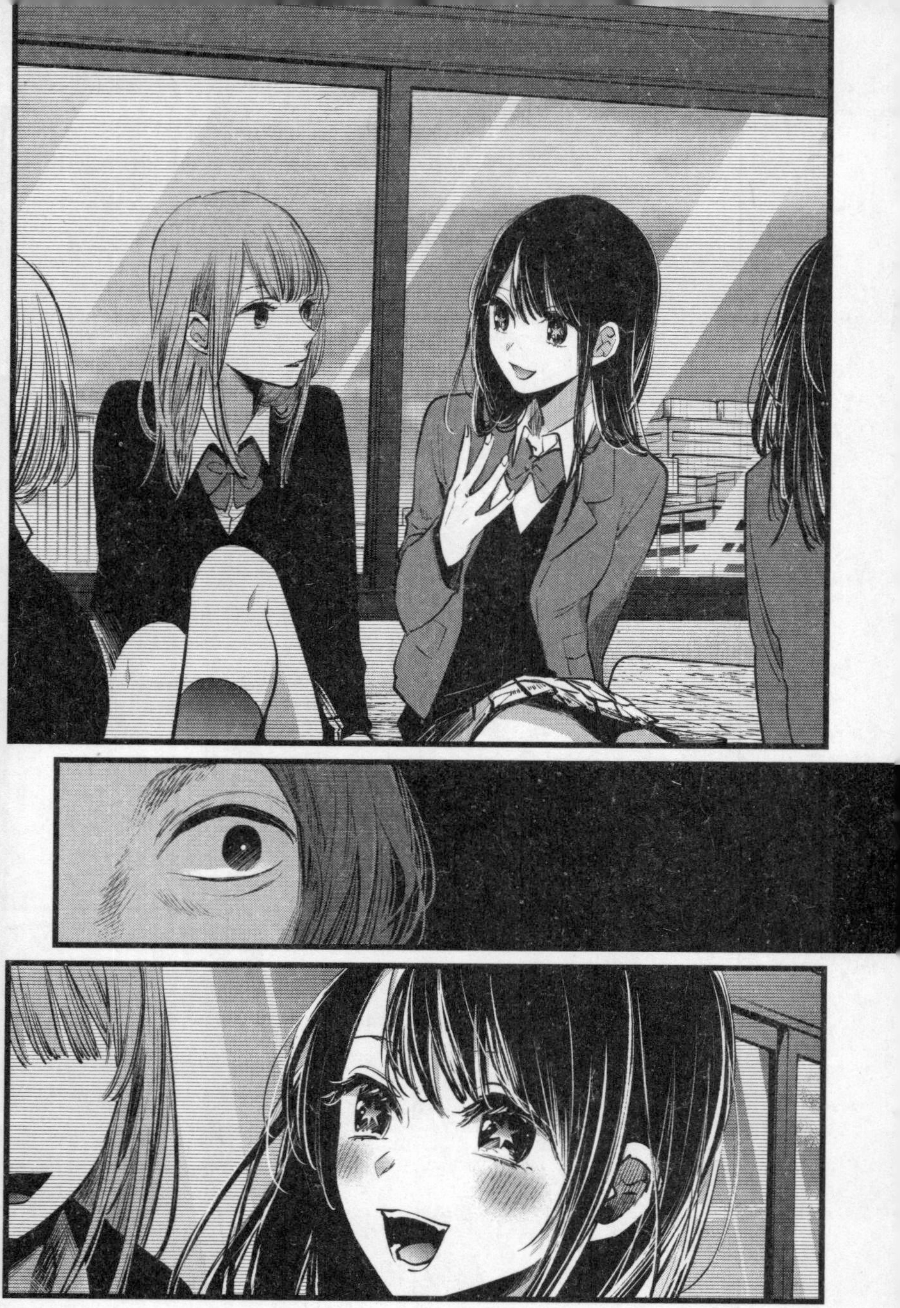

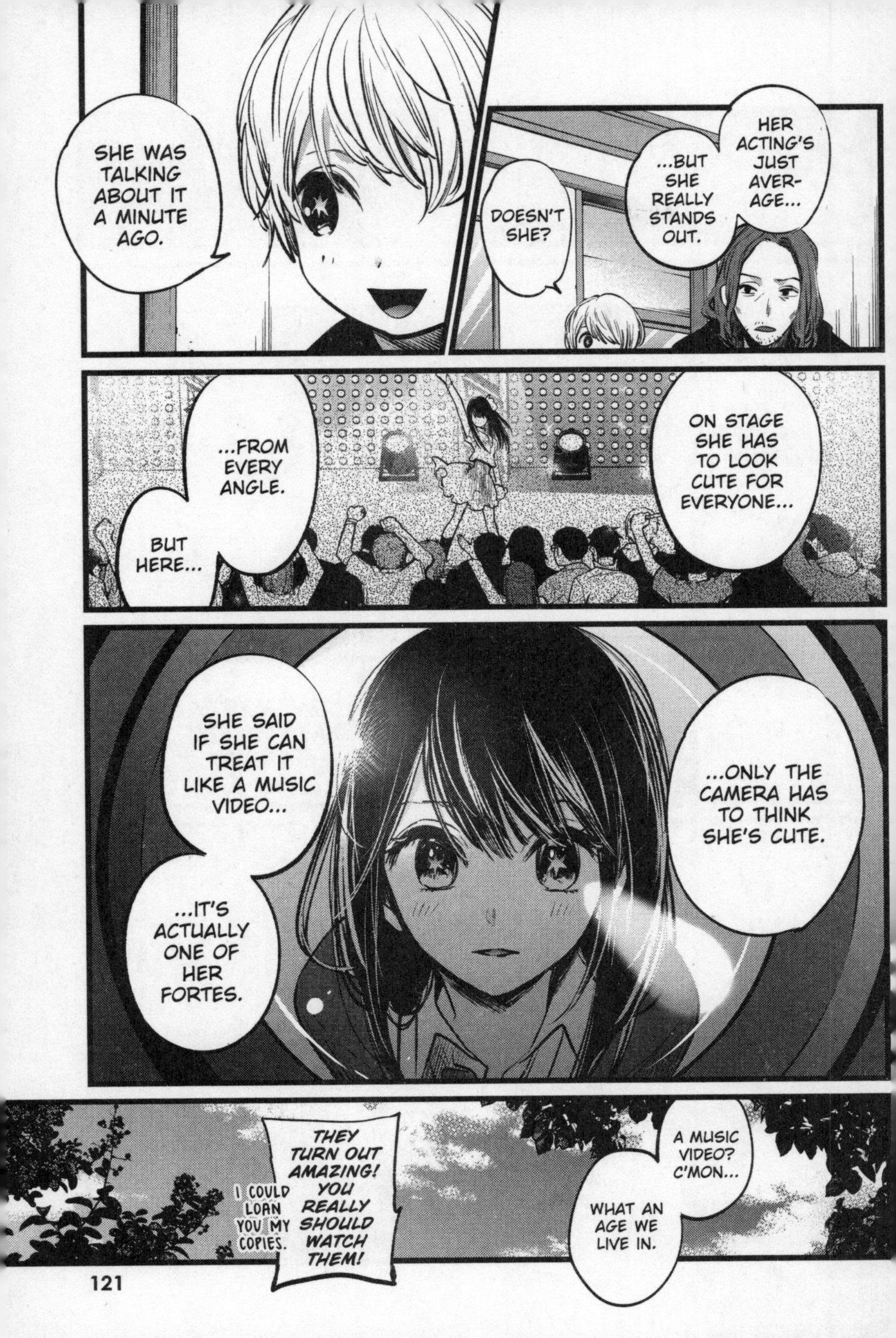
HER ACTING'S JUST AVER-AGE...
...BUT SHE REALLY STANDS OUT.
DOESN'T SHE?
SHE WAS TALKING ABOUT IT A MINUTE AGO.
ON STAGE SHE HAS TO LOOK CUTE FOR EVERYONE...
...FROM EVERY ANGLE.
BUT HERE...
...ONLY THE CAMERA HAS TO THINK SHE'S CUTE.
SHE SAID IF SHE CAN TREAT IT LIKE A MUSIC VIDEO...
...IT'S ACTUALLY ONE OF HER FORTES.
A MUSIC VIDEO? C'MON...
WHAT AN AGE WE LIVE IN.
THEY TURN OUT AMAZING! YOU REALLY SHOULD WATCH THEM!
I COULD LOAN YOU MY COPIES.

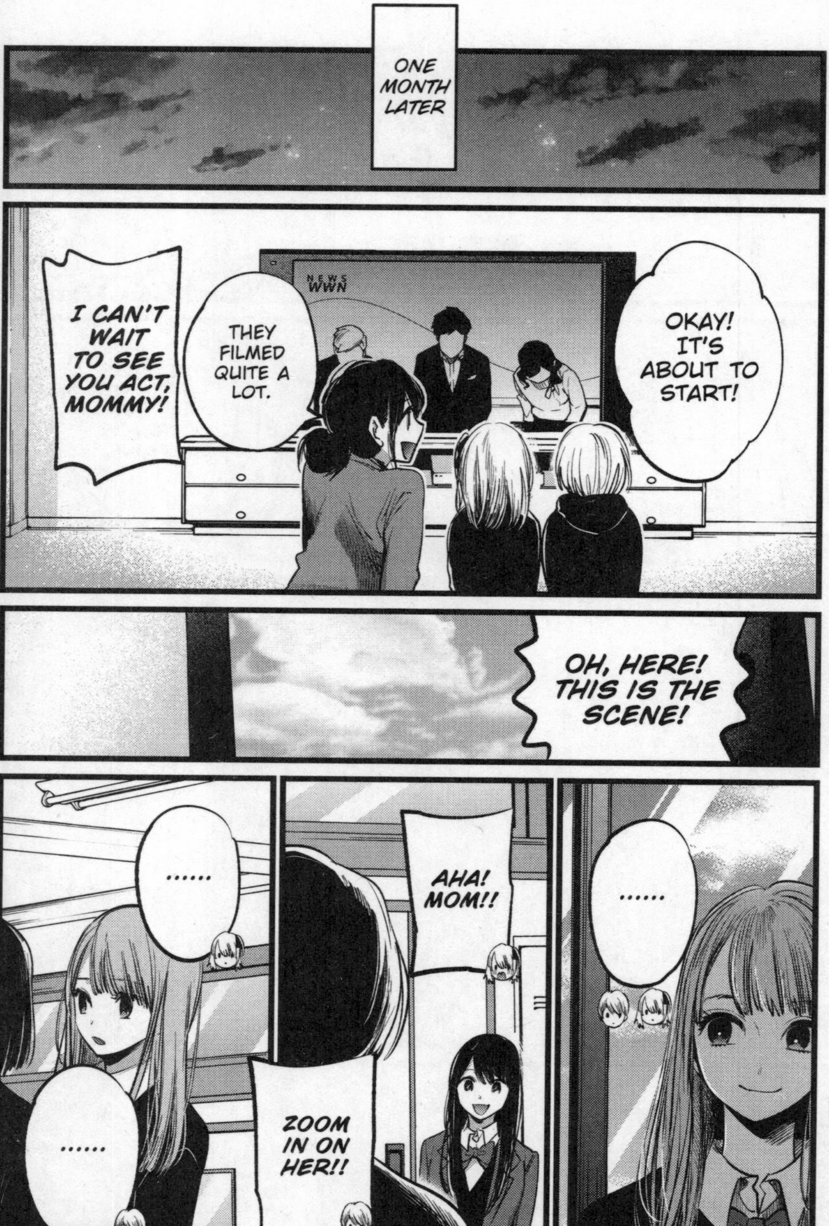
ONE MONTH LATER
OKAY! IT'S ABOUT TO START!
NEWS WWN
THEY FILMED QUITE A LOT.
I CAN'T WAIT TO SEE YOU ACT, MOMMY!
OH, HERE! THIS IS THE SCENE!
......
AHA! MOM!!
ZOOM IN ON HER!!
......
......

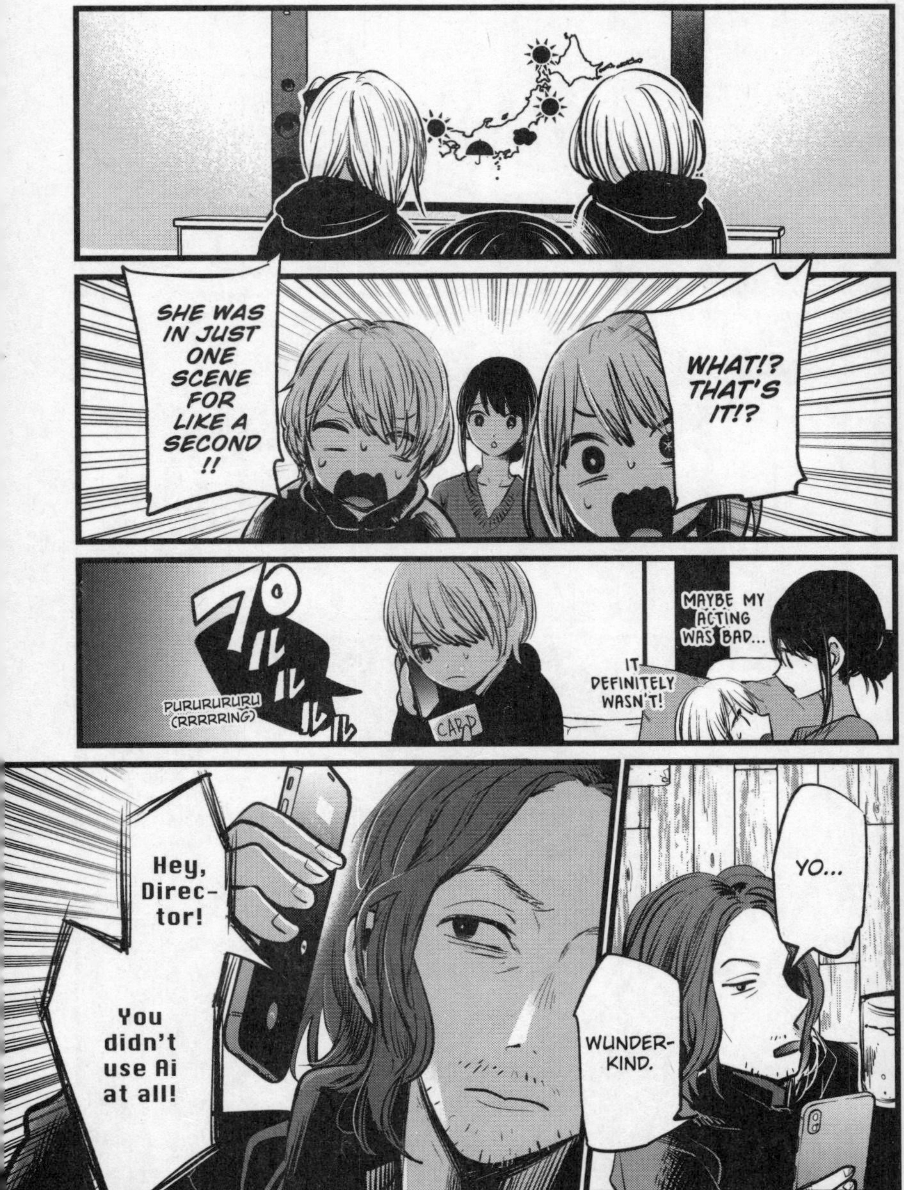
WHAT!? THAT'S IT!?
SHE WAS IN JUST ONE SCENE FOR LIKE A SECOND!!
MAYBE MY ACTING WAS BAD...
IT DEFINITELY WASN'T!
PURURURURU (RRRRRING)
CARD
YO...
WUNDERKIND.
Hey, Director!
You didn't use Ai at all!

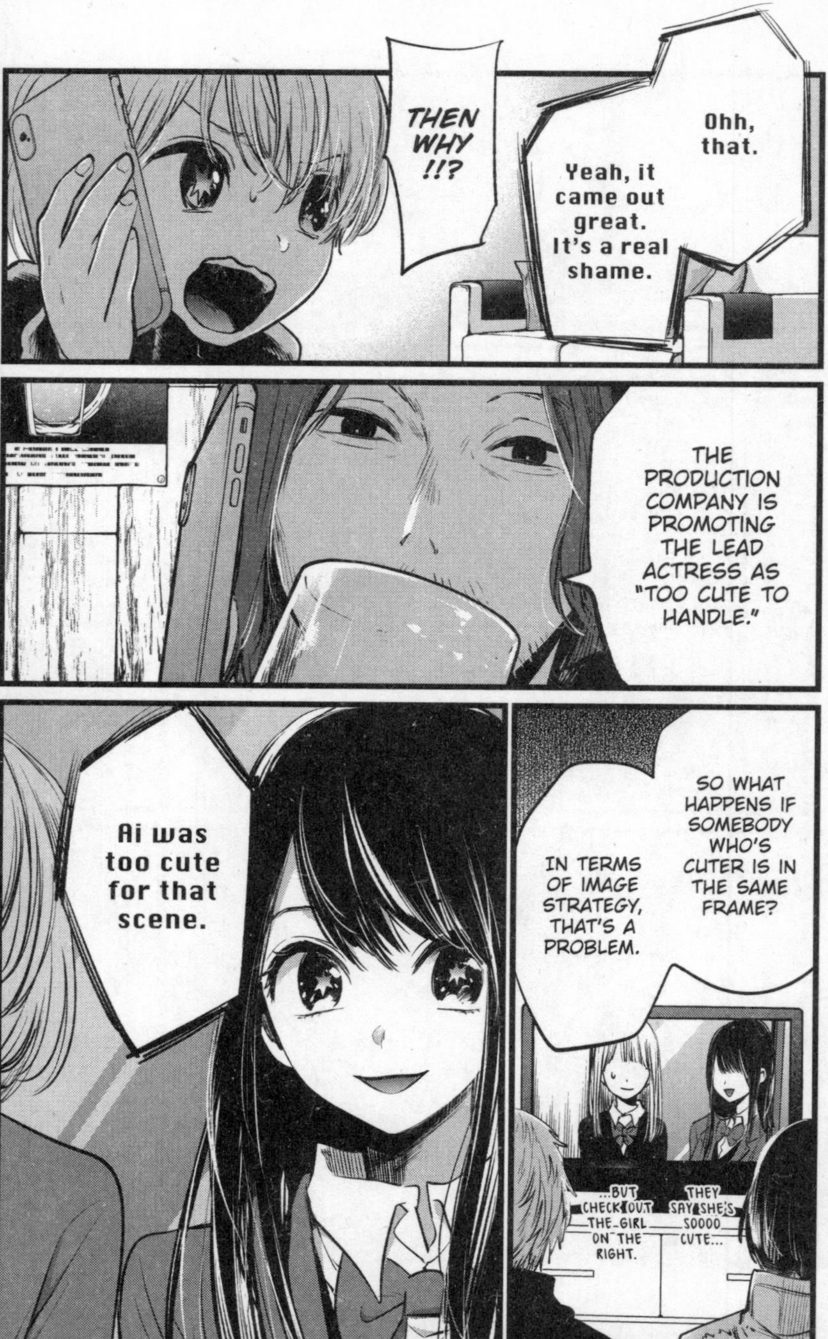
Ohh, that.
Yeah, it came out great. It's a real shame.
THEN WHY !!?
THE PRODUCTION COMPANY IS PROMOTING THE LEAD ACTRESS AS "TOO CUTE TO HANDLE."
SO WHAT HAPPENS IF SOMEBODY WHO'S CUTER IS IN THE SAME FRAME?
IN TERMS OF IMAGE STRATEGY, THAT'S A PROBLEM.
THEY SAY SHE'S SOOOO CUTE...
...BUT CHECK OUT THE GIRL ON THE RIGHT.
Ai was too cute for that scene.

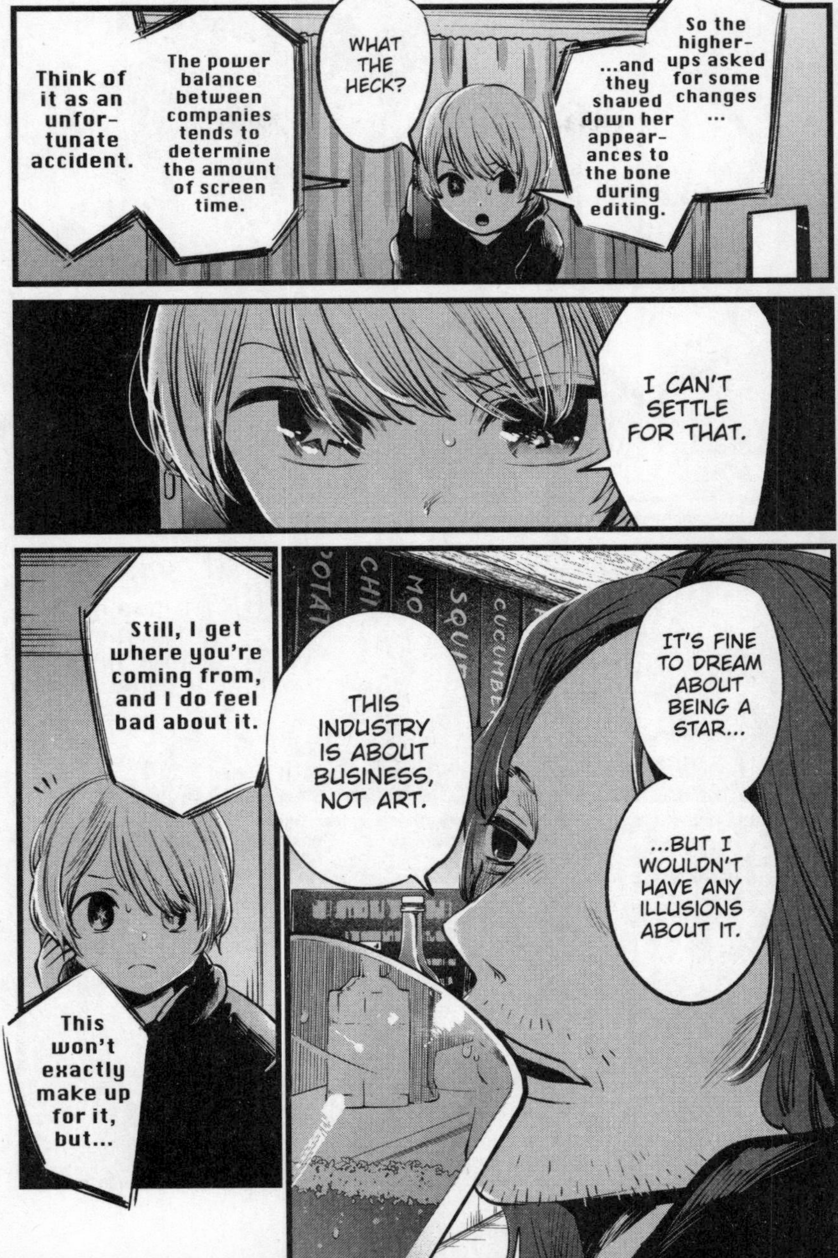
So the higher-ups asked for some changes...
...and they shaved down her appearances to the bone during editing.
WHAT THE HECK?
The power balance between companies tends to determine the amount of screen time.
Think of it as an unfortunate accident.
I CAN'T SETTLE FOR THAT.
IT'S FINE TO DREAM ABOUT BEING A STAR...
...BUT I WOULDN'T HAVE ANY ILLUSIONS ABOUT IT.
THIS INDUSTRY IS ABOUT BUSINESS, NOT ART.
Still, I get where you're coming from, and I do feel bad about it.
This won't exactly make up for it, but...

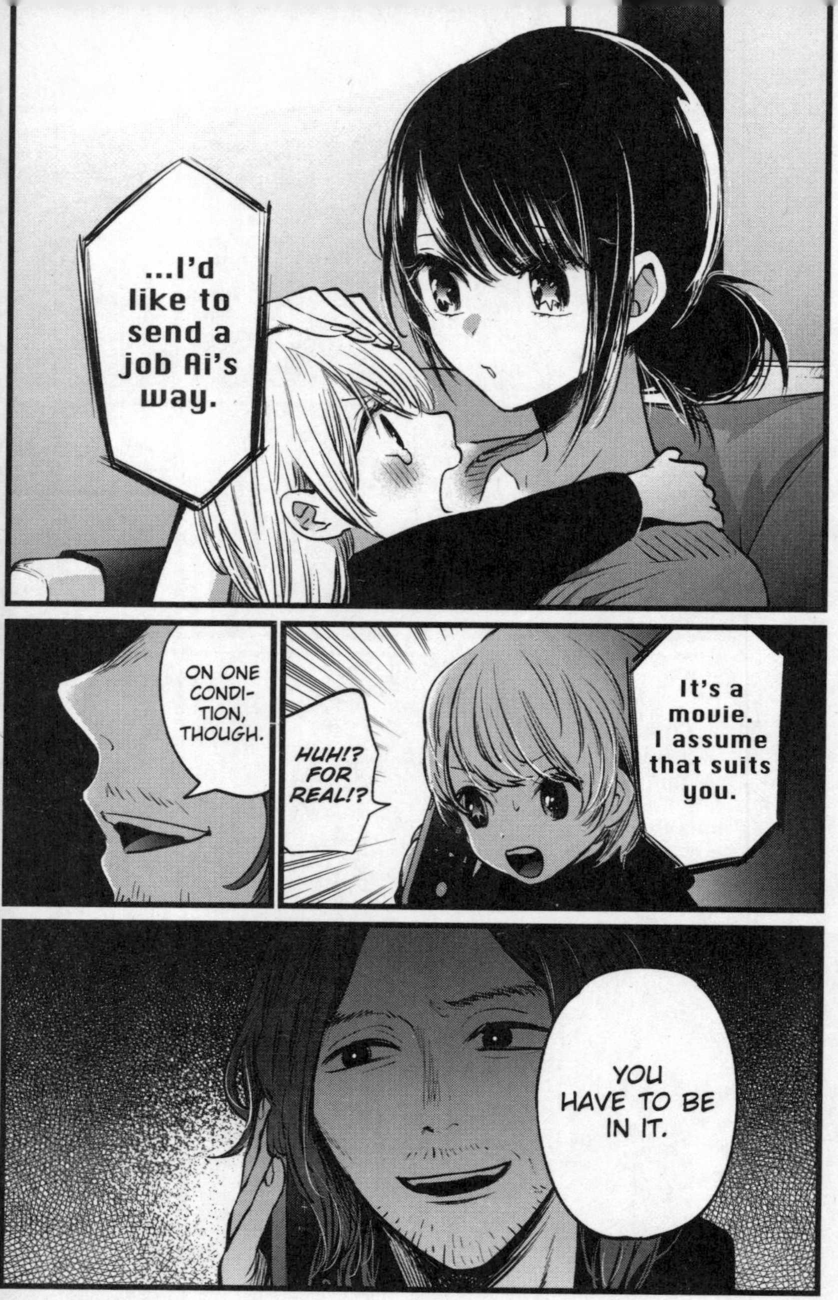
...I'd like to send a job Ai's way.
It's a movie. I assume that suits you.
HUH!? FOR REAL!?
ON ONE CONDITION, THOUGH.
YOU HAVE TO BE IN IT.

【Chapter 6】

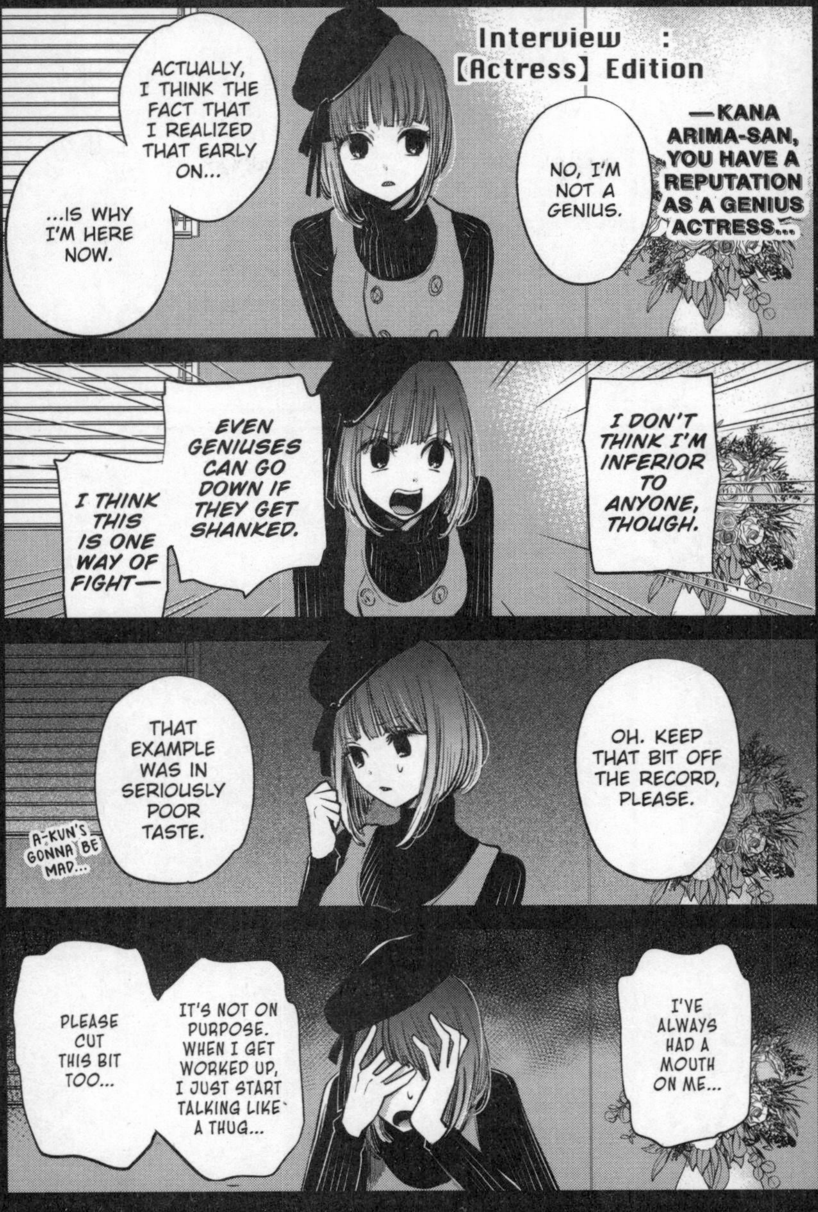
Interview : 【Actress】 Edition
—KANA ARIMA-SAN, YOU HAVE A REPUTATION AS A GENIUS ACTRESS...
NO, I'M NOT A GENIUS.
ACTUALLY, I THINK THE FACT THAT I REALIZED THAT EARLY ON...
...IS WHY I'M HERE NOW.
I DON'T THINK I'M INFERIOR TO ANYONE, THOUGH.
EVEN GENIUSES CAN GO DOWN IF THEY GET SHANKED.
I THINK THIS IS ONE WAY OF FIGHT—
OH. KEEP THAT BIT OFF THE RECORD, PLEASE.
THAT EXAMPLE WAS IN SERIOUSLY POOR TASTE.
A-KUN'S GONNA BE MAD...
I'VE ALWAYS HAD A MOUTH ON ME...
IT'S NOT ON PURPOSE. WHEN I GET WORKED UP, I JUST START TALKING LIKE A THUG...
PLEASE CUT THIS BIT TOO...

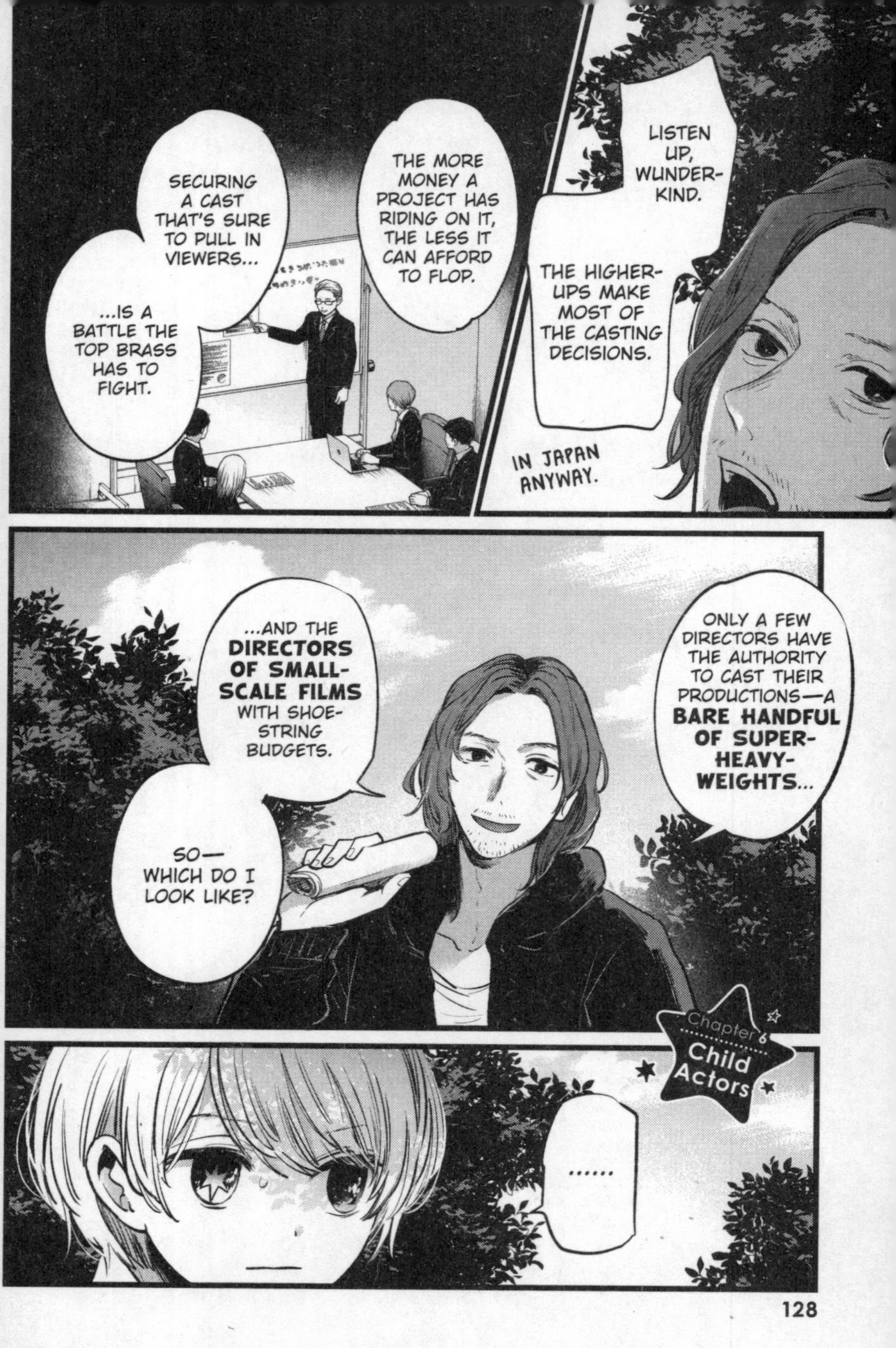
LISTEN UP, WUNDER-KIND.
THE HIGHER-UPS MAKE MOST OF THE CASTING DECISIONS.
IN JAPAN ANYWAY.
THE MORE MONEY A PROJECT HAS RIDING ON IT, THE LESS IT CAN AFFORD TO FLOP.
SECURING A CAST THAT'S SURE TO PULL IN VIEWERS...
...IS A BATTLE THE TOP BRASS HAS TO FIGHT.
ONLY A FEW DIRECTORS HAVE THE AUTHORITY TO CAST THEIR PRODUCTIONS—A **BARE HANDFUL OF SUPER-HEAVY-WEIGHTS**...
...AND THE **DIRECTORS OF SMALL-SCALE FILMS** WITH SHOE-STRING BUDGETS.
SO—WHICH DO I LOOK LIKE?
Chapter 6
Child Actors
......

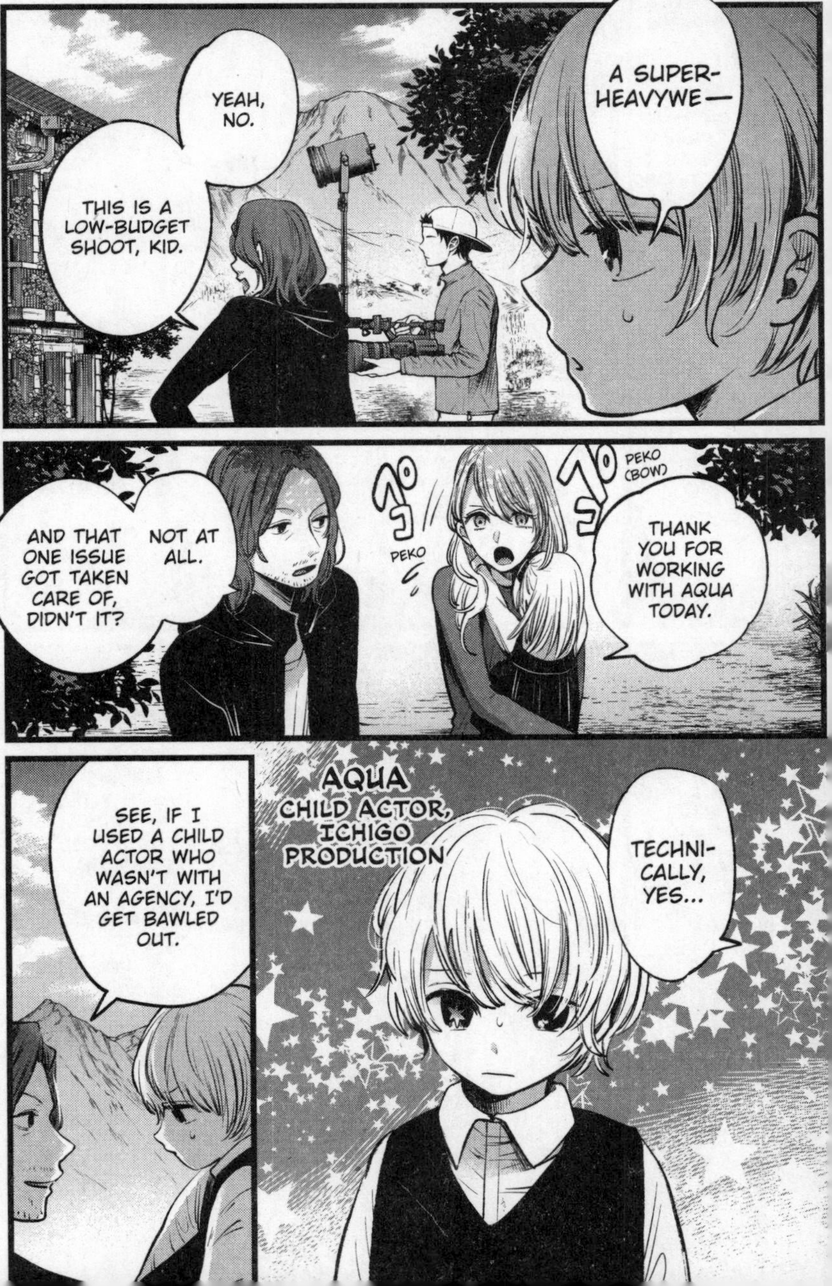
A SUPER-HEAVYWE—
YEAH, NO.
THIS IS A LOW-BUDGET SHOOT, KID.
ペコ
PEKO (BOW)
THANK YOU FOR WORKING WITH AQUA TODAY.
ペコ
PEKO
NOT AT ALL.
AND THAT ONE ISSUE GOT TAKEN CARE OF, DIDN'T IT?
TECHNI-CALLY, YES...
AQUA
CHILD ACTOR, ICHIGO PRODUCTION
SEE, IF I USED A CHILD ACTOR WHO WASN'T WITH AN AGENCY, I'D GET BAWLED OUT.

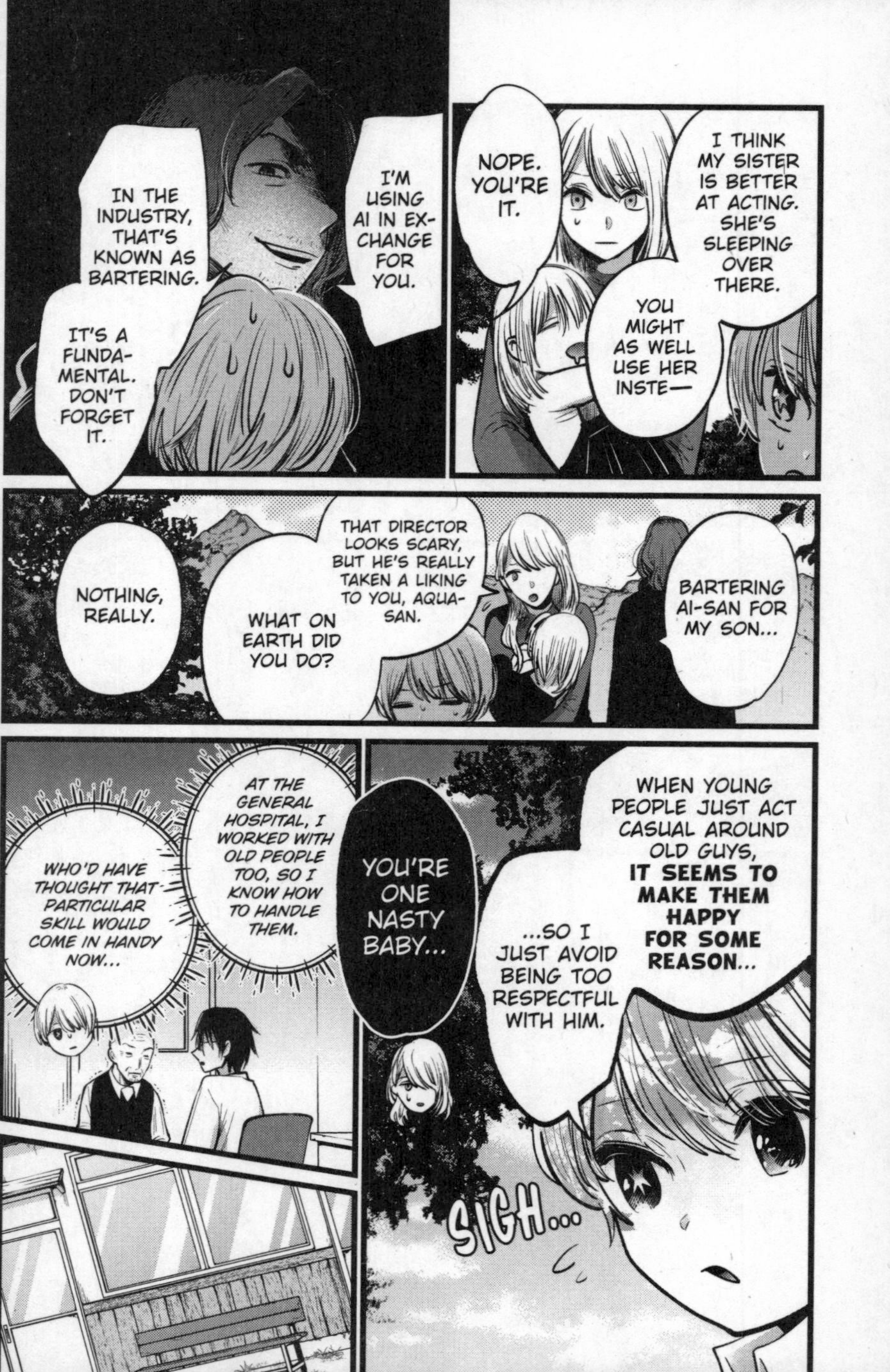
I THINK MY SISTER IS BETTER AT ACTING. SHE'S SLEEPING OVER THERE.
YOU MIGHT AS WELL USE HER INSTE—
NOPE. YOU'RE IT.
I'M USING AI IN EX-CHANGE FOR YOU.
IN THE INDUSTRY, THAT'S KNOWN AS BARTERING.
IT'S A FUNDA-MENTAL. DON'T FORGET IT.
BARTERING AI-SAN FOR MY SON...
THAT DIRECTOR LOOKS SCARY, BUT HE'S REALLY TAKEN A LIKING TO YOU, AQUA-SAN.
WHAT ON EARTH DID YOU DO?
NOTHING, REALLY.
WHEN YOUNG PEOPLE JUST ACT CASUAL AROUND OLD GUYS, **IT SEEMS TO MAKE THEM HAPPY FOR SOME REASON...**
...SO I JUST AVOID BEING TOO RESPECTFUL WITH HIM.
YOU'RE ONE NASTY BABY...
SIGH...
AT THE GENERAL HOSPITAL, I WORKED WITH OLD PEOPLE TOO, SO I KNOW HOW TO HANDLE THEM.
WHO'D HAVE THOUGHT THAT PARTICULAR SKILL WOULD COME IN HANDY NOW...

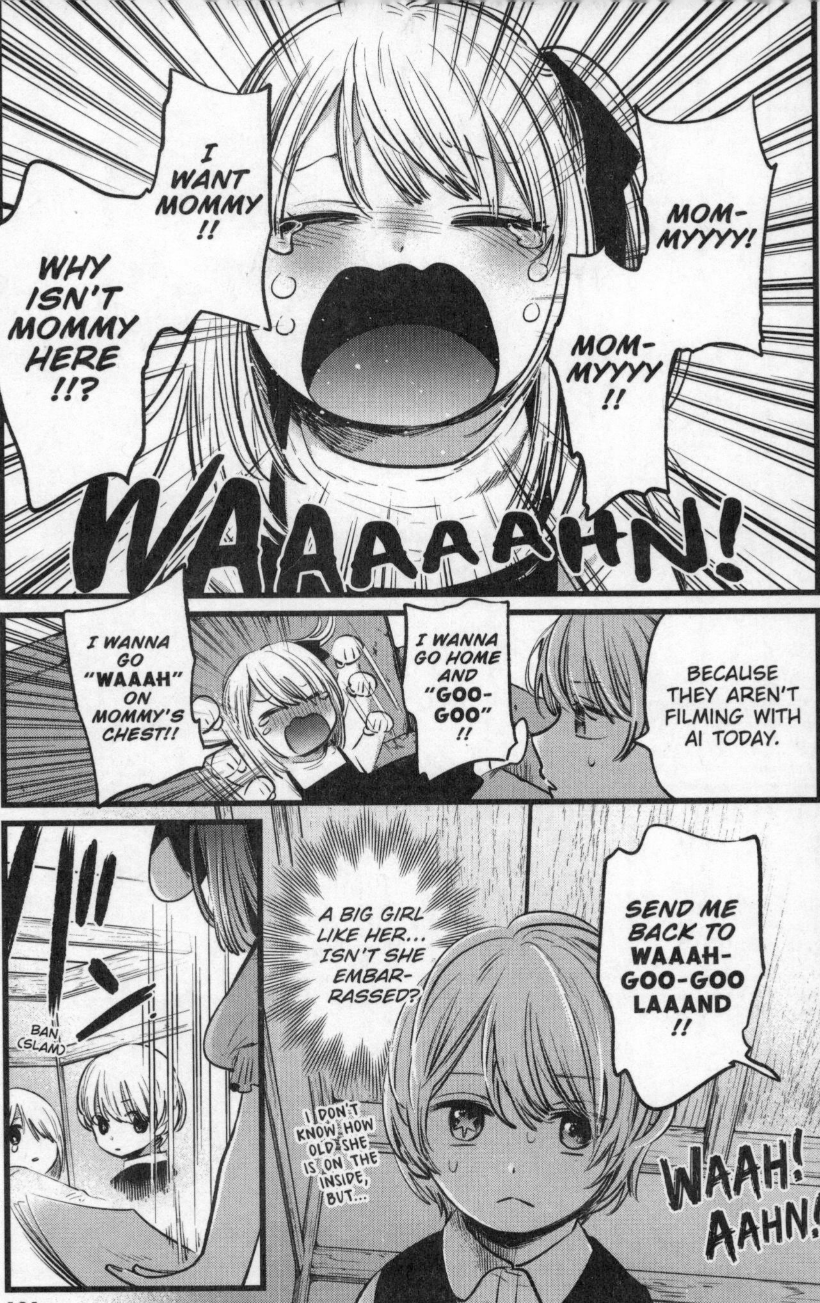
MOM-MYYYY!
I WANT MOMMY!!
MOM-MYYYY!!
WHY ISN'T MOMMY HERE!!?
WAAAAAHN!
BECAUSE THEY AREN'T FILMING WITH AI TODAY.
I WANNA GO HOME AND "GOO-GOO"!!
I WANNA GO "WAAAH" ON MOMMY'S CHEST!!
SEND ME BACK TO WAAAH-GOO-GOO LAAAND!!
A BIG GIRL LIKE HER... ISN'T SHE EMBARRASSED?
WAAH! AAHN!
I DON'T KNOW HOW OLD SHE IS ON THE INSIDE, BUT...
BAN (SLAM)

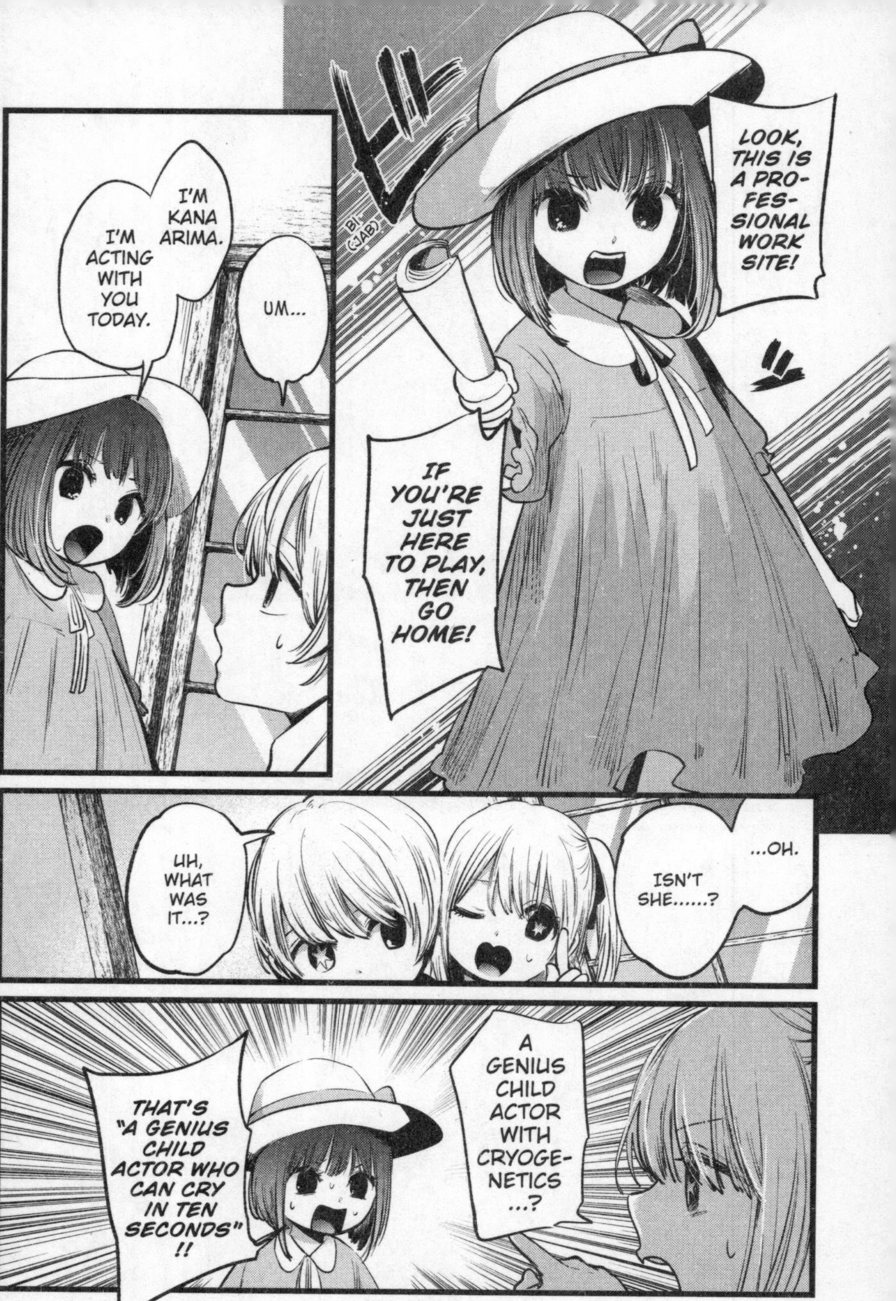

LOOK, THIS IS A PROFESSIONAL WORK SITE!
BI (JAB)
IF YOU'RE JUST HERE TO PLAY, THEN GO HOME!
UM...
I'M KANA ARIMA. I'M ACTING WITH YOU TODAY.
...OH. ISN'T SHE......?
UH, WHAT WAS IT...?
A GENIUS CHILD ACTOR WITH CRYOGENETICS ...?
THAT'S "A GENIUS CHILD ACTOR WHO CAN CRY IN TEN SECONDS"!!

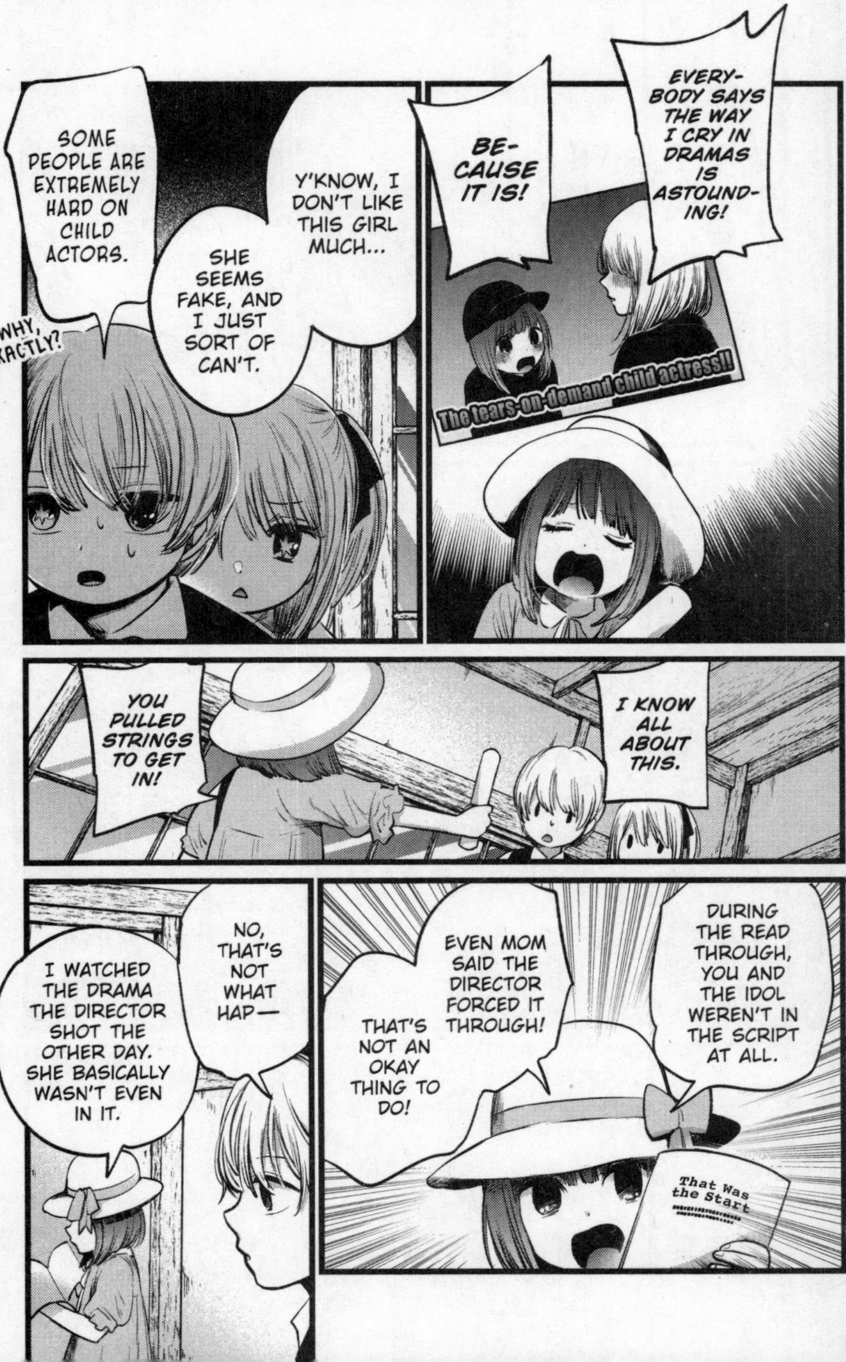
EVERYBODY SAYS THE WAY I CRY IN DRAMAS IS ASTOUNDING!
BECAUSE IT IS!
The tears-on-demand child actress!!
Y'KNOW, I DON'T LIKE THIS GIRL MUCH...
SHE SEEMS FAKE, AND I JUST SORT OF CAN'T.
SOME PEOPLE ARE EXTREMELY HARD ON CHILD ACTORS.
WHY, EXACTLY?
I KNOW ALL ABOUT THIS.
YOU PULLED STRINGS TO GET IN!
DURING THE READ THROUGH, YOU AND THE IDOL WEREN'T IN THE SCRIPT AT ALL.
EVEN MOM SAID THE DIRECTOR FORCED IT THROUGH!
THAT'S NOT AN OKAY THING TO DO!
That Was the Start
NO, THAT'S NOT WHAT HAP—
I WATCHED THE DRAMA THE DIRECTOR SHOT THE OTHER DAY. SHE BASICALLY WASN'T EVEN IN IT.

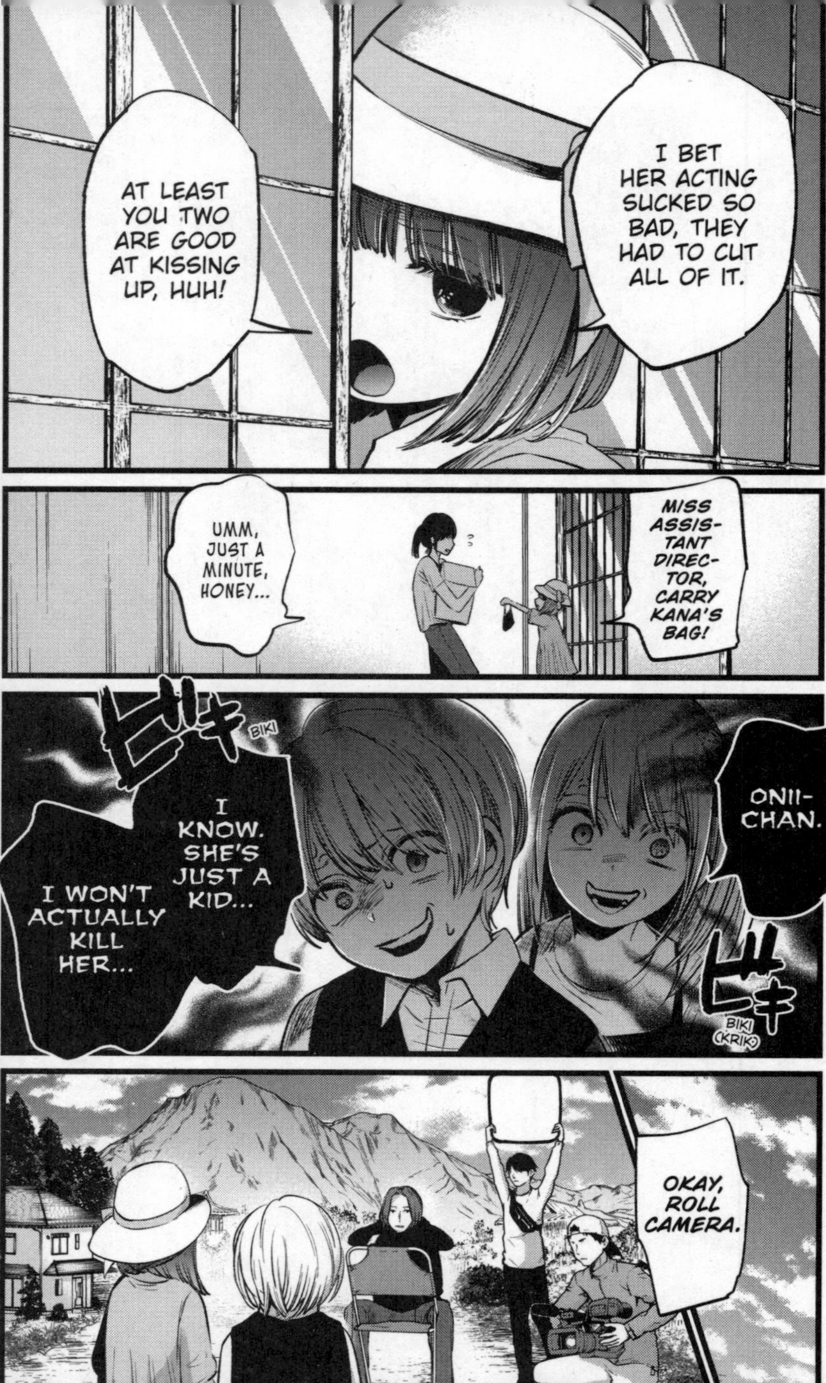
I BET HER ACTING SUCKED SO BAD, THEY HAD TO CUT ALL OF IT.
AT LEAST YOU TWO ARE GOOD AT KISSING UP, HUH!
MISS ASSISTANT DIRECTOR, CARRY KANA'S BAG!
UMM, JUST A MINUTE, HONEY...
ONII-CHAN.
BIKI (KRIK)
I KNOW. SHE'S JUST A KID...
I WON'T ACTUALLY KILL HER...
BIKI
OKAY, ROLL CAMERA.

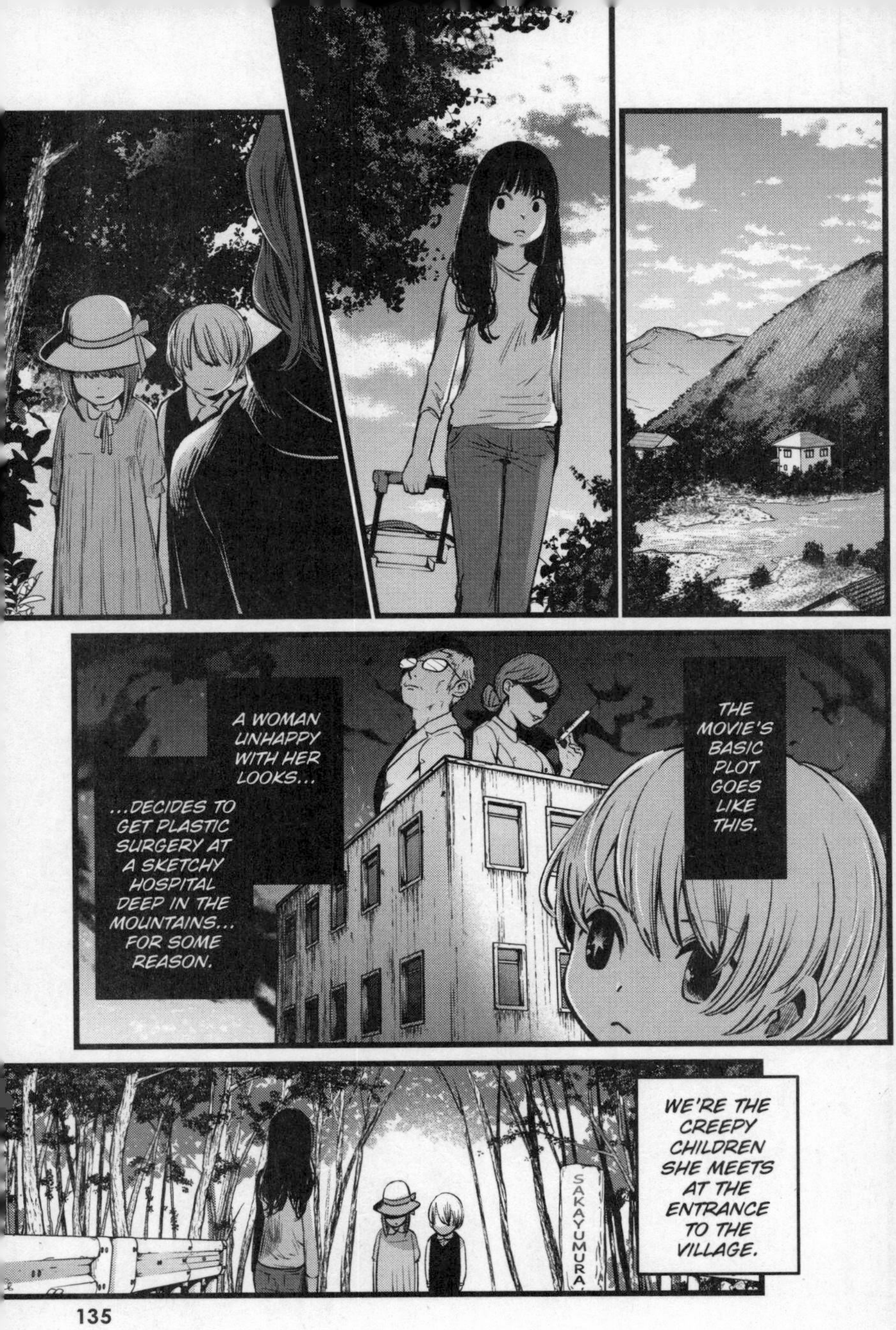
THE MOVIE'S BASIC PLOT GOES LIKE THIS.
A WOMAN UNHAPPY WITH HER LOOKS...
...DECIDES TO GET PLASTIC SURGERY AT A SKETCHY HOSPITAL DEEP IN THE MOUNTAINS... FOR SOME REASON.
WE'RE THE CREEPY CHILDREN SHE MEETS AT THE ENTRANCE TO THE VILLAGE.
SAKAYUMURA

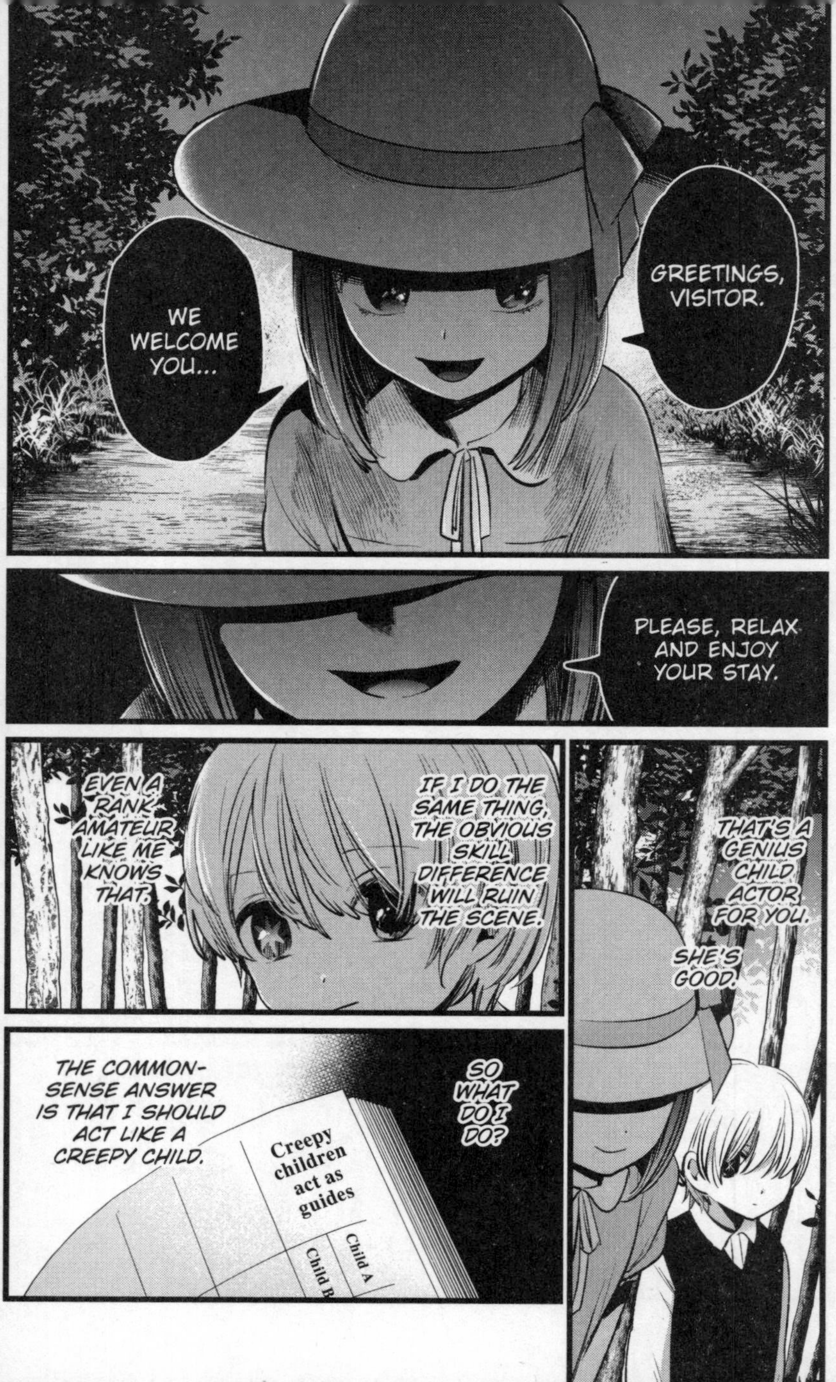
GREETINGS, VISITOR.
WE WELCOME YOU...
PLEASE, RELAX AND ENJOY YOUR STAY.
THAT'S A GENIUS CHILD ACTOR FOR YOU.
SHE'S GOOD.
IF I DO THE SAME THING, THE OBVIOUS SKILL DIFFERENCE WILL RUIN THE SCENE.
EVEN A RANK AMATEUR LIKE ME KNOWS THAT.
SO WHAT DO I DO?
THE COMMON-SENSE ANSWER IS THAT I SHOULD ACT LIKE A CREEPY CHILD.
Creepy children act as guides
Child A
Child B

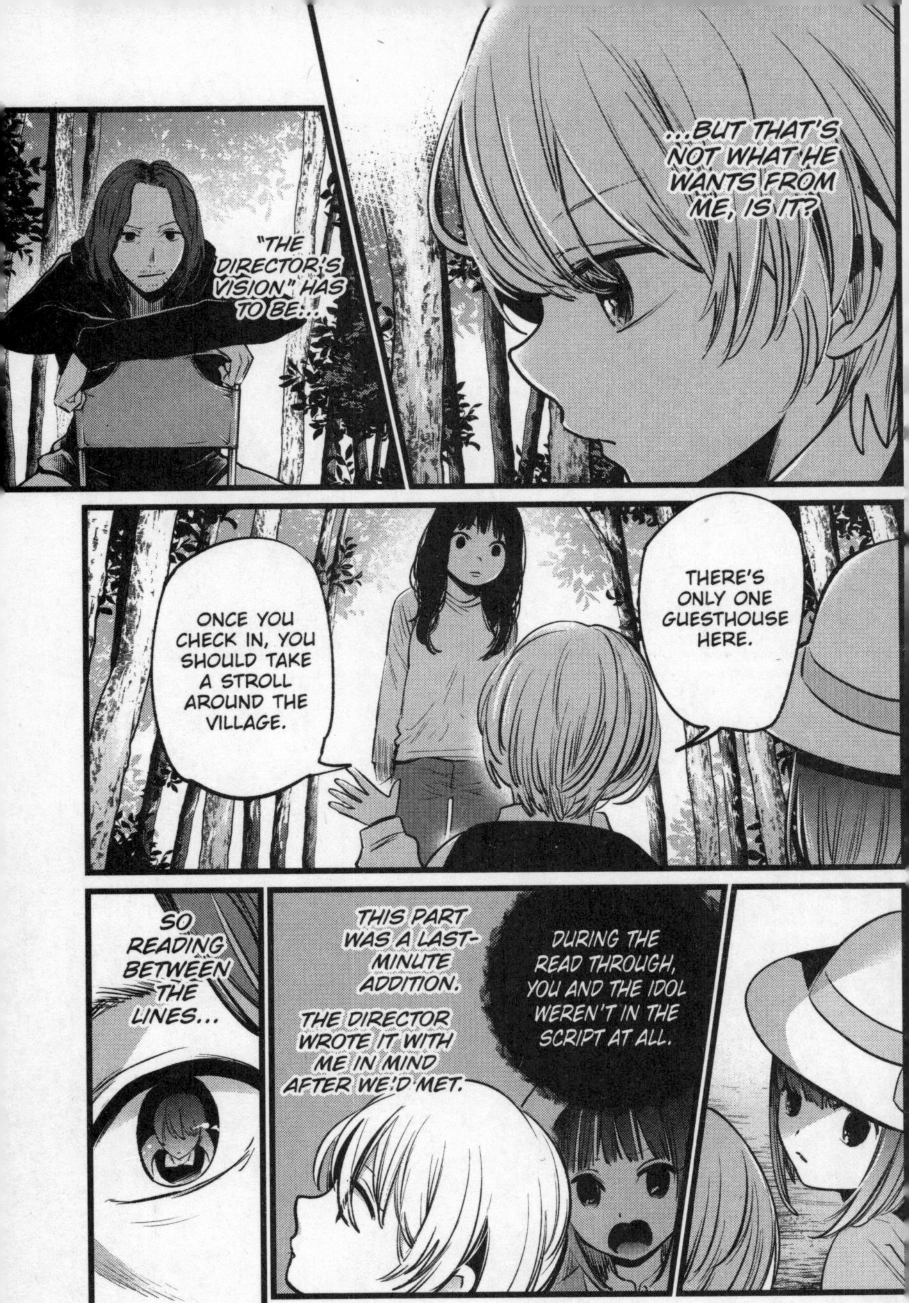
...BUT THAT'S NOT WHAT HE WANTS FROM ME, IS IT?
"THE DIRECTOR'S VISION" HAS TO BE...
THERE'S ONLY ONE GUESTHOUSE HERE.
ONCE YOU CHECK IN, YOU SHOULD TAKE A STROLL AROUND THE VILLAGE.
DURING THE READ THROUGH, YOU AND THE IDOL WEREN'T IN THE SCRIPT AT ALL.
THIS PART WAS A LAST-MINUTE ADDITION.
THE DIRECTOR WROTE IT WITH ME IN MIND AFTER WE'D MET.
SO READING BETWEEN THE LINES...

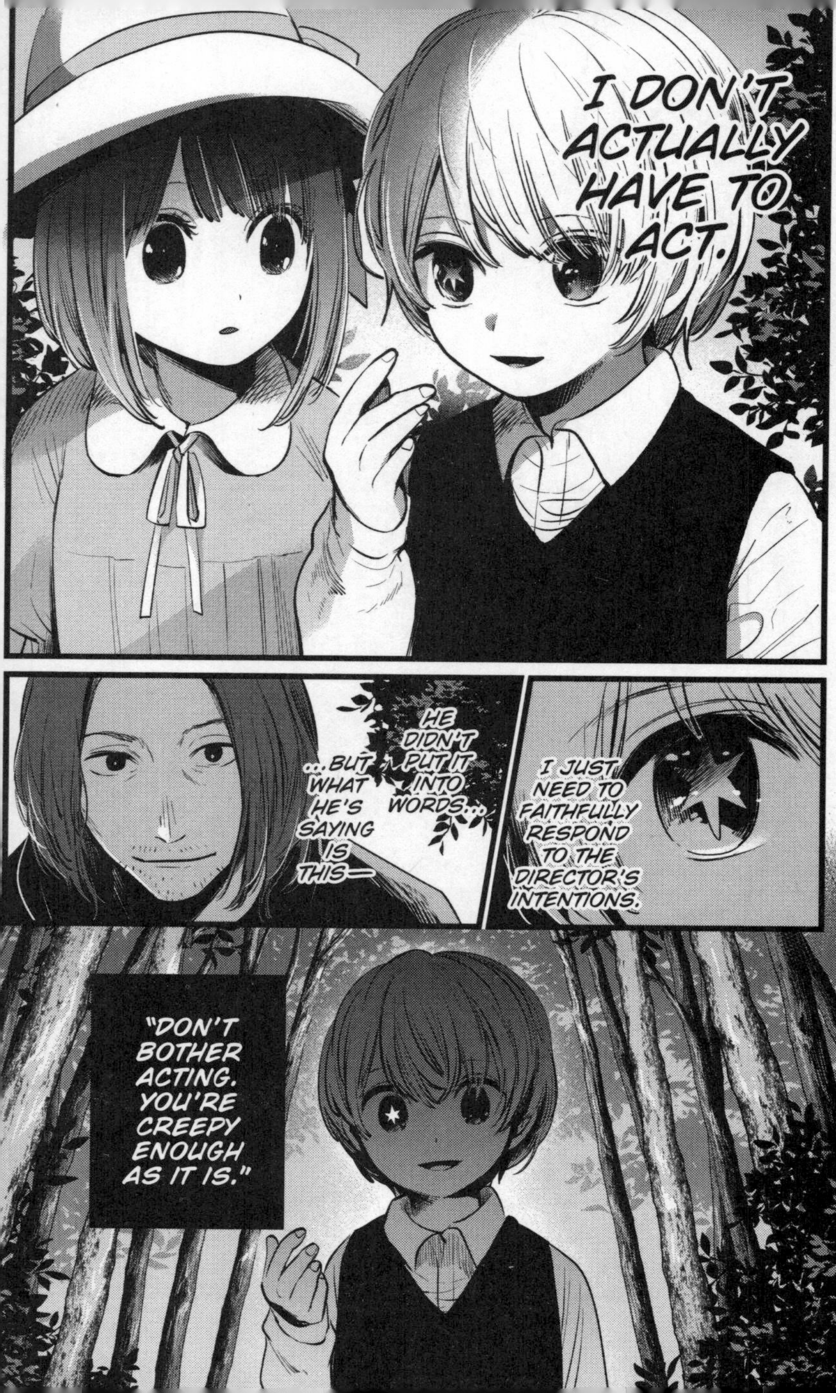
I DON'T ACTUALLY HAVE TO ACT.
I JUST NEED TO FAITHFULLY RESPOND TO THE DIRECTOR'S INTENTIONS.
HE DIDN'T PUT IT INTO WORDS...
...BUT WHAT HE'S SAYING IS THIS—
"DON'T BOTHER ACTING. YOU'RE CREEPY ENOUGH AS IT IS."

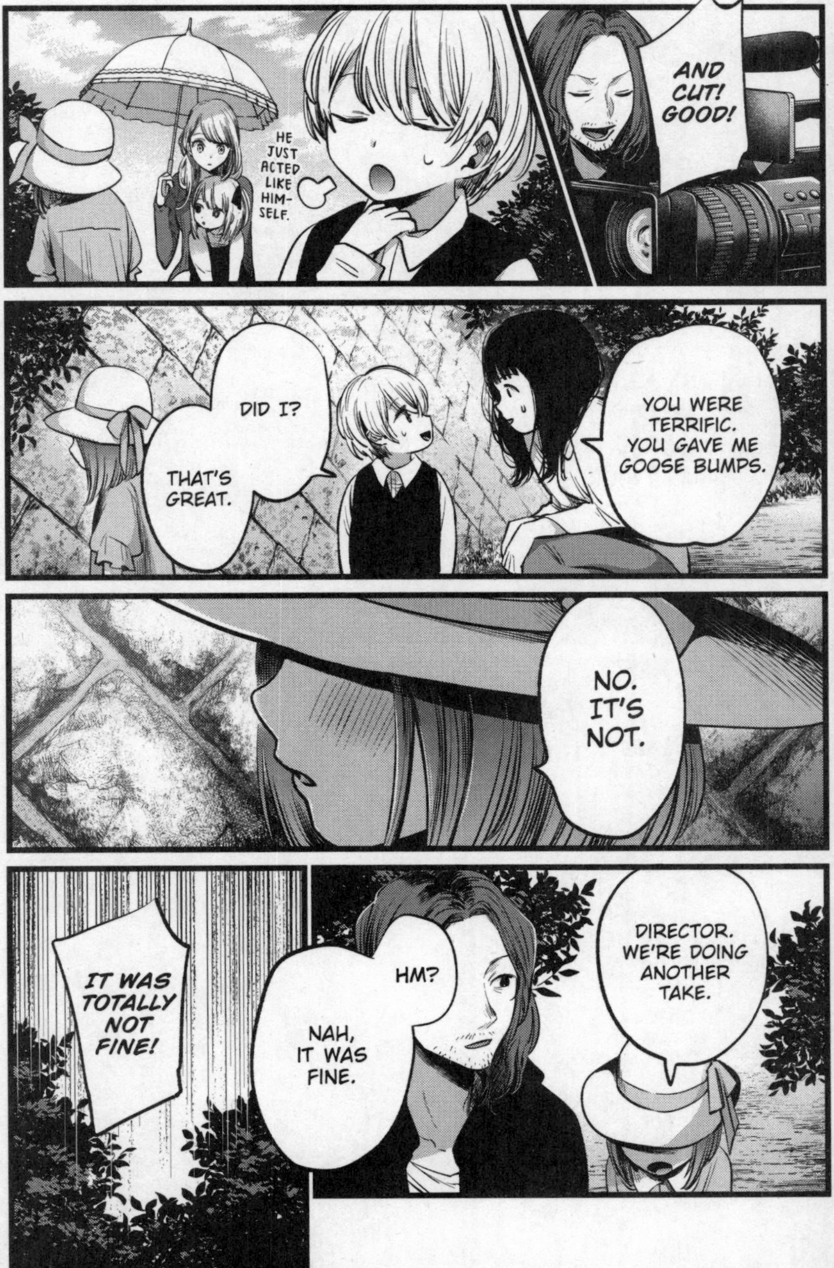
AND CUT! GOOD!
HE JUST ACTED LIKE HIM-SELF.
YOU WERE TERRIFIC. YOU GAVE ME GOOSE BUMPS.
DID I? THAT'S GREAT.
NO. IT'S NOT.
DIRECTOR. WE'RE DOING ANOTHER TAKE.
HM? NAH, IT WAS FINE.
IT WAS TOTALLY NOT FINE!

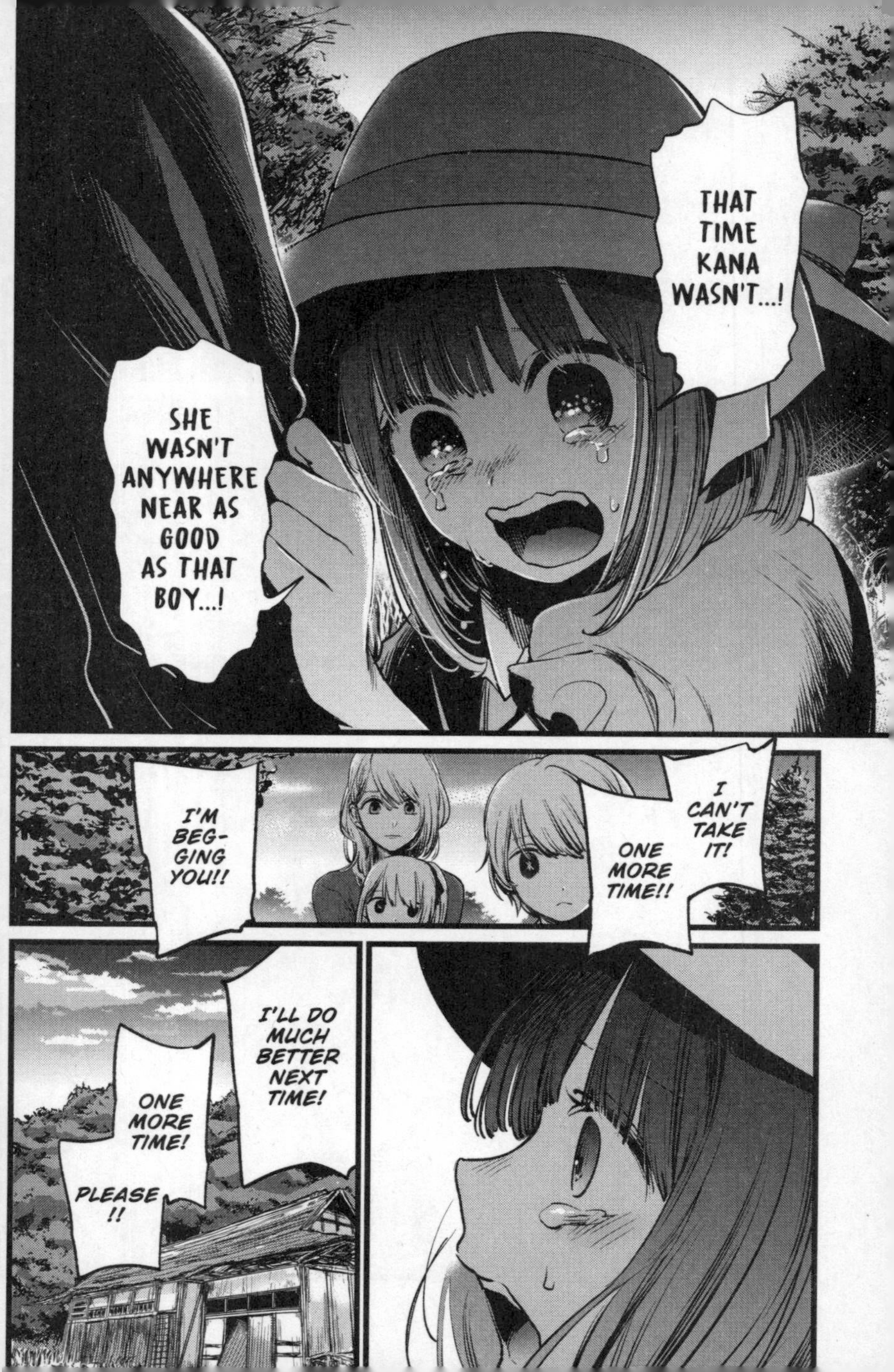
THAT TIME KANA WASN'T...!
SHE WASN'T ANYWHERE NEAR AS GOOD AS THAT BOY...!
I CAN'T TAKE IT!
ONE MORE TIME!!
I'M BEG-GING YOU!!
I'LL DO MUCH BETTER NEXT TIME!
ONE MORE TIME!
PLEASE!!

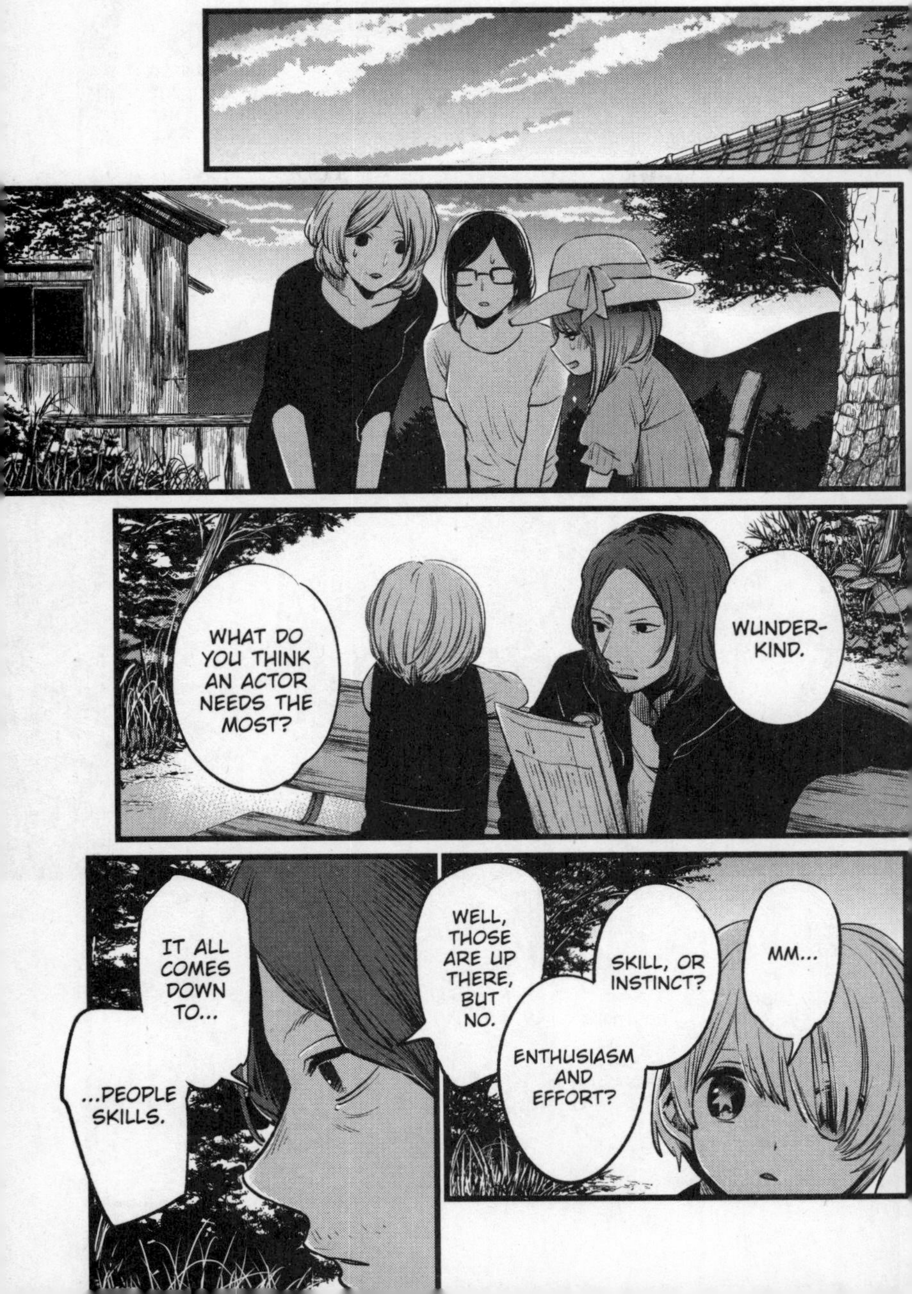
WUNDER-KIND.
WHAT DO YOU THINK AN ACTOR NEEDS THE MOST?
MM...
SKILL, OR INSTINCT?
ENTHUSIASM AND EFFORT?
WELL, THOSE ARE UP THERE, BUT NO.
IT ALL COMES DOWN TO...
...PEOPLE SKILLS.

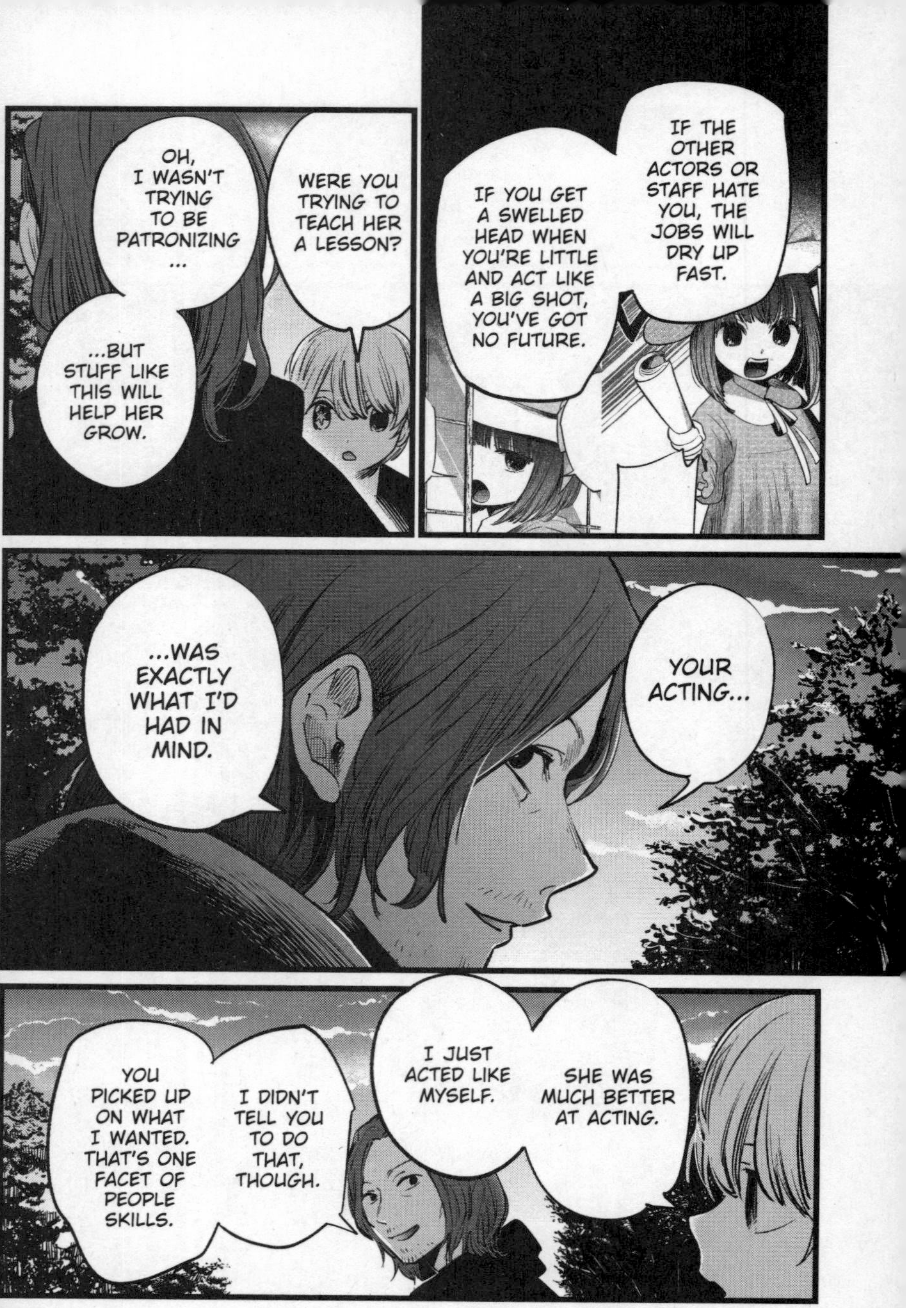
IF THE OTHER ACTORS OR STAFF HATE YOU, THE JOBS WILL DRY UP FAST.
IF YOU GET A SWELLED HEAD WHEN YOU'RE LITTLE AND ACT LIKE A BIG SHOT, YOU'VE GOT NO FUTURE.
WERE YOU TRYING TO TEACH HER A LESSON?
OH, I WASN'T TRYING TO BE PATRONIZING ...
...BUT STUFF LIKE THIS WILL HELP HER GROW.
YOUR ACTING...
...WAS EXACTLY WHAT I'D HAD IN MIND.
SHE WAS MUCH BETTER AT ACTING.
I JUST ACTED LIKE MYSELF.
I DIDN'T TELL YOU TO DO THAT, THOUGH.
YOU PICKED UP ON WHAT I WANTED. THAT'S ONE FACET OF PEOPLE SKILLS.

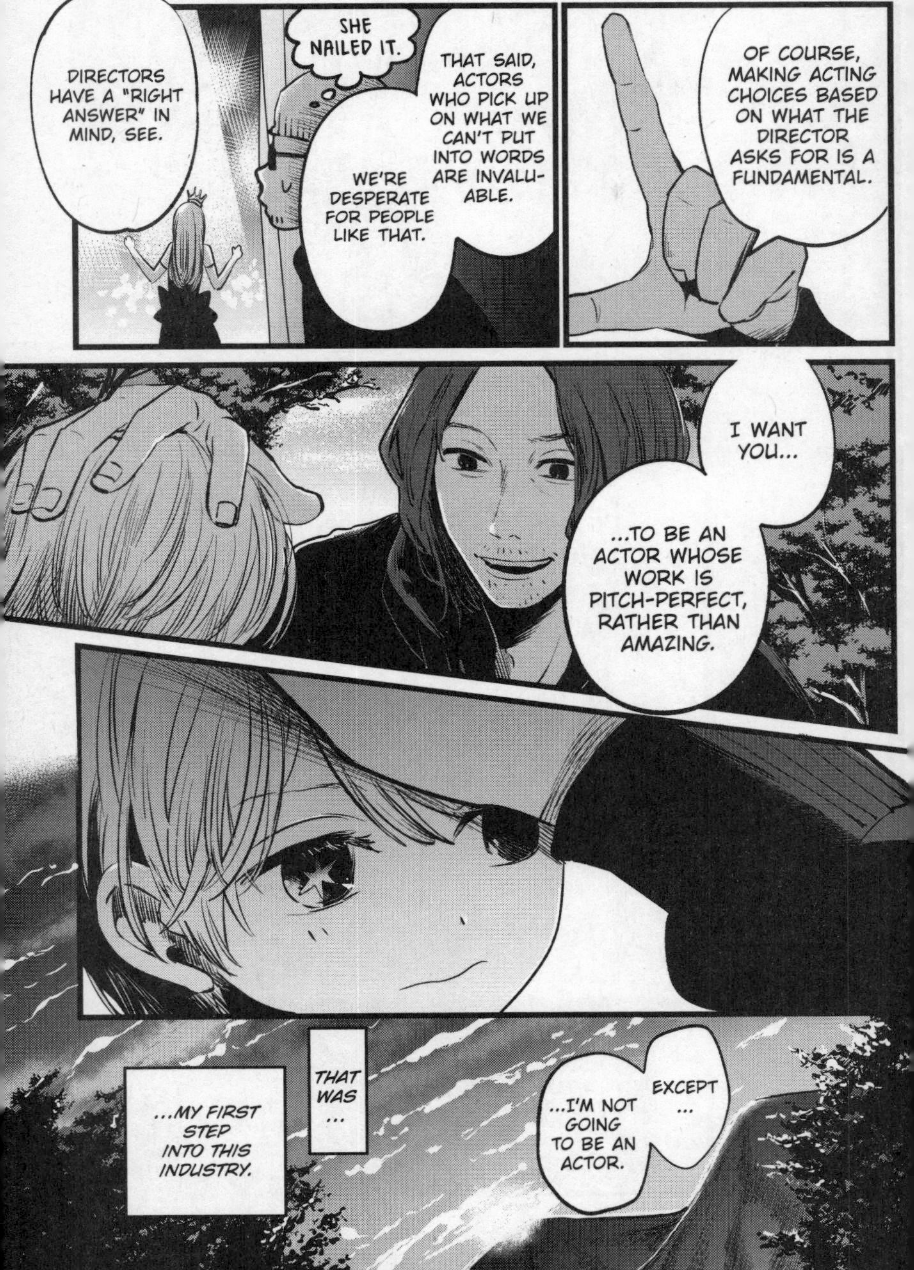
OF COURSE, MAKING ACTING CHOICES BASED ON WHAT THE DIRECTOR ASKS FOR IS A FUNDAMENTAL.
DIRECTORS HAVE A "RIGHT ANSWER" IN MIND, SEE.
SHE NAILED IT.
THAT SAID, ACTORS WHO PICK UP ON WHAT WE CAN'T PUT INTO WORDS ARE INVALUABLE.
WE'RE DESPERATE FOR PEOPLE LIKE THAT.
I WANT YOU...
...TO BE AN ACTOR WHOSE WORK IS PITCH-PERFECT, RATHER THAN AMAZING.
EXCEPT...
...I'M NOT GOING TO BE AN ACTOR.
THAT WAS...
...MY FIRST STEP INTO THIS INDUSTRY.

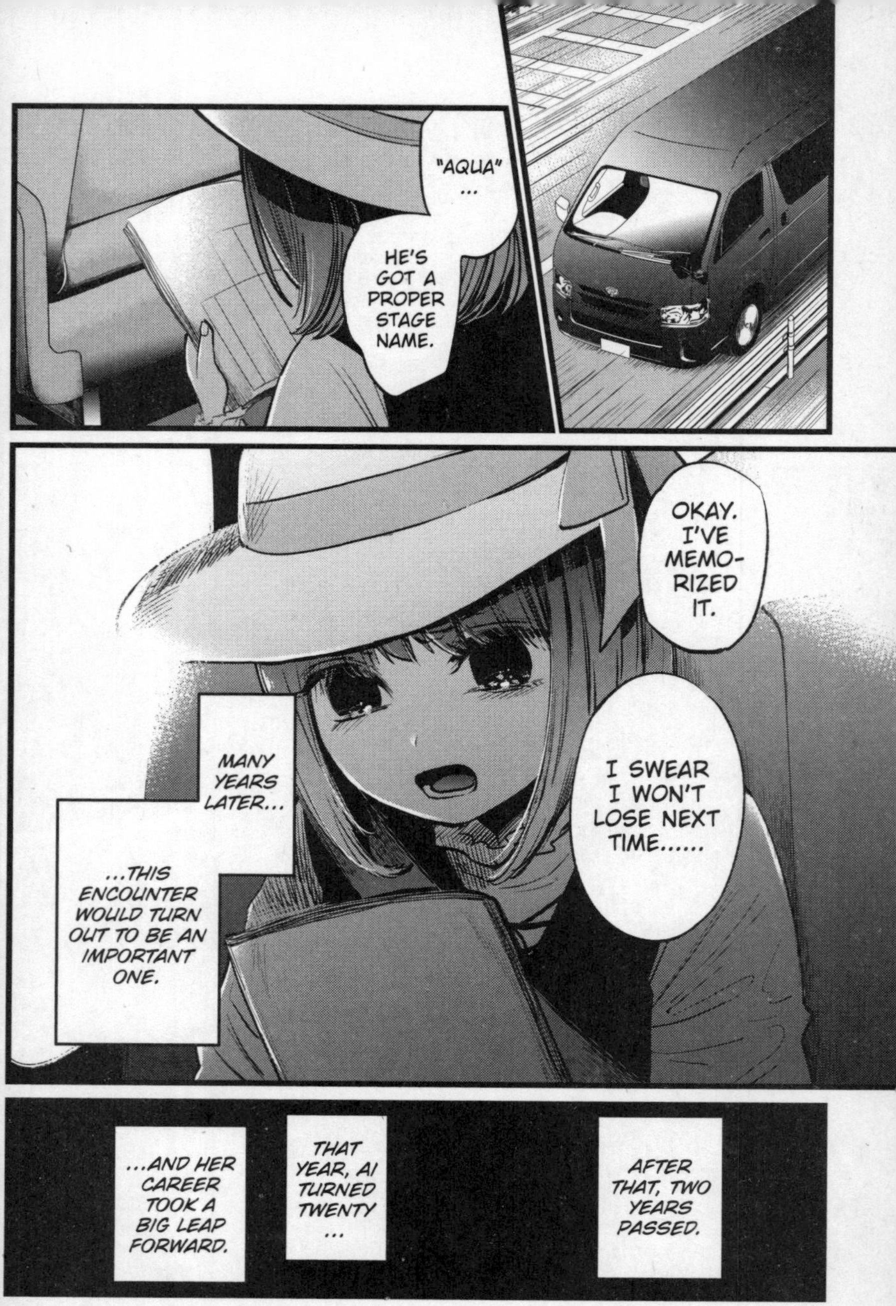
"AQUA" ...
HE'S GOT A PROPER STAGE NAME.
OKAY. I'VE MEMO-RIZED IT.
I SWEAR I WON'T LOSE NEXT TIME......
MANY YEARS LATER...
...THIS ENCOUNTER WOULD TURN OUT TO BE AN IMPORTANT ONE.
AFTER THAT, TWO YEARS PASSED.
THAT YEAR, AI TURNED TWENTY ...
...AND HER CAREER TOOK A BIG LEAP FORWARD.

Interview: [Kindergarten Staff] Edition

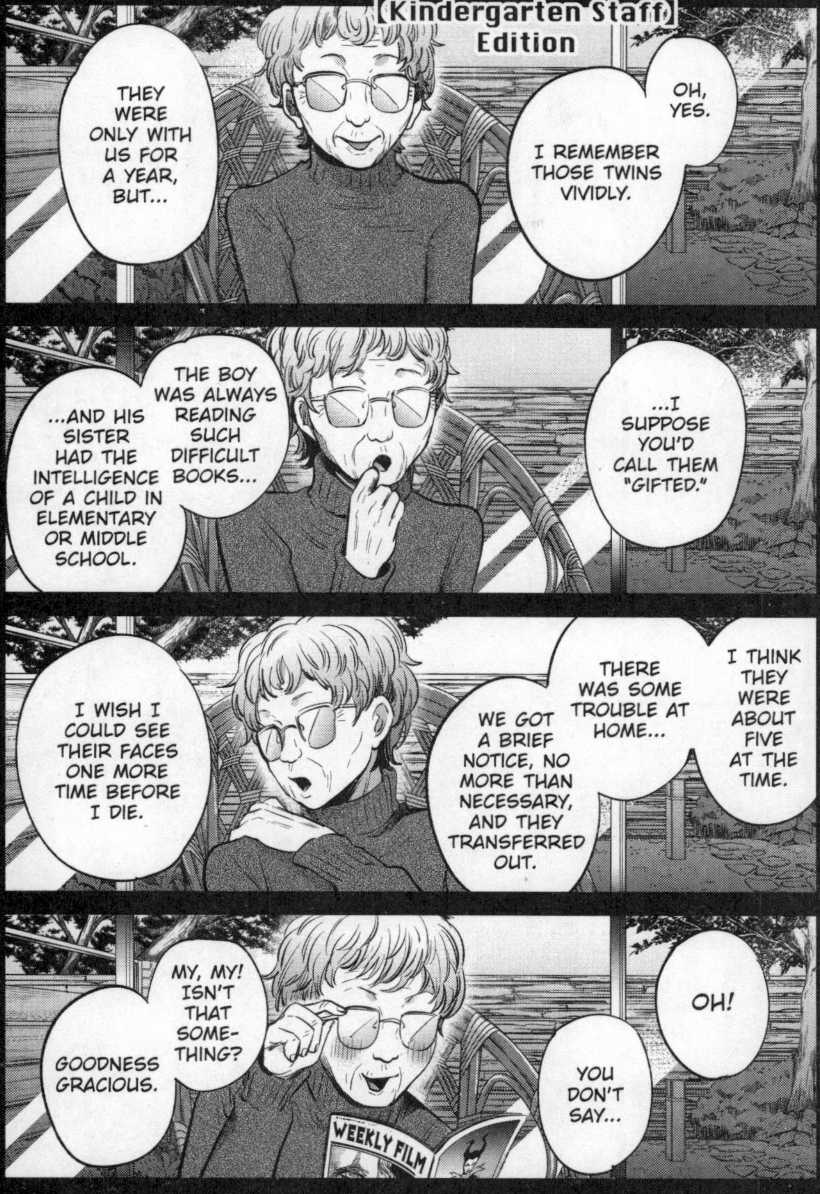
OH, YES.
I REMEMBER THOSE TWINS VIVIDLY.
THEY WERE ONLY WITH US FOR A YEAR, BUT...
...I SUPPOSE YOU'D CALL THEM "GIFTED."
THE BOY WAS ALWAYS READING SUCH DIFFICULT BOOKS...
...AND HIS SISTER HAD THE INTELLIGENCE OF A CHILD IN ELEMENTARY OR MIDDLE SCHOOL.
I THINK THEY WERE ABOUT FIVE AT THE TIME.
THERE WAS SOME TROUBLE AT HOME...
WE GOT A BRIEF NOTICE, NO MORE THAN NECESSARY, AND THEY TRANSFERRED OUT.
I WISH I COULD SEE THEIR FACES ONE MORE TIME BEFORE I DIE.
OH!
YOU DON'T SAY...
MY, MY! ISN'T THAT SOME-THING?
GOODNESS GRACIOUS.
WEEKLY FILM

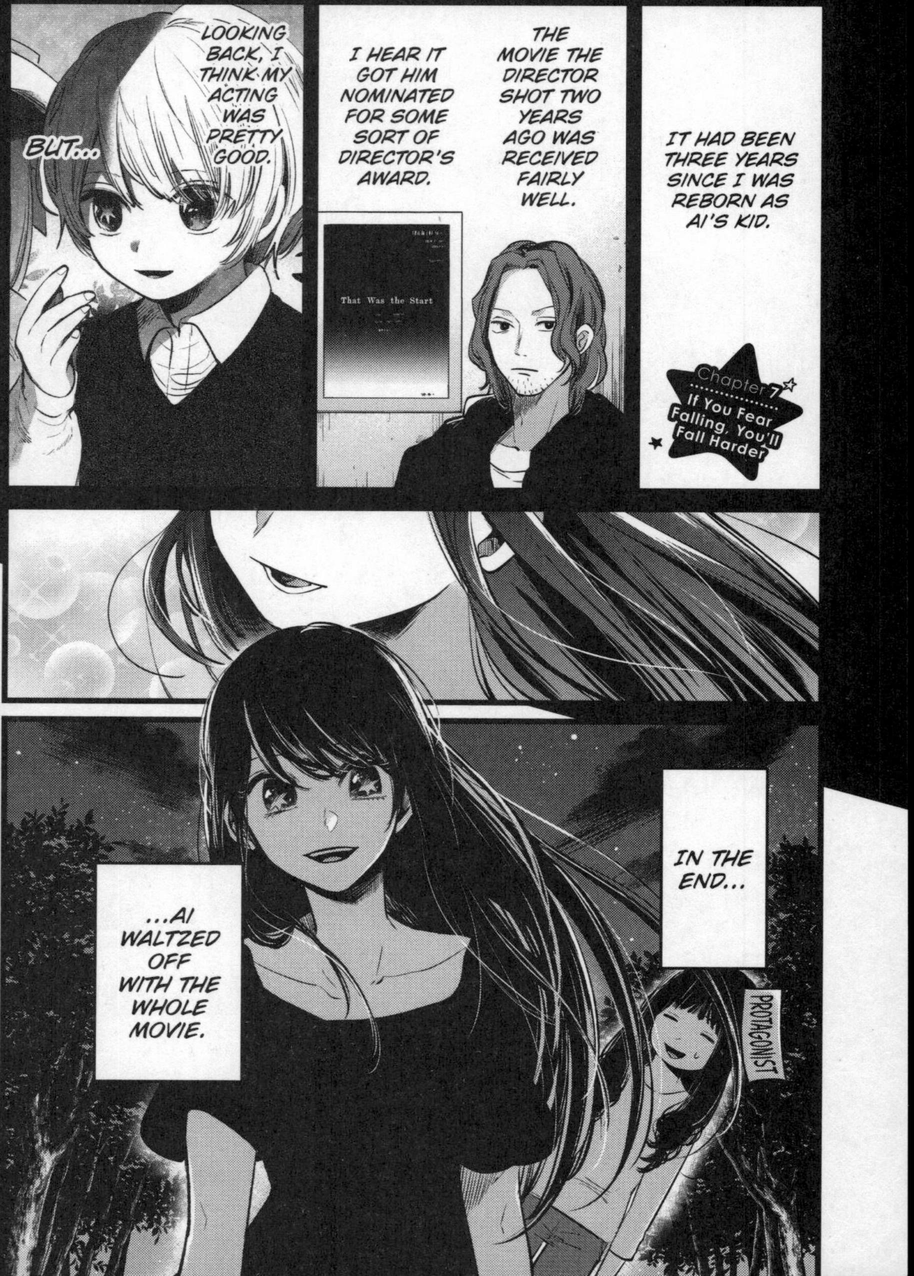
IT HAD BEEN THREE YEARS SINCE I WAS REBORN AS AI'S KID.
Chapter 7
If You Fear Falling, You'll Fall Harder
THE MOVIE THE DIRECTOR SHOT TWO YEARS AGO WAS RECEIVED FAIRLY WELL.
I HEAR IT GOT HIM NOMINATED FOR SOME SORT OF DIRECTOR'S AWARD.
That Was the Start
LOOKING BACK, I THINK MY ACTING WAS PRETTY GOOD.
BUT...
IN THE END...
...AI WALTZED OFF WITH THE WHOLE MOVIE.
PROTAGONIST

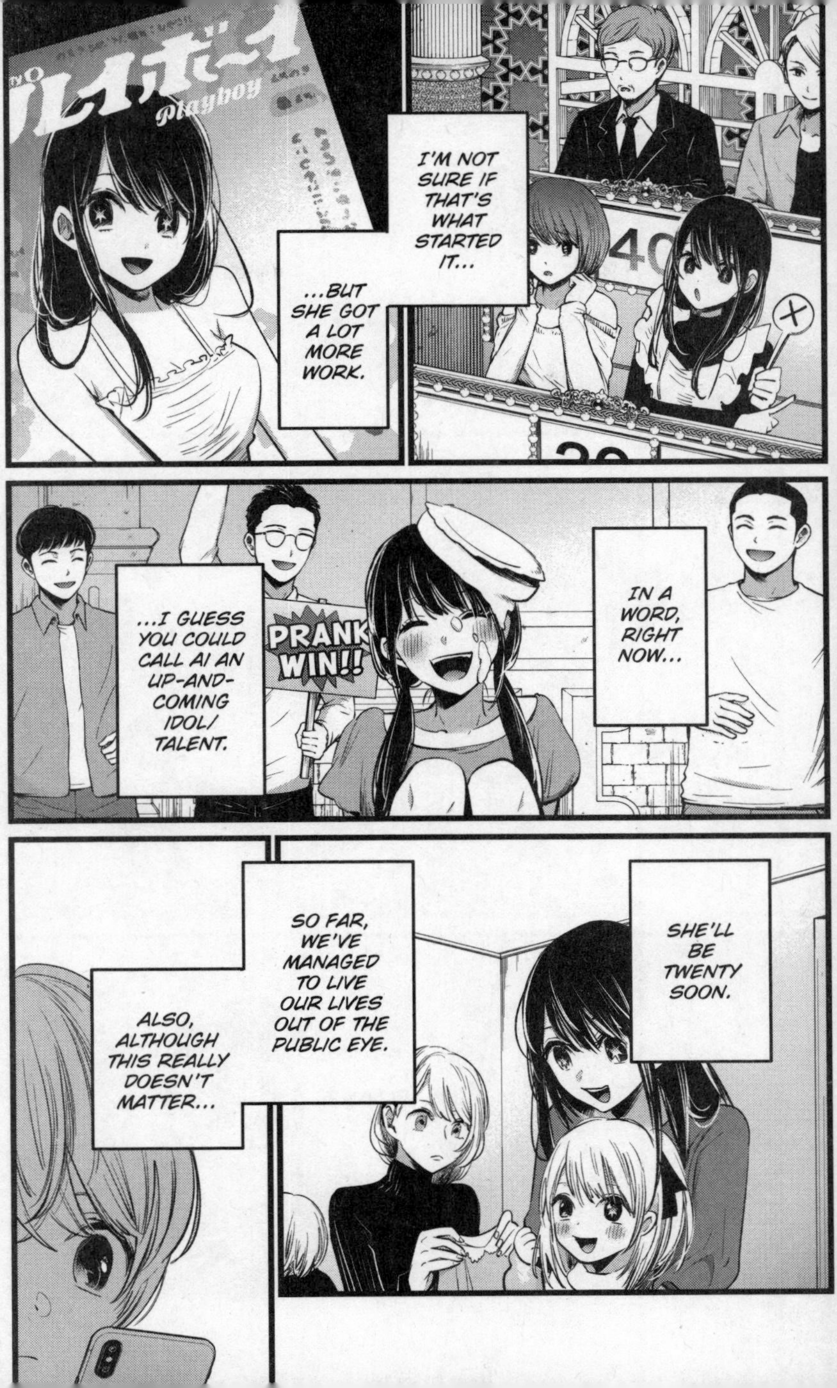
I'M NOT SURE IF THAT'S WHAT STARTED IT...
40
...BUT SHE GOT A LOT MORE WORK.
Playboy
IN A WORD, RIGHT NOW...
...I GUESS YOU COULD CALL AI AN UP-AND-COMING IDOL/TALENT.
PRANK WIN!!
SHE'LL BE TWENTY SOON.
SO FAR, WE'VE MANAGED TO LIVE OUR LIVES OUT OF THE PUBLIC EYE.
ALSO, ALTHOUGH THIS REALLY DOESN'T MATTER...

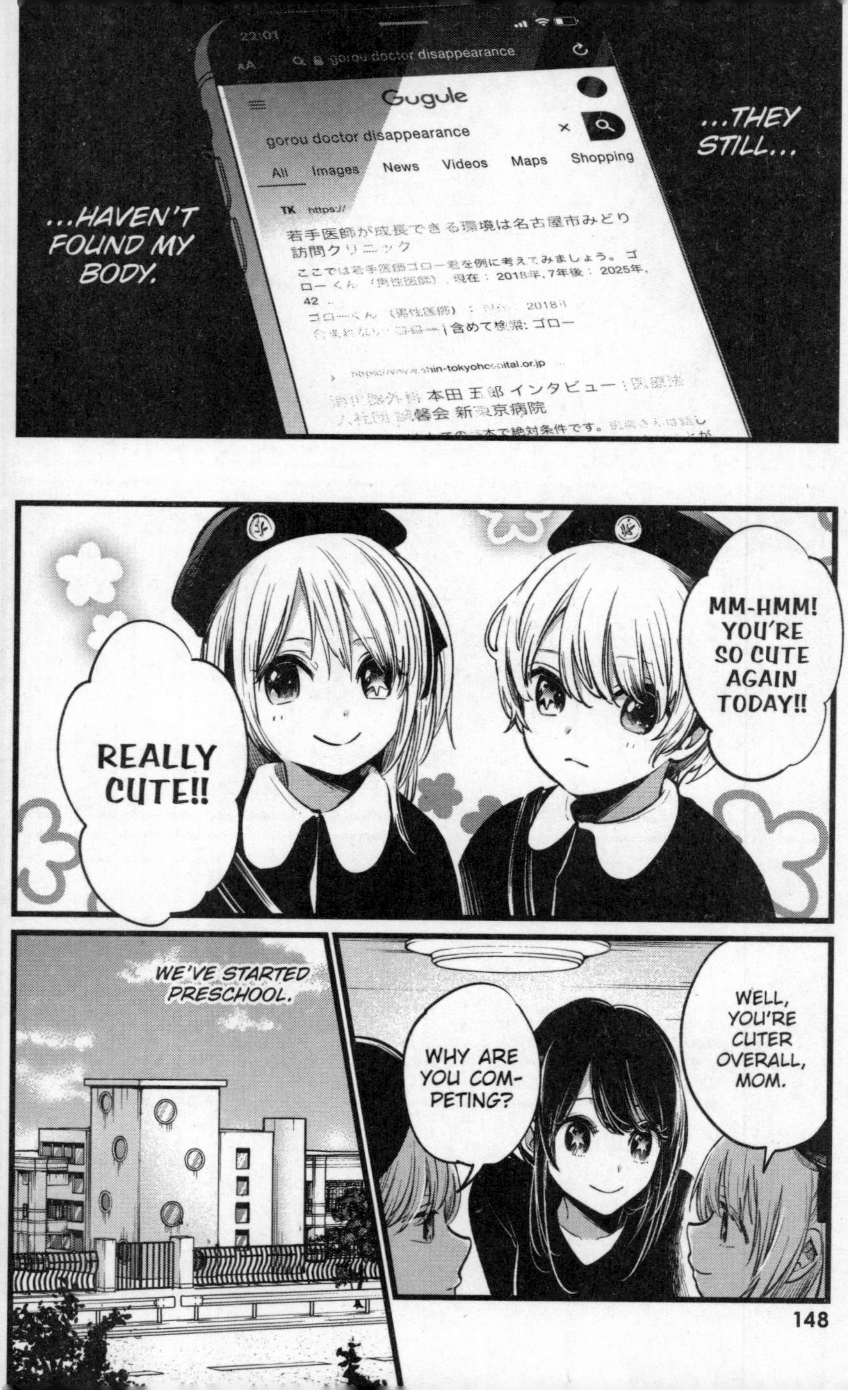
...THEY STILL...
...HAVEN'T FOUND MY BODY.
gorou doctor disappearance
Gugule
gorou doctor disappearance
All Images News Videos Maps Shopping
若手医師が成長できる環境は名古屋市みどり訪問クリニック
本田 王郎 インタビュー
新東京病院
MM-HMM! YOU'RE SO CUTE AGAIN TODAY!!
REALLY CUTE!!
WELL, YOU'RE CUTER OVERALL, MOM.
WHY ARE YOU COM-PETING?
WE'VE STARTED PRESCHOOL.

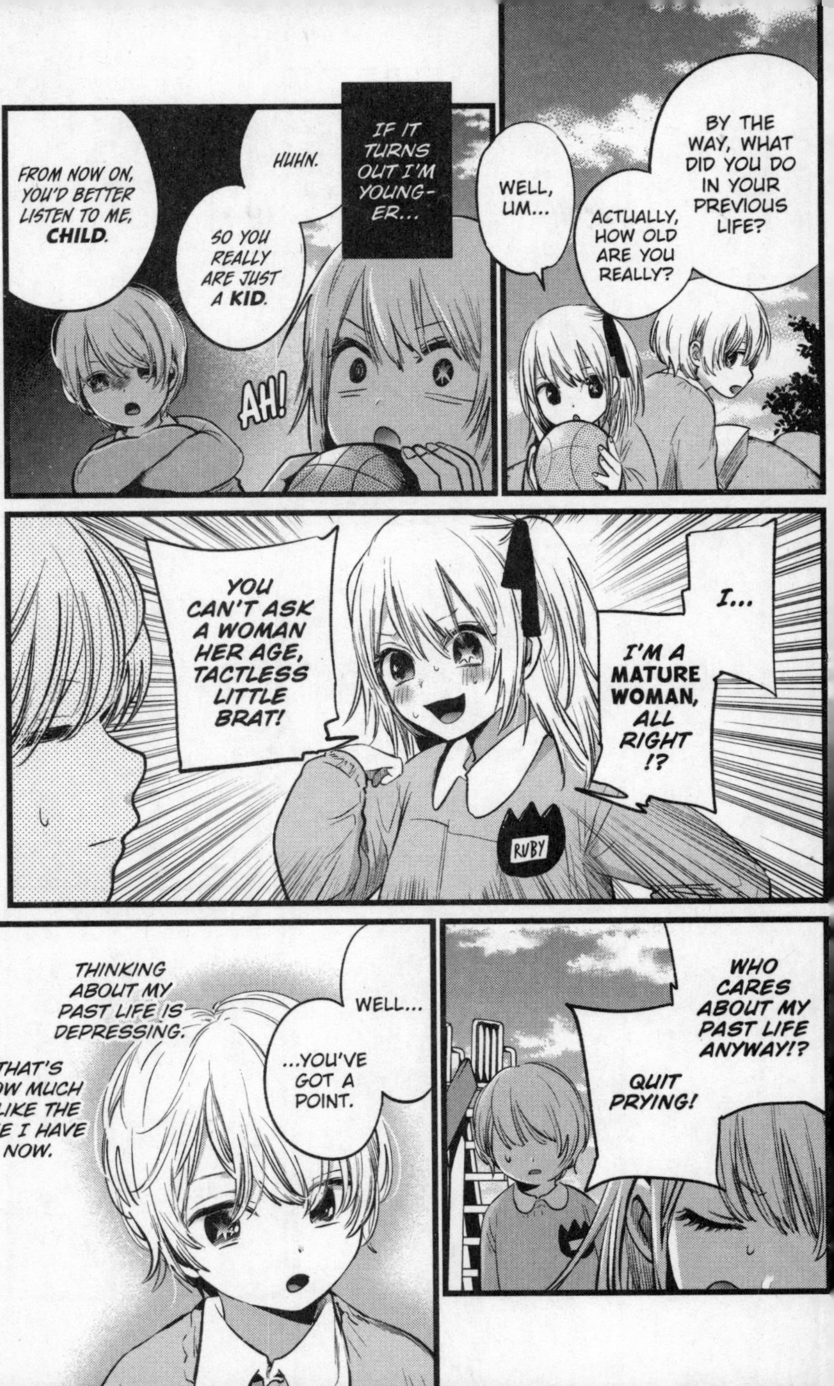

BY THE WAY, WHAT DID YOU DO IN YOUR PREVIOUS LIFE?
ACTUALLY, HOW OLD ARE YOU REALLY?
WELL, UM...
IF IT TURNS OUT I'M YOUNG-ER...
HUHN.
SO YOU REALLY ARE JUST A KID.
AH!
FROM NOW ON, YOU'D BETTER LISTEN TO ME, CHILD.
I...
I'M A MATURE WOMAN, ALL RIGHT!?
YOU CAN'T ASK A WOMAN HER AGE, TACTLESS LITTLE BRAT!
RUBY
WHO CARES ABOUT MY PAST LIFE ANYWAY!?
QUIT PRYING!
WELL...
...YOU'VE GOT A POINT.
THINKING ABOUT MY PAST LIFE IS DEPRESSING.
THAT'S HOW MUCH I LIKE THE LIFE I HAVE NOW.

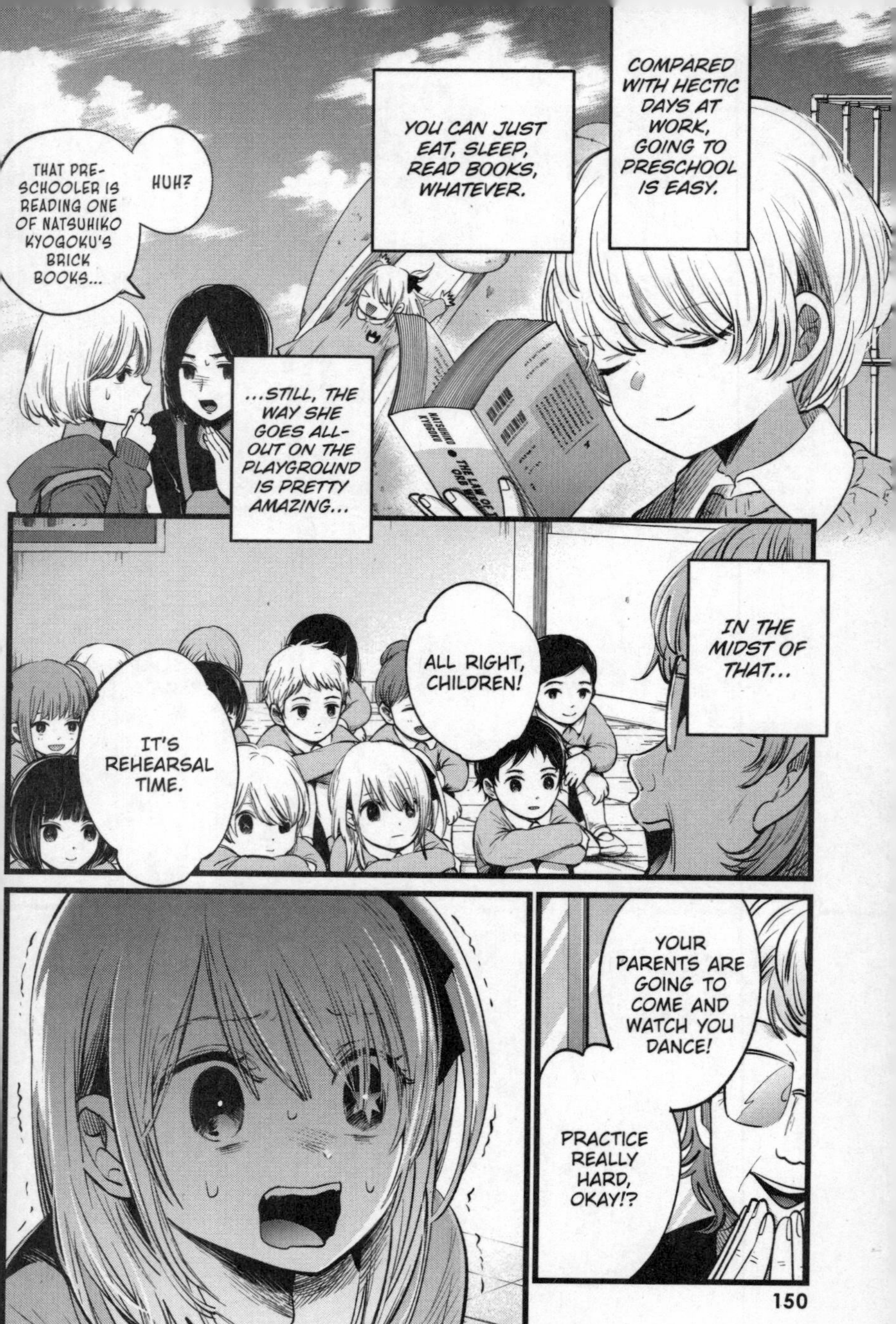
COMPARED WITH HECTIC DAYS AT WORK, GOING TO PRESCHOOL IS EASY.
YOU CAN JUST EAT, SLEEP, READ BOOKS, WHATEVER.
HUH?
THAT PRE-SCHOOLER IS READING ONE OF NATSUHIKO KYOGOKU'S BRICK BOOKS...
...STILL, THE WAY SHE GOES ALL-OUT ON THE PLAYGROUND IS PRETTY AMAZING...
IN THE MIDST OF THAT...
ALL RIGHT, CHILDREN!
IT'S REHEARSAL TIME.
YOUR PARENTS ARE GOING TO COME AND WATCH YOU DANCE!
PRACTICE REALLY HARD, OKAY!?

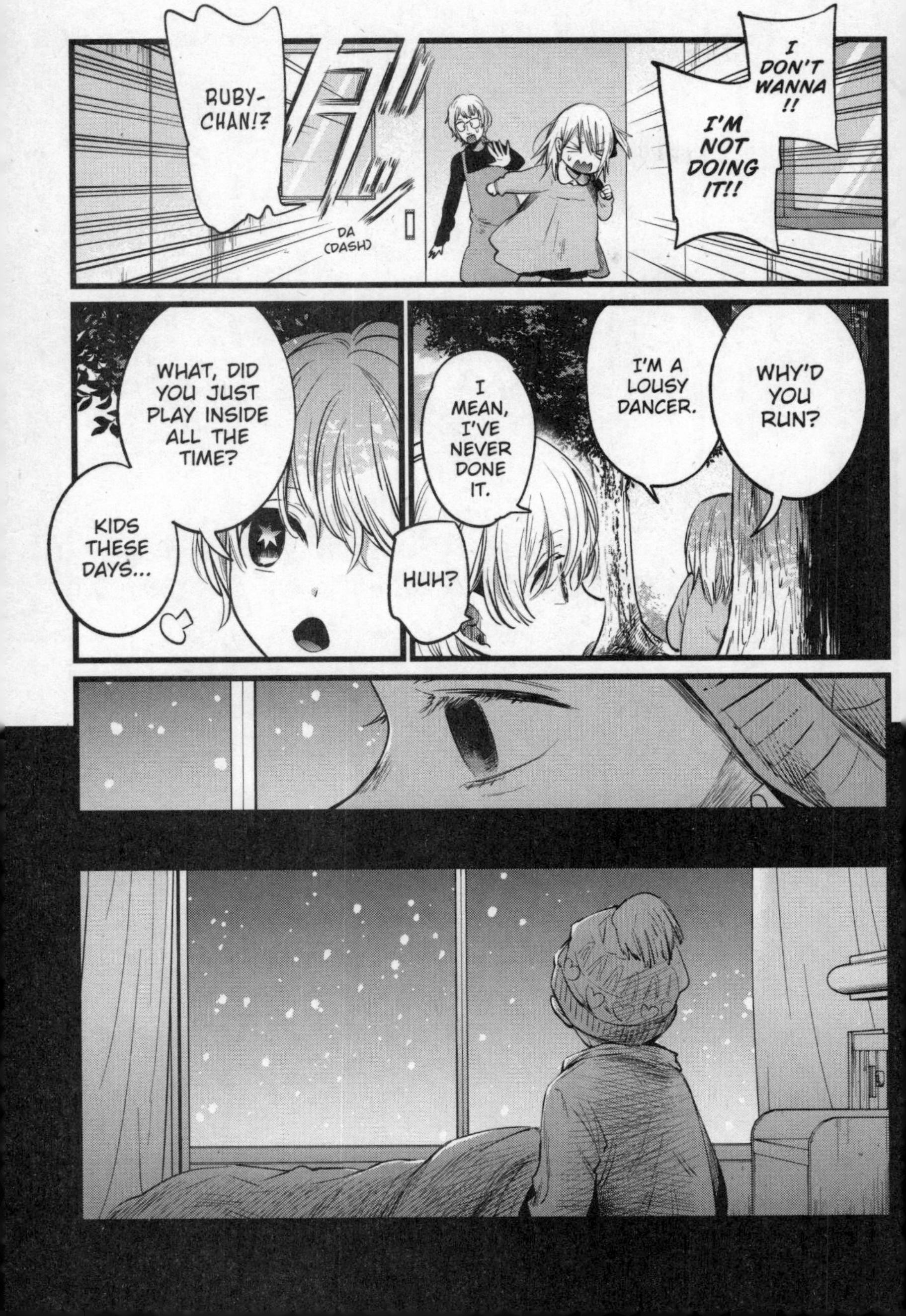
I DON'T WANNA!!
I'M NOT DOING IT!!
DA (DASH)
RUBY-CHAN!?
WHY'D YOU RUN?
I'M A LOUSY DANCER.
I MEAN, I'VE NEVER DONE IT.
HUH?
WHAT, DID YOU JUST PLAY INSIDE ALL THE TIME?
KIDS THESE DAYS...

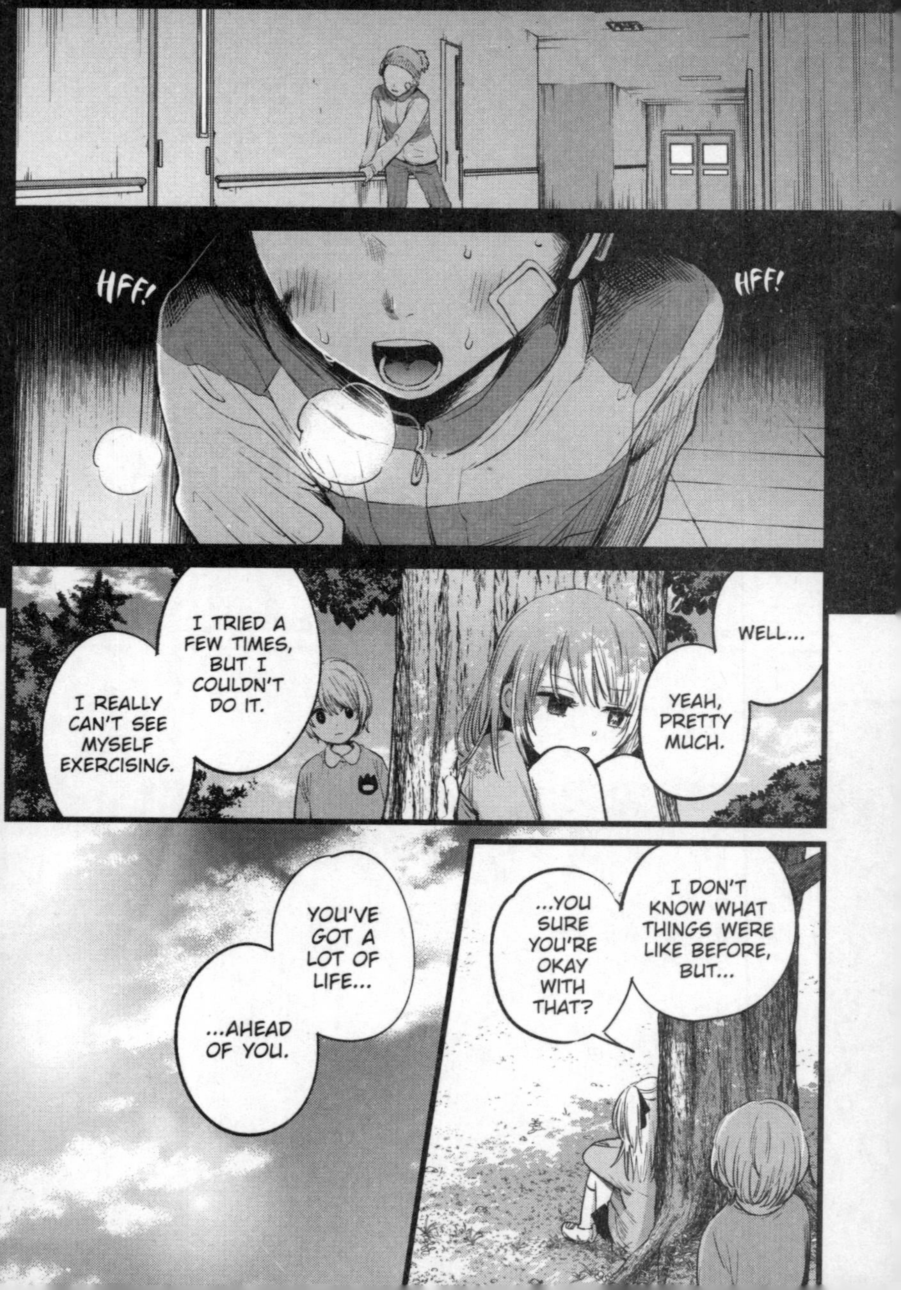
HFF!
HFF!
WELL... YEAH, PRETTY MUCH.
I TRIED A FEW TIMES, BUT I COULDN'T DO IT.
I REALLY CAN'T SEE MYSELF EXERCISING.
I DON'T KNOW WHAT THINGS WERE LIKE BEFORE, BUT...
...YOU SURE YOU'RE OKAY WITH THAT?
YOU'VE GOT A LOT OF LIFE...
...AHEAD OF YOU.

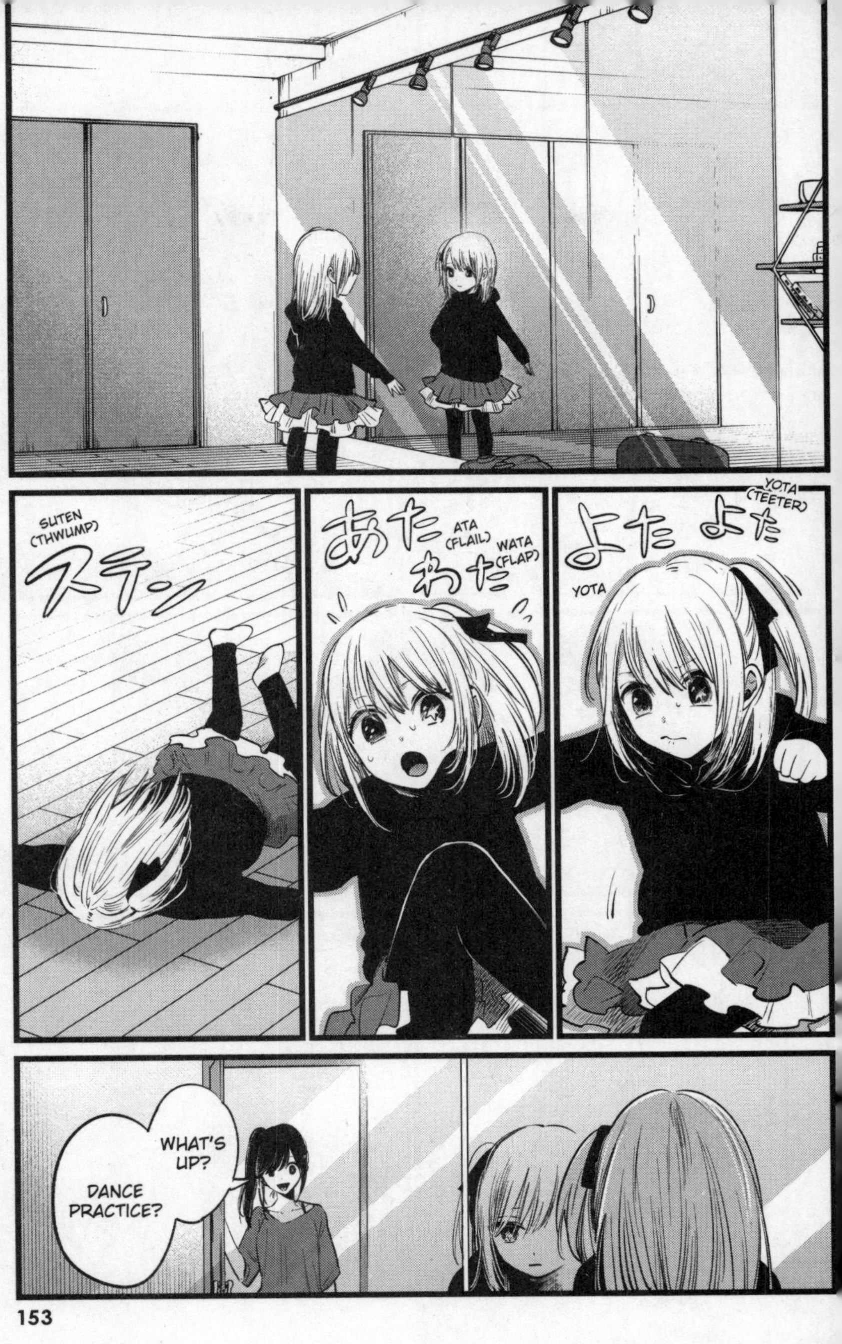
よた よた
YOTA (TEETER)
YOTA
あたわた
ATA (FLAIL)
WATA (FLAP)
ステン
SUTEN (THWUMP)
WHAT'S UP?
DANCE PRACTICE?

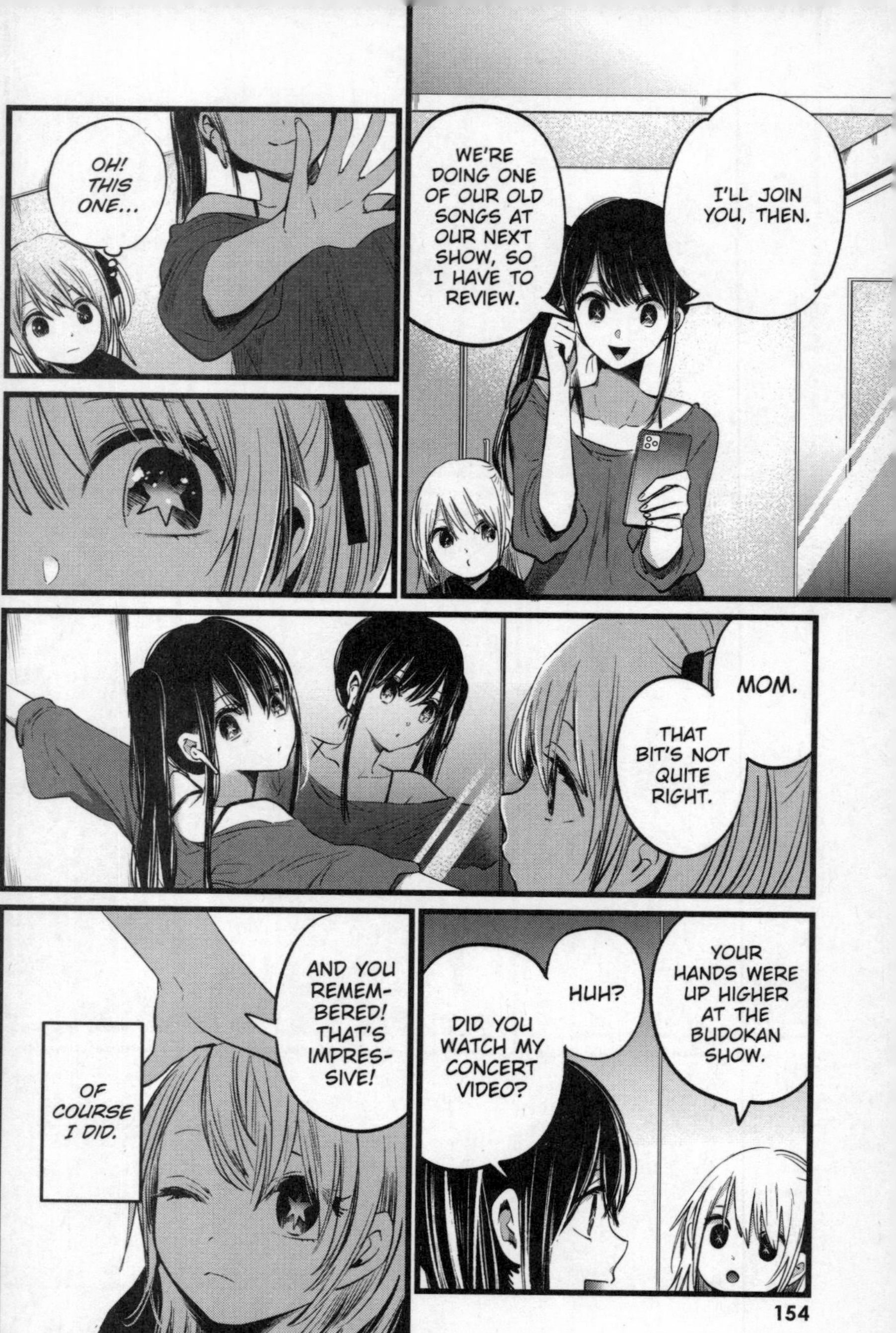
I'LL JOIN YOU, THEN.
WE'RE DOING ONE OF OUR OLD SONGS AT OUR NEXT SHOW, SO I HAVE TO REVIEW.
OH! THIS ONE...
MOM.
THAT BIT'S NOT QUITE RIGHT.
YOUR HANDS WERE UP HIGHER AT THE BUDOKAN SHOW.
HUH?
DID YOU WATCH MY CONCERT VIDEO?
AND YOU REMEMBERED! THAT'S IMPRESSIVE!
OF COURSE I DID.

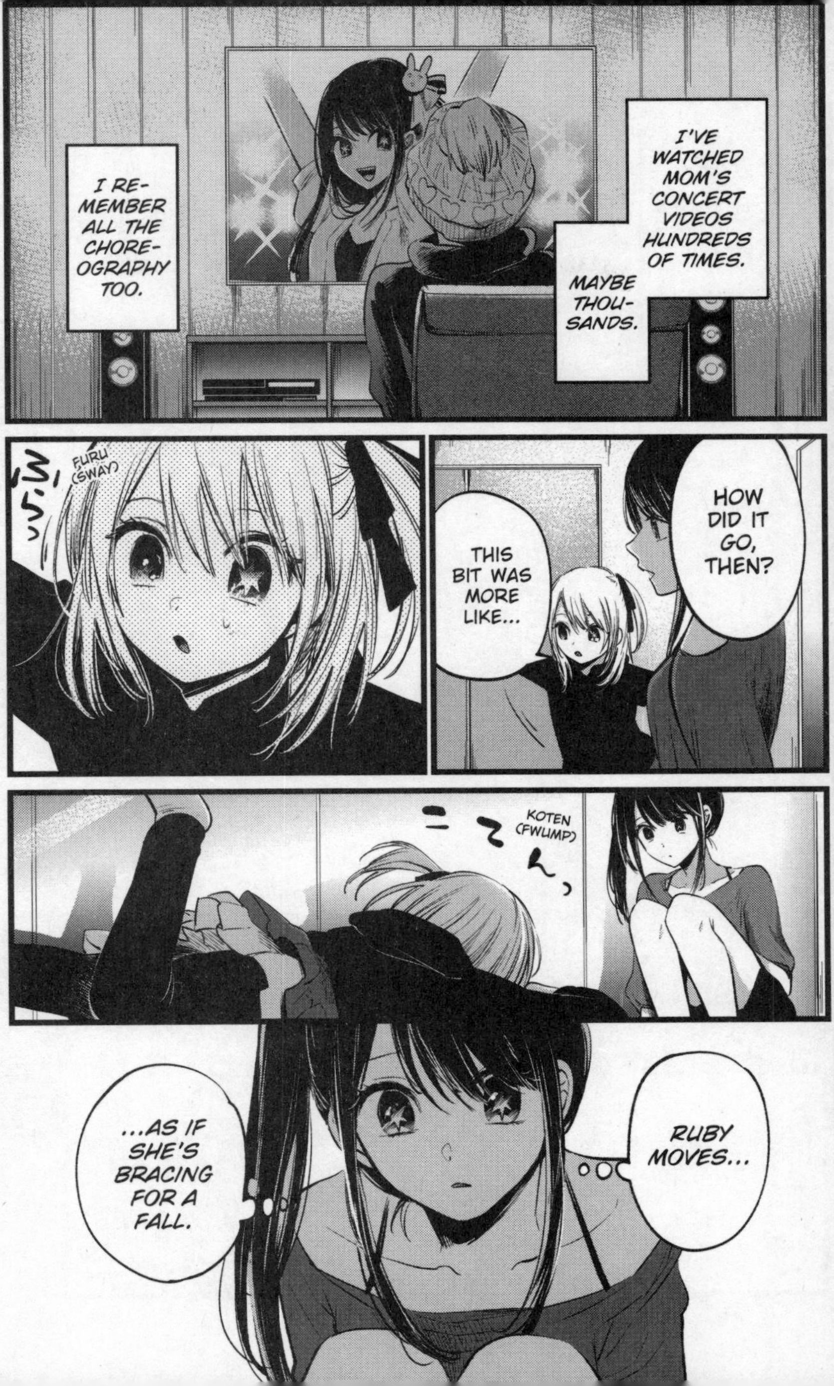
I'VE WATCHED MOM'S CONCERT VIDEOS HUNDREDS OF TIMES.
MAYBE THOUSANDS.
I REMEMBER ALL THE CHOREOGRAPHY TOO.
HOW DID IT GO, THEN?
THIS BIT WAS MORE LIKE...
FURU (SWAY)
KOTEN (FWUMP)
RUBY MOVES...
...AS IF SHE'S BRACING FOR A FALL.

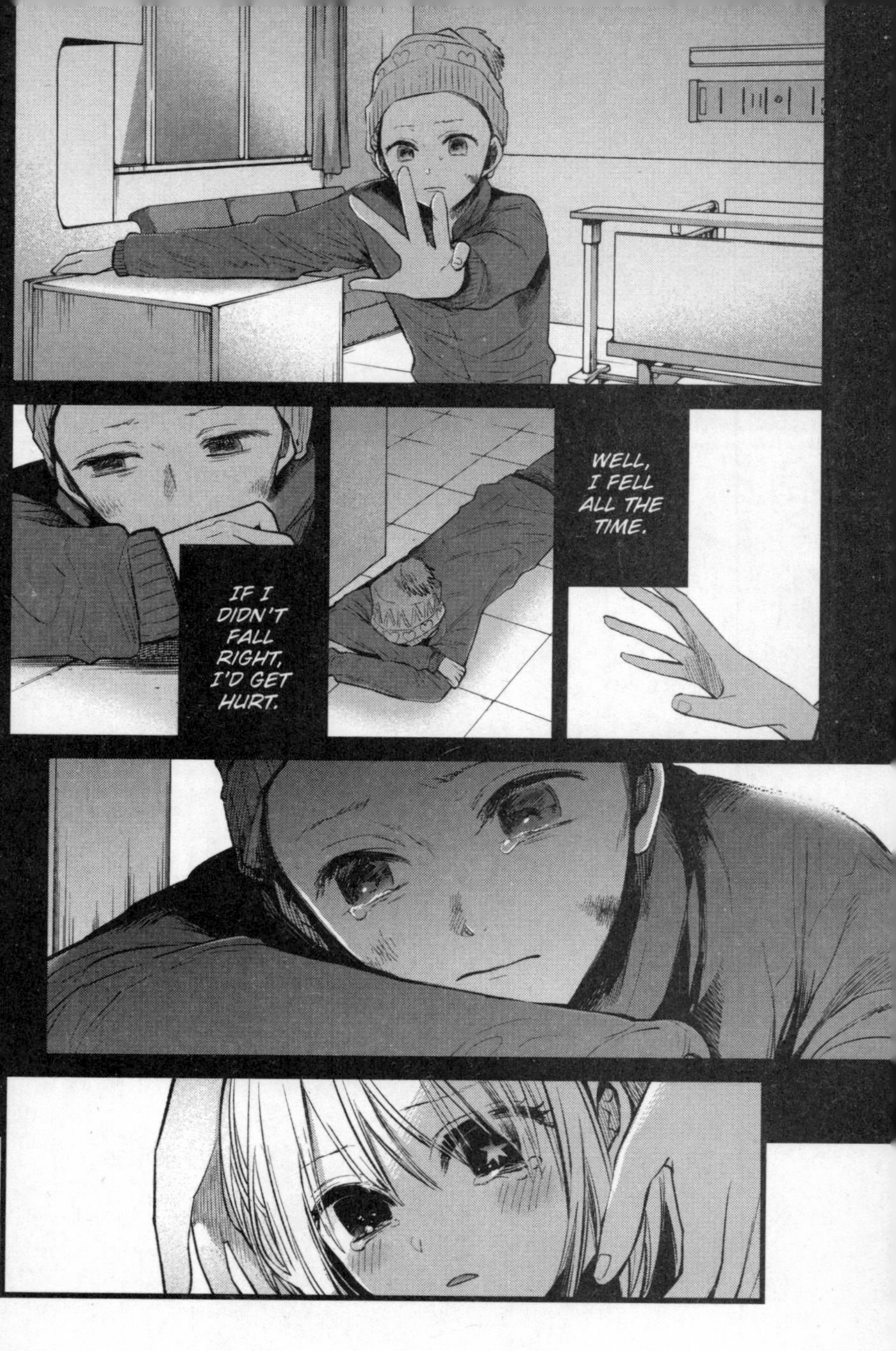
WELL, I FELL ALL THE TIME.
IF I DIDN'T FALL RIGHT, I'D GET HURT.

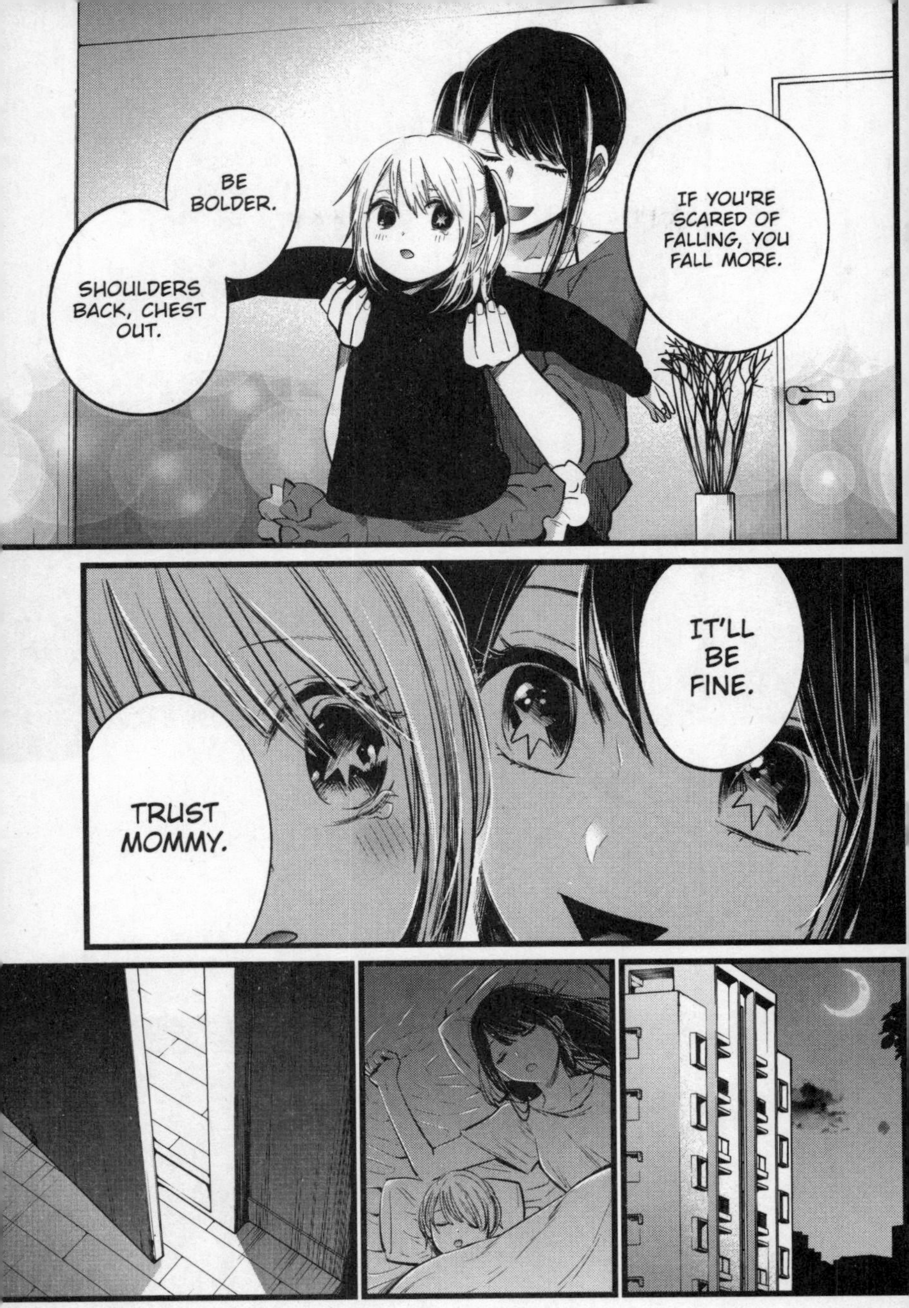
IF YOU'RE SCARED OF FALLING, YOU FALL MORE.
BE BOLDER.
SHOULDERS BACK, CHEST OUT.
IT'LL BE FINE.
TRUST MOMMY.

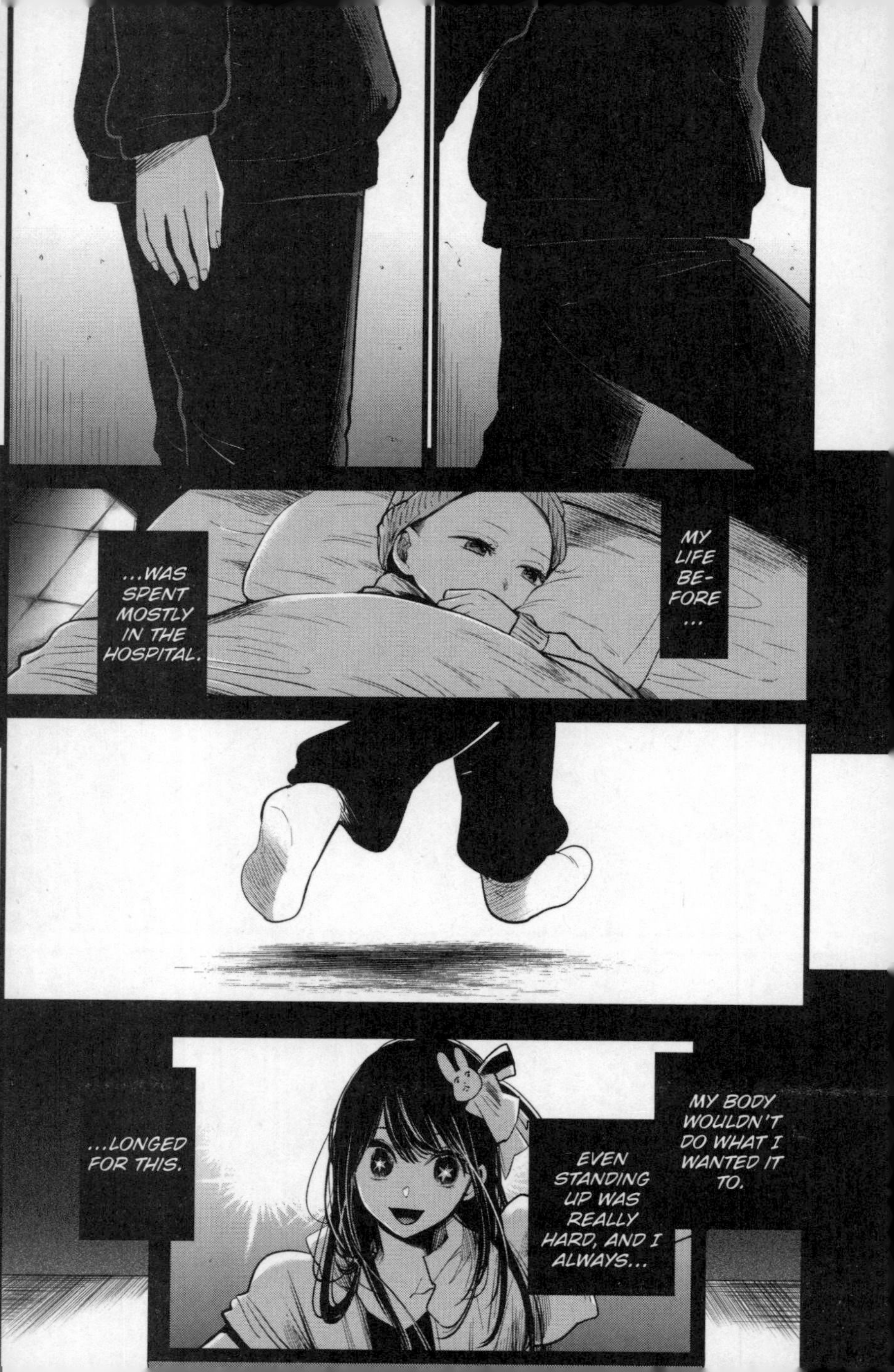
MY LIFE BE-FORE...
...WAS SPENT MOSTLY IN THE HOSPITAL.
MY BODY WOULDN'T DO WHAT I WANTED IT TO.
EVEN STANDING UP WAS REALLY HARD, AND I ALWAYS...
...LONGED FOR THIS.

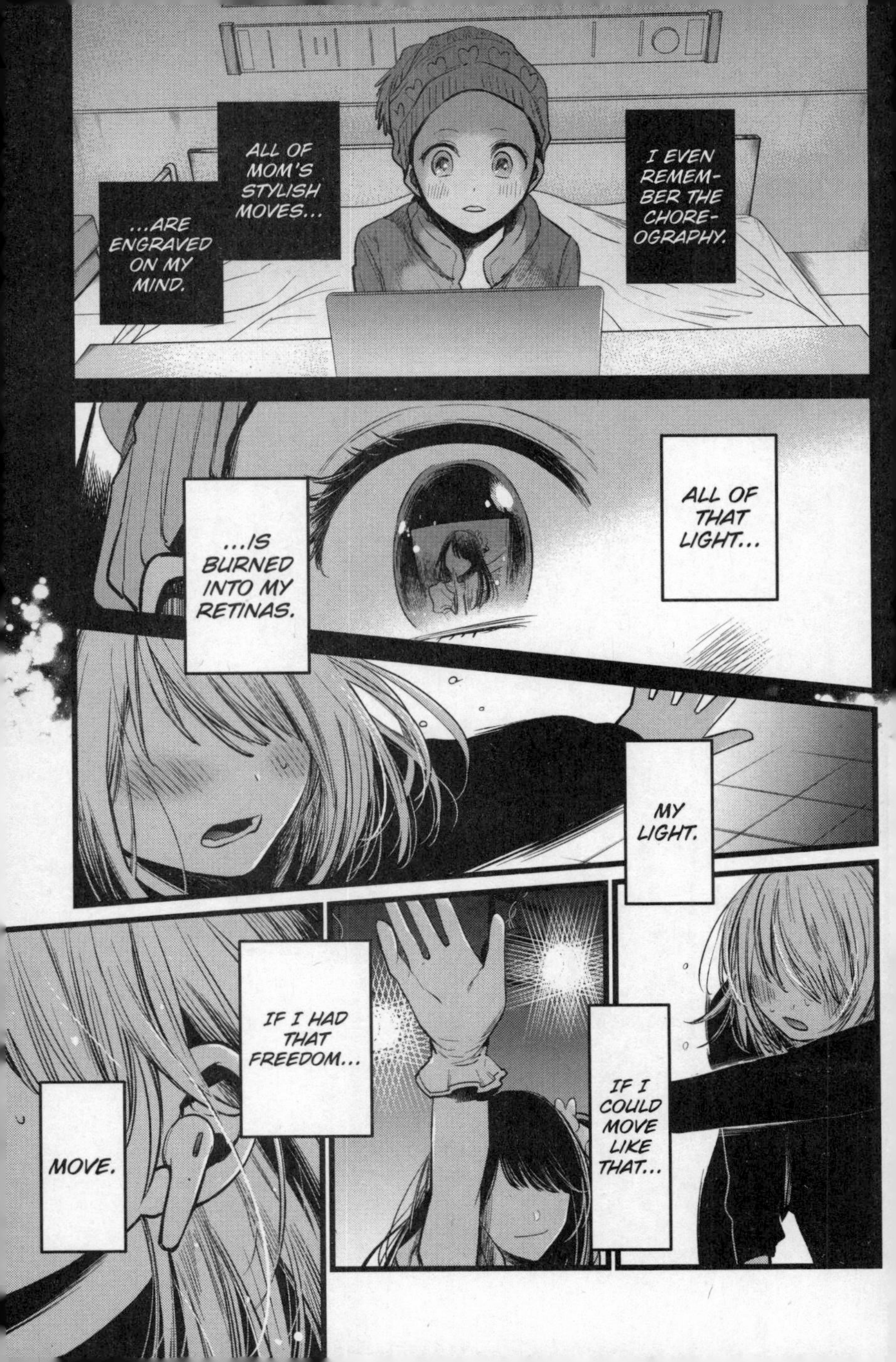
I EVEN REMEMBER THE CHOREOGRAPHY.
ALL OF MOM'S STYLISH MOVES...
...ARE ENGRAVED ON MY MIND.
ALL OF THAT LIGHT...
...IS BURNED INTO MY RETINAS.
MY LIGHT.
IF I COULD MOVE LIKE THAT...
IF I HAD THAT FREEDOM...
MOVE.

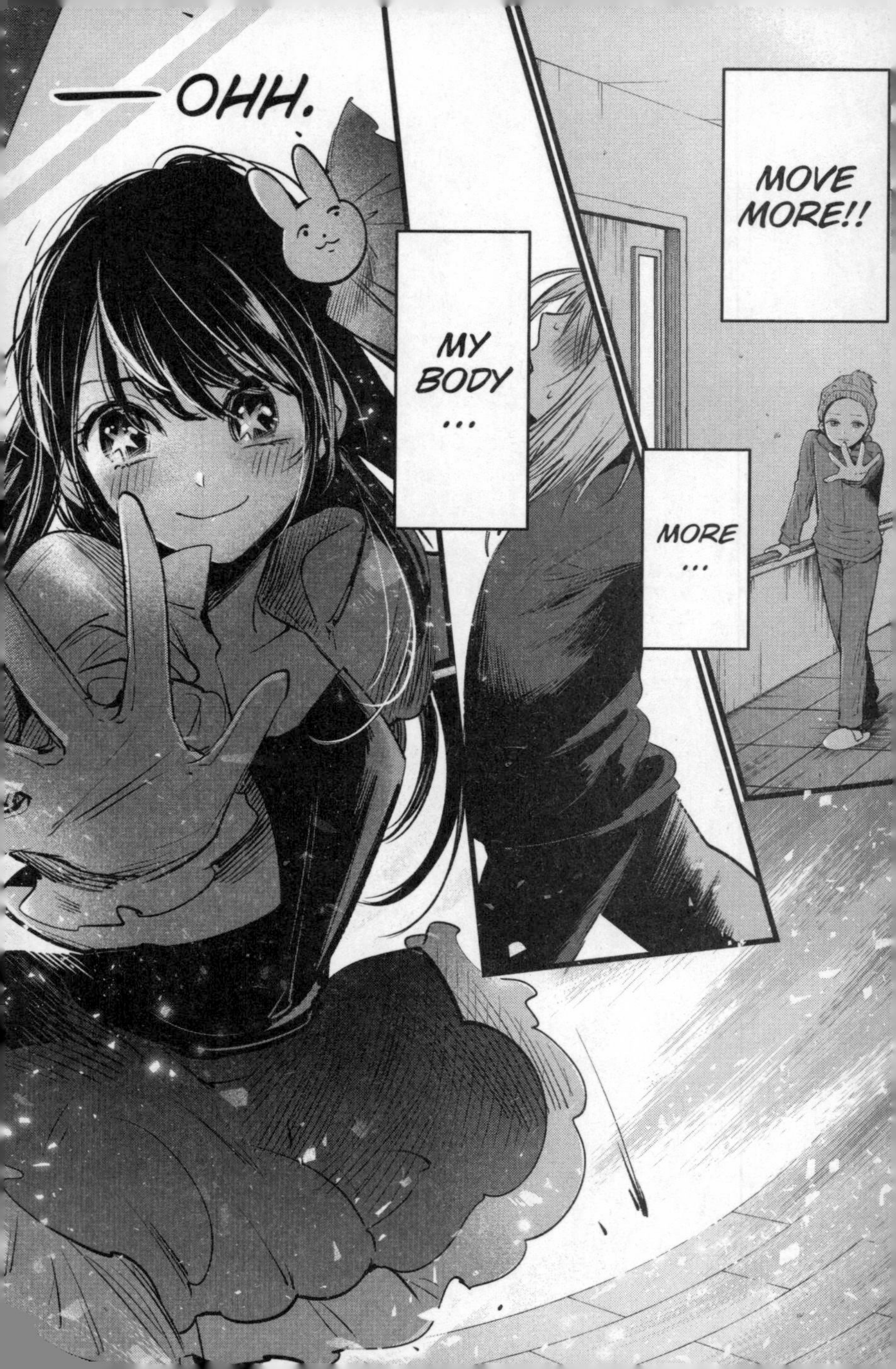
MOVE MORE!!
MORE ...
MY BODY ...
—OHH.

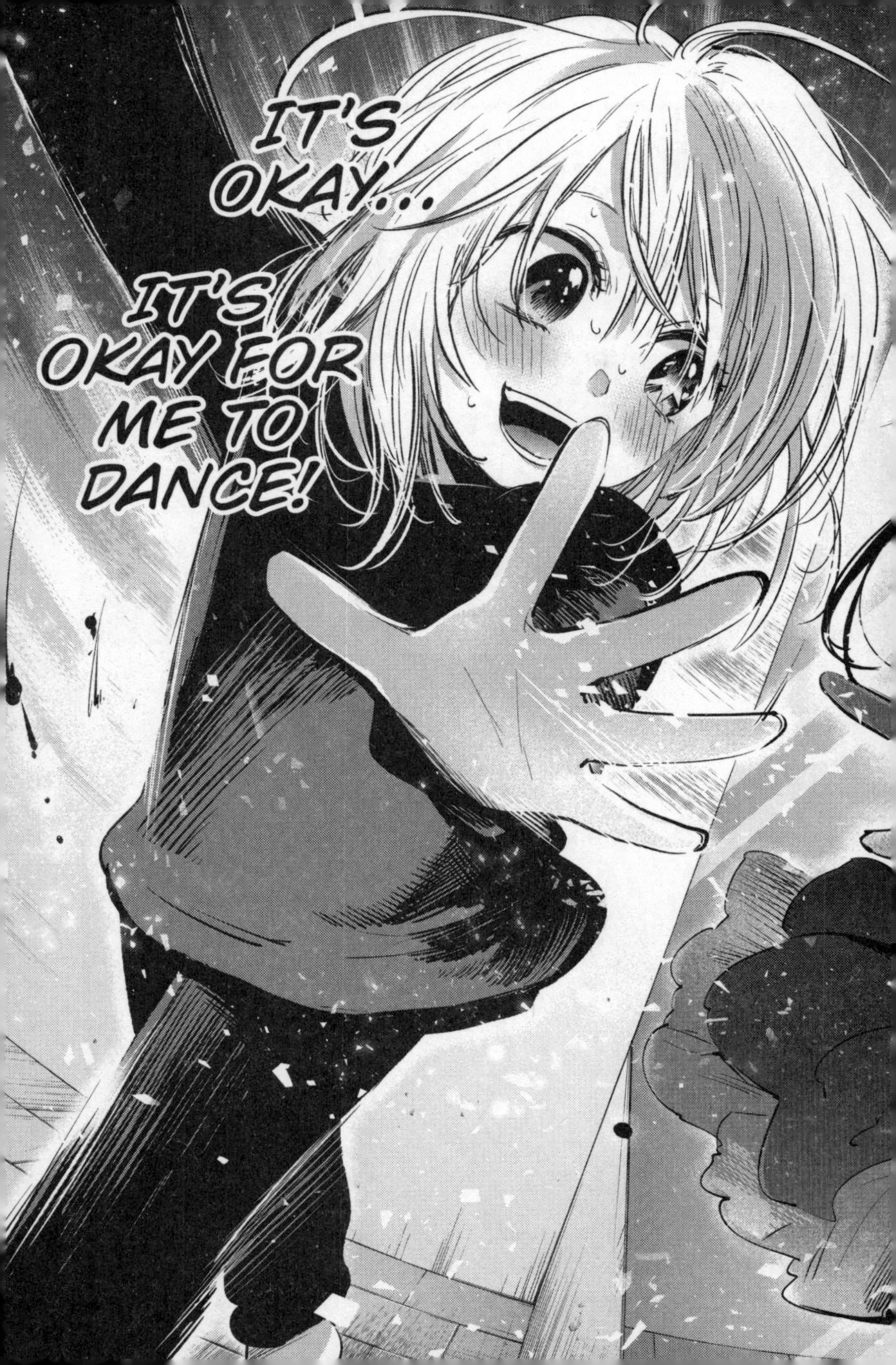
IT'S OKAY...
IT'S OKAY FOR ME TO DANCE!

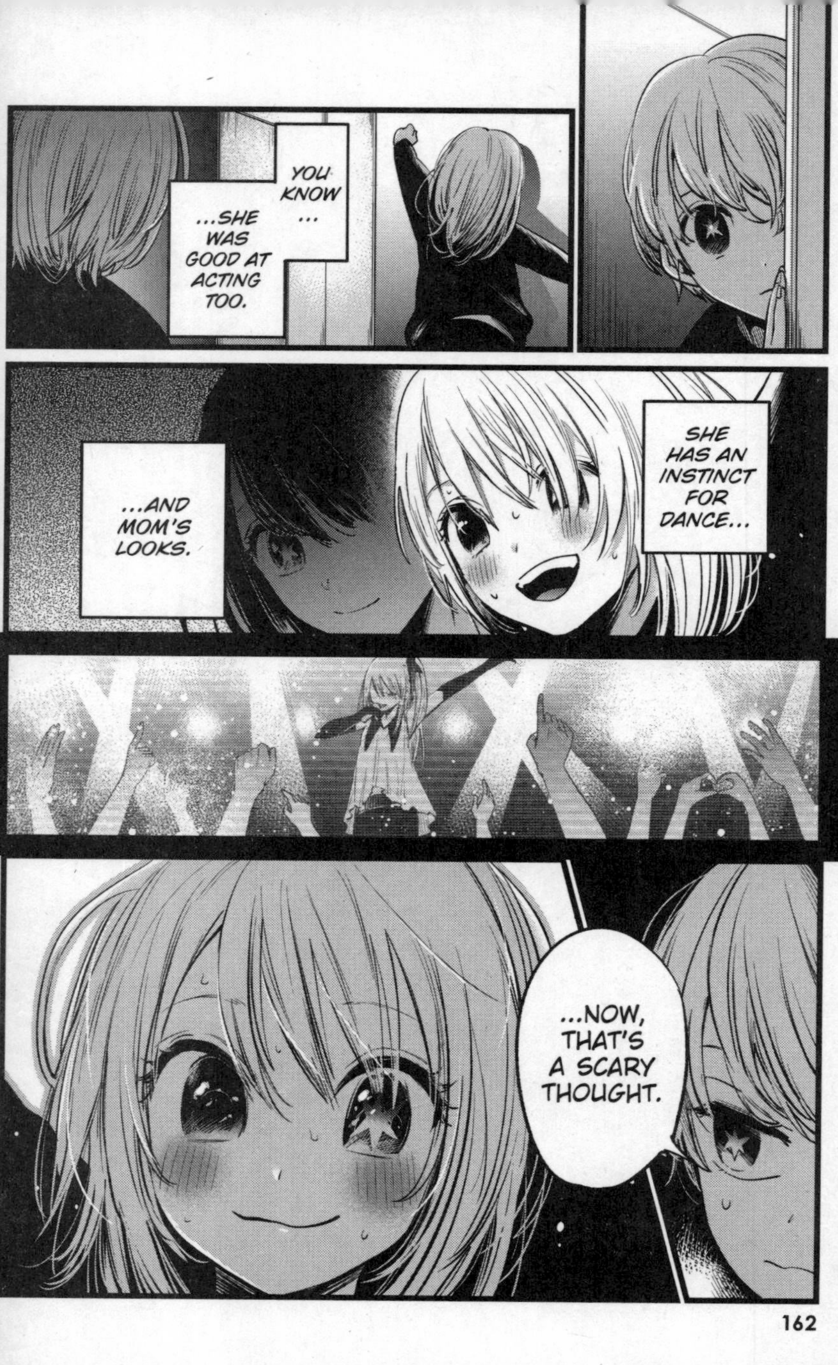
YOU KNOW ...
...SHE WAS GOOD AT ACTING TOO.
SHE HAS AN INSTINCT FOR DANCE...
...AND MOM'S LOOKS.
...NOW, THAT'S A SCARY THOUGHT.

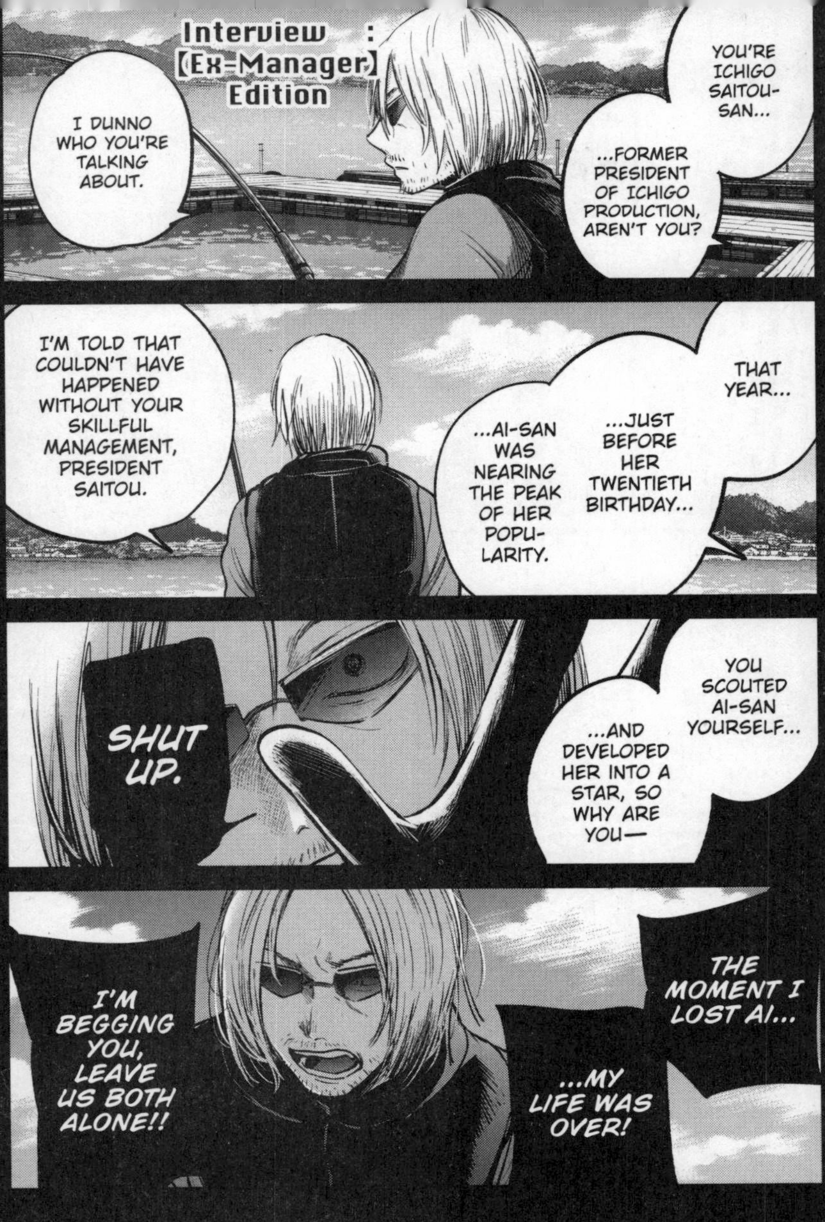

Interview : 【Ex-Manager】 Edition
YOU'RE ICHIGO SAITOU-SAN...
...FORMER PRESIDENT OF ICHIGO PRODUCTION, AREN'T YOU?
I DUNNO WHO YOU'RE TALKING ABOUT.
THAT YEAR...
...JUST BEFORE HER TWENTIETH BIRTHDAY...
...AI-SAN WAS NEARING THE PEAK OF HER POPULARITY.
I'M TOLD THAT COULDN'T HAVE HAPPENED WITHOUT YOUR SKILLFUL MANAGEMENT, PRESIDENT SAITOU.
YOU SCOUTED AI-SAN YOURSELF...
...AND DEVELOPED HER INTO A STAR, SO WHY ARE YOU—
SHUT UP.
THE MOMENT I LOST AI...
...MY LIFE WAS OVER!
I'M BEGGING YOU, LEAVE US BOTH ALONE!!

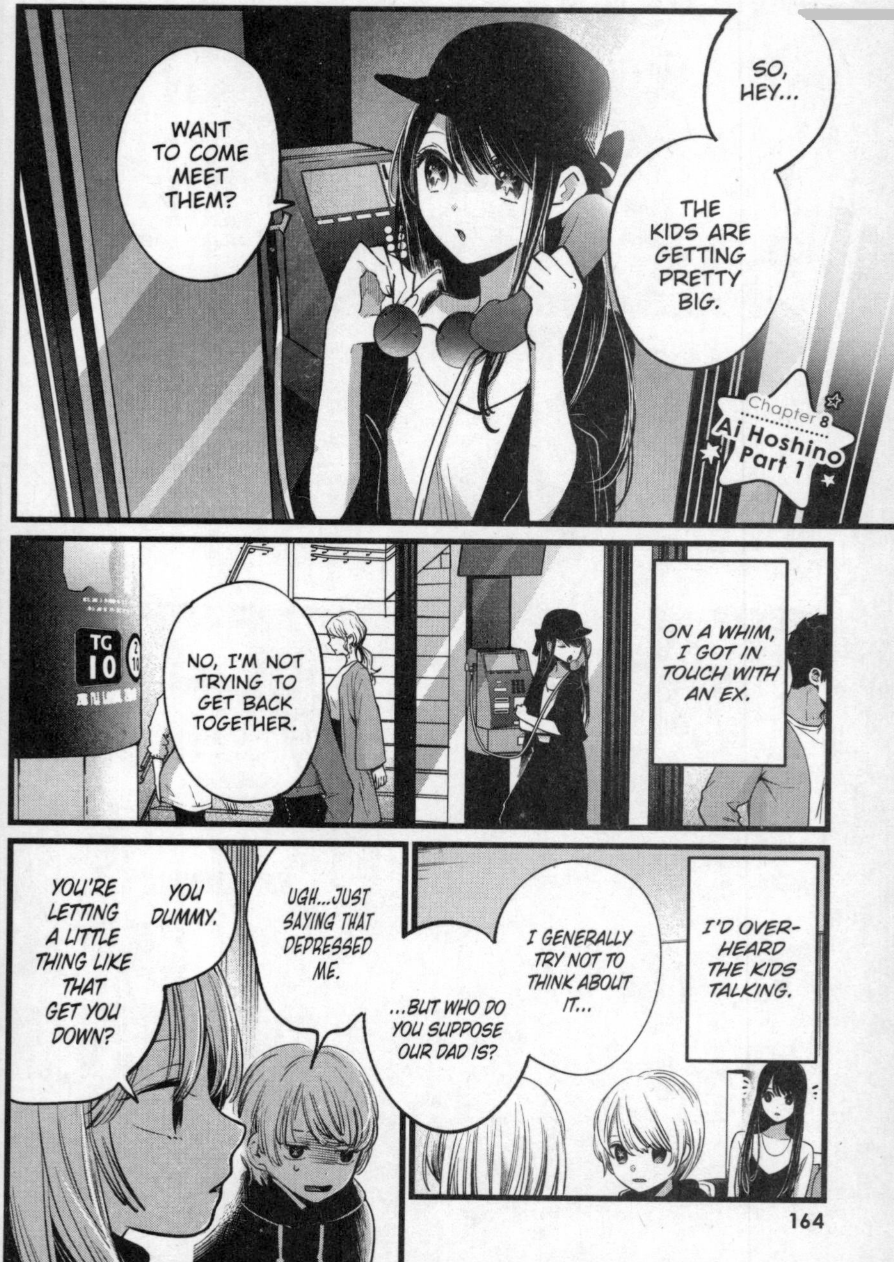
SO, HEY...
THE KIDS ARE GETTING PRETTY BIG.
WANT TO COME MEET THEM?
Chapter 8 Ai Hoshino Part 1
ON A WHIM, I GOT IN TOUCH WITH AN EX.
NO, I'M NOT TRYING TO GET BACK TOGETHER.
TG 10
I'D OVERHEARD THE KIDS TALKING.
I GENERALLY TRY NOT TO THINK ABOUT IT...
...BUT WHO DO YOU SUPPOSE OUR DAD IS?
UGH...JUST SAYING THAT DEPRESSED ME.
YOU DUMMY.
YOU'RE LETTING A LITTLE THING LIKE THAT GET YOU DOWN?

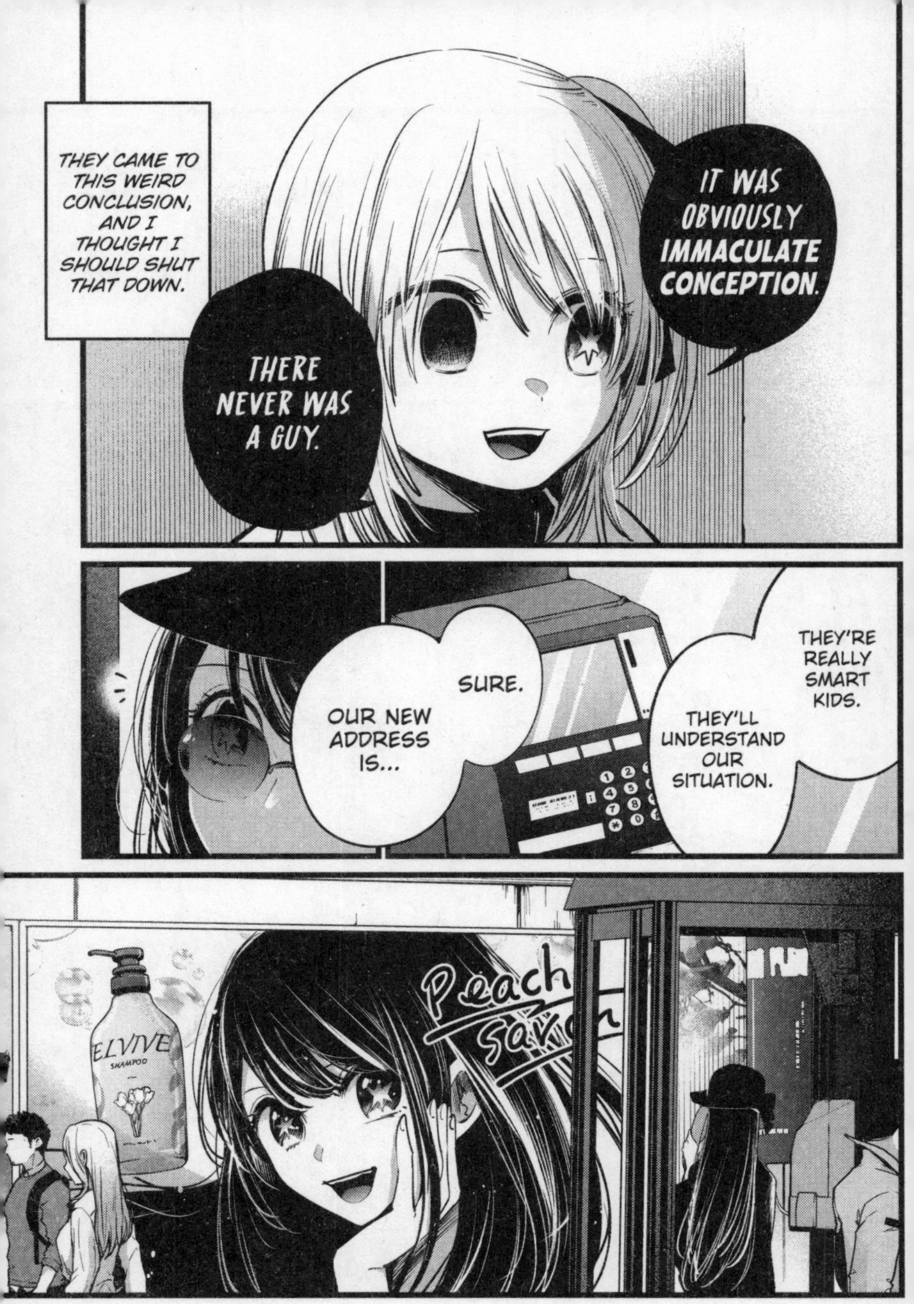
THEY CAME TO THIS WEIRD CONCLUSION, AND I THOUGHT I SHOULD SHUT THAT DOWN.
IT WAS OBVIOUSLY IMMACULATE CONCEPTION.
THERE NEVER WAS A GUY.
THEY'RE REALLY SMART KIDS.
THEY'LL UNDERSTAND OUR SITUATION.
SURE.
OUR NEW ADDRESS IS...
Peach saron
ELVIVE
SHAMPOO

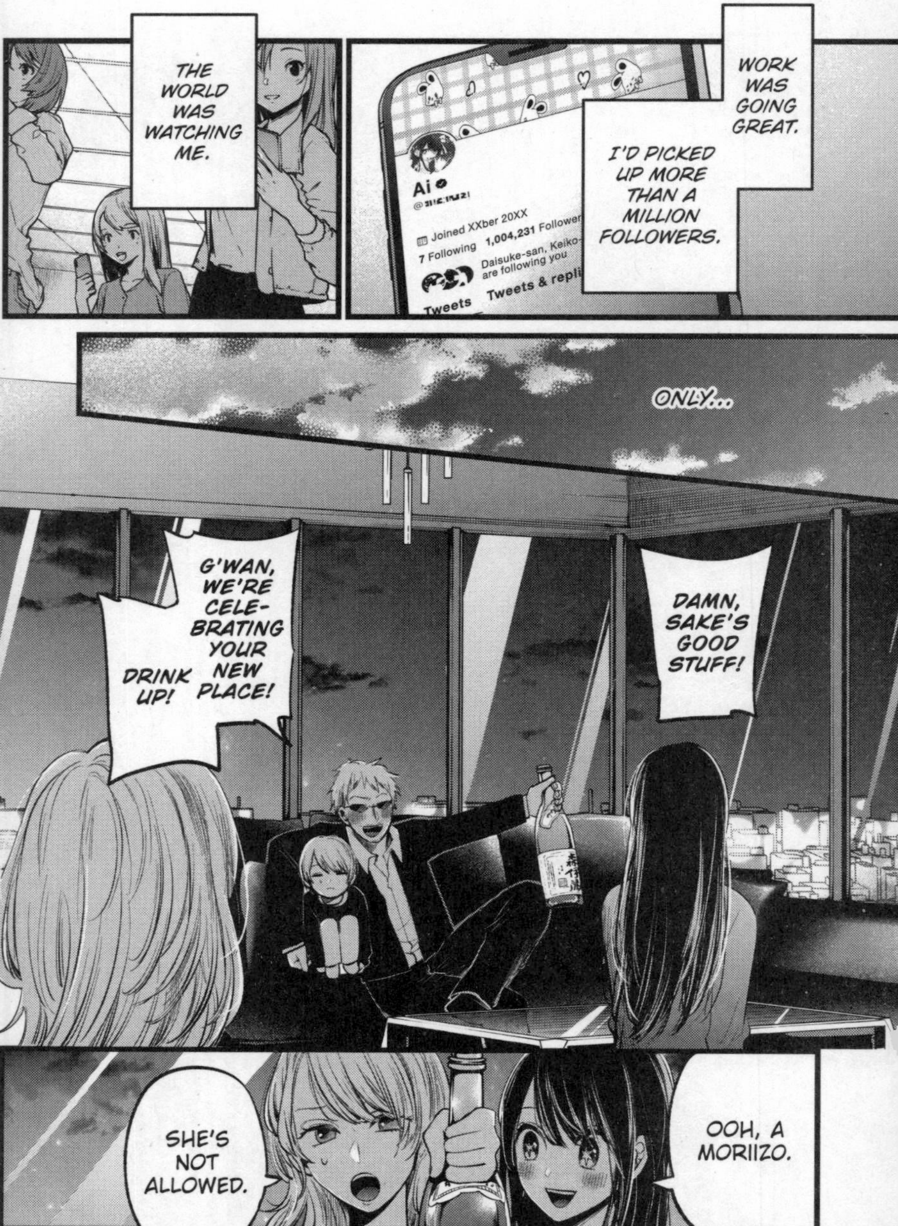
WORK WAS GOING GREAT.
I'D PICKED UP MORE THAN A MILLION FOLLOWERS.
Ai
Joined XXber 20XX
7 Following
1,004,231
Daisuke-san,
are following you
Tweets
THE WORLD WAS WATCHING ME.
ONLY...
DAMN, SAKE'S GOOD STUFF!
G'WAN, WE'RE CELE-BRATING YOUR NEW PLACE!
DRINK UP!
OOH, A MORIIZO.
SHE'S NOT ALLOWED.

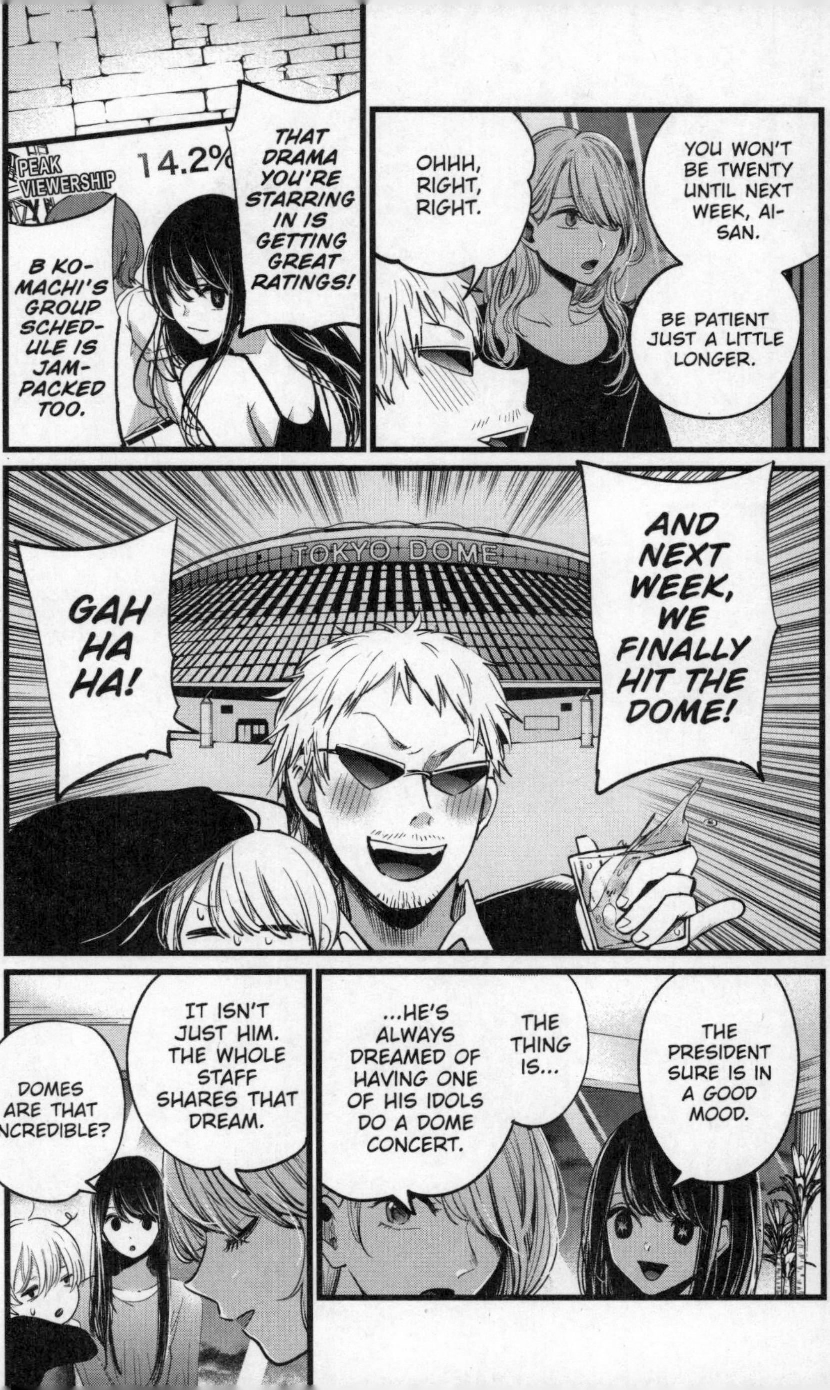
YOU WON'T BE TWENTY UNTIL NEXT WEEK, AI-SAN.
BE PATIENT JUST A LITTLE LONGER.
OHHH, RIGHT, RIGHT.
THAT DRAMA YOU'RE STARRING IN IS GETTING GREAT RATINGS!
14.2%
PEAK VIEWERSHIP
B KOMACHI'S GROUP SCHEDULE IS JAM-PACKED TOO.
AND NEXT WEEK, WE FINALLY HIT THE DOME!
TOKYO DOME
GAH HA HA!
THE PRESIDENT SURE IS IN A GOOD MOOD.
THE THING IS...
...HE'S ALWAYS DREAMED OF HAVING ONE OF HIS IDOLS DO A DOME CONCERT.
IT ISN'T JUST HIM. THE WHOLE STAFF SHARES THAT DREAM.
DOMES ARE THAT INCREDIBLE?

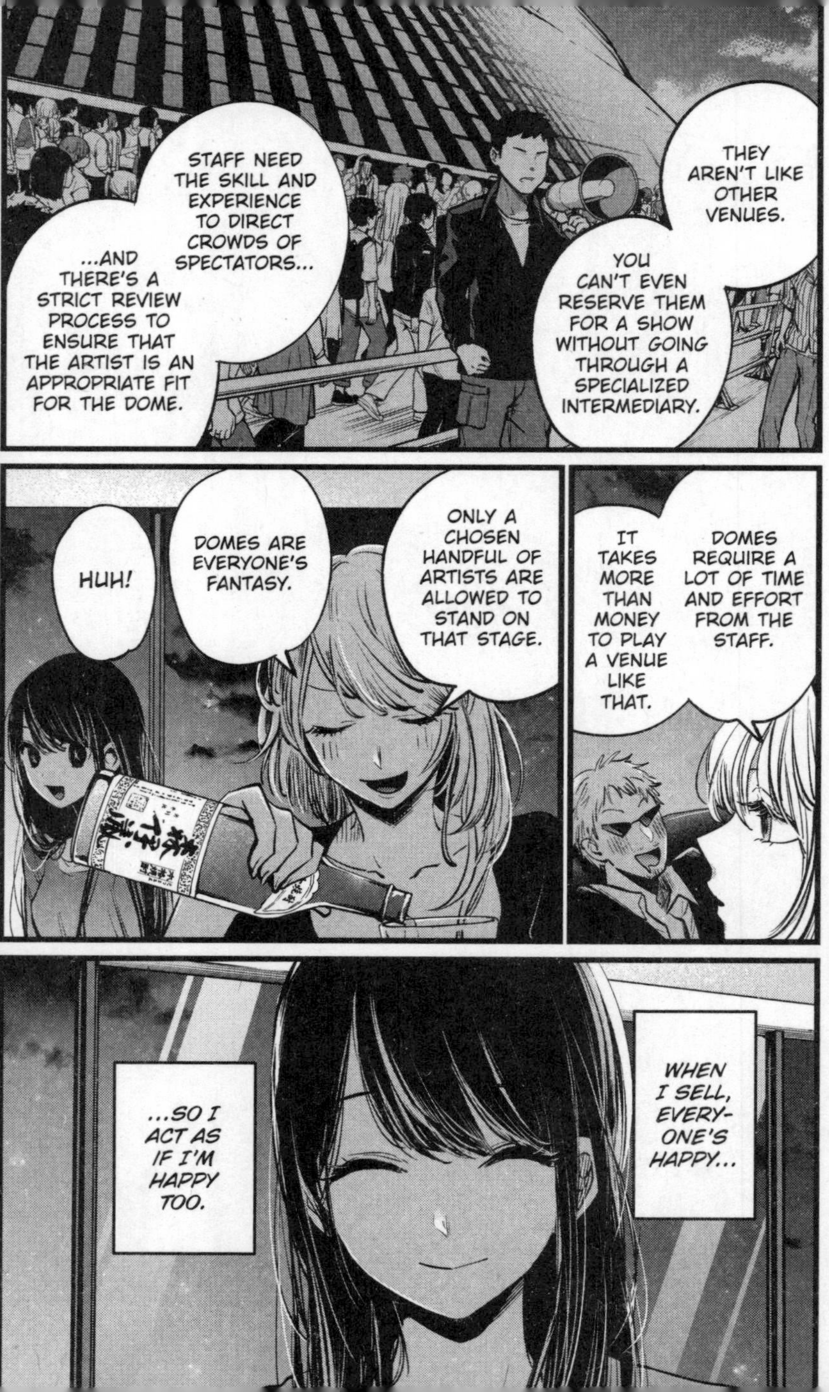
THEY AREN'T LIKE OTHER VENUES.
YOU CAN'T EVEN RESERVE THEM FOR A SHOW WITHOUT GOING THROUGH A SPECIALIZED INTERMEDIARY.
STAFF NEED THE SKILL AND EXPERIENCE TO DIRECT CROWDS OF SPECTATORS...
...AND THERE'S A STRICT REVIEW PROCESS TO ENSURE THAT THE ARTIST IS AN APPROPRIATE FIT FOR THE DOME.
DOMES REQUIRE A LOT OF TIME AND EFFORT FROM THE STAFF.
IT TAKES MORE THAN MONEY TO PLAY A VENUE LIKE THAT.
ONLY A CHOSEN HANDFUL OF ARTISTS ARE ALLOWED TO STAND ON THAT STAGE.
DOMES ARE EVERYONE'S FANTASY.
HUH!
WHEN I SELL, EVERYONE'S HAPPY...
...SO I ACT AS IF I'M HAPPY TOO.

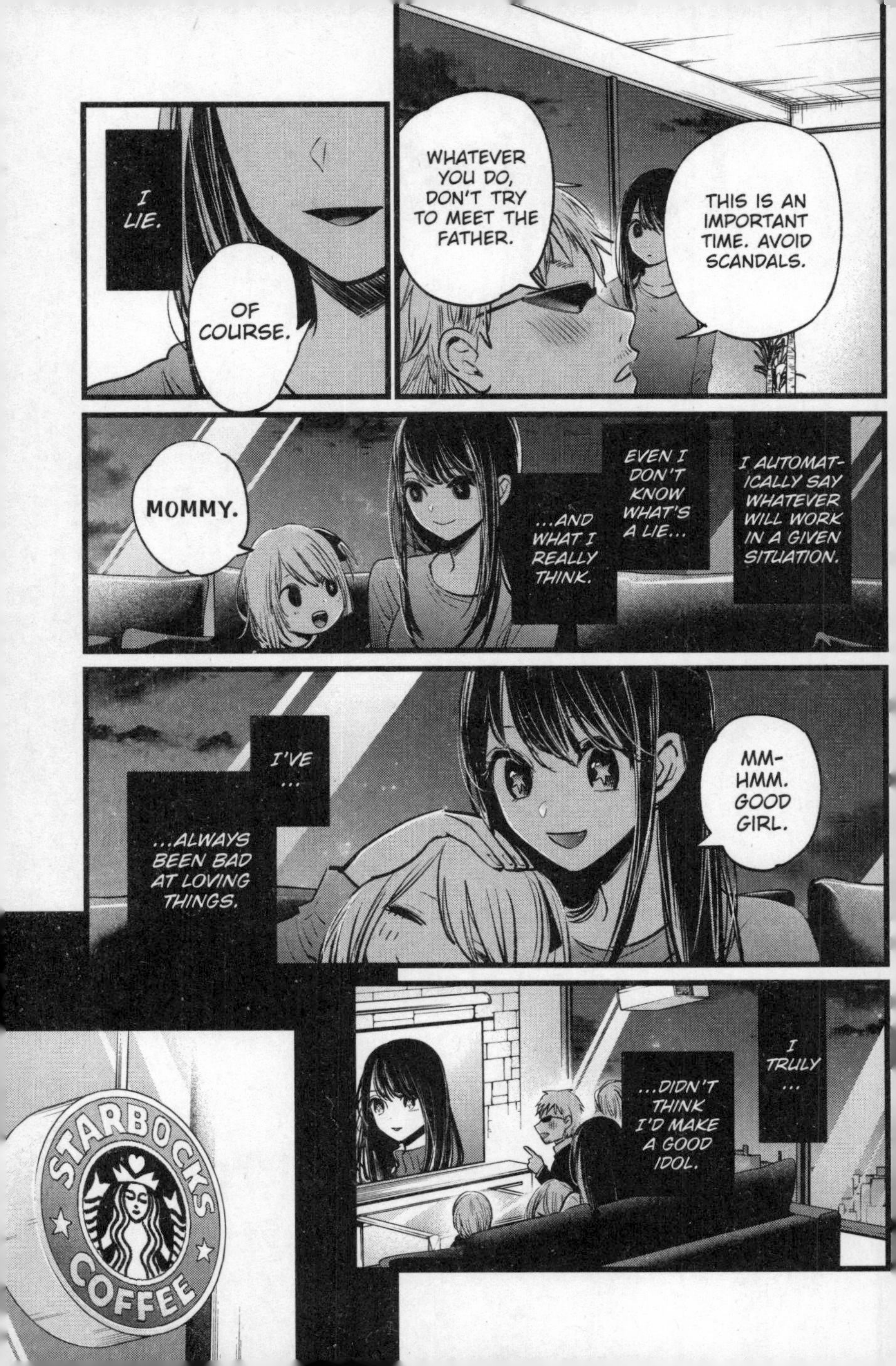
THIS IS AN IMPORTANT TIME. AVOID SCANDALS.
WHATEVER YOU DO, DON'T TRY TO MEET THE FATHER.
OF COURSE.
I LIE.
I AUTOMATICALLY SAY WHATEVER WILL WORK IN A GIVEN SITUATION.
EVEN I DON'T KNOW WHAT'S A LIE...
...AND WHAT I REALLY THINK.
MOMMY.
MM-HMM. GOOD GIRL.
I'VE...
...ALWAYS BEEN BAD AT LOVING THINGS.
I TRULY...
...DIDN'T THINK I'D MAKE A GOOD IDOL.
STARBOCKS COFFEE

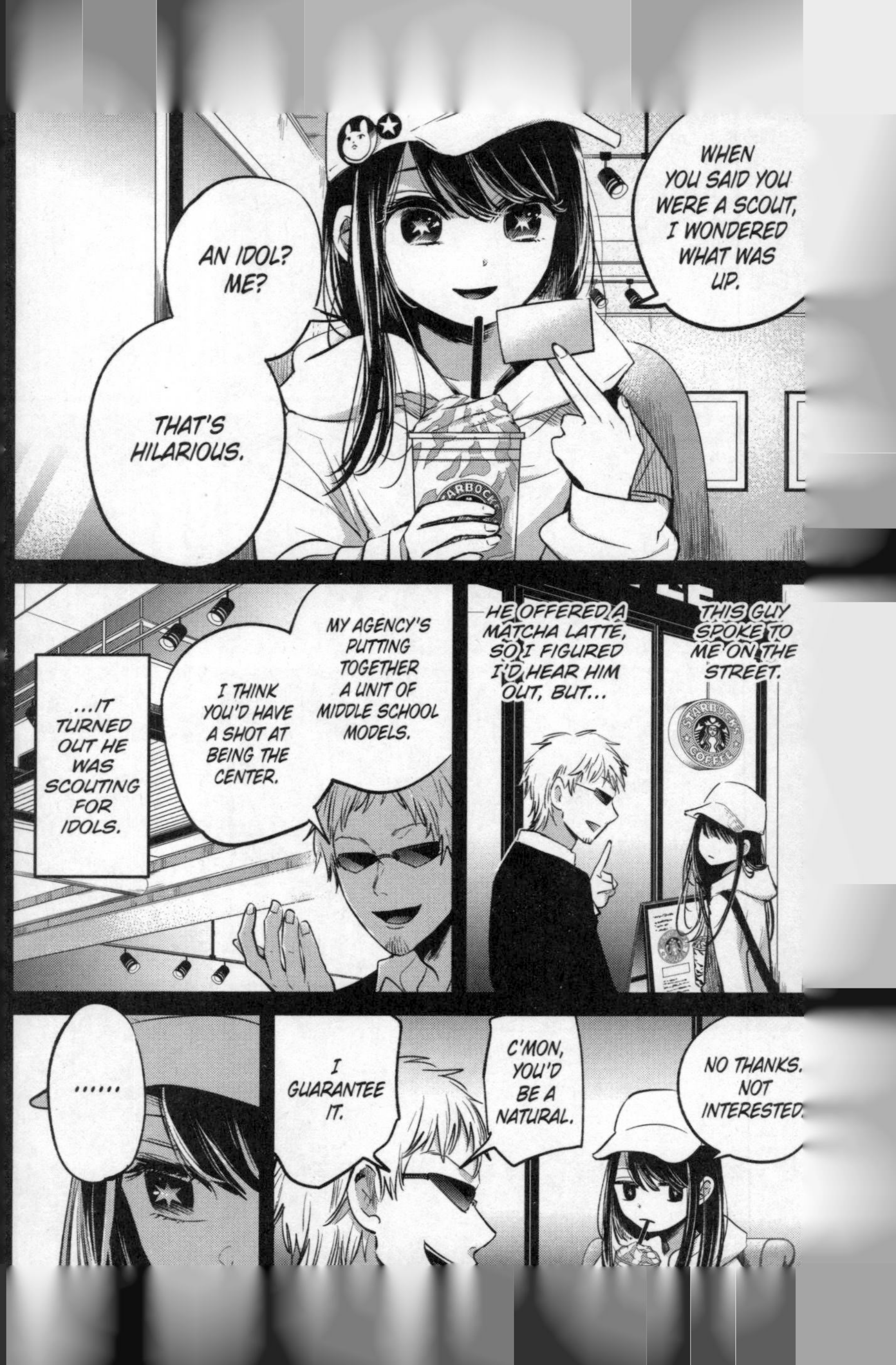
WHEN YOU SAID YOU WERE A SCOUT, I WONDERED WHAT WAS UP.
AN IDOL? ME?
THAT'S HILARIOUS.
THIS GUY SPOKE TO ME ON THE STREET.
HE OFFERED A MATCHA LATTE, SO I FIGURED I'D HEAR HIM OUT, BUT...
STARBOCKS COFFEE
MY AGENCY'S PUTTING TOGETHER A UNIT OF MIDDLE SCHOOL MODELS.
I THINK YOU'D HAVE A SHOT AT BEING THE CENTER.
...IT TURNED OUT HE WAS SCOUTING FOR IDOLS.
NO THANKS. NOT INTERESTED.
C'MON, YOU'D BE A NATURAL.
I GUARANTEE IT.
......

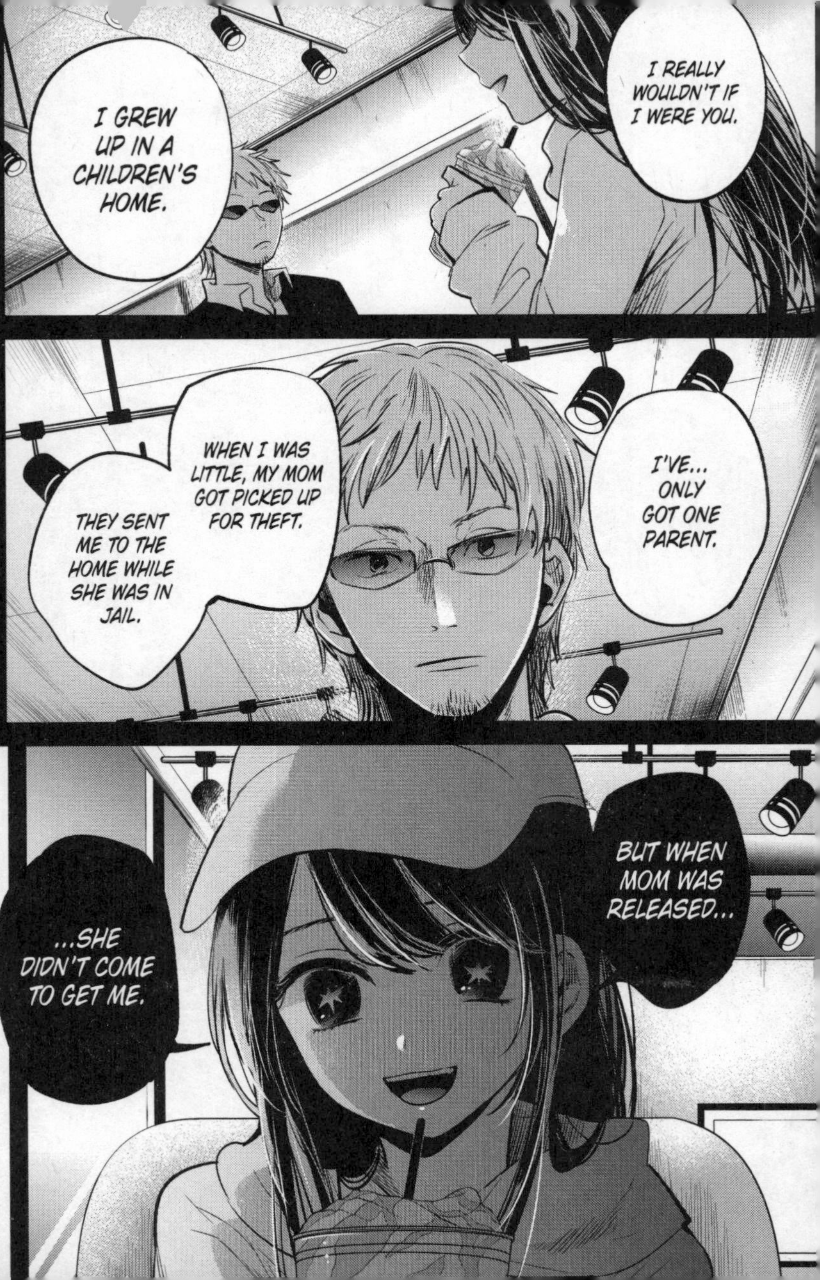
I REALLY WOULDN'T IF I WERE YOU.
I GREW UP IN A CHILDREN'S HOME.
I'VE... ONLY GOT ONE PARENT.
WHEN I WAS LITTLE, MY MOM GOT PICKED UP FOR THEFT.
THEY SENT ME TO THE HOME WHILE SHE WAS IN JAIL.
BUT WHEN MOM WAS RELEASED...
...SHE DIDN'T COME TO GET ME.

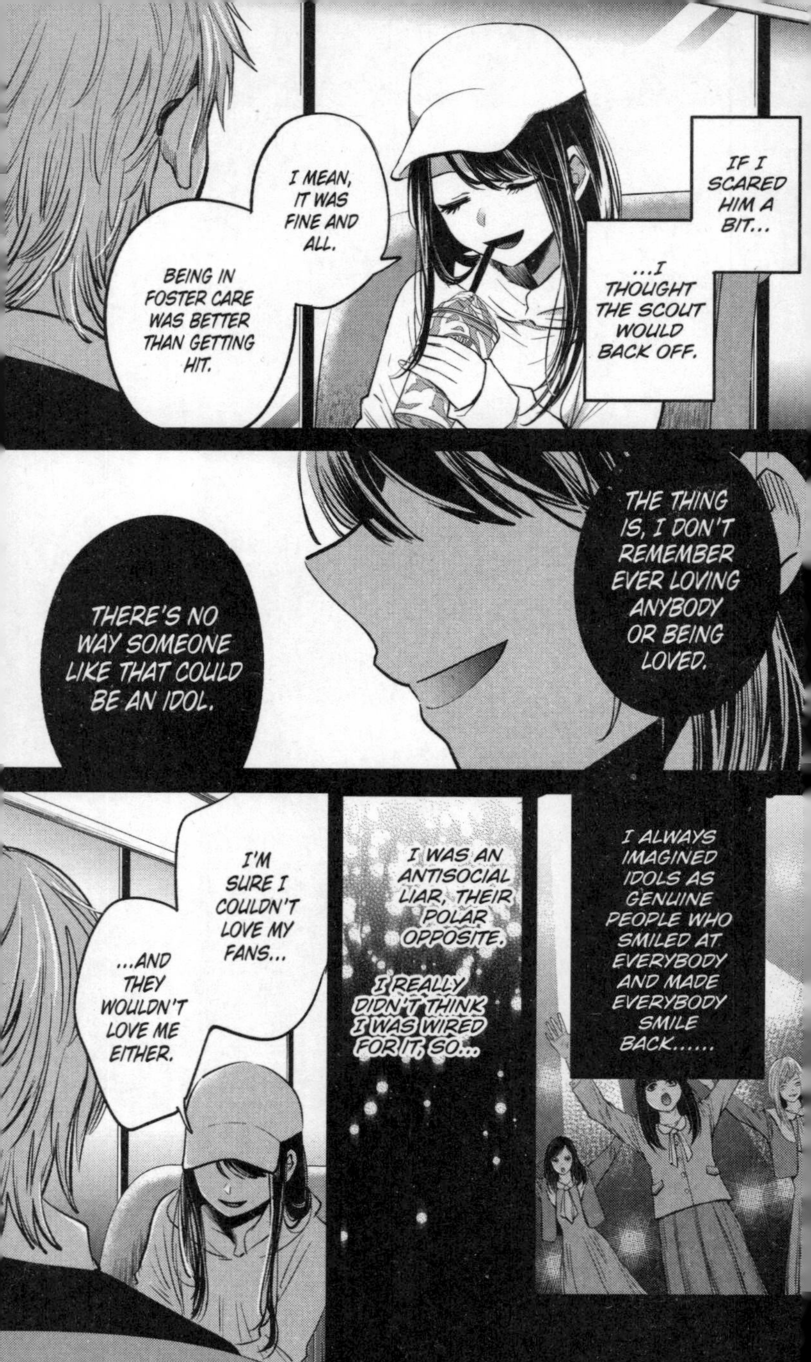
IF I SCARED HIM A BIT...
...I THOUGHT THE SCOUT WOULD BACK OFF.
I MEAN, IT WAS FINE AND ALL.
BEING IN FOSTER CARE WAS BETTER THAN GETTING HIT.
THE THING IS, I DON'T REMEMBER EVER LOVING ANYBODY OR BEING LOVED.
THERE'S NO WAY SOMEONE LIKE THAT COULD BE AN IDOL.
I ALWAYS IMAGINED IDOLS AS GENUINE PEOPLE WHO SMILED AT EVERYBODY AND MADE EVERYBODY SMILE BACK......
I WAS AN ANTISOCIAL LIAR, THEIR POLAR OPPOSITE.
I REALLY DIDN'T THINK I WAS WIRED FOR IT, SO...
I'M SURE I COULDN'T LOVE MY FANS...
...AND THEY WOULDN'T LOVE ME EITHER.

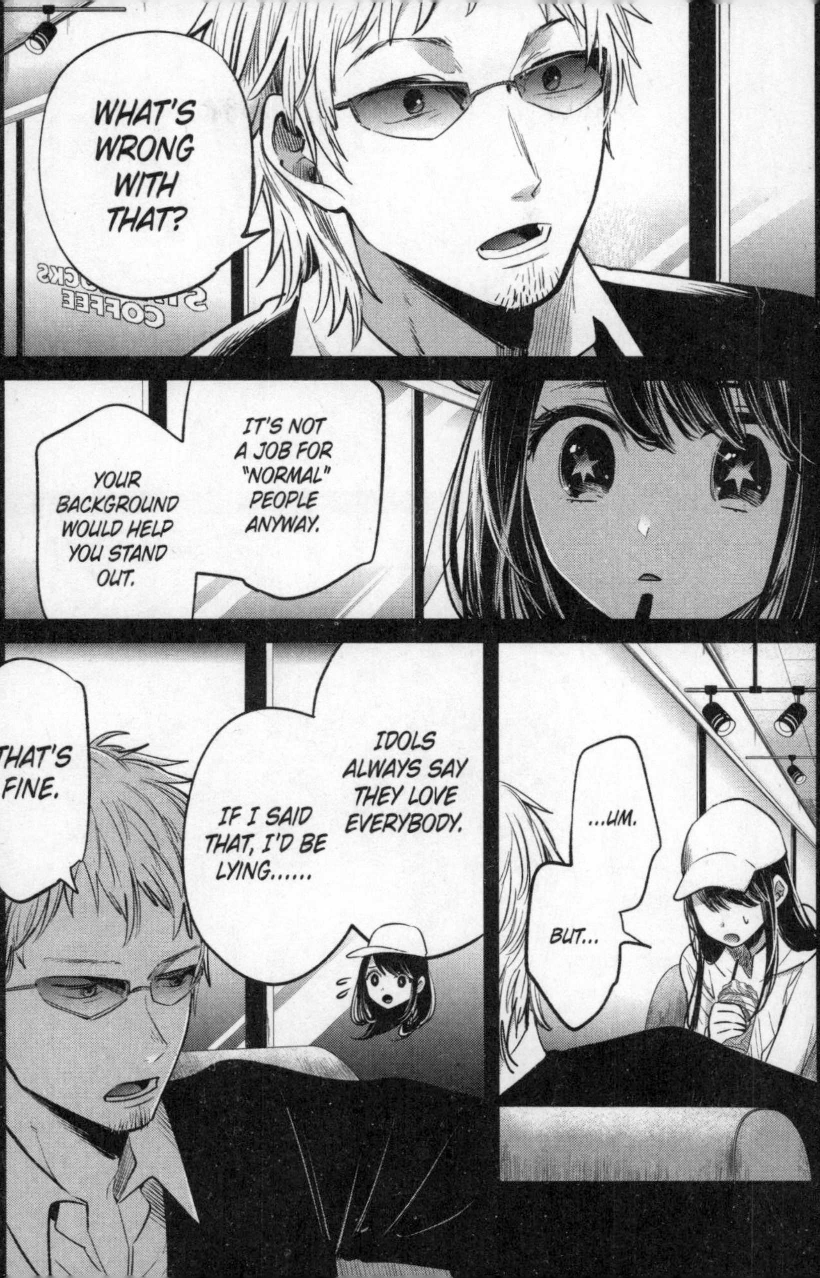
WHAT'S WRONG WITH THAT?
IT'S NOT A JOB FOR "NORMAL" PEOPLE ANYWAY.
YOUR BACKGROUND WOULD HELP YOU STAND OUT.
...UM.
BUT...
IDOLS ALWAYS SAY THEY LOVE EVERYBODY.
IF I SAID THAT, I'D BE LYING......
THAT'S FINE.

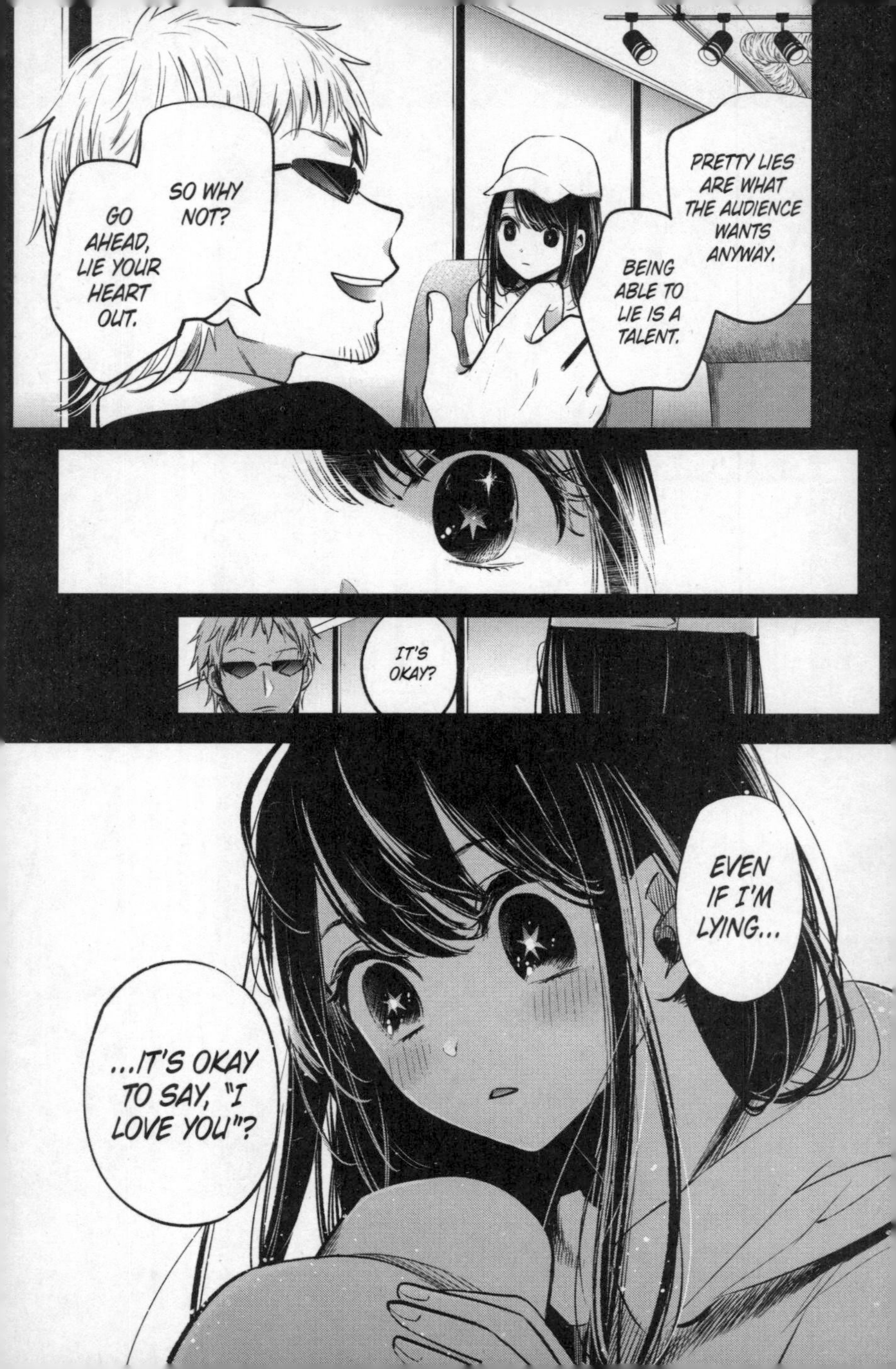
PRETTY LIES ARE WHAT THE AUDIENCE WANTS ANYWAY.
BEING ABLE TO LIE IS A TALENT.
SO WHY NOT?
GO AHEAD, LIE YOUR HEART OUT.
IT'S OKAY?
EVEN IF I'M LYING...
...IT'S OKAY TO SAY, "I LOVE YOU"?

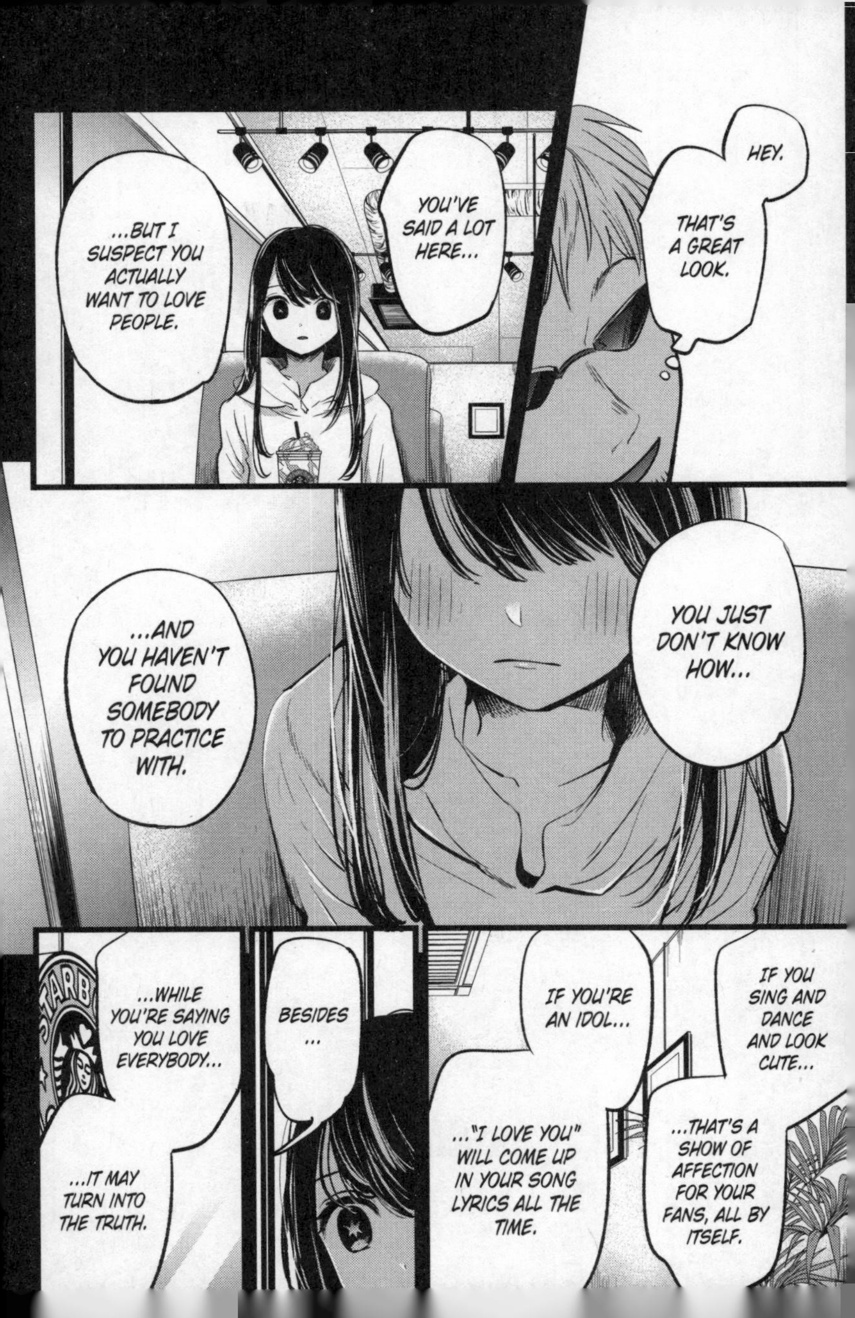
HEY.
THAT'S A GREAT LOOK.
YOU'VE SAID A LOT HERE...
...BUT I SUSPECT YOU ACTUALLY WANT TO LOVE PEOPLE.
YOU JUST DON'T KNOW HOW...
...AND YOU HAVEN'T FOUND SOMEBODY TO PRACTICE WITH.
IF YOU SING AND DANCE AND LOOK CUTE...
IF YOU'RE AN IDOL...
...THAT'S A SHOW OF AFFECTION FOR YOUR FANS, ALL BY ITSELF.
..."I LOVE YOU" WILL COME UP IN YOUR SONG LYRICS ALL THE TIME.
BESIDES...
...WHILE YOU'RE SAYING YOU LOVE EVERYBODY...
...IT MAY TURN INTO THE TRUTH.

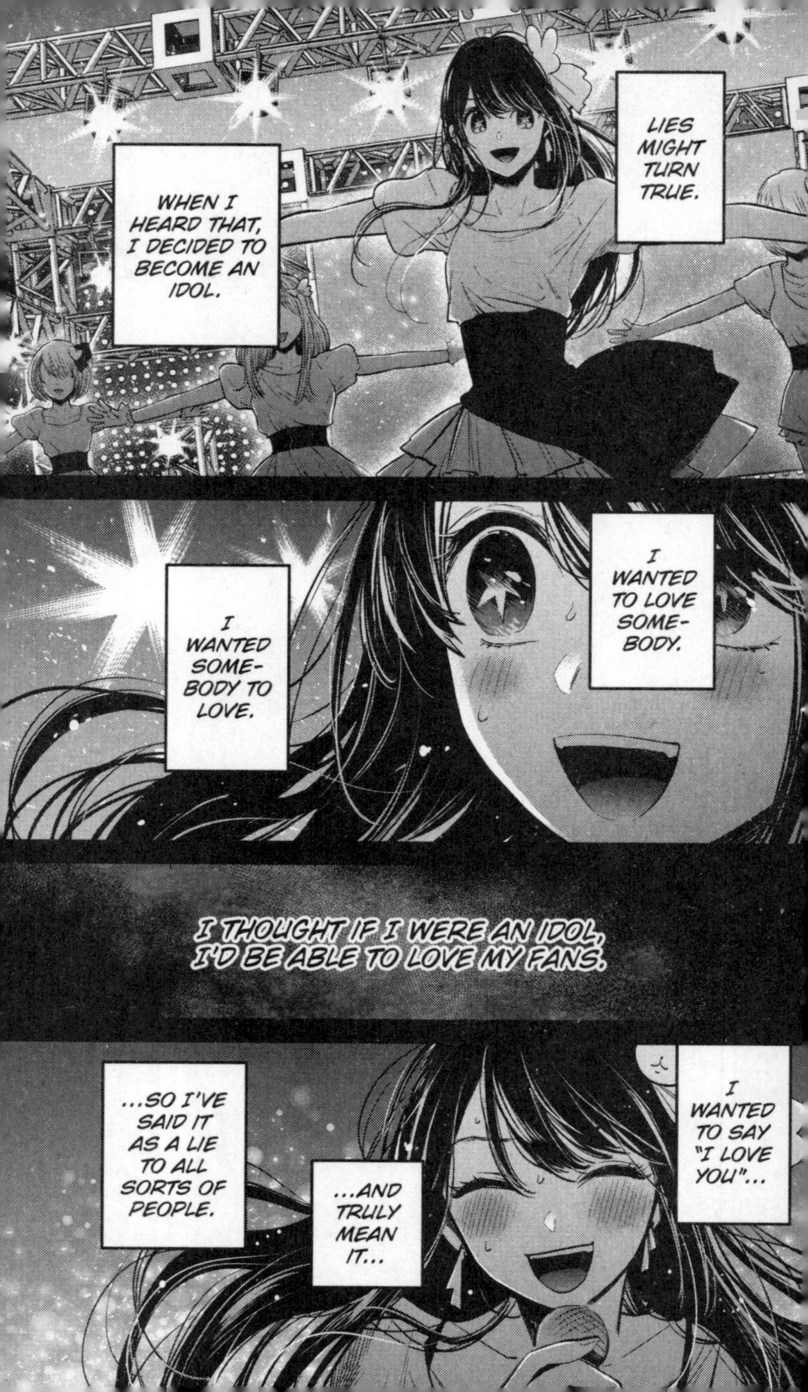
LIES MIGHT TURN TRUE.
WHEN I HEARD THAT, I DECIDED TO BECOME AN IDOL.
I WANTED TO LOVE SOMEBODY.
I WANTED SOMEBODY TO LOVE.
I THOUGHT IF I WERE AN IDOL, I'D BE ABLE TO LOVE MY FANS.
I WANTED TO SAY "I LOVE YOU"...
...AND TRULY MEAN IT...
...SO I'VE SAID IT AS A LIE TO ALL SORTS OF PEOPLE.

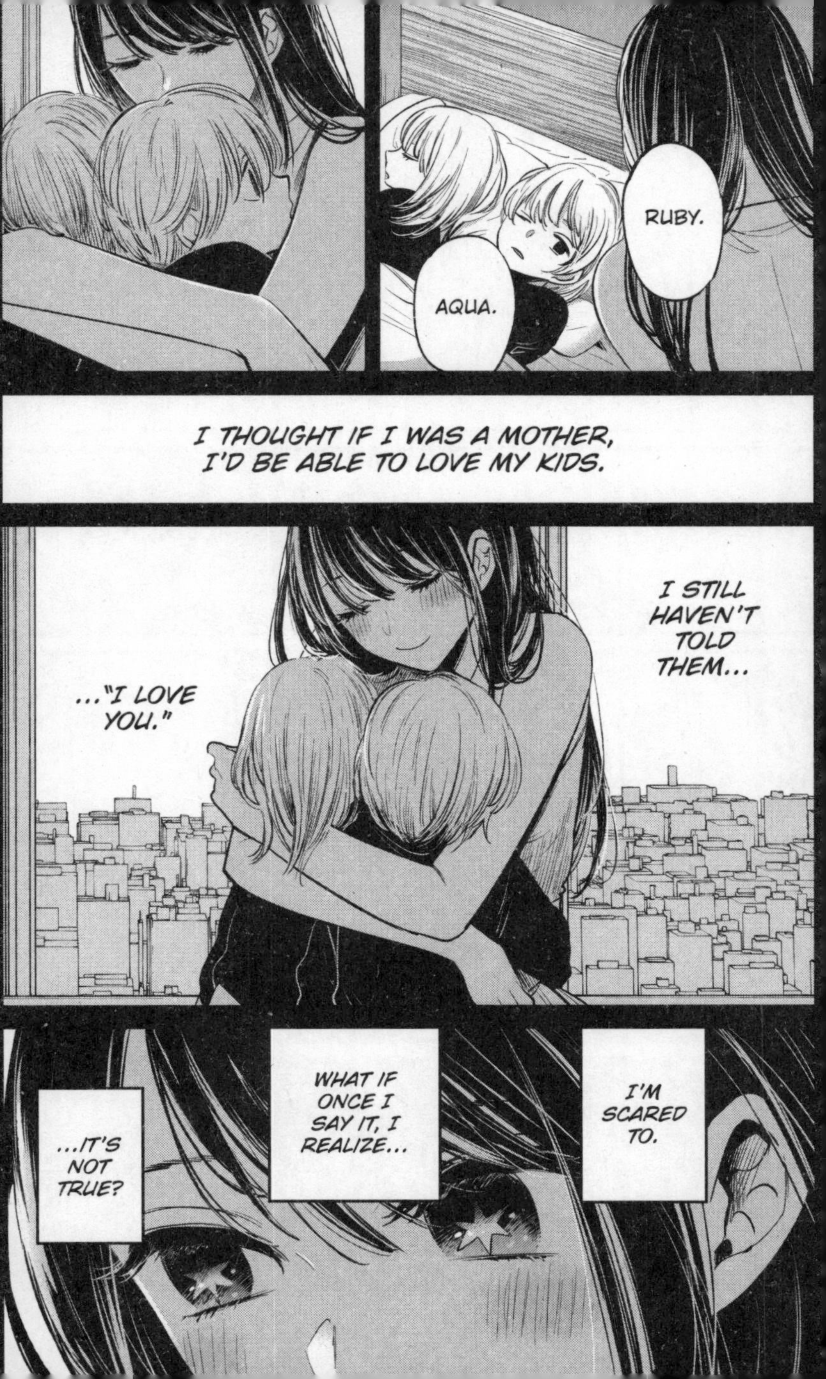
RUBY.
AQUA.
I THOUGHT IF I WAS A MOTHER, I'D BE ABLE TO LOVE MY KIDS.
I STILL HAVEN'T TOLD THEM...
..."I LOVE YOU."
I'M SCARED TO.
WHAT IF ONCE I SAY IT, I REALIZE...
...IT'S NOT TRUE?

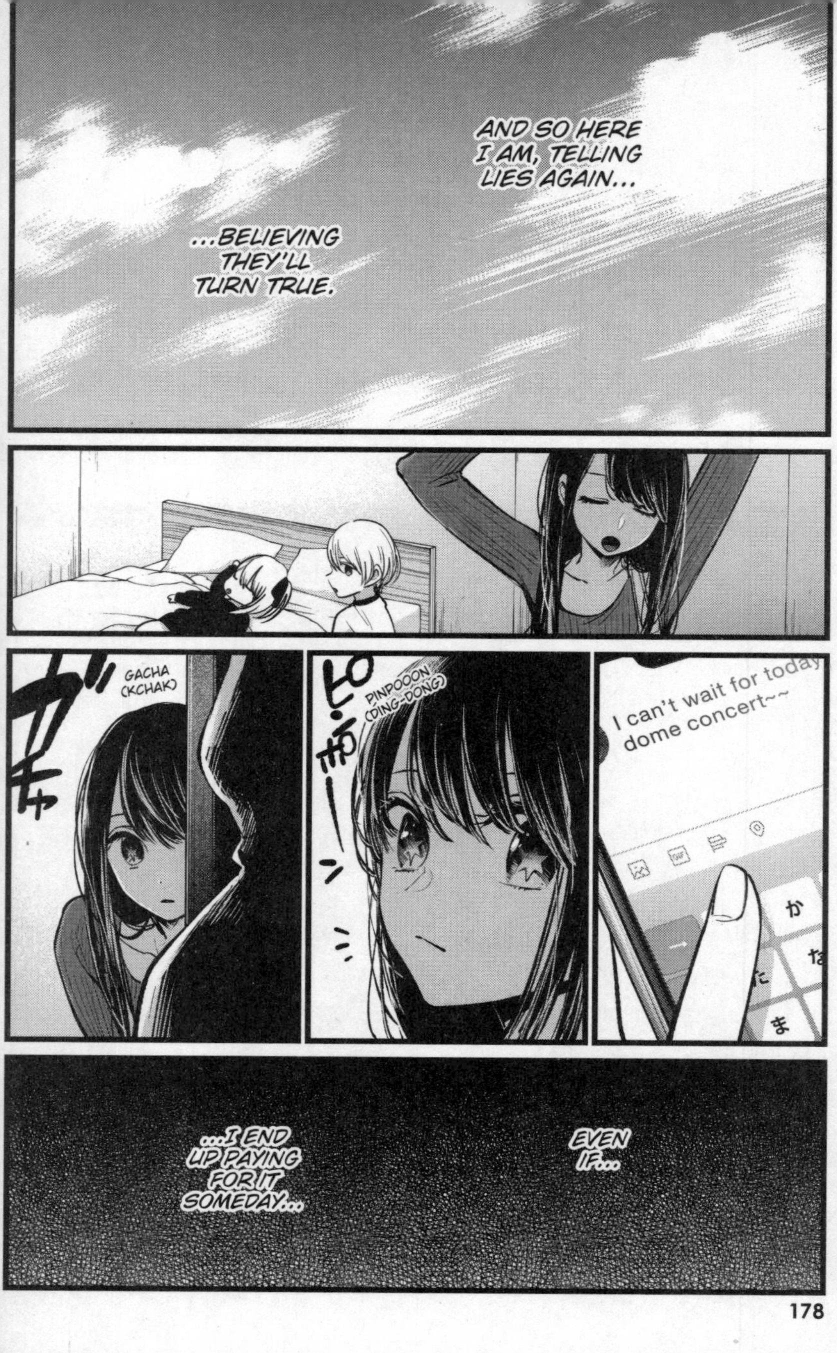
AND SO HERE I AM, TELLING LIES AGAIN...
...BELIEVING THEY'LL TURN TRUE.
I can't wait for today
dome concert~~
PINPOOON (DING-DONG)
GACHA (KCHAK)
EVEN IF...
...I END UP PAYING FOR IT SOMEDAY...

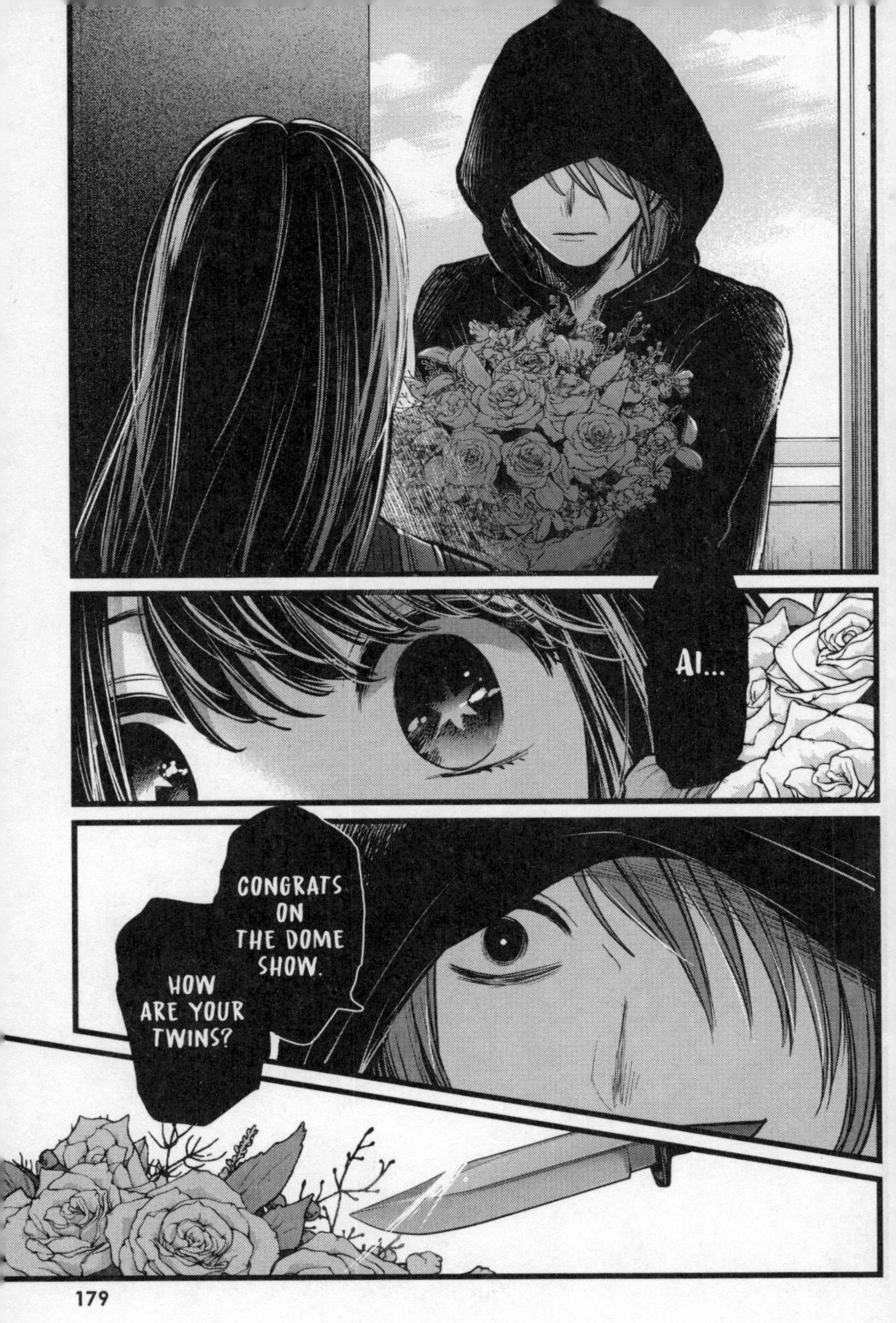
AI...
CONGRATS ON THE DOME SHOW.
HOW ARE YOUR TWINS?

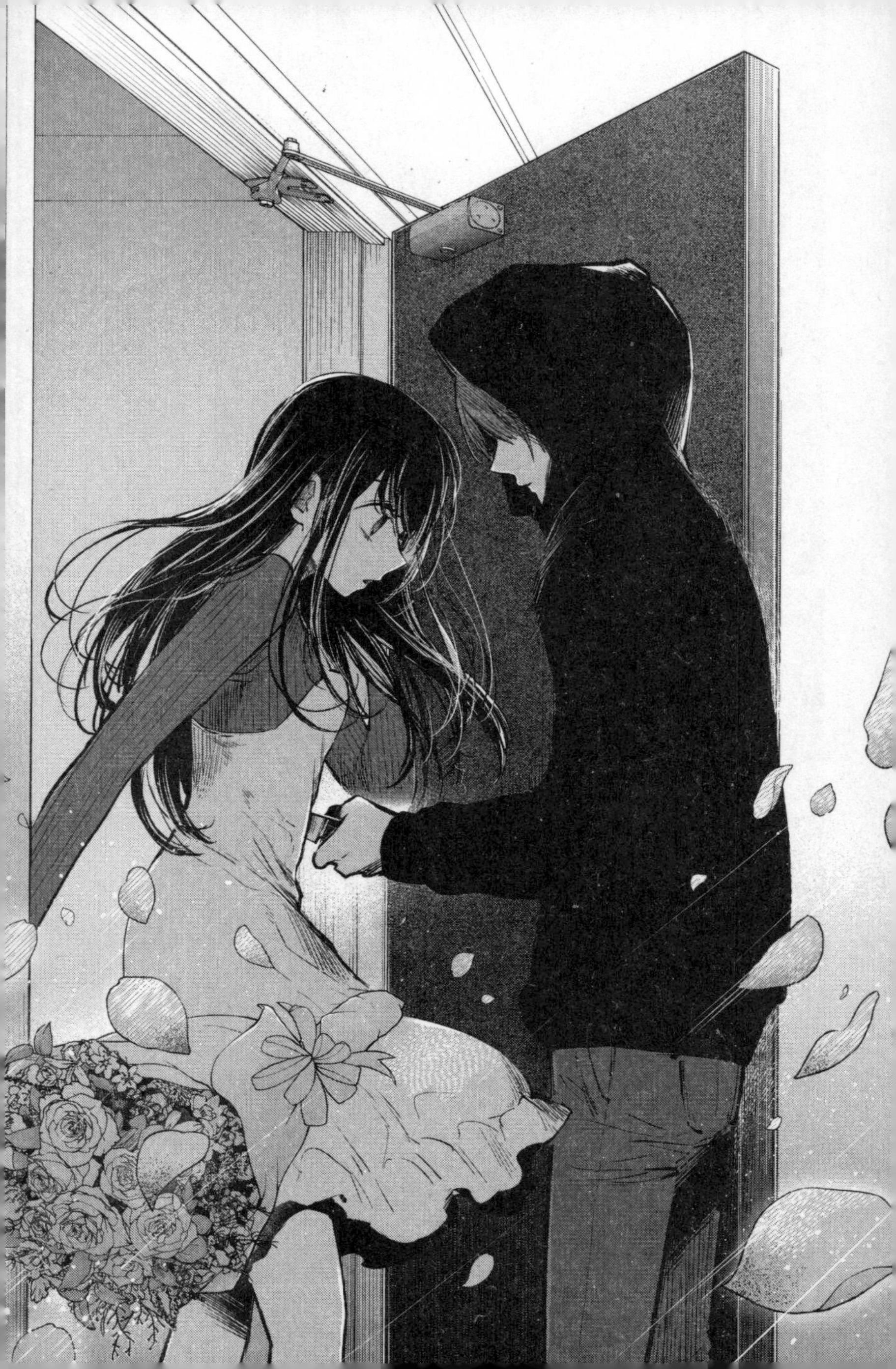

【Chapter 9】

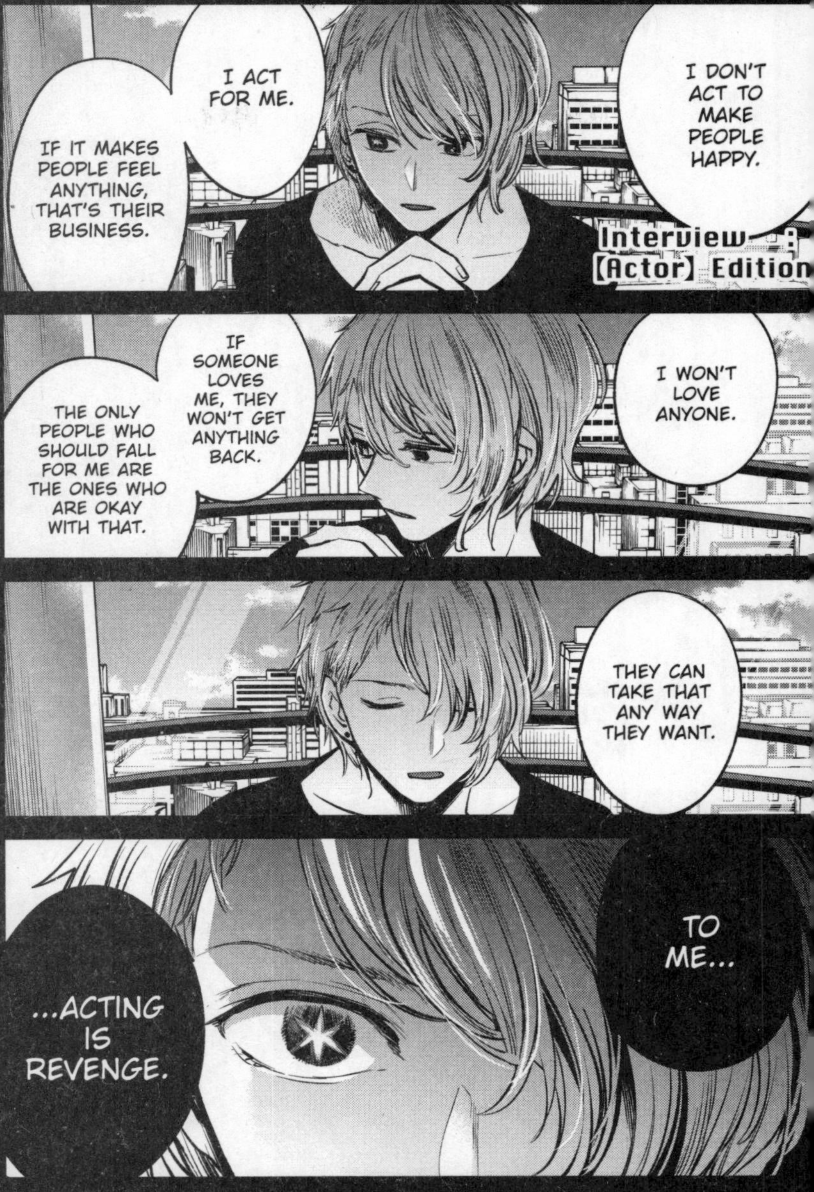
I DON'T ACT TO MAKE PEOPLE HAPPY.
I ACT FOR ME.
IF IT MAKES PEOPLE FEEL ANYTHING, THAT'S THEIR BUSINESS.
Interview: 【Actor】 Edition
I WON'T LOVE ANYONE.
IF SOMEONE LOVES ME, THEY WON'T GET ANYTHING BACK.
THE ONLY PEOPLE WHO SHOULD FALL FOR ME ARE THE ONES WHO ARE OKAY WITH THAT.
THEY CAN TAKE THAT ANY WAY THEY WANT.
TO ME...
...ACTING IS REVENGE.

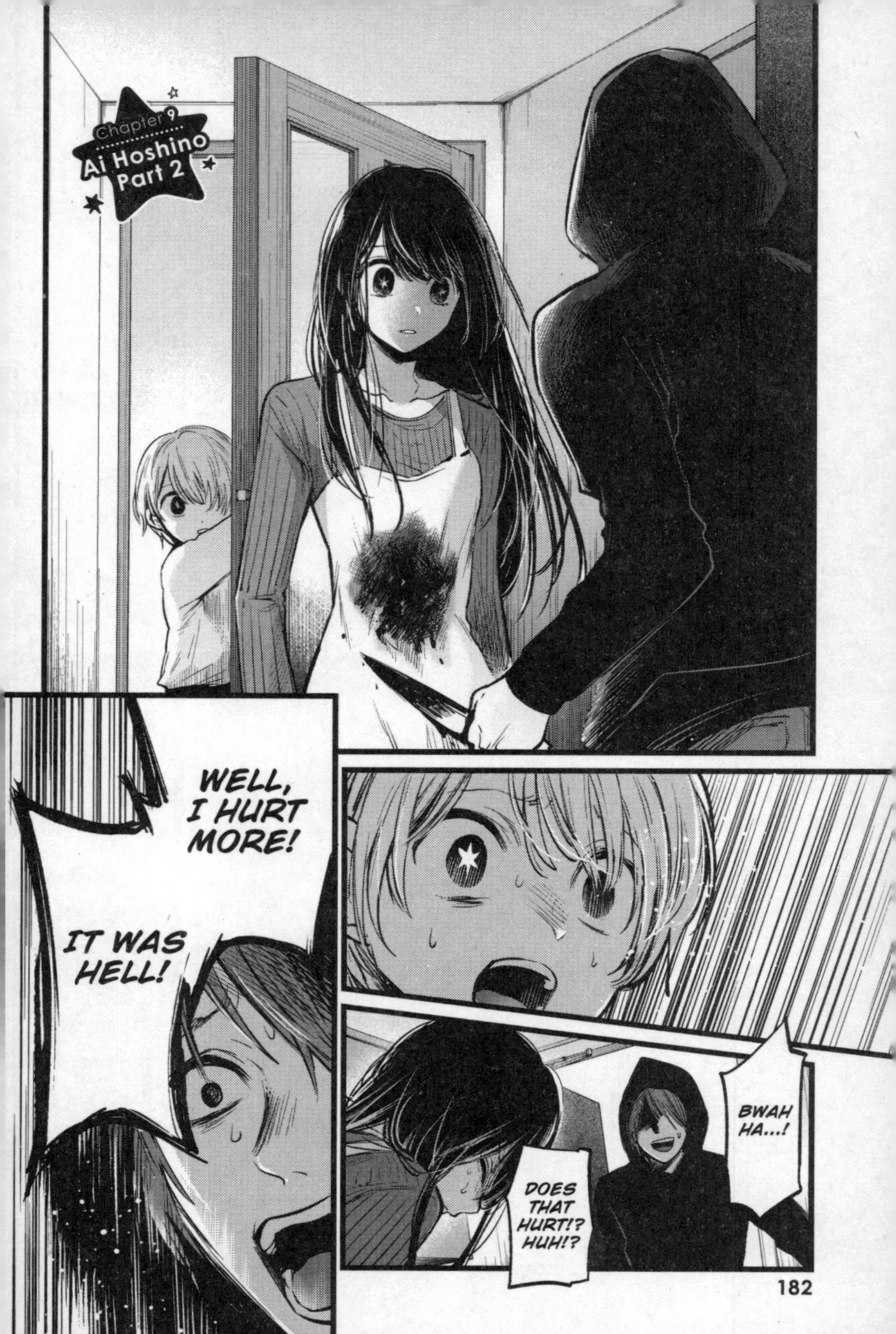
Chapter 9
Ai Hoshino Part 2
BWAH HA...!
DOES THAT HURT!? HUH!?
WELL, I HURT MORE!
IT WAS HELL!

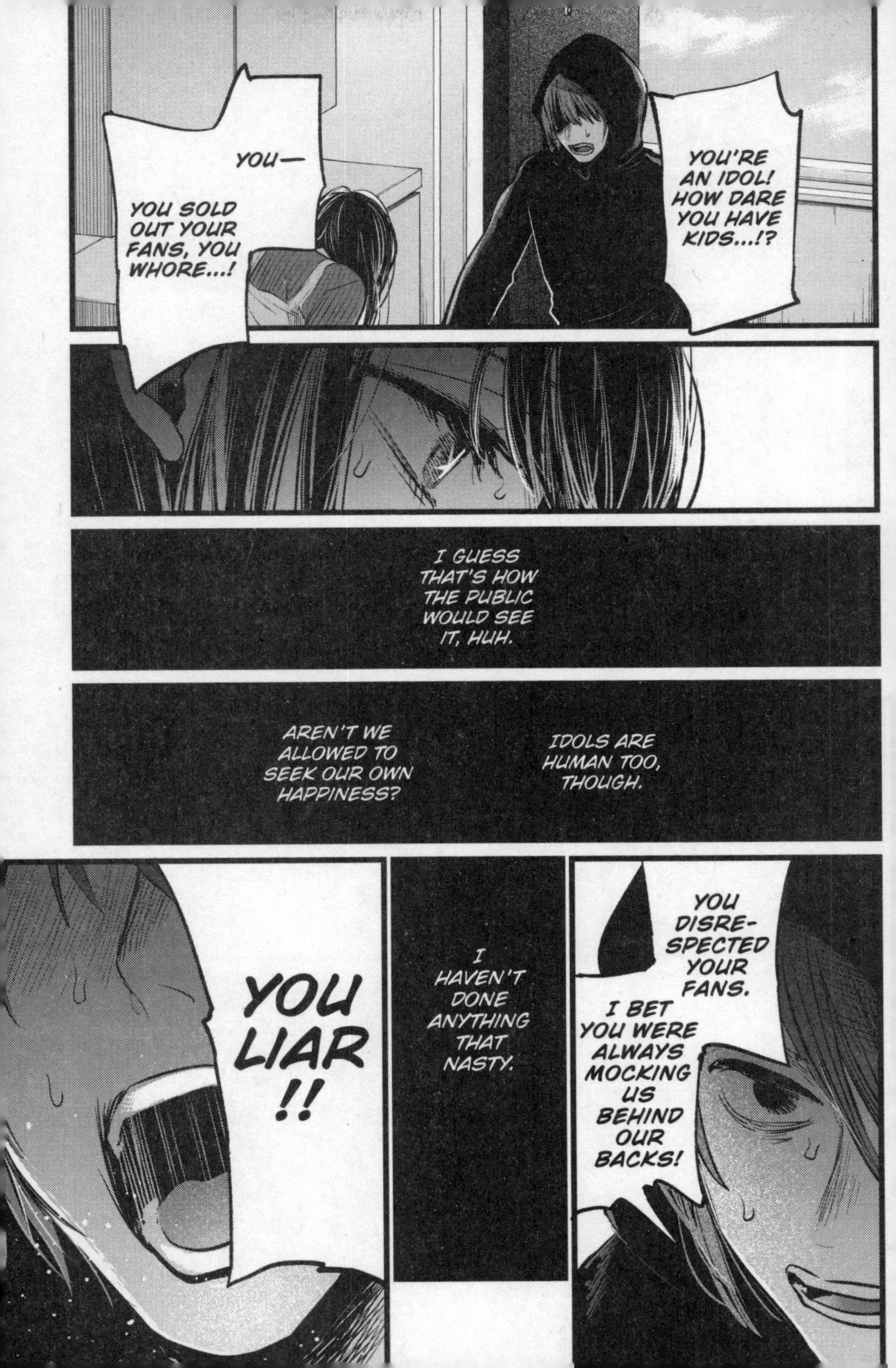
YOU'RE AN IDOL! HOW DARE YOU HAVE KIDS...!?
YOU—
YOU SOLD OUT YOUR FANS, YOU WHORE...!
I GUESS THAT'S HOW THE PUBLIC WOULD SEE IT, HUH.
IDOLS ARE HUMAN TOO, THOUGH.
AREN'T WE ALLOWED TO SEEK OUR OWN HAPPINESS?
YOU DISRE-SPECTED YOUR FANS.
I BET YOU WERE ALWAYS MOCKING US BEHIND OUR BACKS!
I HAVEN'T DONE ANYTHING THAT NASTY.
YOU LIAR!!

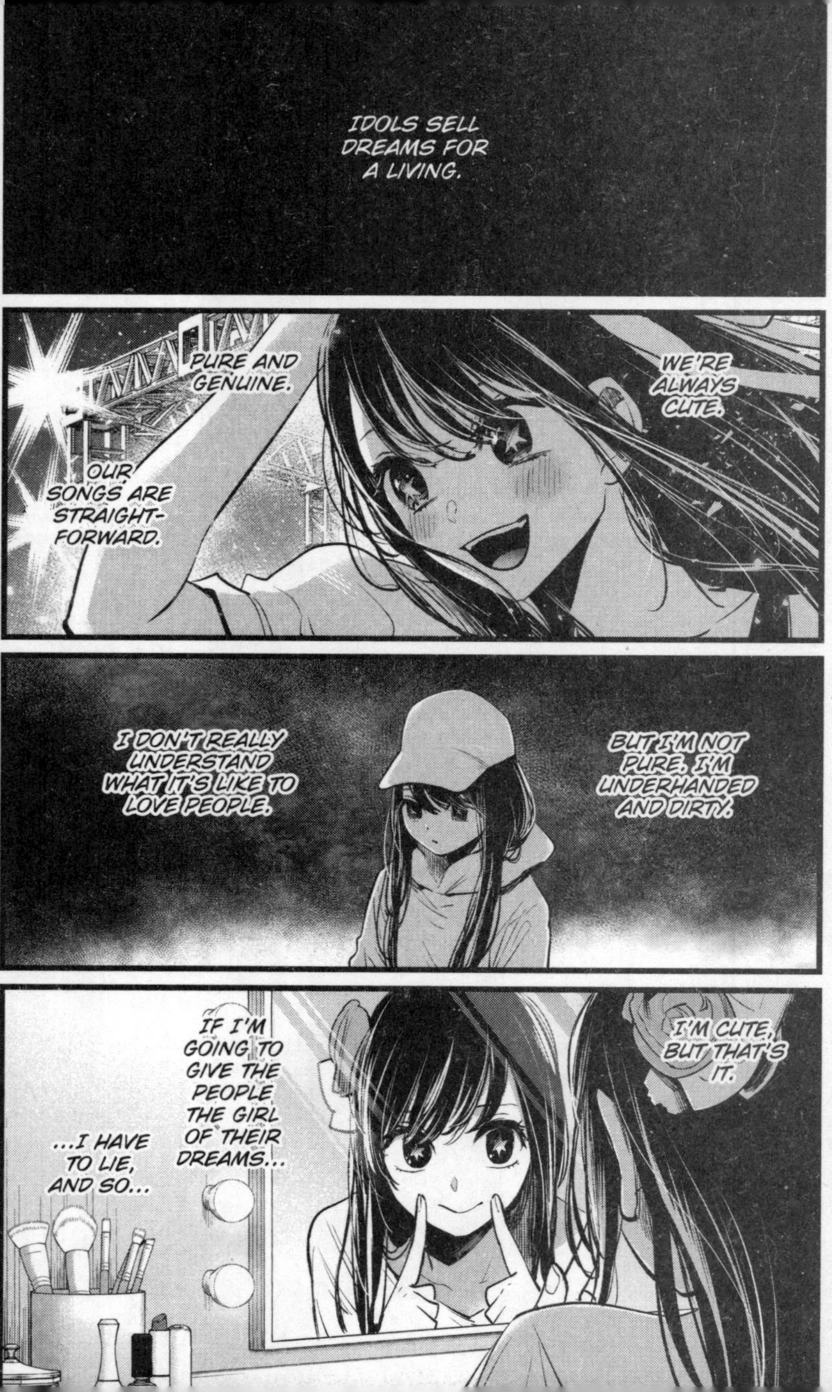
IDOLS SELL DREAMS FOR A LIVING.
WE'RE ALWAYS CUTE.
PURE AND GENUINE.
OUR SONGS ARE STRAIGHT-FORWARD.
BUT I'M NOT PURE. I'M UNDERHANDED AND DIRTY.
I DON'T REALLY UNDERSTAND WHAT IT'S LIKE TO LOVE PEOPLE.
I'M CUTE, BUT THAT'S IT.
IF I'M GOING TO GIVE THE PEOPLE THE GIRL OF THEIR DREAMS...
...I HAVE TO LIE, AND SO...

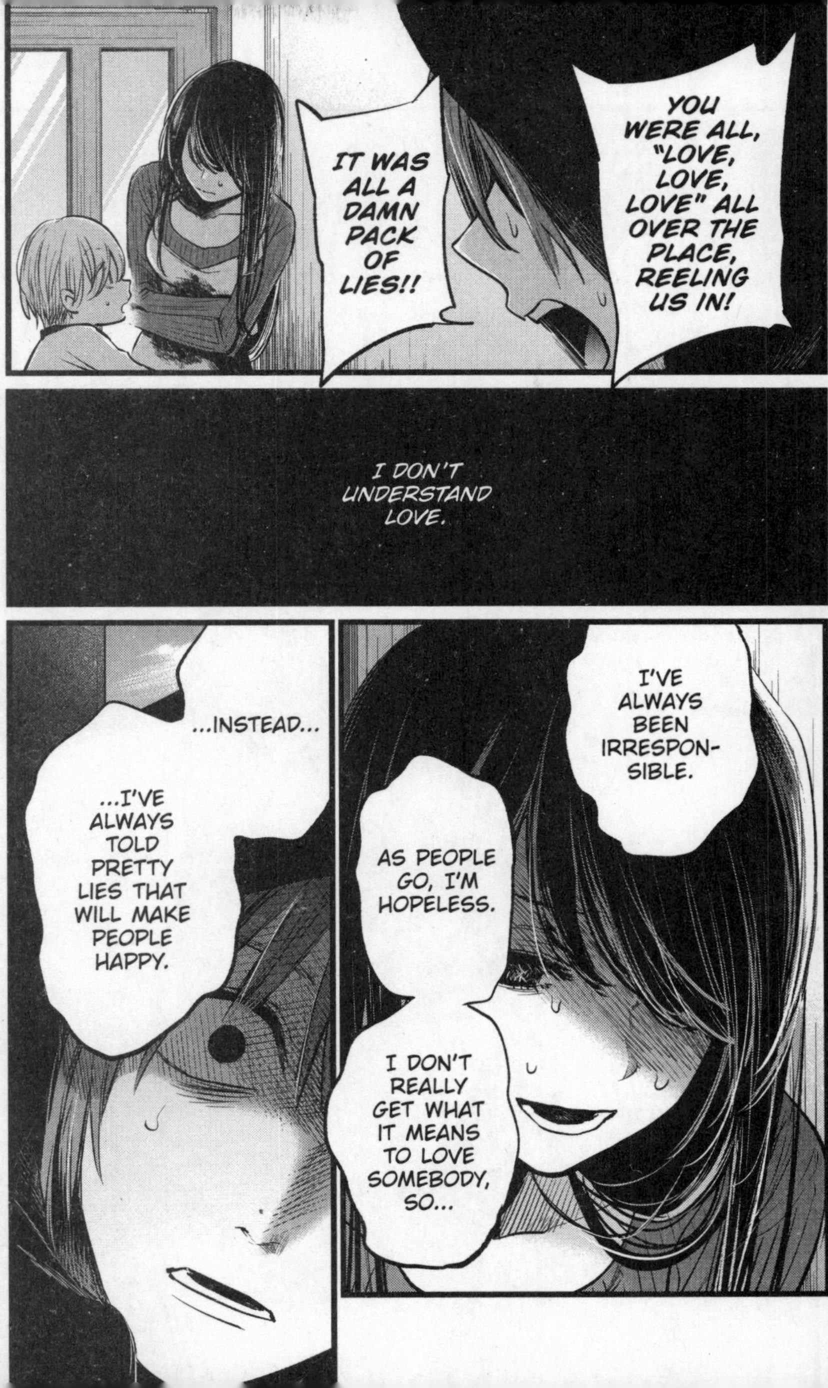
YOU WERE ALL, "LOVE, LOVE, LOVE" ALL OVER THE PLACE, REELING US IN!
IT WAS ALL A DAMN PACK OF LIES!!
I DON'T UNDERSTAND LOVE.
I'VE ALWAYS BEEN IRRESPONSIBLE.
AS PEOPLE GO, I'M HOPELESS.
I DON'T REALLY GET WHAT IT MEANS TO LOVE SOMEBODY, SO...
...INSTEAD...
...I'VE ALWAYS TOLD PRETTY LIES THAT WILL MAKE PEOPLE HAPPY.

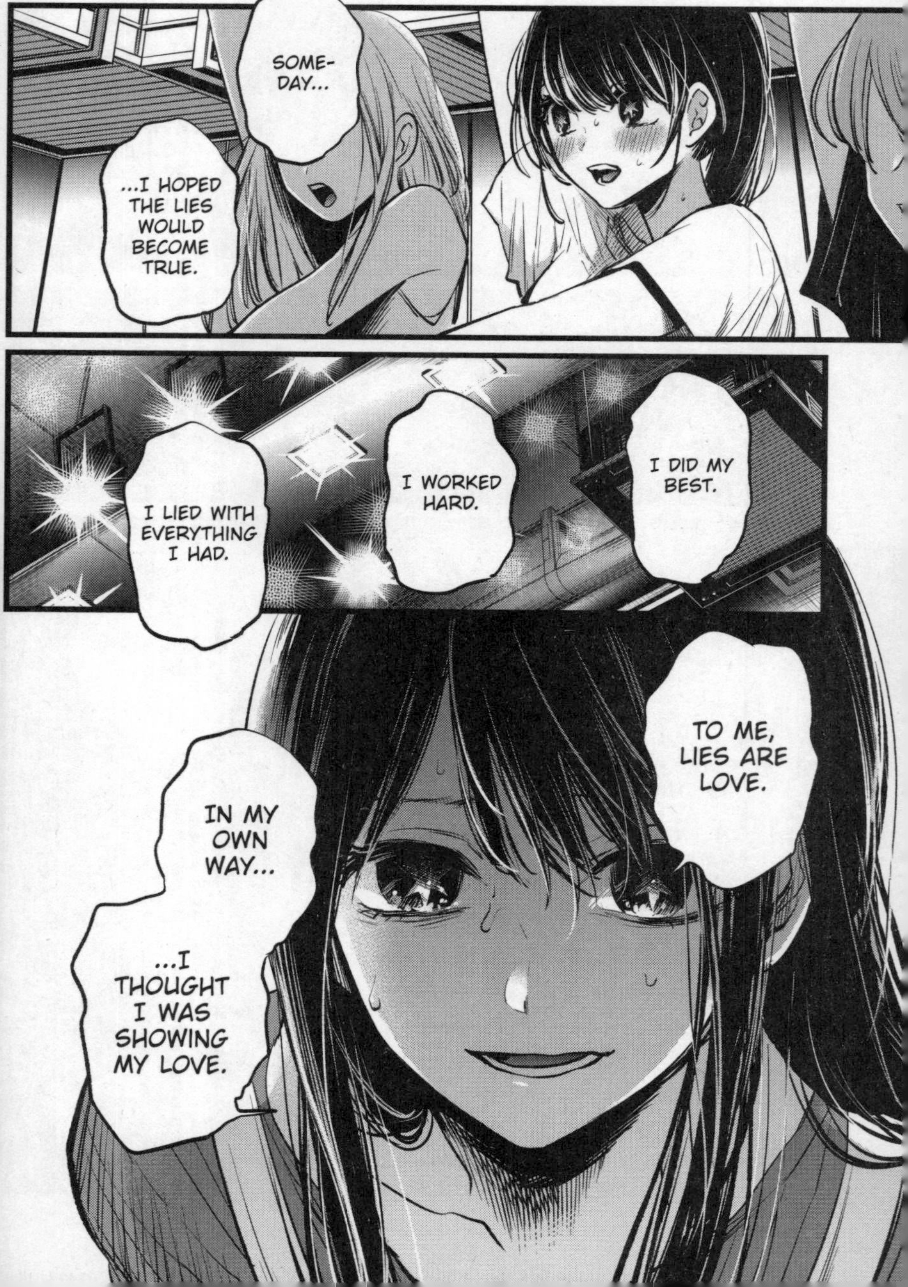
SOME-DAY...
...I HOPED THE LIES WOULD BECOME TRUE.
I DID MY BEST.
I WORKED HARD.
I LIED WITH EVERYTHING I HAD.
TO ME, LIES ARE LOVE.
IN MY OWN WAY...
...I THOUGHT I WAS SHOWING MY LOVE.

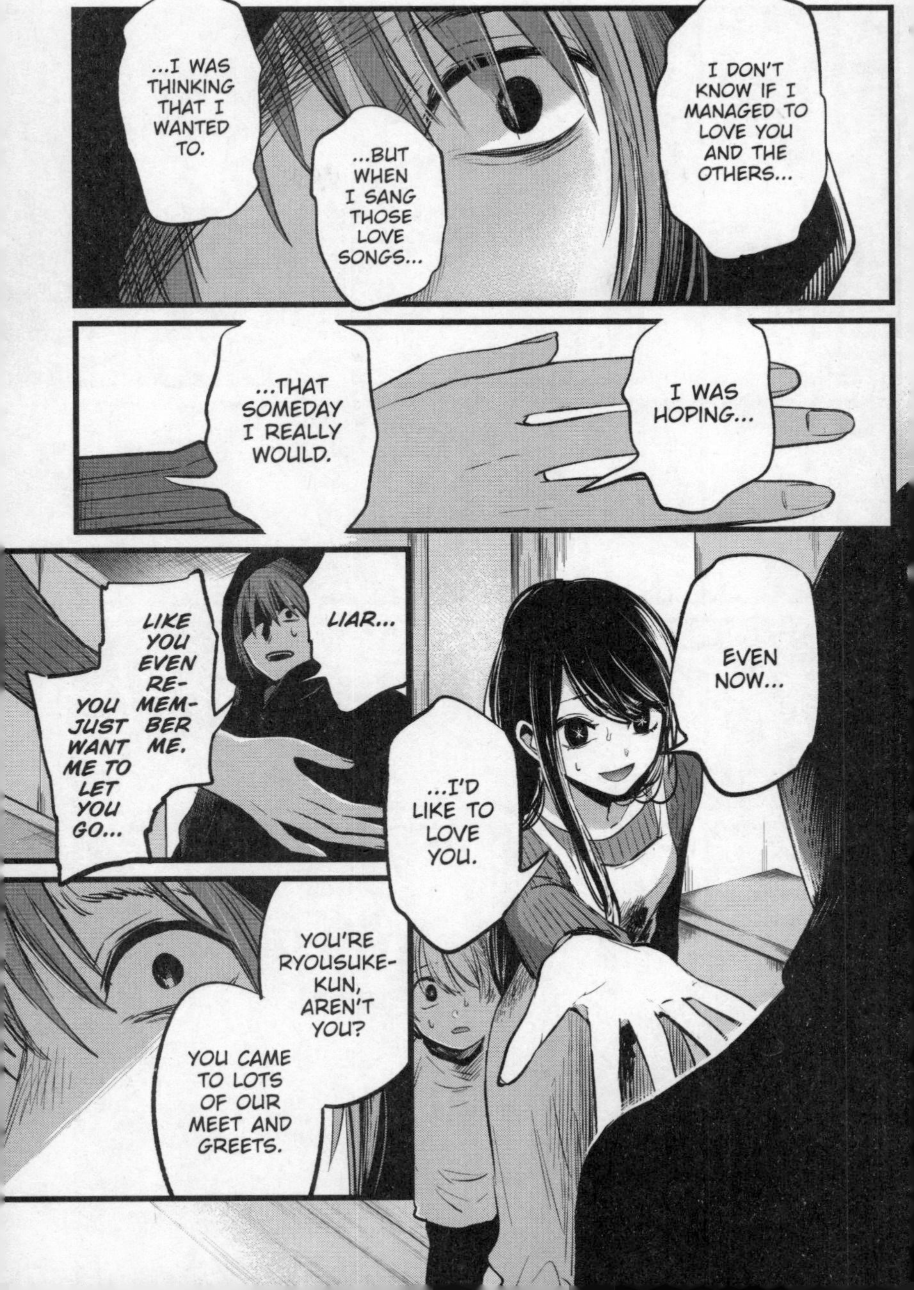
I DON'T KNOW IF I MANAGED TO LOVE YOU AND THE OTHERS...
...BUT WHEN I SANG THOSE LOVE SONGS...
...I WAS THINKING THAT I WANTED TO.
I WAS HOPING...
...THAT SOMEDAY I REALLY WOULD.
EVEN NOW...
...I'D LIKE TO LOVE YOU.
LIAR...
LIKE YOU EVEN RE-MEM-BER ME.
YOU JUST WANT ME TO LET YOU GO...
YOU'RE RYOUSUKE-KUN, AREN'T YOU?
YOU CAME TO LOTS OF OUR MEET AND GREETS.

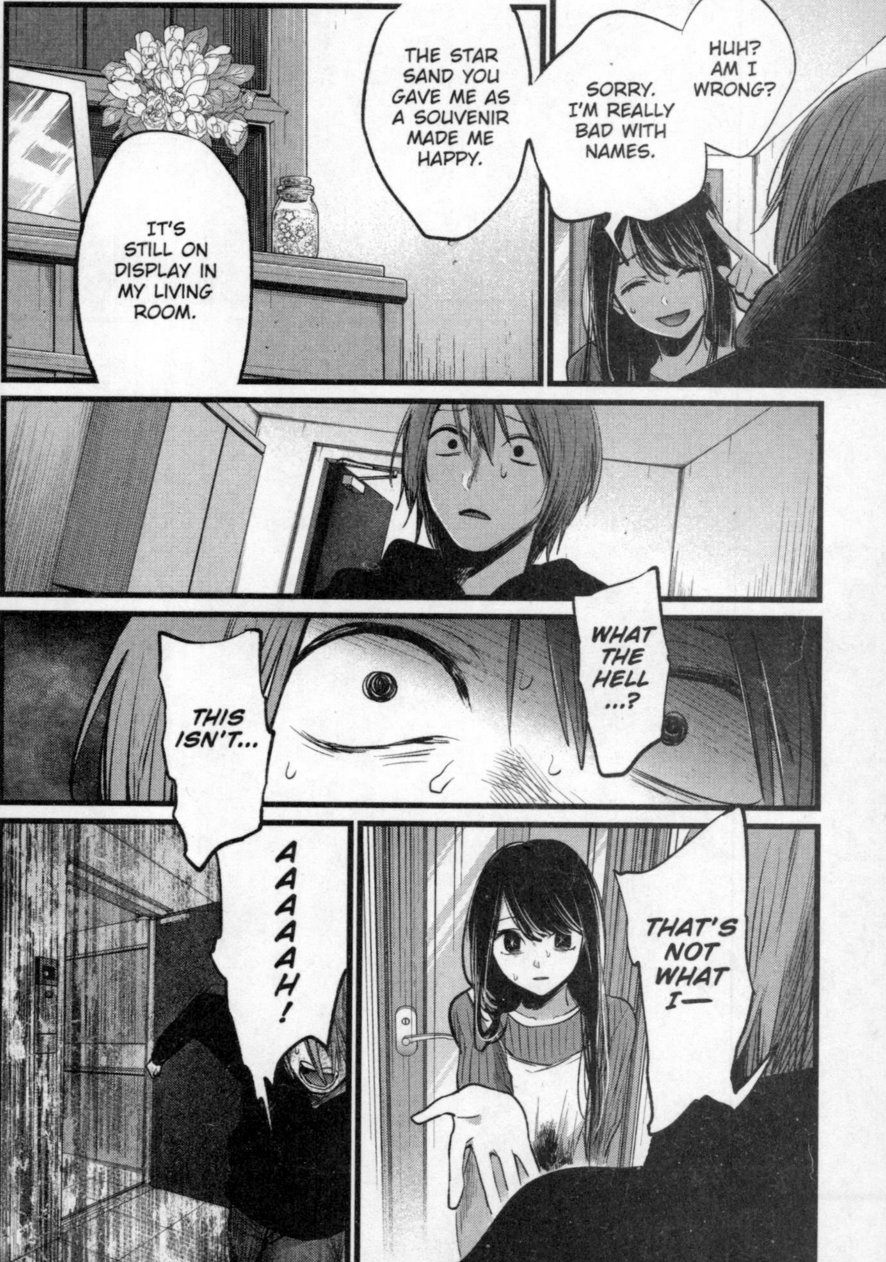
HUH? AM I WRONG?
SORRY. I'M REALLY BAD WITH NAMES.
THE STAR SAND YOU GAVE ME AS A SOUVENIR MADE ME HAPPY.
IT'S STILL ON DISPLAY IN MY LIVING ROOM.
WHAT THE HELL ...?
THIS ISN'T...
THAT'S NOT WHAT I—
AAAAAAH!

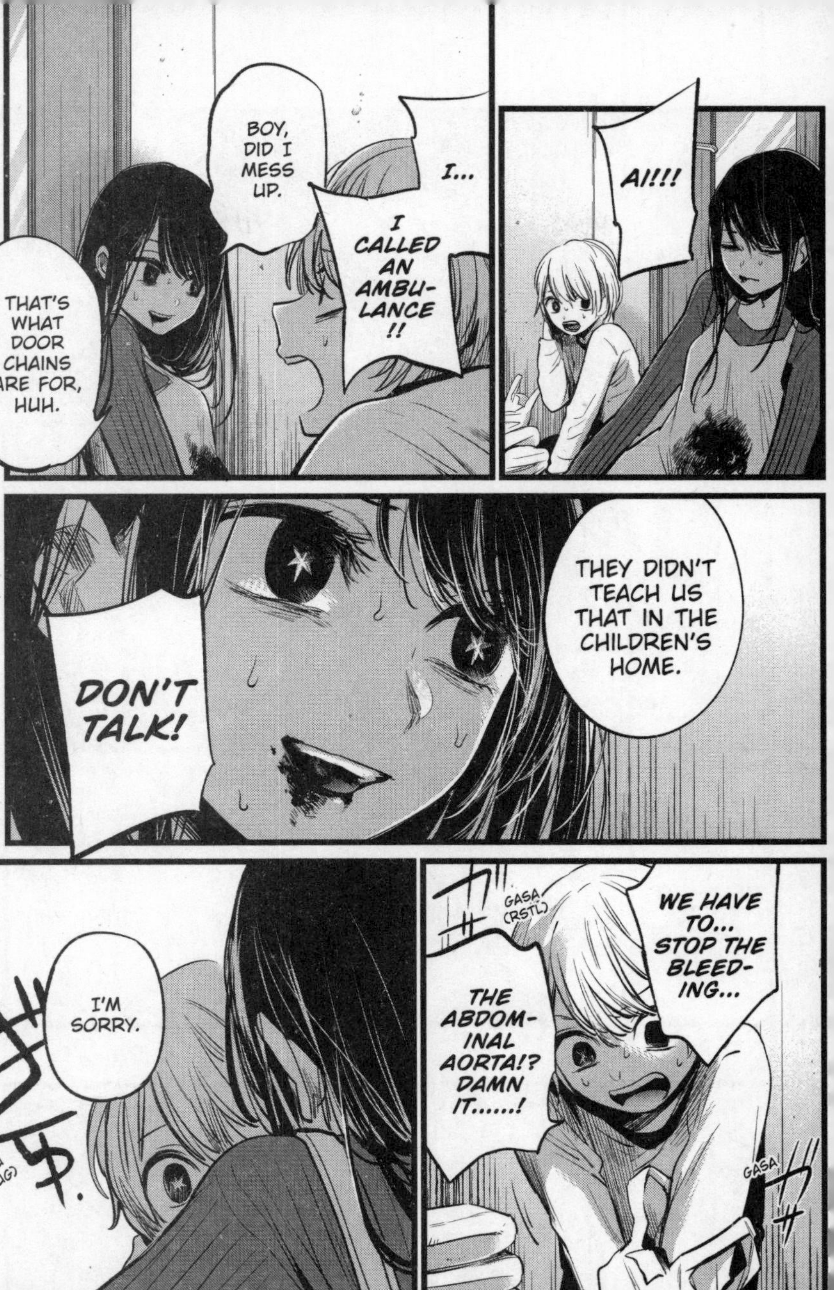
AI!!!
I...
I CALLED AN AMBULANCE!!
BOY, DID I MESS UP.
THAT'S WHAT DOOR CHAINS ARE FOR, HUH.
THEY DIDN'T TEACH US THAT IN THE CHILDREN'S HOME.
DON'T TALK!
GASA (RSTL)
WE HAVE TO... STOP THE BLEEDING...
THE ABDOMINAL AORTA!? DAMN IT......!
GASA
I'M SORRY.
GYU (HUG)

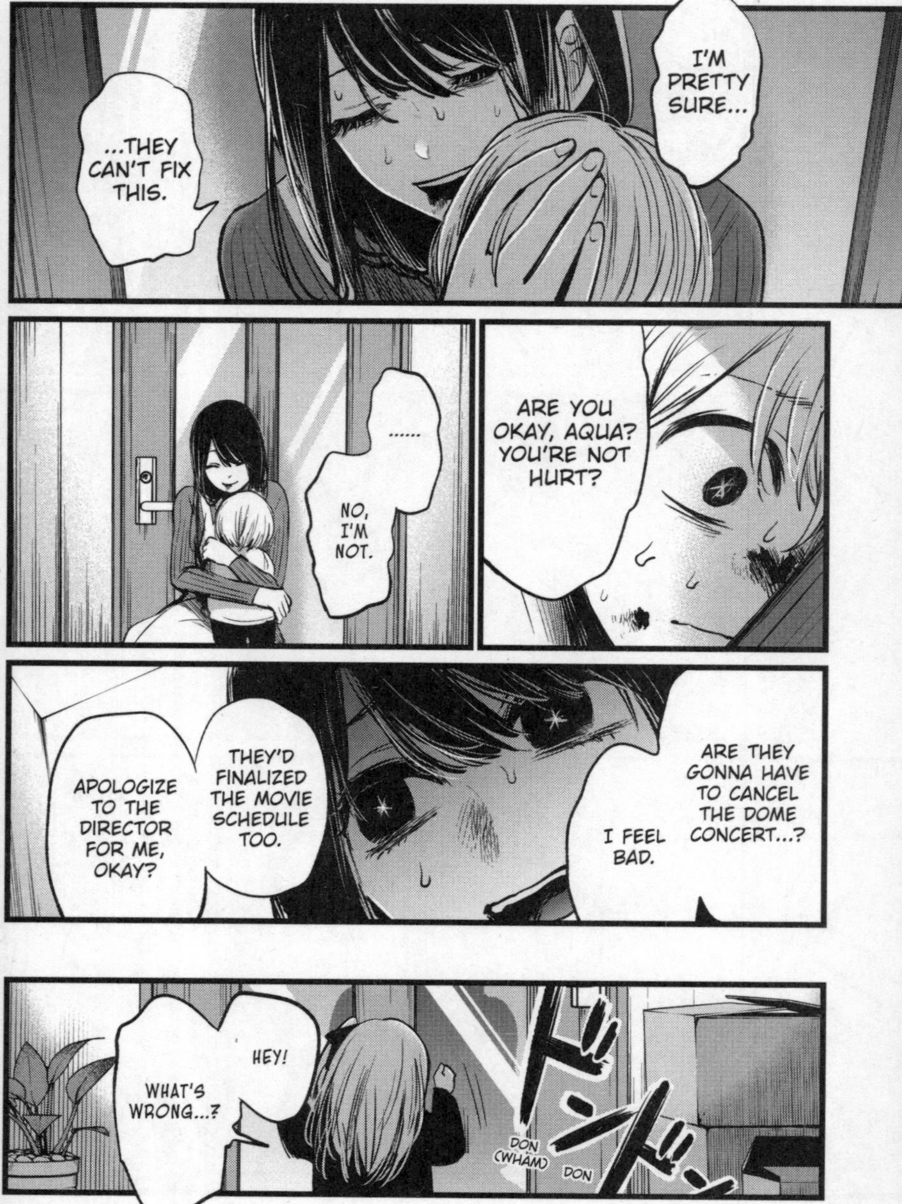

I'M PRETTY SURE...
...THEY CAN'T FIX THIS.
ARE YOU OKAY, AQUA? YOU'RE NOT HURT?
......
NO, I'M NOT.
ARE THEY GONNA HAVE TO CANCEL THE DOME CONCERT...?
I FEEL BAD.
THEY'D FINALIZED THE MOVIE SCHEDULE TOO.
APOLOGIZE TO THE DIRECTOR FOR ME, OKAY?
DON (WHAM)
DON
HEY!
WHAT'S WRONG...?

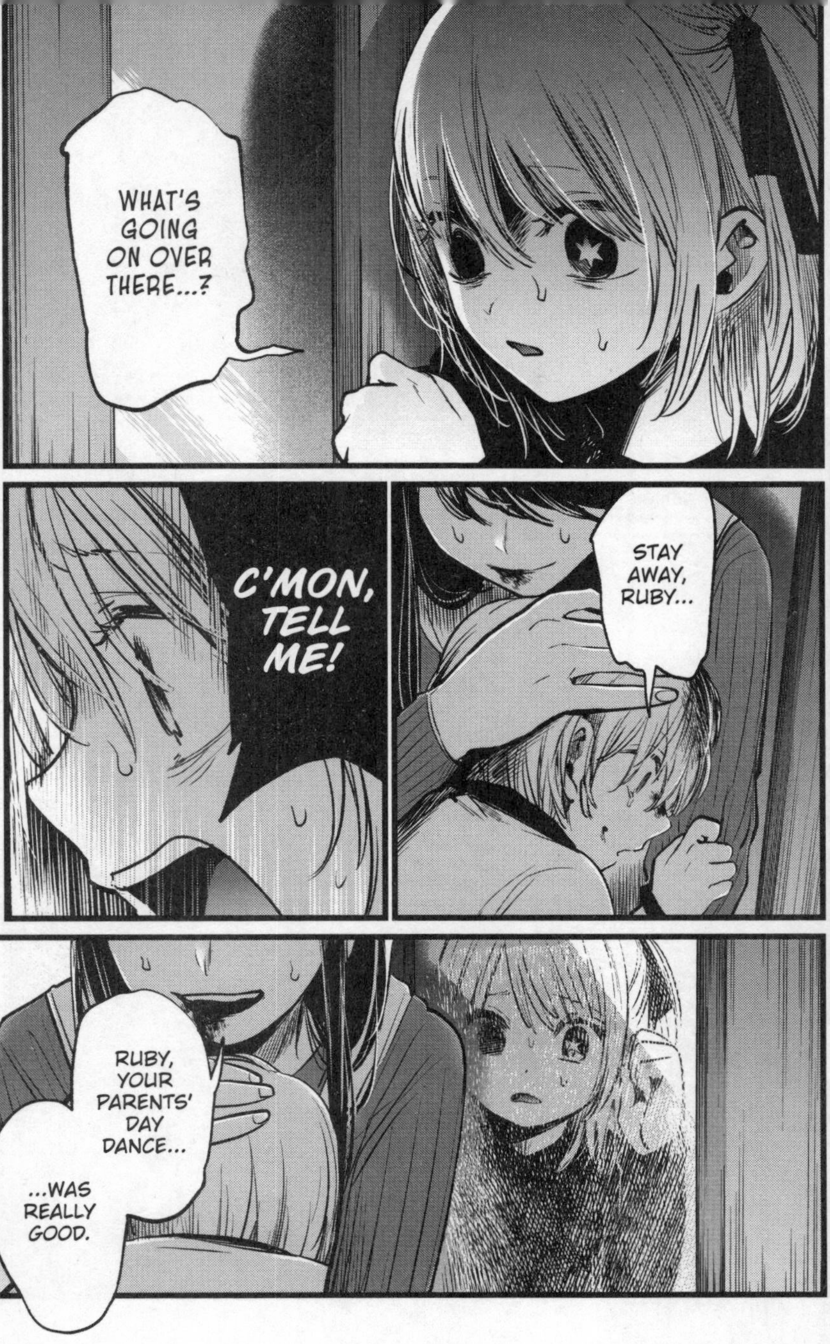
WHAT'S GOING ON OVER THERE...?
STAY AWAY, RUBY...
C'MON, TELL ME!
RUBY, YOUR PARENTS' DAY DANCE...
...WAS REALLY GOOD.

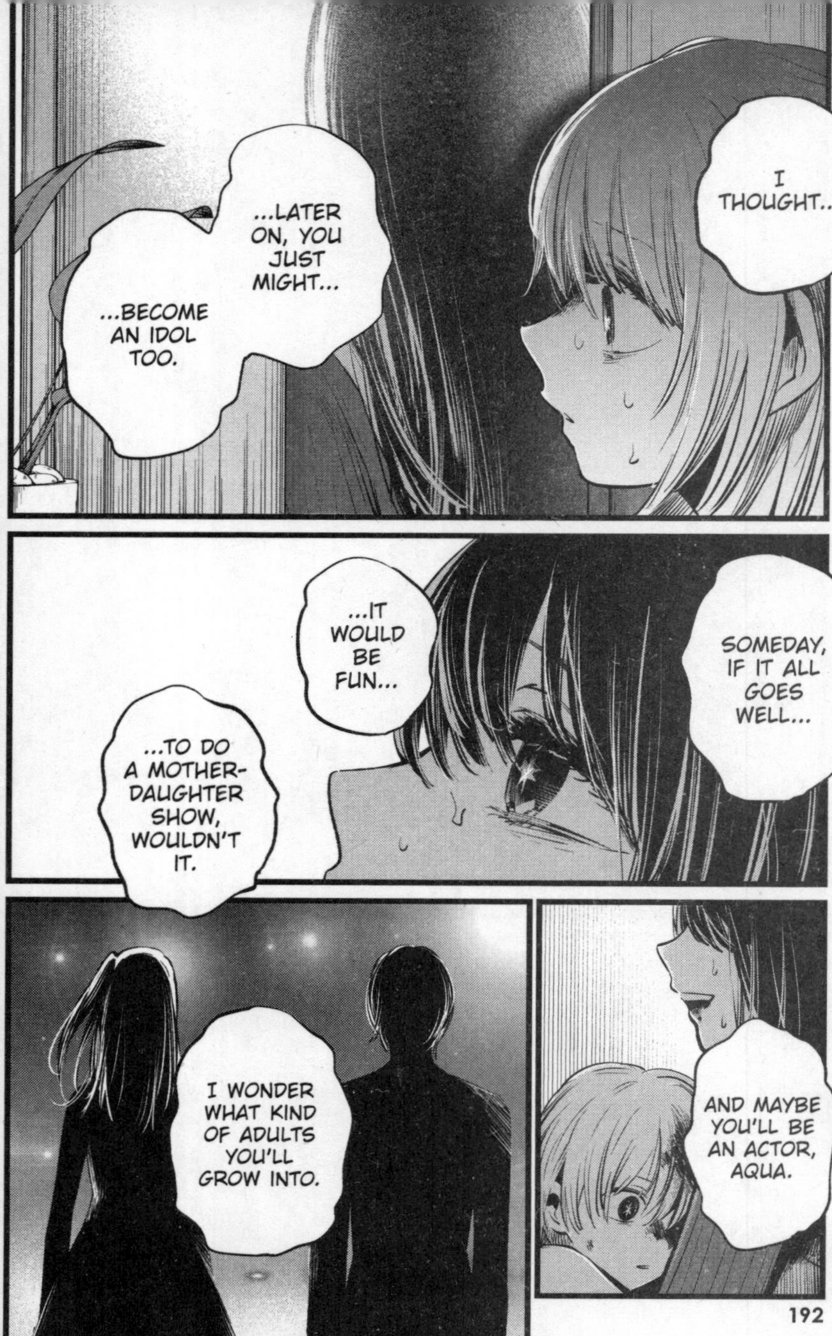
I THOUGHT...
...LATER ON, YOU JUST MIGHT...
...BECOME AN IDOL TOO.
SOMEDAY, IF IT ALL GOES WELL...
...IT WOULD BE FUN...
...TO DO A MOTHER-DAUGHTER SHOW, WOULDN'T IT.
AND MAYBE YOU'LL BE AN ACTOR, AQUA.
I WONDER WHAT KIND OF ADULTS YOU'LL GROW INTO.

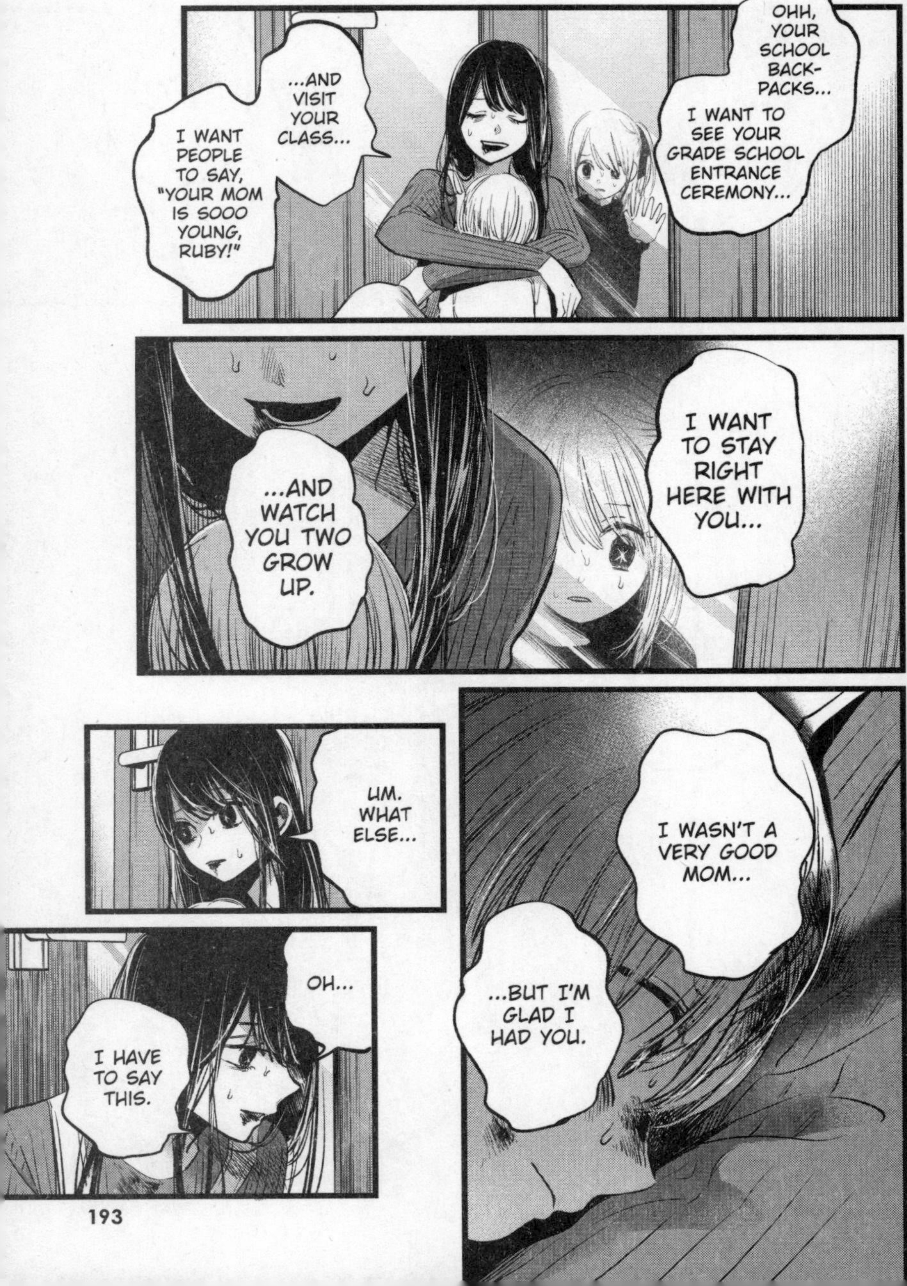

OHH, YOUR SCHOOL BACK-PACKS...
I WANT TO SEE YOUR GRADE SCHOOL ENTRANCE CEREMONY...
...AND VISIT YOUR CLASS...
I WANT PEOPLE TO SAY, "YOUR MOM IS SOOO YOUNG, RUBY!"
I WANT TO STAY RIGHT HERE WITH YOU...
...AND WATCH YOU TWO GROW UP.
I WASN'T A VERY GOOD MOM...
...BUT I'M GLAD I HAD YOU.
UM. WHAT ELSE...
OH...
I HAVE TO SAY THIS.

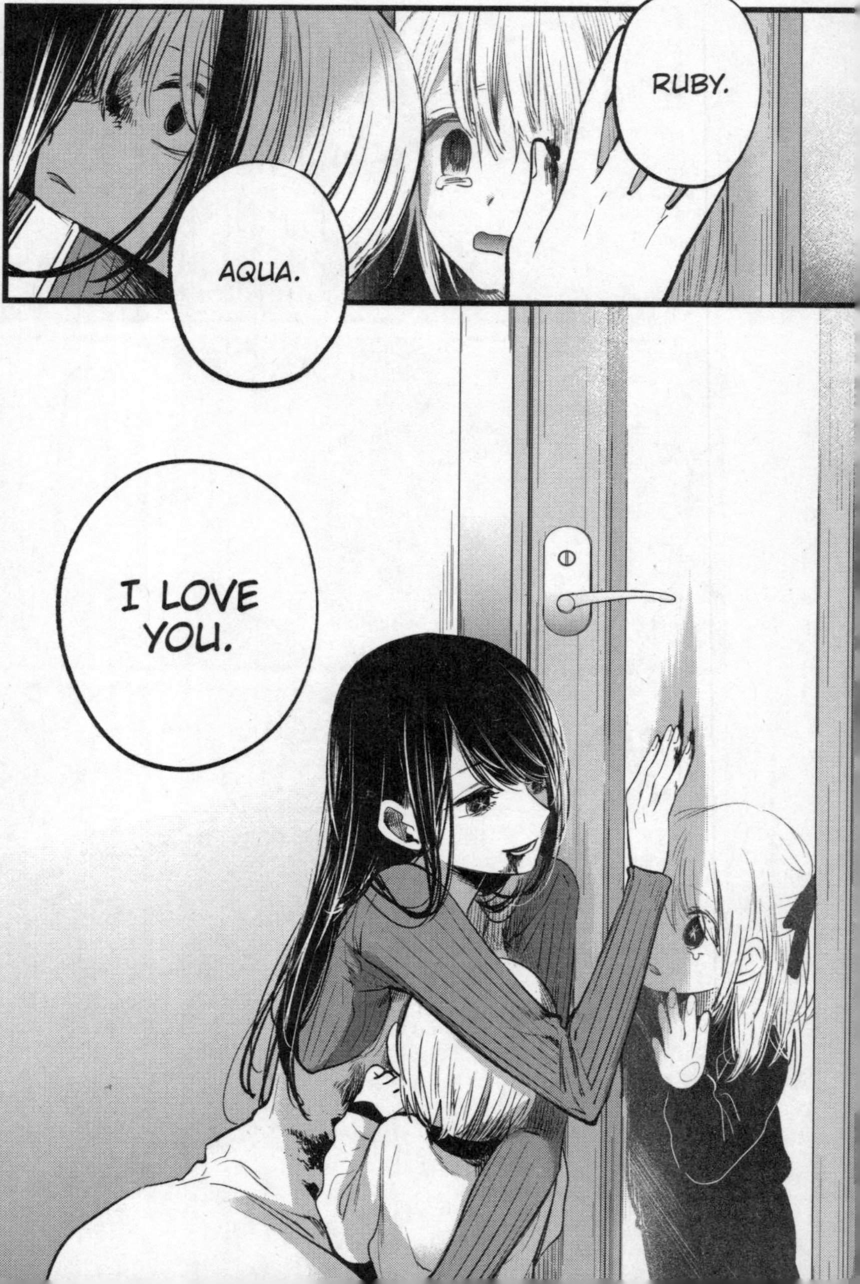
RUBY.
AQUA.
I LOVE YOU.

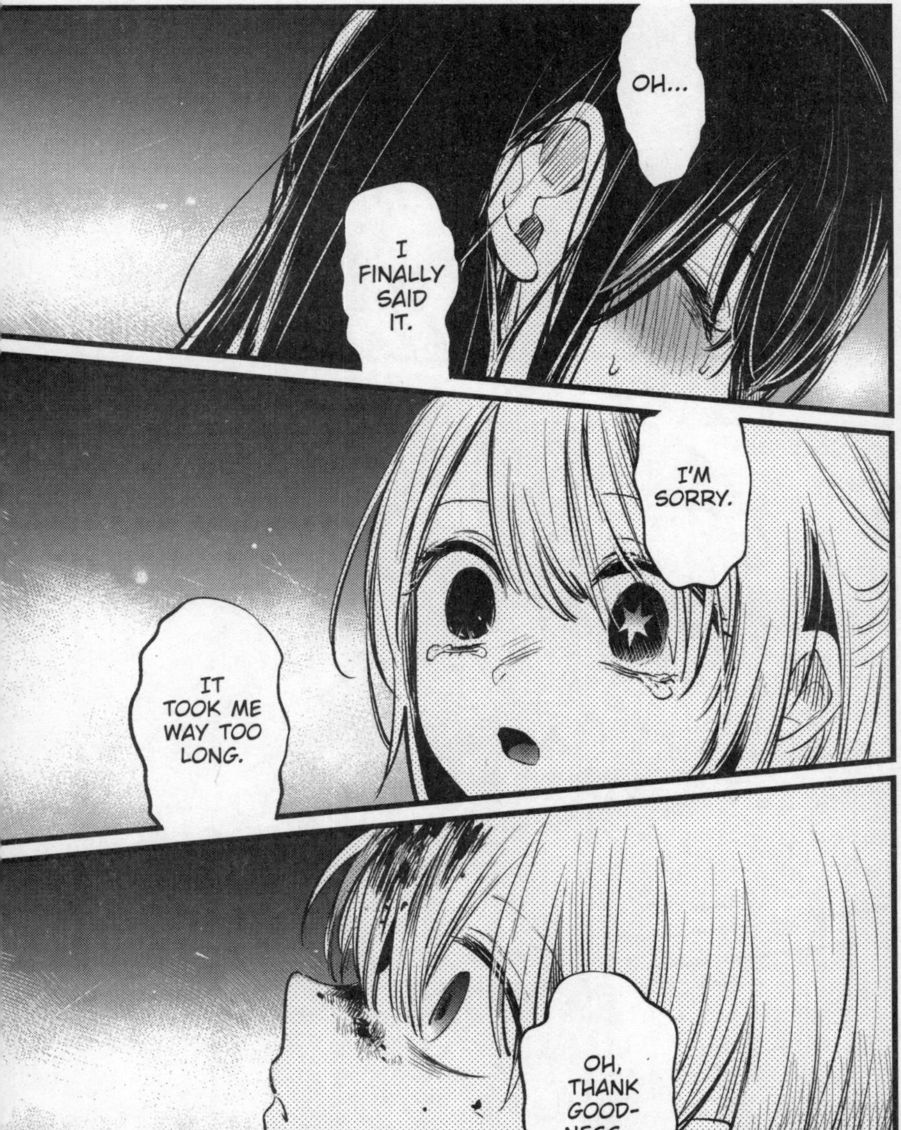
OH...
I FINALLY SAID IT.
I'M SORRY.
IT TOOK ME WAY TOO LONG.
OH, THANK GOOD-NESS...

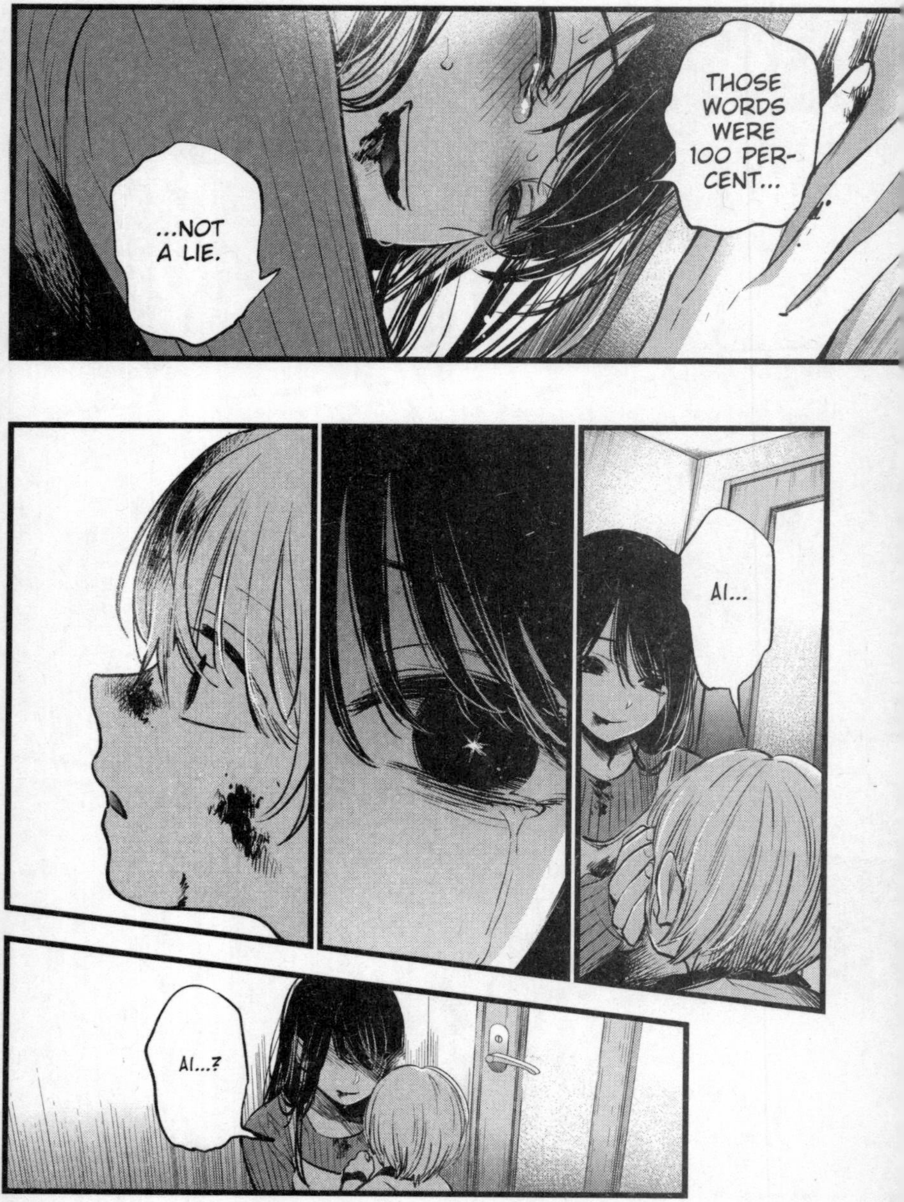
THOSE WORDS WERE 100 PERCENT...
...NOT A LIE.
AI...
AI...?

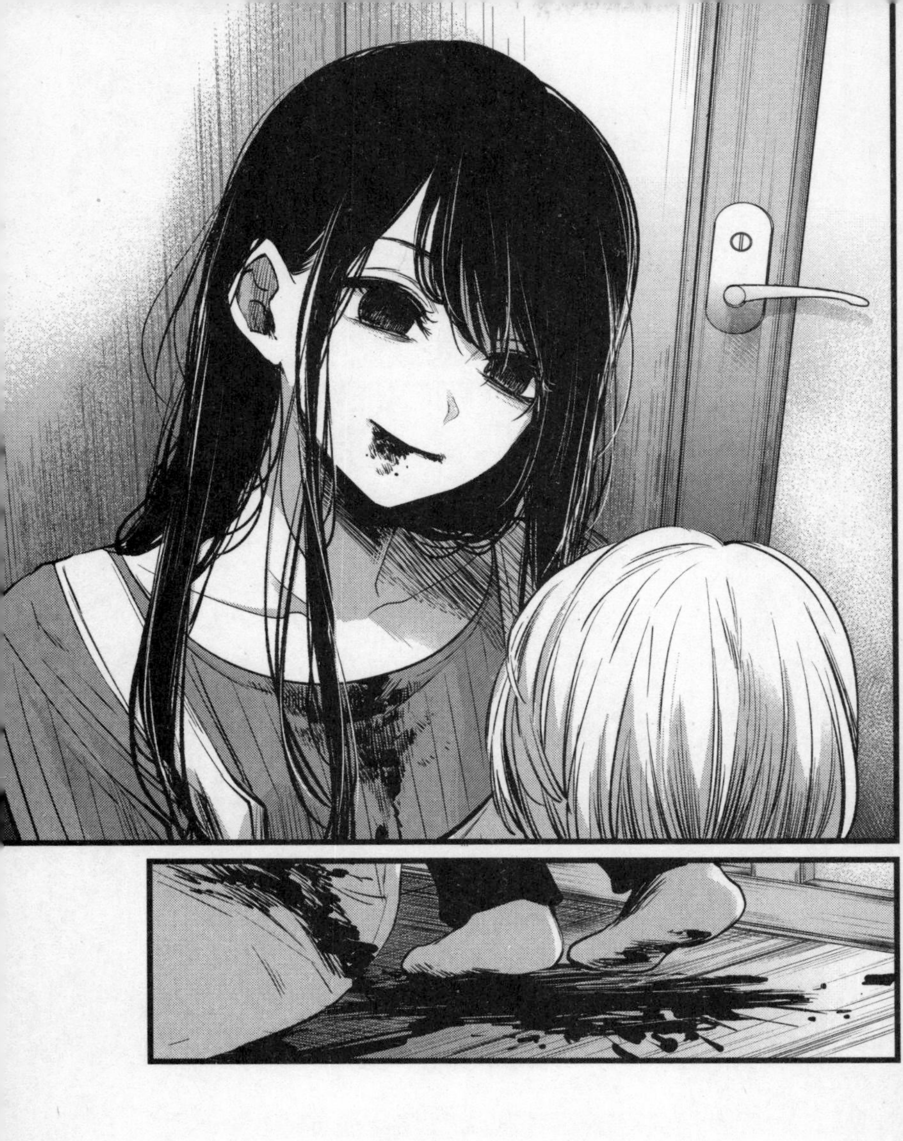

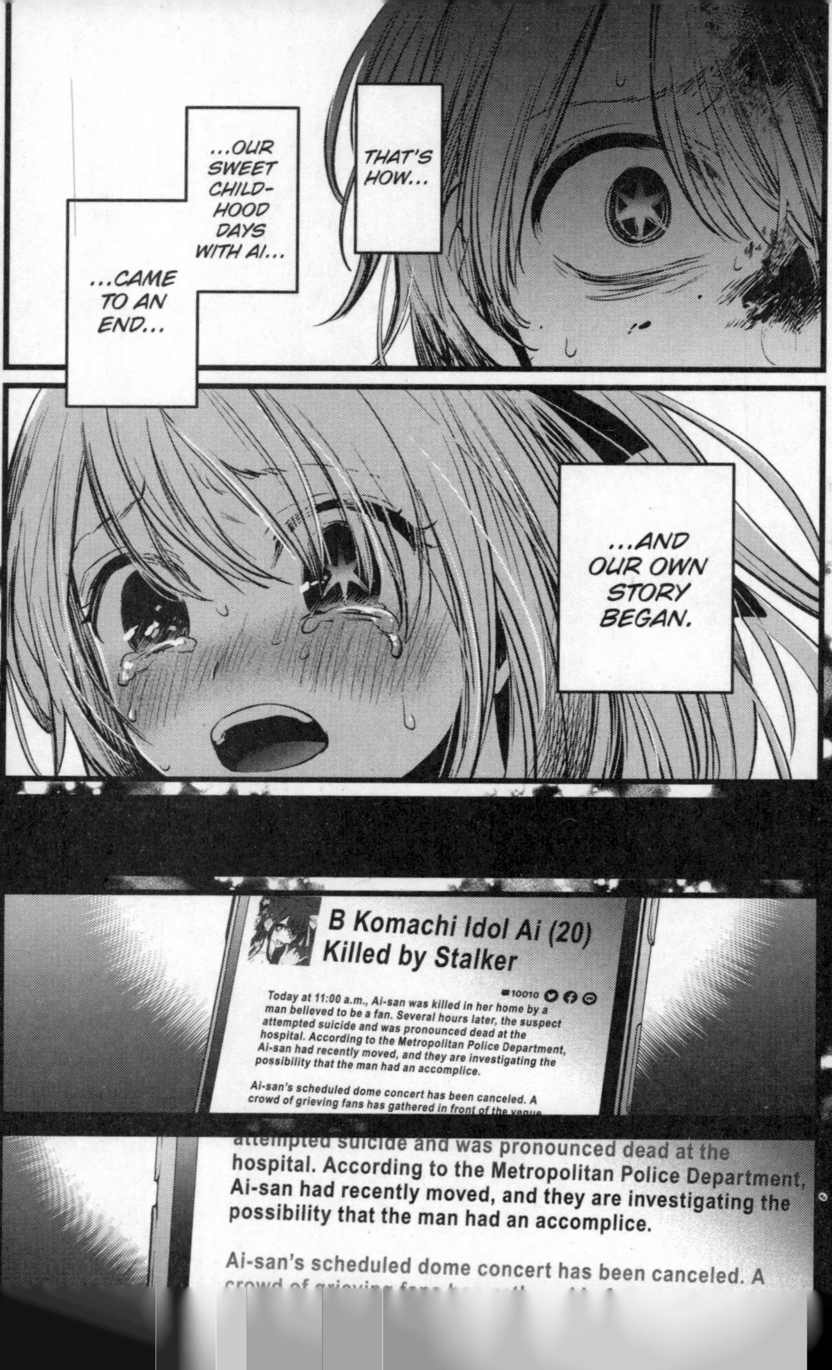
THAT'S HOW...
...OUR SWEET CHILD-HOOD DAYS WITH AI...
...CAME TO AN END...
...AND OUR OWN STORY BEGAN.
B Komachi Idol Ai (20) Killed by Stalker
10010
Today at 11:00 a.m., Ai-san was killed in her home by a man believed to be a fan. Several hours later, the suspect attempted suicide and was pronounced dead at the hospital. According to the Metropolitan Police Department, Ai-san had recently moved, and they are investigating the possibility that the man had an accomplice.
Ai-san's scheduled dome concert has been canceled. A crowd of grieving fans has gathered in front of the venue
attempted suicide and was pronounced dead at the hospital. According to the Metropolitan Police Department, Ai-san had recently moved, and they are investigating the possibility that the man had an accomplice.
Ai-san's scheduled dome concert has been canceled. A

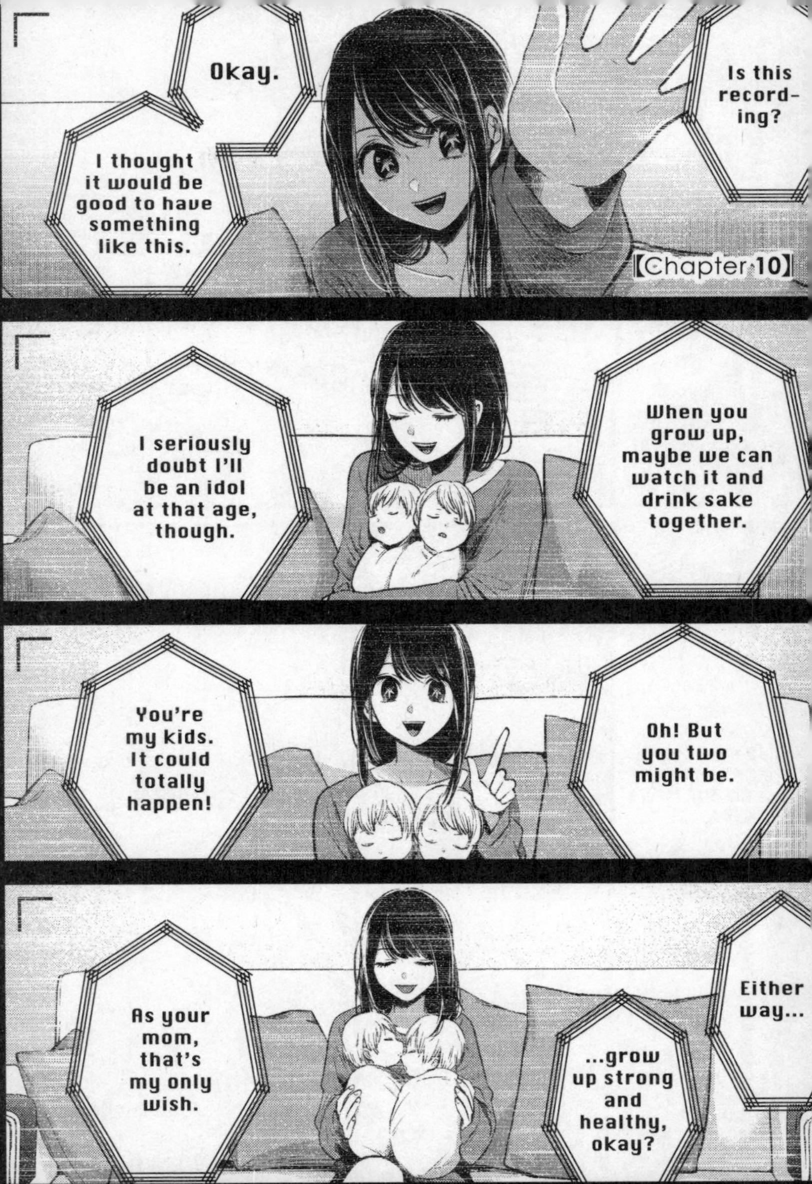

Is this recording?
Okay.
I thought it would be good to have something like this.
【Chapter 10】
When you grow up, maybe we can watch it and drink sake together.
I seriously doubt I'll be an idol at that age, though.
Oh! But you two might be.
You're my kids. It could totally happen!
Either way...
...grow up strong and healthy, okay?
As your mom, that's my only wish.

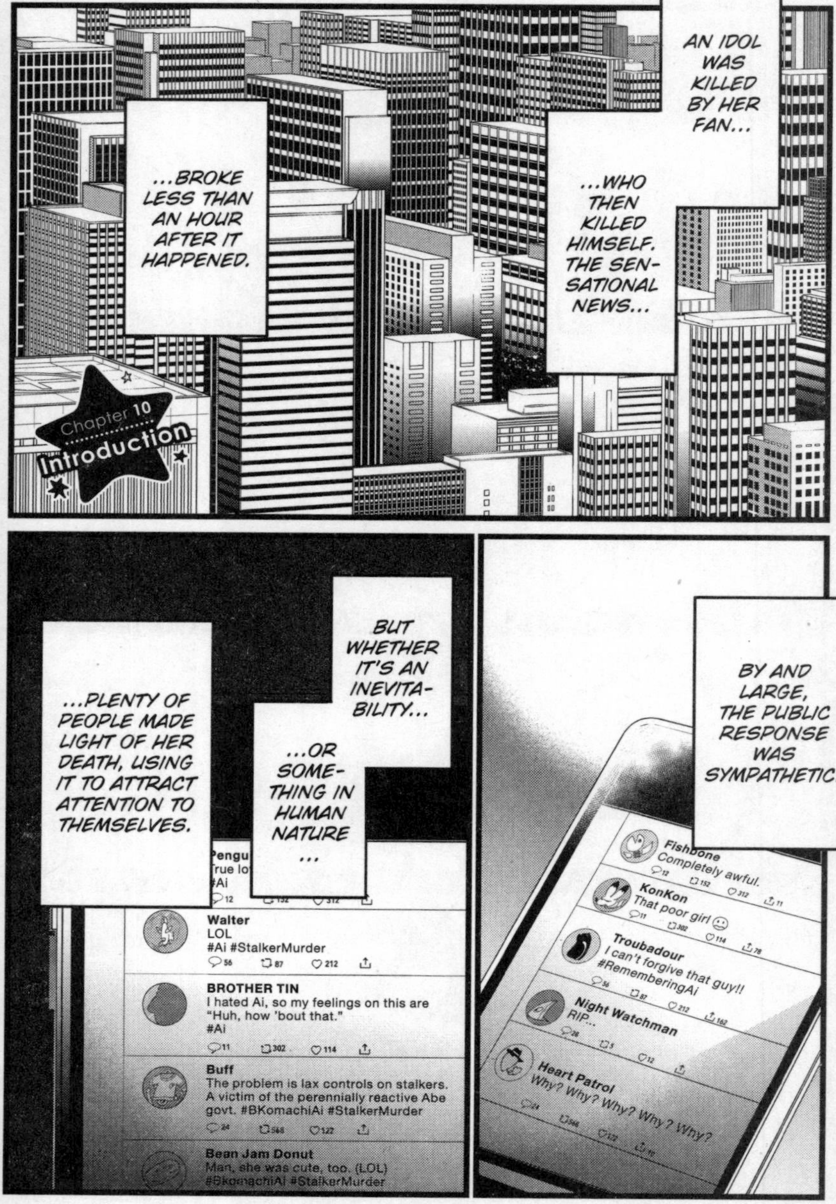
AN IDOL WAS KILLED BY HER FAN...
...WHO THEN KILLED HIMSELF. THE SEN-SATIONAL NEWS...
...BROKE LESS THAN AN HOUR AFTER IT HAPPENED.
Chapter 10
Introduction
BY AND LARGE, THE PUBLIC RESPONSE WAS SYMPATHETIC.
Fishbone
Completely awful.
KonKon
That poor girl
Troubadour
I can't forgive that guy!!
#RememberingAi
Night Watchman
RIP...
Heart Patrol
Why? Why? Why? Why? Why?
BUT WHETHER IT'S AN INEVITA-BILITY...
...OR SOME-THING IN HUMAN NATURE...
...PLENTY OF PEOPLE MADE LIGHT OF HER DEATH, USING IT TO ATTRACT ATTENTION TO THEMSELVES.
Walter
LOL
#Ai #StalkerMurder
BROTHER TIN
I hated Ai, so my feelings on this are "Huh, how 'bout that."
#Ai
Buff
The problem is lax controls on stalkers. A victim of the perennially reactive Abe govt. #BKomachiAi #StalkerMurder
Bean Jam Donut
Man, she was cute, too. (LOL)
#BKomachiAi #StalkerMurder

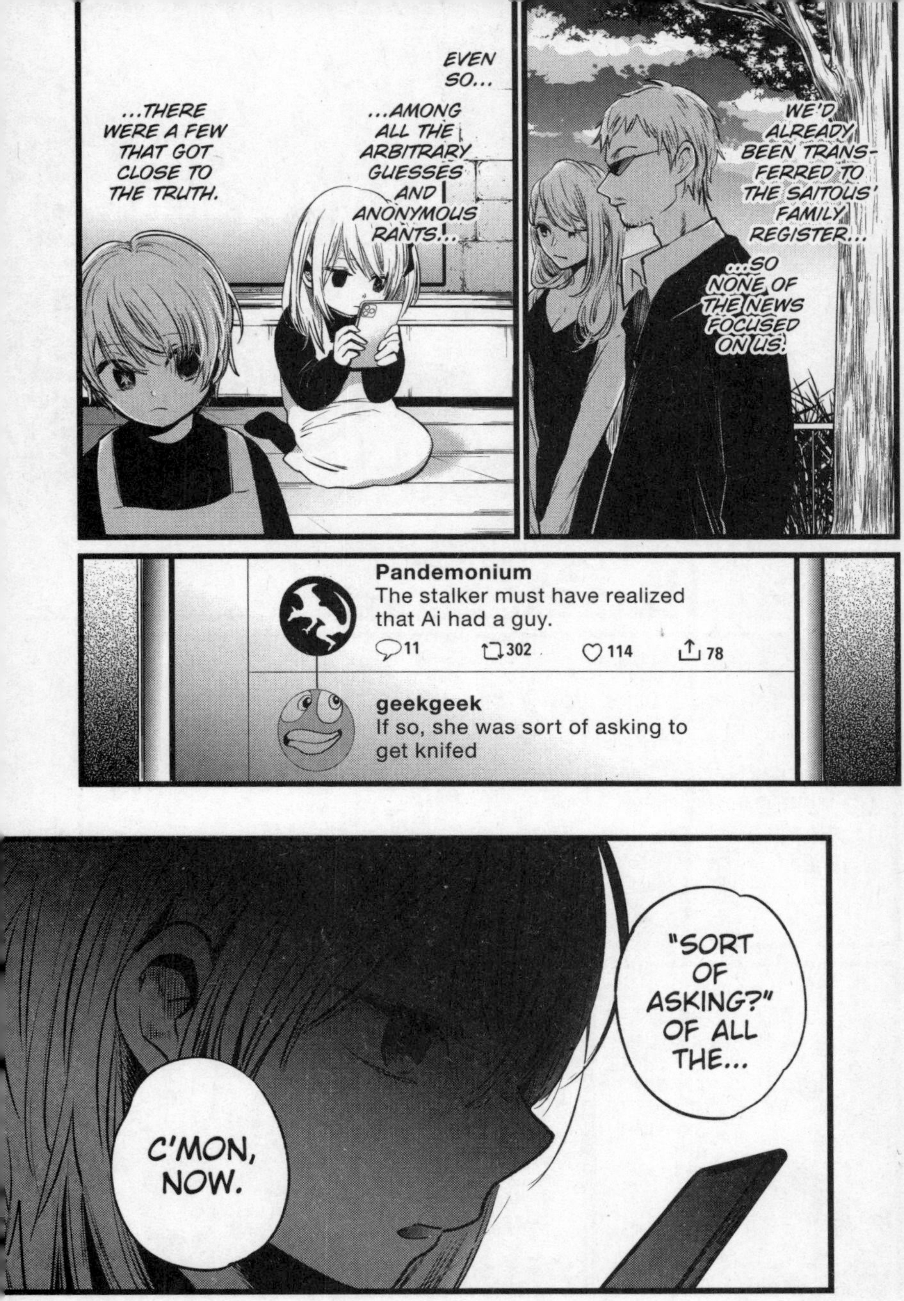
WE'D ALREADY BEEN TRANS-FERRED TO THE SAITOUS' FAMILY REGISTER...
...SO NONE OF THE NEWS FOCUSED ON US.
EVEN SO...
...AMONG ALL THE ARBITRARY GUESSES AND ANONYMOUS RANTS...
...THERE WERE A FEW THAT GOT CLOSE TO THE TRUTH.
Pandemonium
The stalker must have realized that Ai had a guy.
11
302
114
78
geekgeek
If so, she was sort of asking to get knifed
"SORT OF ASKING?" OF ALL THE...
C'MON, NOW.

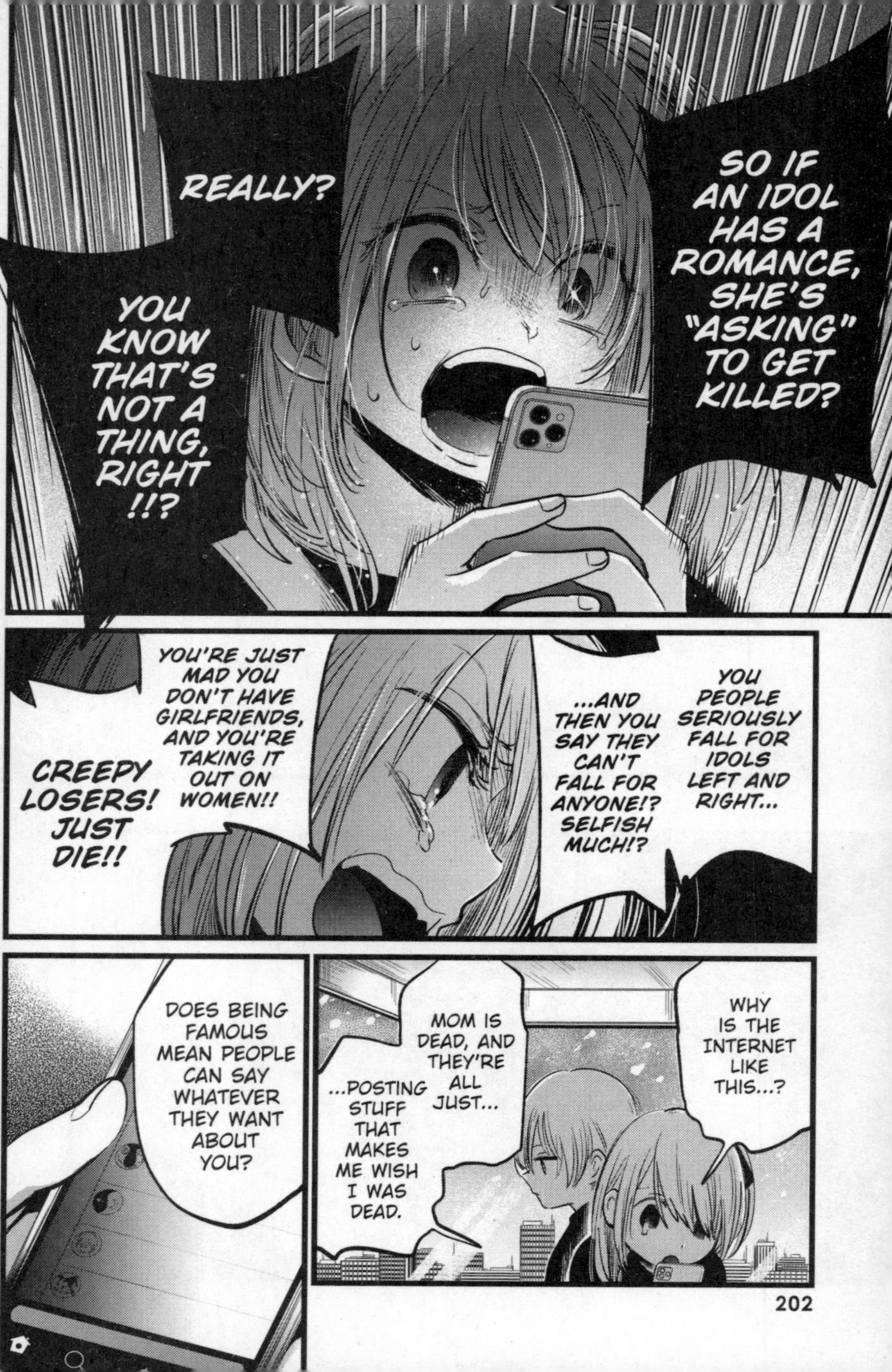
SO IF AN IDOL HAS A ROMANCE, SHE'S "ASKING" TO GET KILLED?
REALLY?
YOU KNOW THAT'S NOT A THING, RIGHT!!?
YOU PEOPLE SERIOUSLY FALL FOR IDOLS LEFT AND RIGHT...
...AND THEN YOU SAY THEY CAN'T FALL FOR ANYONE!? SELFISH MUCH!?
YOU'RE JUST MAD YOU DON'T HAVE GIRLFRIENDS, AND YOU'RE TAKING IT OUT ON WOMEN!!
CREEPY LOSERS! JUST DIE!!
WHY IS THE INTERNET LIKE THIS...?
MOM IS DEAD, AND THEY'RE ALL JUST...
...POSTING STUFF THAT MAKES ME WISH I WAS DEAD.
DOES BEING FAMOUS MEAN PEOPLE CAN SAY WHATEVER THEY WANT ABOUT YOU?

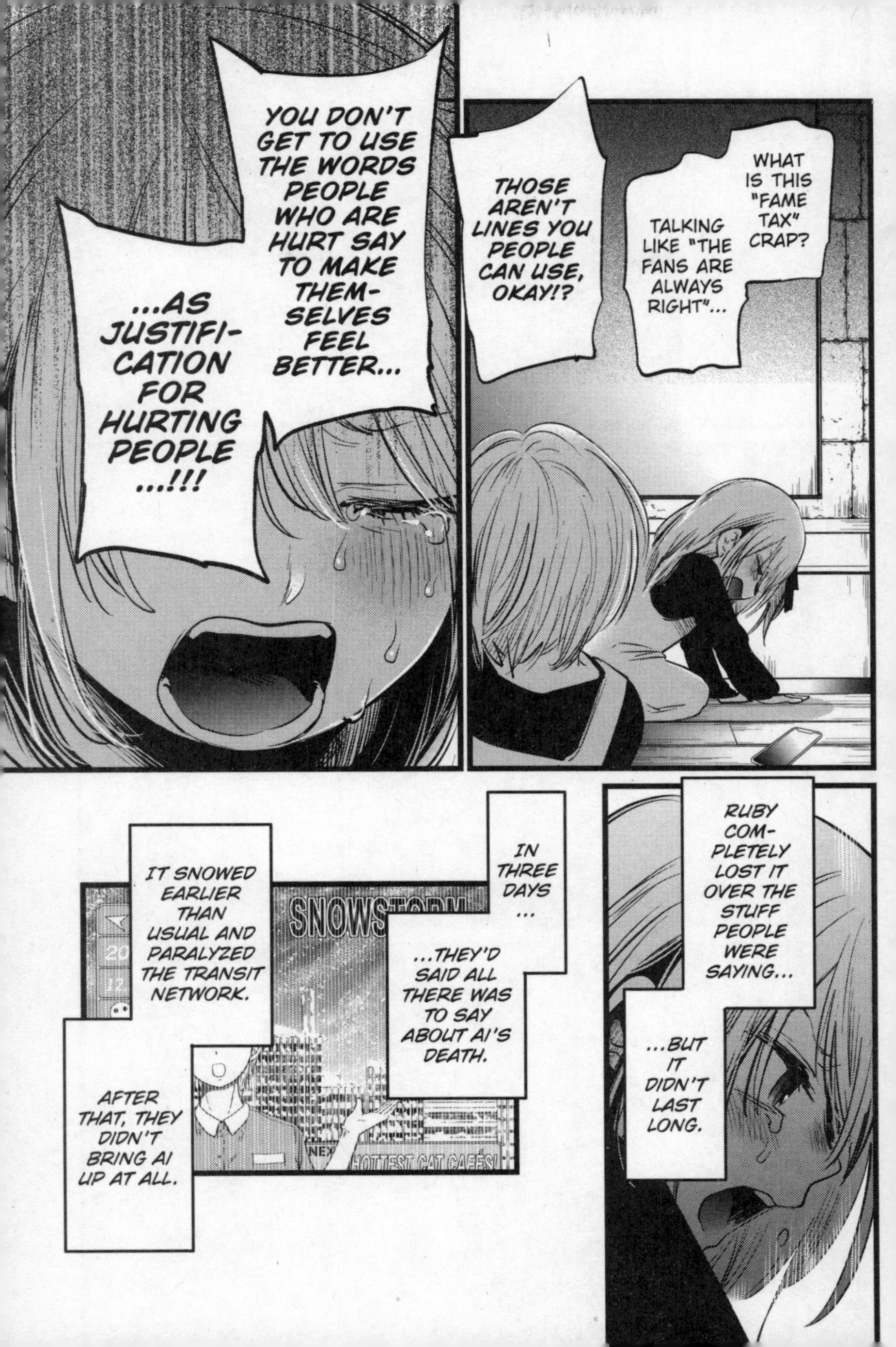
WHAT IS THIS "FAME TAX" CRAP?
TALKING LIKE "THE FANS ARE ALWAYS RIGHT"...
THOSE AREN'T LINES YOU PEOPLE CAN USE, OKAY!?
YOU DON'T GET TO USE THE WORDS PEOPLE WHO ARE HURT SAY TO MAKE THEMSELVES FEEL BETTER...
...AS JUSTIFICATION FOR HURTING PEOPLE ...!!!
RUBY COMPLETELY LOST IT OVER THE STUFF PEOPLE WERE SAYING...
...BUT IT DIDN'T LAST LONG.
IN THREE DAYS...
...THEY'D SAID ALL THERE WAS TO SAY ABOUT AI'S DEATH.
IT SNOWED EARLIER THAN USUAL AND PARALYZED THE TRANSIT NETWORK.
AFTER THAT, THEY DIDN'T BRING AI UP AT ALL.
HOTTEST CAT CAFÉS!

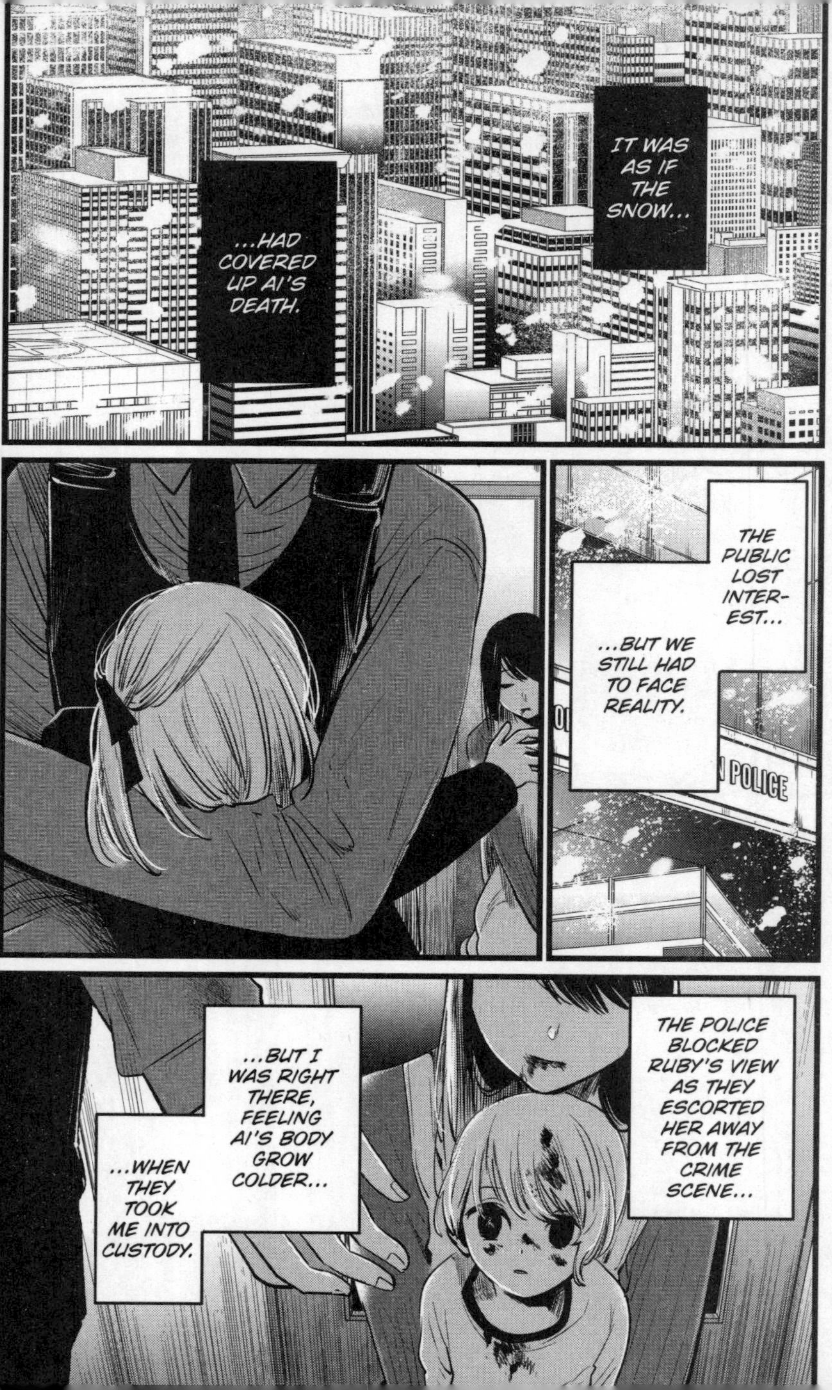
IT WAS AS IF THE SNOW...
...HAD COVERED UP AI'S DEATH.
THE PUBLIC LOST INTER-EST...
...BUT WE STILL HAD TO FACE REALITY.
N POLICE
THE POLICE BLOCKED RUBY'S VIEW AS THEY ESCORTED HER AWAY FROM THE CRIME SCENE...
...BUT I WAS RIGHT THERE, FEELING AI'S BODY GROW COLDER...
...WHEN THEY TOOK ME INTO CUSTODY.

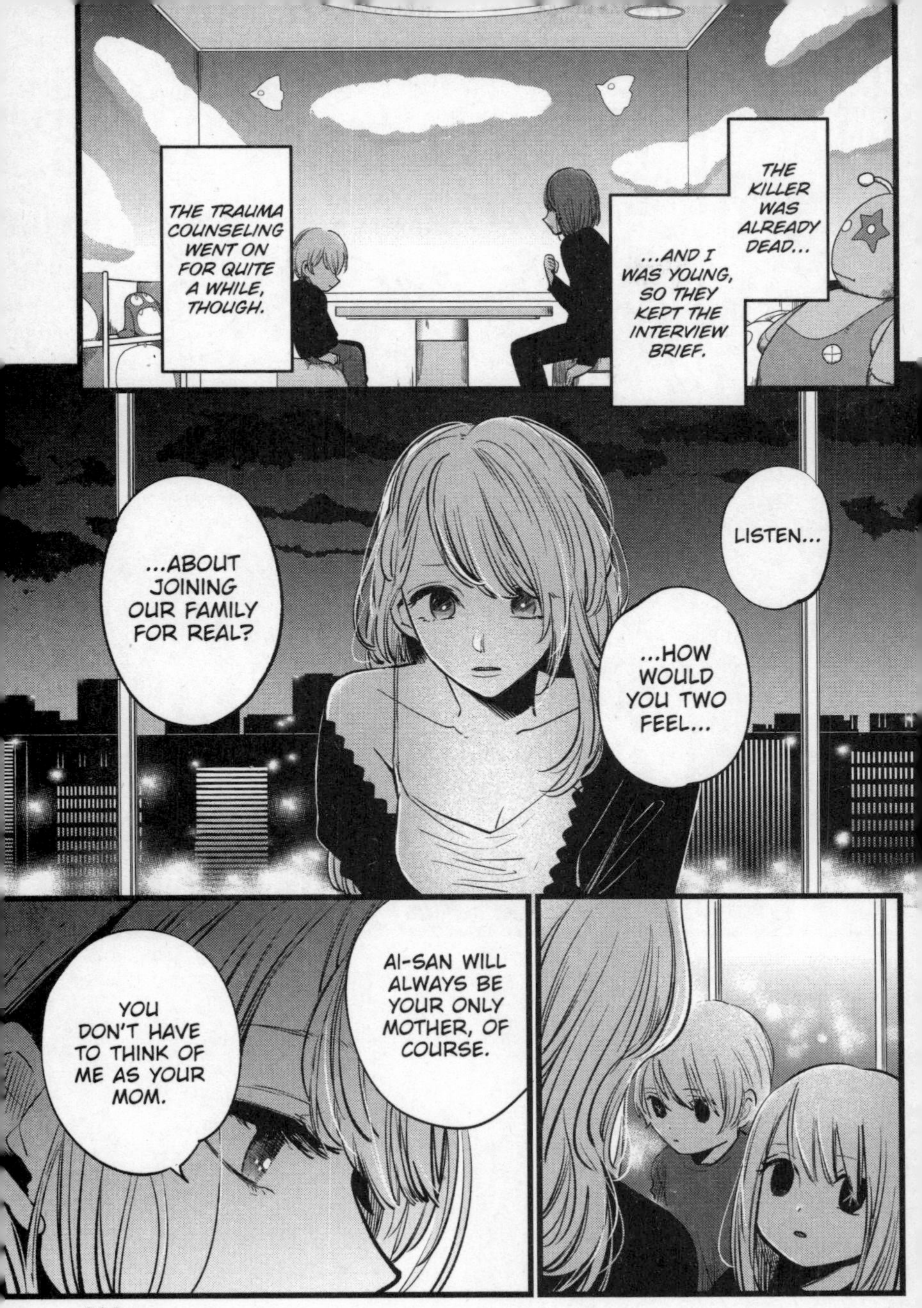
THE KILLER WAS ALREADY DEAD...
...AND I WAS YOUNG, SO THEY KEPT THE INTERVIEW BRIEF.
THE TRAUMA COUNSELING WENT ON FOR QUITE A WHILE, THOUGH.
LISTEN...
...HOW WOULD YOU TWO FEEL...
...ABOUT JOINING OUR FAMILY FOR REAL?
AI-SAN WILL ALWAYS BE YOUR ONLY MOTHER, OF COURSE.
YOU DON'T HAVE TO THINK OF ME AS YOUR MOM.

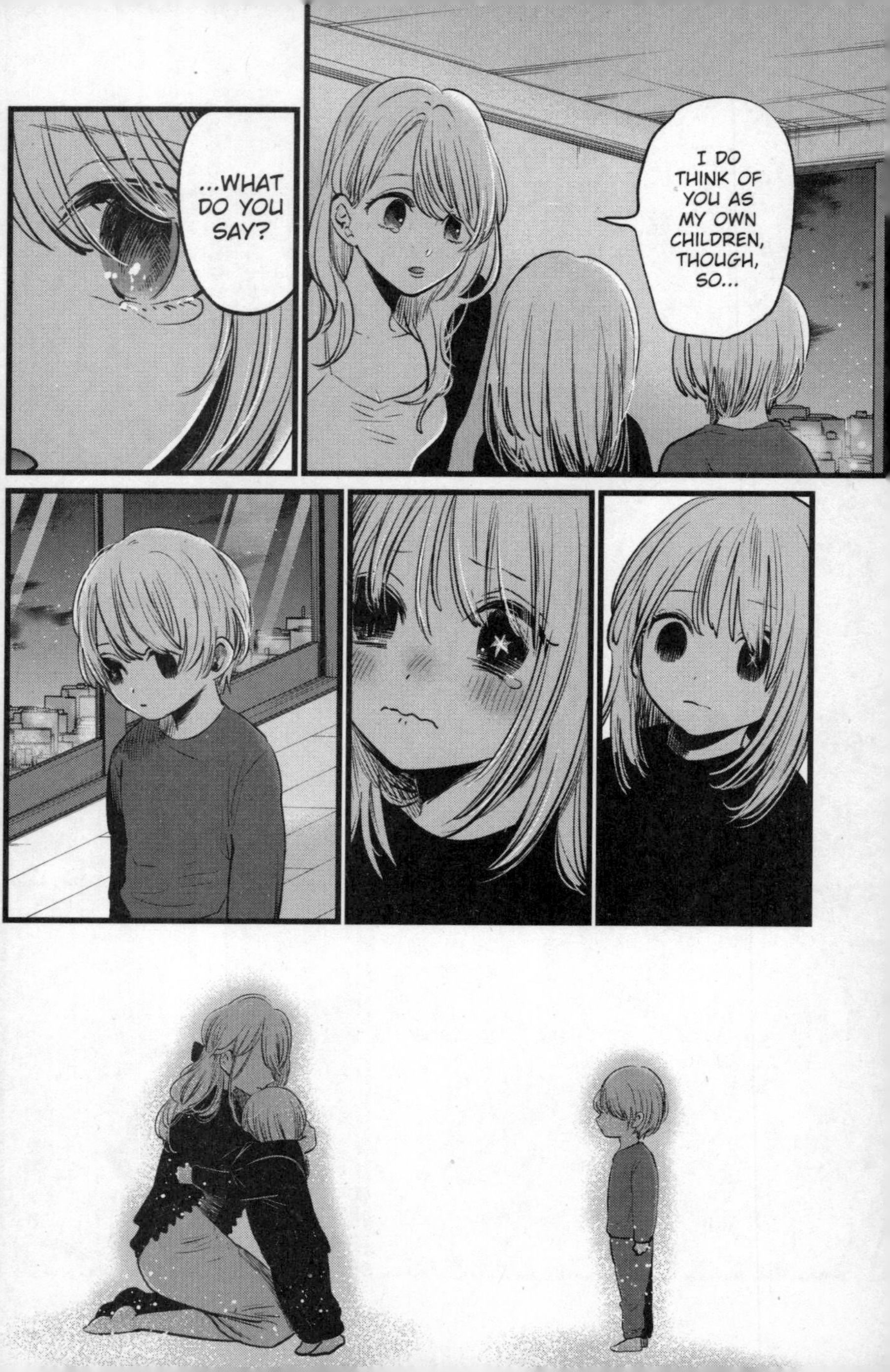
I DO THINK OF YOU AS MY OWN CHILDREN, THOUGH, SO...
...WHAT DO YOU SAY?

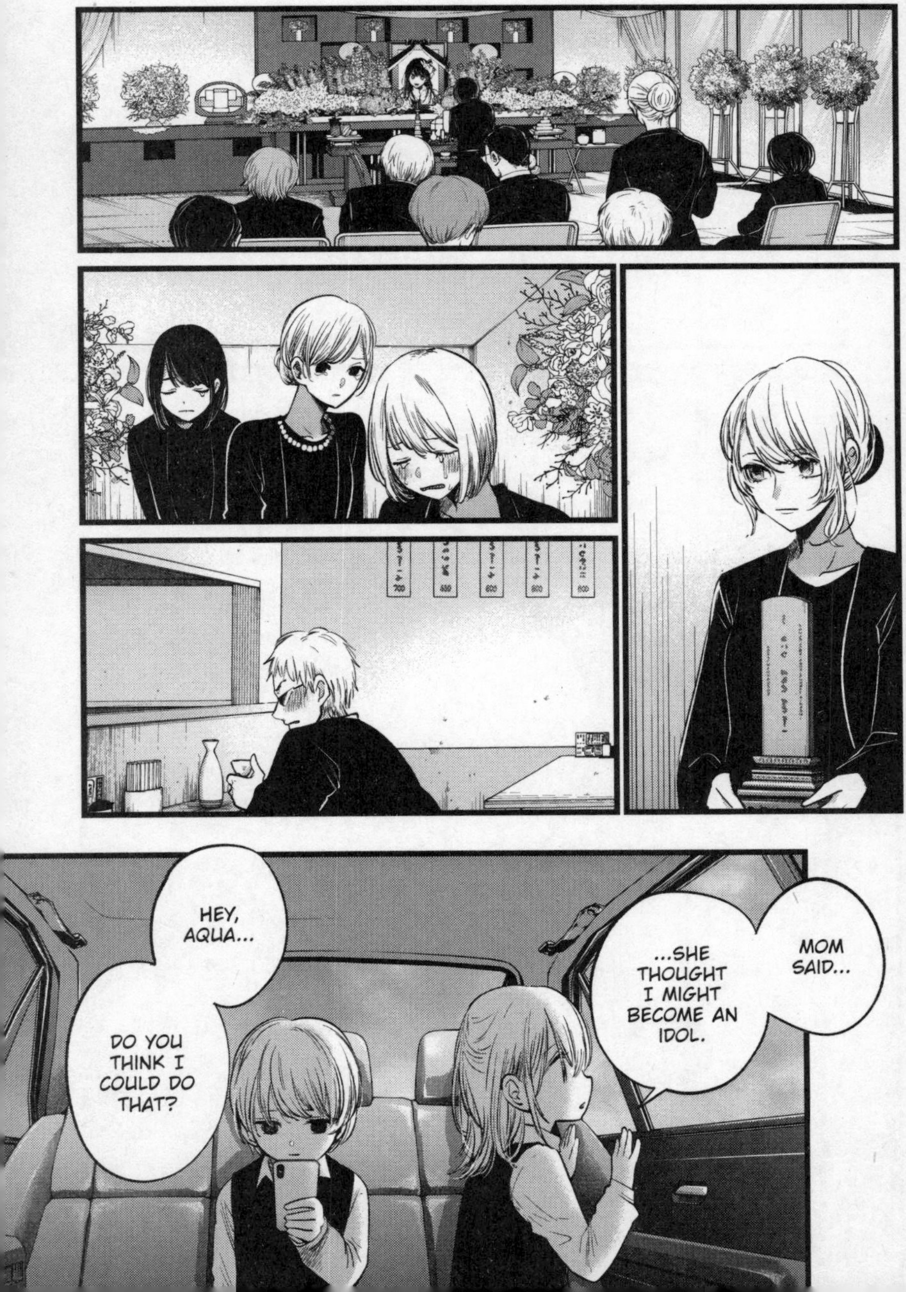
MOM SAID...
...SHE THOUGHT I MIGHT BECOME AN IDOL.
HEY, AQUA...
DO YOU THINK I COULD DO THAT?

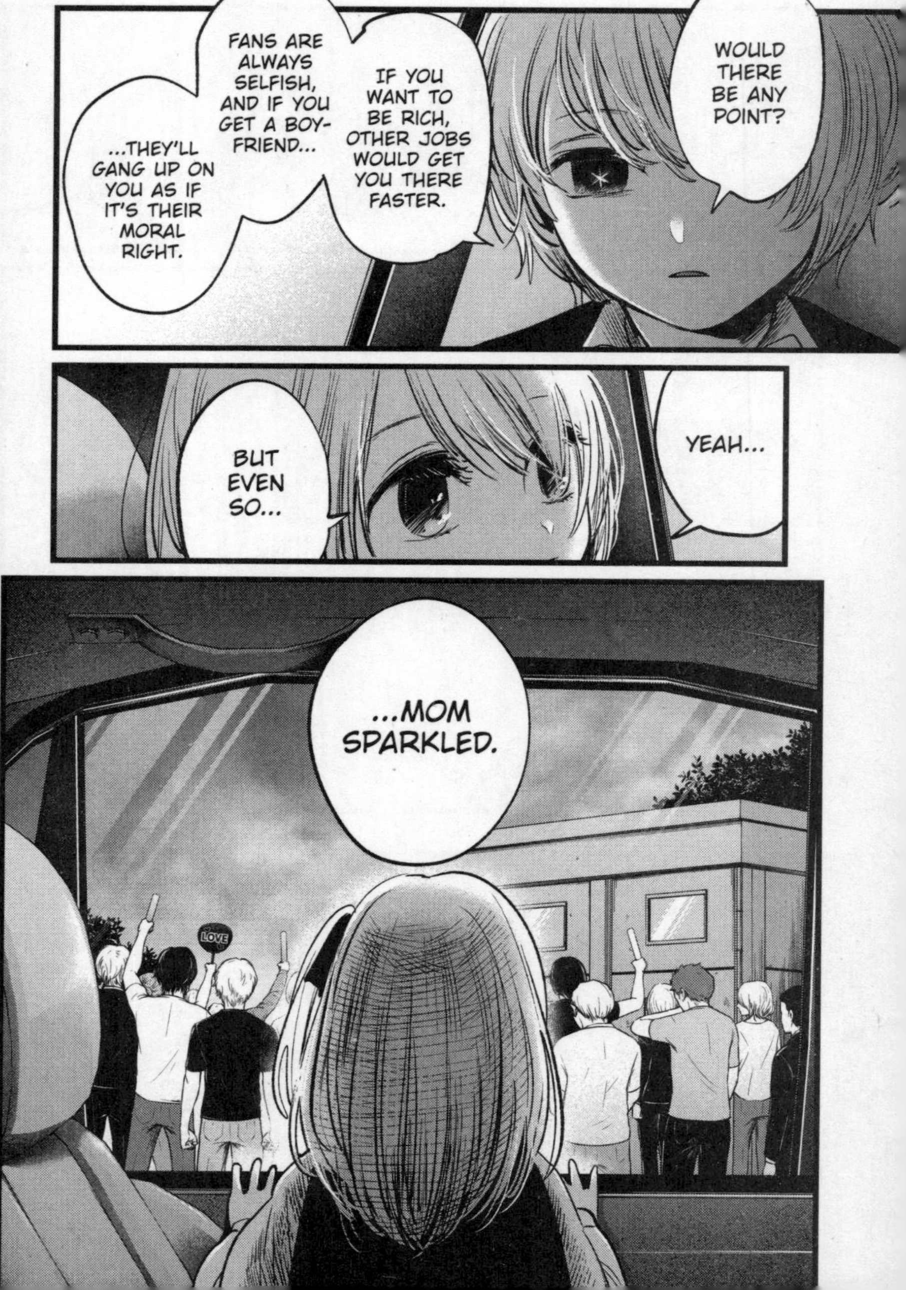
WOULD THERE BE ANY POINT?
IF YOU WANT TO BE RICH, OTHER JOBS WOULD GET YOU THERE FASTER.
FANS ARE ALWAYS SELFISH, AND IF YOU GET A BOY-FRIEND...
...THEY'LL GANG UP ON YOU AS IF IT'S THEIR MORAL RIGHT.
YEAH...
BUT EVEN SO...
...MOM SPARKLED.
LOVE

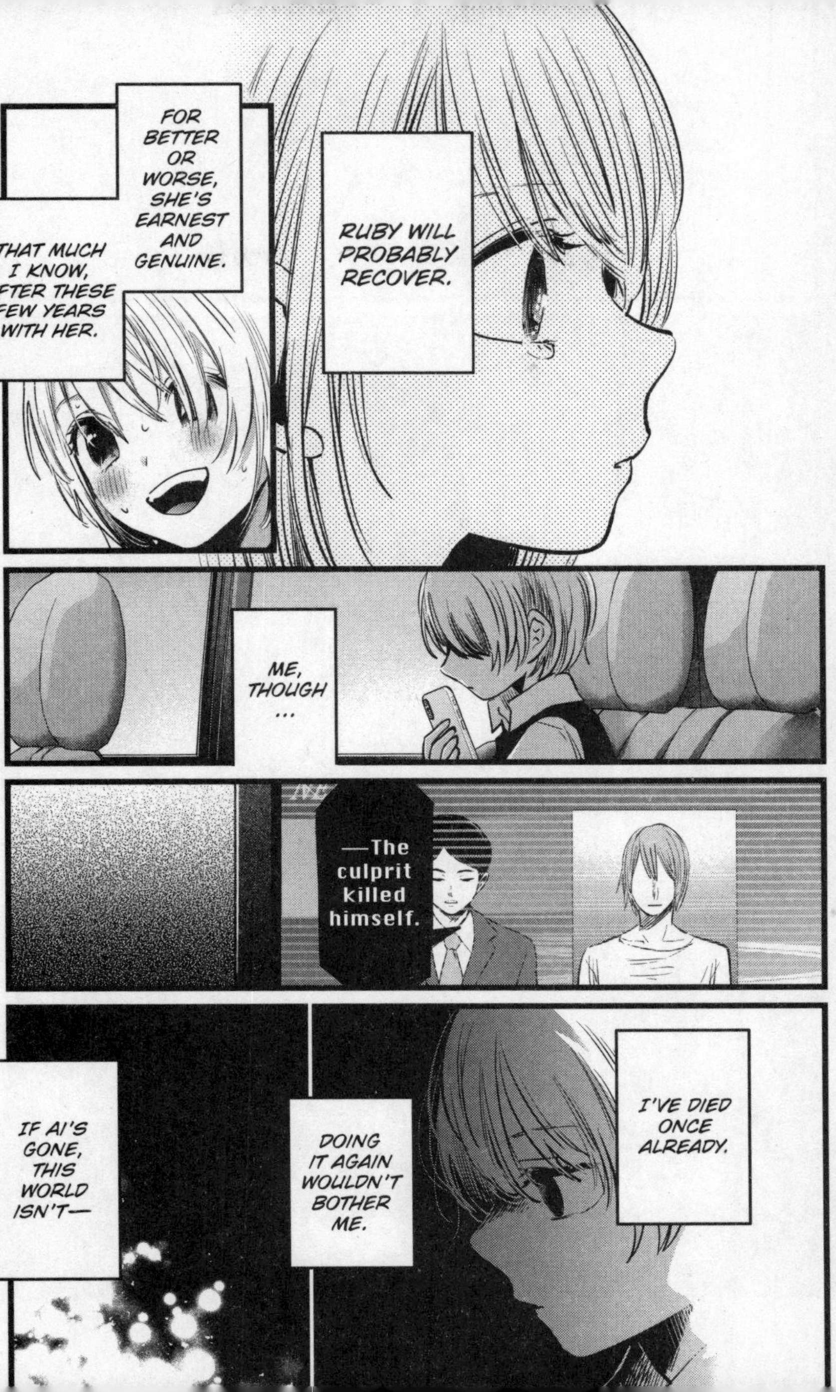
RUBY WILL PROBABLY RECOVER.
FOR BETTER OR WORSE, SHE'S EARNEST AND GENUINE.
THAT MUCH I KNOW, AFTER THESE FEW YEARS WITH HER.
ME, THOUGH...
—The culprit killed himself.
I'VE DIED ONCE ALREADY.
DOING IT AGAIN WOULDN'T BOTHER ME.
IF AI'S GONE, THIS WORLD ISN'T—

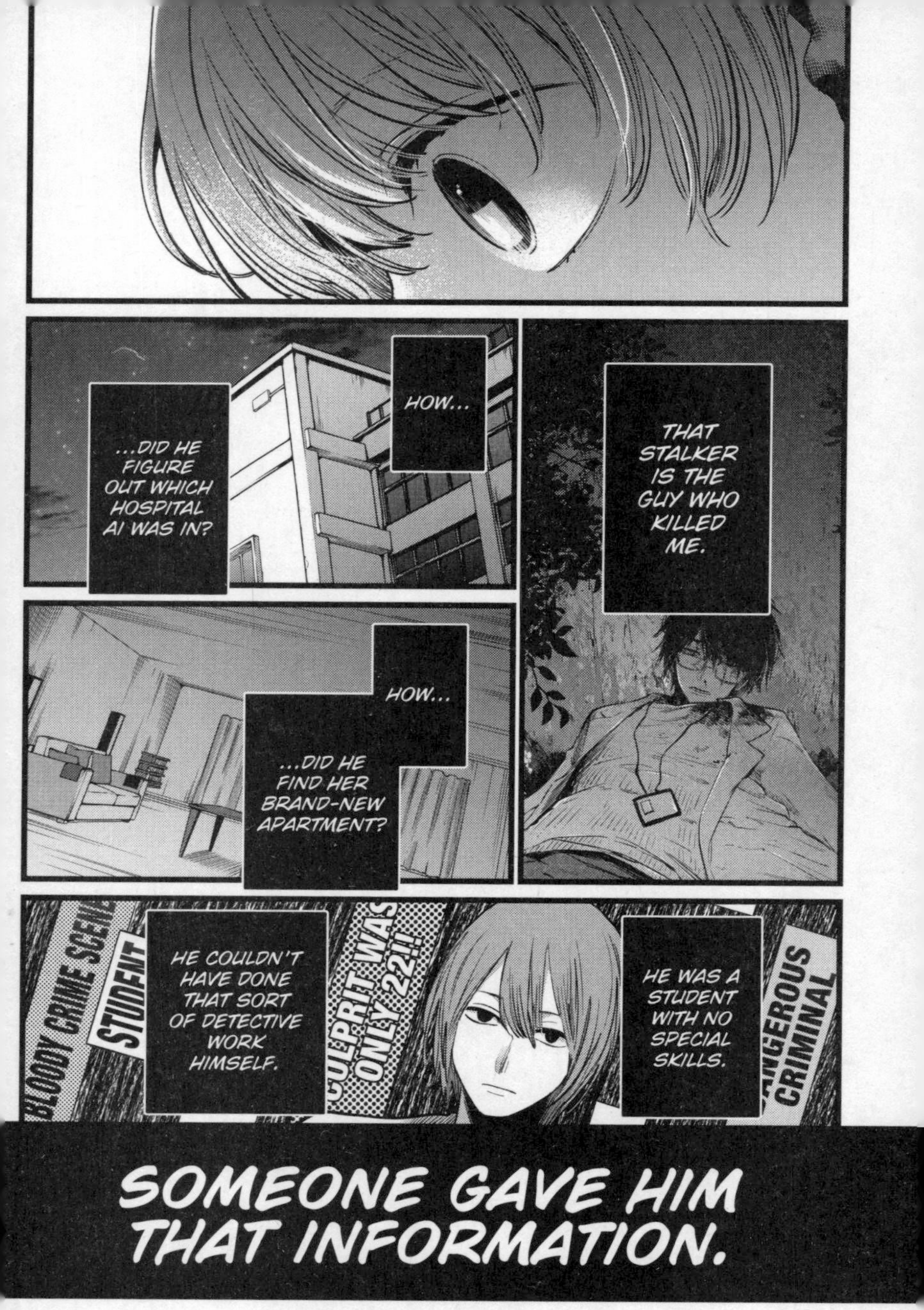

THAT STALKER IS THE GUY WHO KILLED ME.
HOW...
...DID HE FIGURE OUT WHICH HOSPITAL AI WAS IN?
HOW...
...DID HE FIND HER BRAND-NEW APARTMENT?
HE WAS A STUDENT WITH NO SPECIAL SKILLS.
ANGEROUS CRIMINAL
CULPRIT WAS ONLY 22!!
HE COULDN'T HAVE DONE THAT SORT OF DETECTIVE WORK HIMSELF.
STUDENT
BLOODY CRIME SCEN
SOMEONE GAVE HIM THAT INFORMATION.

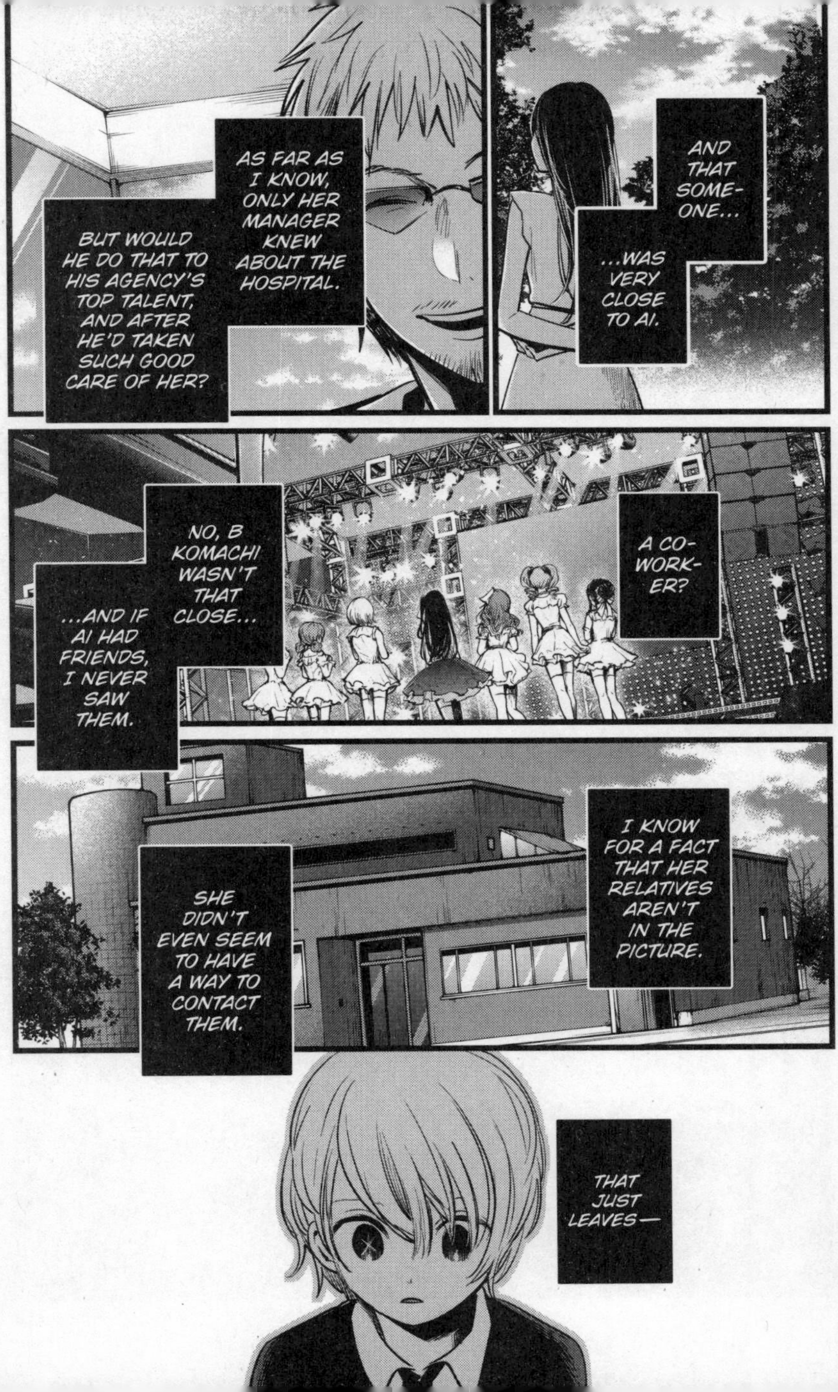
AND THAT SOME-ONE...
...WAS VERY CLOSE TO AI.
AS FAR AS I KNOW, ONLY HER MANAGER KNEW ABOUT THE HOSPITAL.
BUT WOULD HE DO THAT TO HIS AGENCY'S TOP TALENT, AND AFTER HE'D TAKEN SUCH GOOD CARE OF HER?
A CO-WORKER?
NO, B KOMACHI WASN'T THAT CLOSE...
...AND IF AI HAD FRIENDS, I NEVER SAW THEM.
I KNOW FOR A FACT THAT HER RELATIVES AREN'T IN THE PICTURE.
SHE DIDN'T EVEN SEEM TO HAVE A WAY TO CONTACT THEM.
THAT JUST LEAVES—

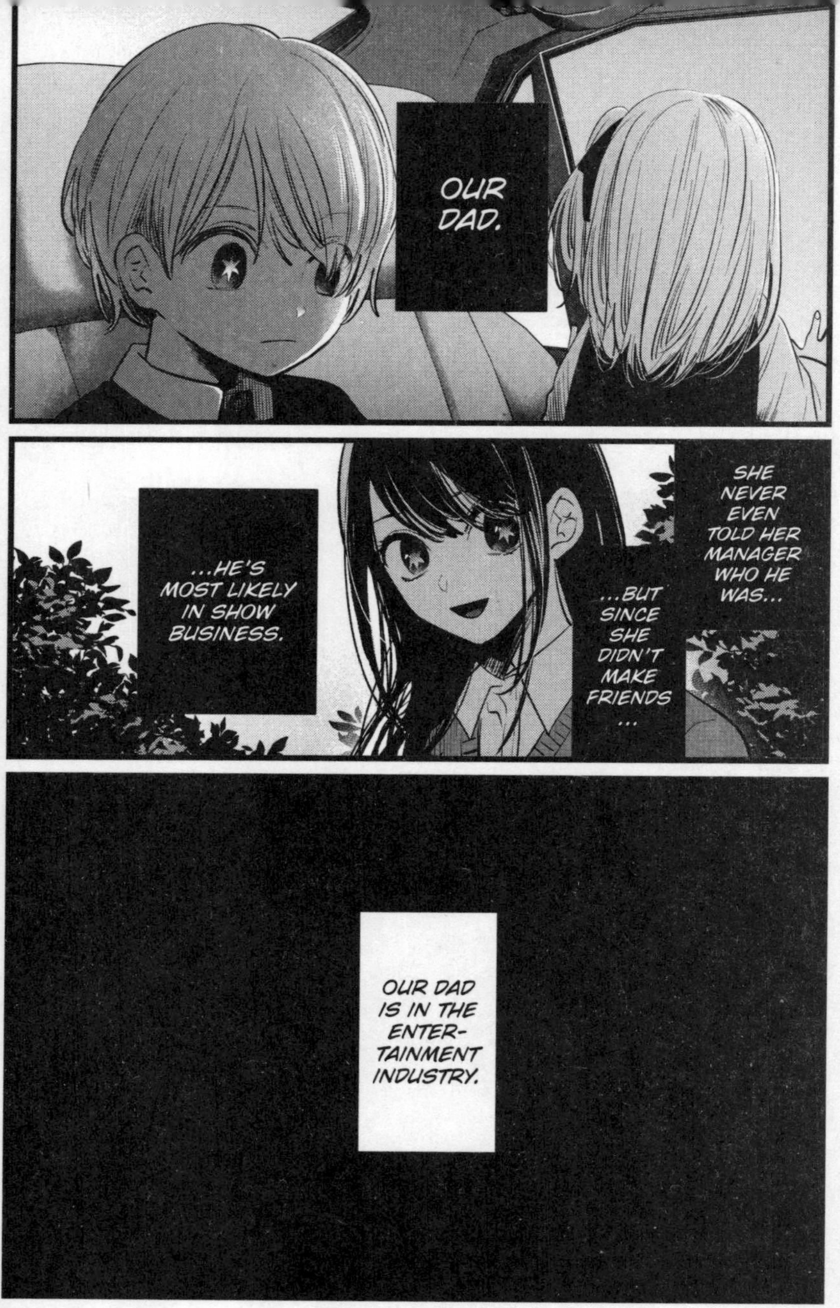
OUR DAD.
SHE NEVER EVEN TOLD HER MANAGER WHO HE WAS...
...BUT SINCE SHE DIDN'T MAKE FRIENDS...
...HE'S MOST LIKELY IN SHOW BUSINESS.
OUR DAD IS IN THE ENTER-TAINMENT INDUSTRY.

THE GUY WHO SET AI UP FOR THAT...

...IS IN THE ENTERTAINMENT INDUSTRY.

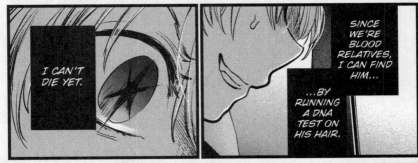

I CAN'T DIE YET.

SINCE WE'RE BLOOD RELATIVES, I CAN FIND HIM...

...BY RUNNING A DNA TEST ON HIS HAIR.

NOT UNTIL I FIND THAT GUY...

...AND KILL HIM MYSELF.

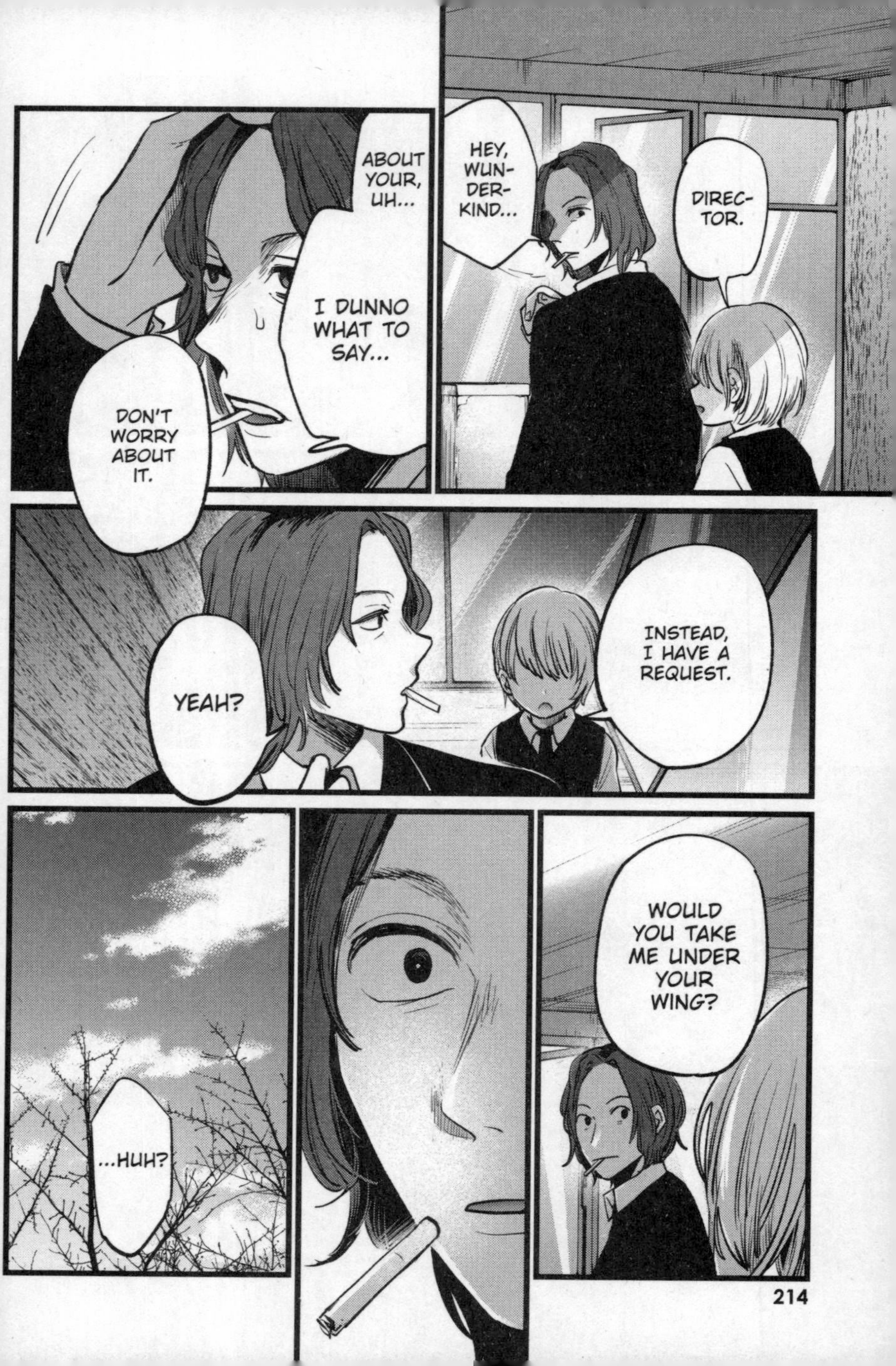
DIREC-TOR.
HEY, WUN-DER-KIND...
ABOUT YOUR, UH...
I DUNNO WHAT TO SAY...
DON'T WORRY ABOUT IT.
INSTEAD, I HAVE A REQUEST.
YEAH?
WOULD YOU TAKE ME UNDER YOUR WING?
...HUH?

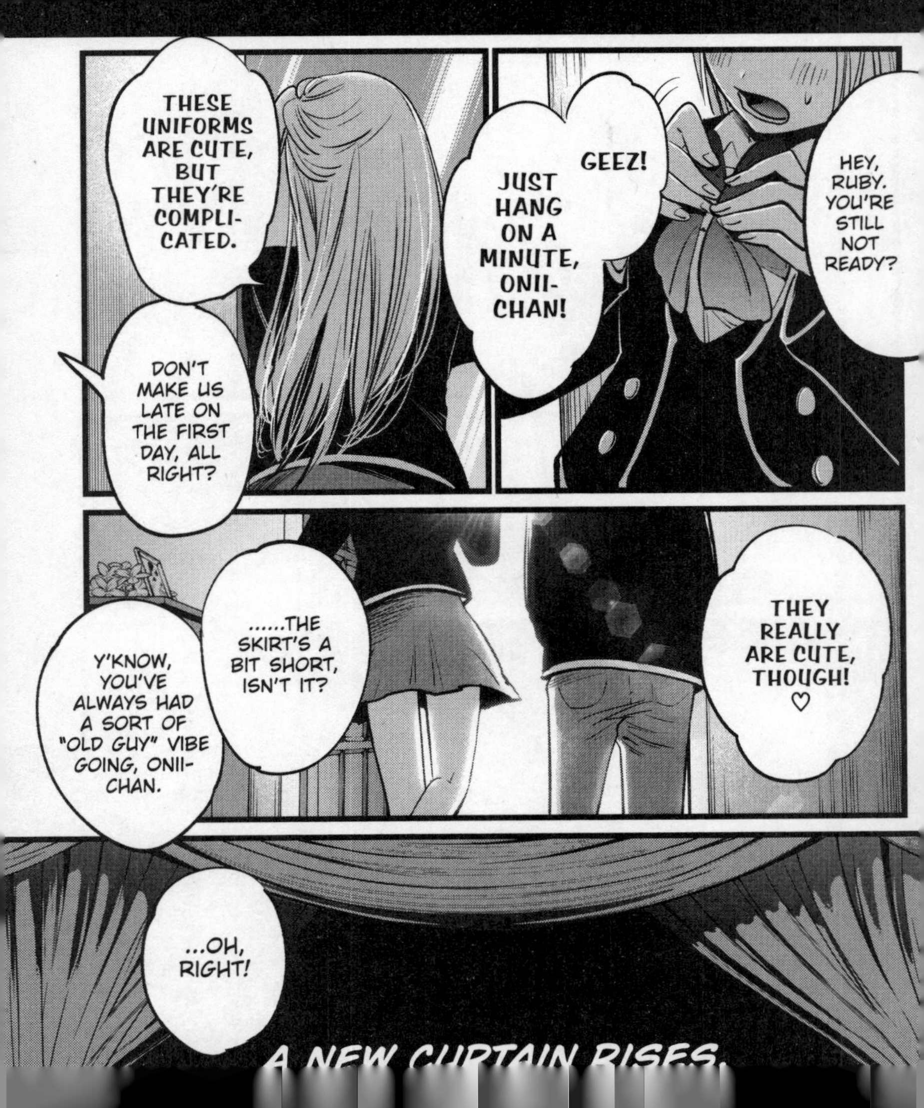
HEY, RUBY. YOU'RE STILL NOT READY?
GEEZ! JUST HANG ON A MINUTE, ONII-CHAN!
THESE UNIFORMS ARE CUTE, BUT THEY'RE COMPLICATED.
DON'T MAKE US LATE ON THE FIRST DAY, ALL RIGHT?
THEY REALLY ARE CUTE, THOUGH! ♡
......THE SKIRT'S A BIT SHORT, ISN'T IT?
Y'KNOW, YOU'VE ALWAYS HAD A SORT OF "OLD GUY" VIBE GOING, ONII-CHAN.
...OH, RIGHT!
A NEW CURTAIN RISES.

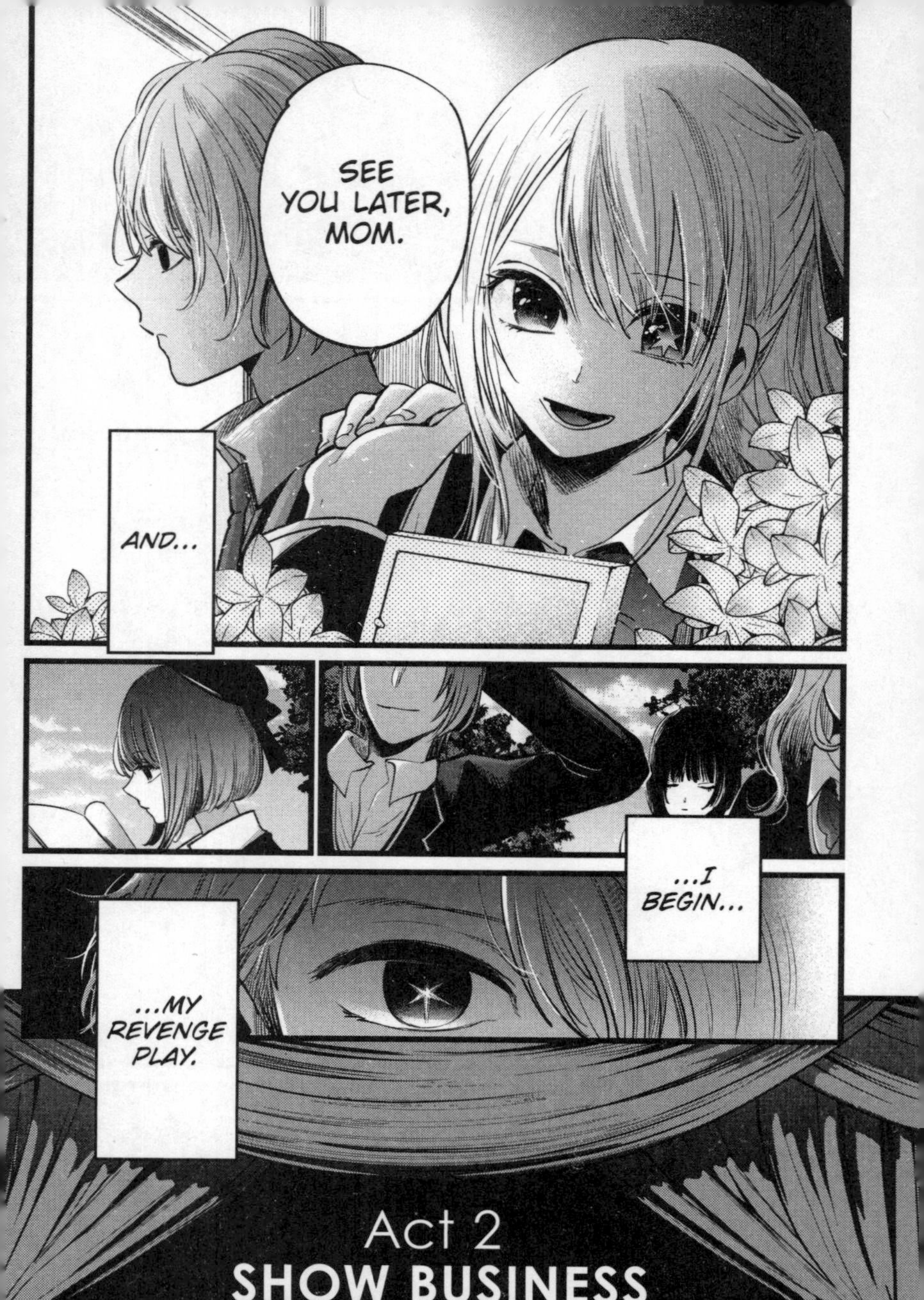
SEE YOU LATER, MOM.
AND...
...I BEGIN...
...MY REVENGE PLAY.
Act 2
SHOW BUSINESS
【OSHI NO KO】 1 END

Aka Akasaka ✕ Mengo Yokoyari

【OSHI NO KO】

★

★

★

Volume 2
COMING SOON

✳ TRANSLATION NOTES ⋆✫

COMMON HONORIFICS
no honorific: Indicates familiarity or closeness; if used without permission or reason, addressing someone in this manner would constitute an insult.
-san: The Japanese equivalent of Mr./Mrs./Miss. If a situation calls for politeness, this is the fail-safe honorific.
-kun: Used most often when referring to boys, this indicates affection or familiarity. Occasionally used by older men among their peers, but it may also be used by anyone referring to a person of lower standing.
-chan: An affectionate honorific indicating familiarity used mostly in reference to girls; also used in reference to cute persons or animals regardless of gender.
-sensei: A respectful term for teachers, artists, or high-level professionals.
-oniisan, onii-san: Used to address an older brother or older brother figure.

CURRENCY CONVERSION
While exchange rates fluctuate daily, a general approximation is ¥100 to 1 USD.

GENERAL
Oshi is a term used by fans of idol groups, bands, and other similar acts to describe one's favorite member.

The title 【Oshi no Ko】 has been left untranslated from the Japanese because the phrase can have multiple meanings depending on context. "The girl who is my favorite performer," "the girl who's a fan of my favorite performer," and "the child/children of my favorite performer"—among others—are all valid interpretations.

PAGE 7
In idol groups, the **center** is the group member who is literally positioned in the middle of the group during performances. They get the most support from their agency, which means they have the most lines in songs and the most screen time in videos, and they get the most attention as a result. The member who occupies that spot may change between performances or tours, but if a member is popular enough in their own right, they may be kept as the center to draw more attention to the group.

PAGE 9
Gorou's hospital is near the southern tip of Kyushu. It's about as far from Tokyo as you can get and still be on one of Japan's four main islands.

PAGE 14
Anaplastic astrocytoma is a type of rare malignant brain tumor.

PAGE 17
About 80% of Japanese children who are orphaned or can't live with their parents grow up in **children's homes**, group homes that are more like orphanages, as opposed to foster care.

PAGE 22
Abortion is only legal up to the 22nd week of **pregnancy in Japan**, so this examination and discussion is happening very close to when Ai will have to make her decision.

PAGE 32
Receiving an **epidural** (an injection delivered in the back to relieve pain) during childbirth is very common in the US (73.1% of births in 2018) but very rare in Japan. Japan's rate in 2019 was 6.1%.

PAGE 47
Gorou and his new sister have been given what are known as "*kira-kira* (or sparkly) **names**." These are nontraditional names that use unusual kanji readings or use kanji characters simply for their phonetic values to spell out names that seem foreign. The trend for giving kids kira-kira names started in the mid '90s, exploded in the 2000s, and had slowed down again by the mid-2010s. Aquamarine's name is written 愛久愛海 for "*a-ku-a-marin*." The first three characters are used for their phonetic values ("*ku*" is a rare reading for its character, while the kanji character used for "*a*" is never read that way). The last one, "ocean," is read as the English "marine."

PAGE 49
Ruby's name is written 瑠美衣 for "*ru-bi-i*." It's still obviously a "foreign" name, but the kanji readings are pretty intuitive, and none of them are original or forced. Her name is much less likely to give clerical workers headaches than Aquamarine's name.

PAGE 51
Ichigo Production is a pun on Saitou's first name: "strawberry" in Japanese is pronounced *ichigo*. However, Saitou's first name is not written the same way as the fruit, but rather using the number "one" and the word "protection."

PAGE 58
The **pinup modeling** mentioned by the production crew is called *gravure* work. *Gravure* models tend to pose in swimsuits or lingerie for men's magazines. They're almost never actually naked, so it isn't technically porn, but their work is very similar to pinup models.

PAGE 66
N-Ste is a parody of N-Sta, a live news and variety show that airs on TBS on weekday and Sunday evenings.

PAGE 80
Weekly Bun●●● is *Shuukan Bunshun*, a weekly magazine with a reputation for exposing political and entertainment scandals.

PAGE 81
Moët is one of the world's largest champagne producers; the company owns the Dom Pérignon brand. At host clubs, buying expensive champagne for (or because of) a host raises his status.

PAGE 84
Amaterasu is the sun goddess in Japanese mythology and one of the most powerful dieties of Shinto.

PAGE 96
Livers are capable of full regeneration, and it is possible to donate part of a liver while still alive. The donor's liver fully regenerates within a few weeks of the surgery, while the transplanted partial liver will also grow to full size.

PAGE 105
The twins' **lightstick choreography** is part of a *wotagei*, or *otagei*, routine, a type of dance that fans perform at idol concerts. The trend originally started in the 1970s and is thought to have its roots in synchronized group cheering. Dances are usually based on the choreography of the idol group and heavily feature lightsticks.

PAGE 137

The word used for **guesthouse** here refers to a private home whose owners rent a room or two to guests, more like a bed-and-breakfast than an inn or hostel.

PAGE 147

The **Playboy** magazine here refers to *Shuukan Playboy*, a weekly variety magazine that includes manga, celebrity interviews, pinup model photos, and more. Although meant for adults, it is not considered pornographic and is not associated with American *Playboy* magazine.

"**Talent**" here refers to a fairly loose category of celebrity; they take part in game shows, participate as panelists, appear on variety shows, and perform in regular TV dramas or movies.

PAGE 150

The Law of the Orb Weaver was published in 1996 by Kodansha. It's a whopping 829 pages long, one of several of similar length written by author Natsuhiko Kyogoku. They're collectively referred to as **"brick books"** ("dice books" in Japanese) for their impressive size.

PAGE 151

In the context of preschool, the children's "**rehearsal**" refers to them a participating in *oyuugi*, a light, full-body exercise routine with moves geared toward the class's age-range (nothing too complicated) and conducted as a group that is a regular part of the school day. The moves are generally performed to music, which makes it similar to a group dance routine and lends itself well to Parents' Day recitals.

PAGE 166

Moriizo is a sake brewer established in Kagoshima in 1885.

PAGE 167

In this case the **dome** they're referring to is the Tokyo Dome, but there are actually five domes in Japan where concerts can be held: Sapporo, Tokyo, Osaka, Nagoya, and Fukuoka.

PAGE 188

Star sand is actually the fossilized skeletons of tiny, star-shaped organisms. The sand is found on the beaches of the Yaeyama Islands and is a popular souvenir from Okinawa Prefecture.

PAGE 207

Miyako is acting as a surviving family member for Ai. The plaque she's holding is a Buddhist mortuary tablet known as an *ihai*. While this one isn't legible, it will be inscribed with Ai's posthumous Buddhist name, the name she used while she was alive, her age at death, and the day she died. After Ai's cremation, it will be placed on a home altar venerating her until the forty-ninth day after her death, when it will be replaced with a more ornate, permanent mortuary tablet.

PAGE 214

When Aqua ask the director to, "take me under your wing," the word he uses can mean either "train" (an employee) or "raise" (a child).

【OSHI NO KO】

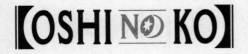

【OSHI NO KO】

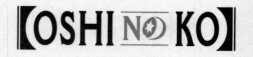

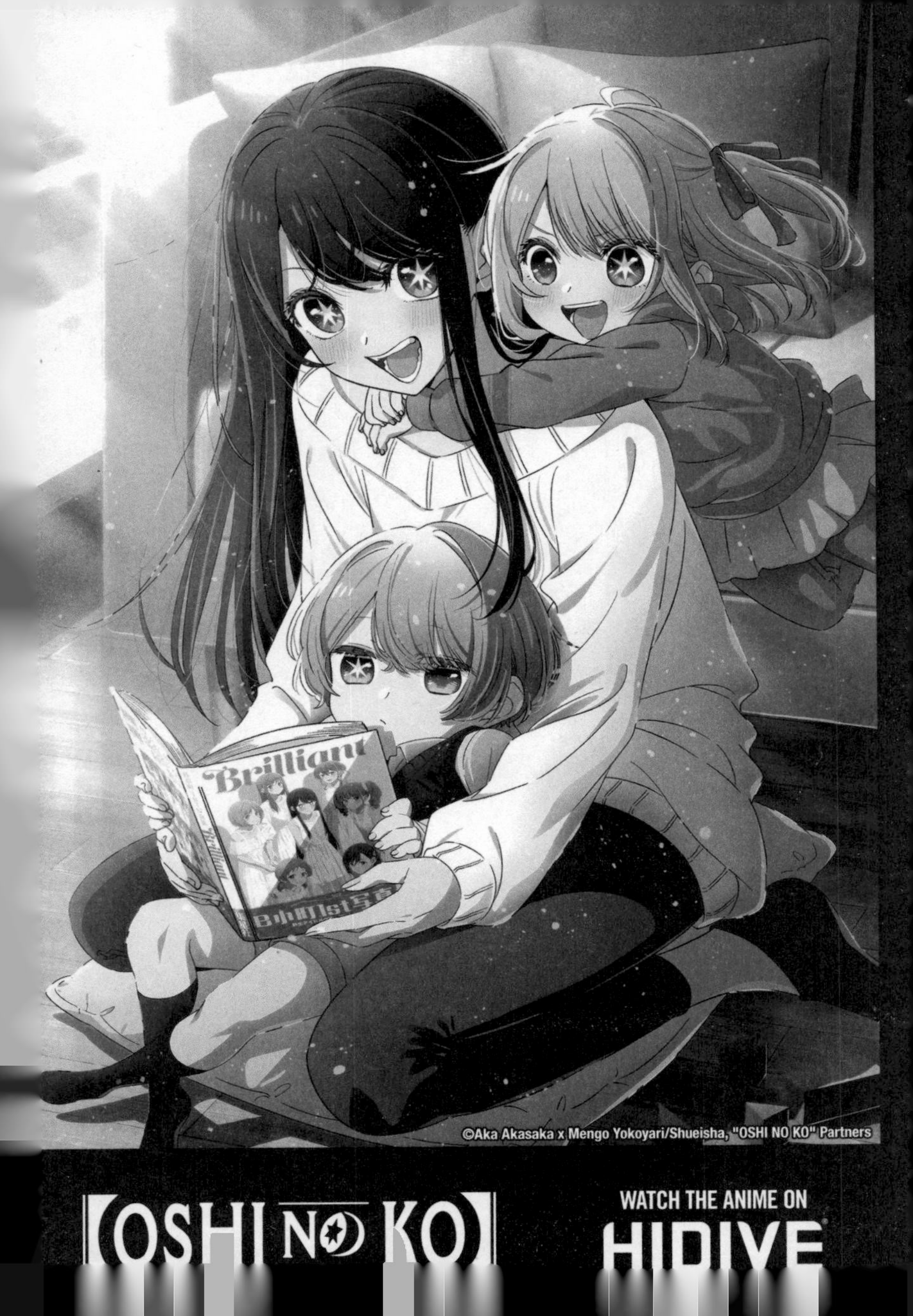
Brilliant

A Loner's Worst Nightmare: Human Interaction!

MY YOUTH R♥MANTIC COMEDY iS WRØNG, AS I EXPECTED

Wataru Watari
Illustration Ponkan⑧

1

Volumes 1–14.5 on sale now!

MY YOUTH R♥MANTIC COMEDY iS WRØNG, AS I EXPECTED

Hachiman Hikigaya is a cynic. He believes "youth" is a crock—a sucker's game, an illusion woven from failure and hypocrisy. But when he turns in an essay for a school assignment espousing this view, he's sentenced to work in the Service Club, an organization dedicated to helping students with problems! Worse, the only other member of the club is the haughty Yukino Yukinoshita, a girl with beauty, brains, and the personality of a garbage fire. How will Hachiman the Cynic cope with a job that requires—*gasp!*—social skills?

Check out the manga too!

There's something really strange about the maid I just hired!

No normal person could be so beautiful, or cook such amazingly delicious food, or know exactly what I want before I even ask. She must be using magic—right, a spell is the only thing that can explain why my chest feels so tight whenever I look at her. I swear, I'm going to get to the bottom of what makes this maid so...mysterious!

Volume 1-4 Now Available!

The Maid I Hired Recently is Mysterious

【OSHI  KO】 1

Aka Akasaka ╳ Mengo Yokoyari

Translation: **Taylor Engel**   Lettering: **Abigail Blackman**

【OSHI NO KO】 © 2020 by Aka Akasaka × Mengo Yokoyari/SHUEISHA Inc. All rights reserved. First published in Japan in 2020 by SHUEISHA, Inc. English translation rights arranged with SHUEISHA, Inc. through Tuttle-Mori Agency, Inc., Tokyo.

English translation © 2023 by Yen Press, LLC

Yen Press
150 West 30th Street, 19th Floor
New York, NY 10001

Visit us at yenpress.com • facebook.com/yenpress • twitter.com/yenpress • yenpress.tumblr.com • instagram.com/yenpress

First Yen Press Edition: January 2023

Edited by Abigail Blackman &
Yen Press Editorial: Carl Li
Designed by Yen Press Design: Andy Swist

Yen Press is an imprint of Yen Press, LLC.
The Yen Press name and logo are trademarks of Yen Press, LLC.

The publisher is not responsible for websites (or their content) that are not owned by the publisher.

Library of Congress Control Number: 2022946522

ISBNs: 978-1-9753-6317-8 (paperback)
       978-1-9753-6318-5 (ebook)

10 9 8 7 6 5

WOR

Printed in the United States of America